28·50

The Text as Thou

THE TEXT AS THOU

Martin Buber's Dialogical Hermeneutics
and Narrative Theology

STEVEN KEPNES

INDIANA UNIVERSITY PRESS

Bloomington and Indianapolis

The paper used in this publication meets the minimum requirements of American
National Standard for Information Sciences—Permanence of Paper for Printed
Library Materials, ANSI Z39.48-1984.

Manufactured in the United States of America

Library of Congress Cataloging-in-Publication Data

Kepnes, Steven, date
    The text as thou : Martin Buber's dialogical hermeneutics and
narrative theology / Steven Kepnes.
      p.   cm.
    Includes bibliographical references (p.) and index.
    ISBN 0-253-33127-7 (cloth : alk. paper)
    1. Buber, Martin, 1878–1965. 2. Hermeneutics—History—20th
century. 3. Language and languages—Religious aspects—
History—20th century. I. Title.
B3213.B84K47 1992
121'.68'092—dc20   92-7725
1 2 3 4 5 96 95 94 93 92

For Arlene

CONTENTS

PREFACE

The Linguistic Turn in Jewish Philosophy

Although we are usually directed toward the French-speaking world—to Saussure, Lévi-Strauss, Barthes, and Derrida—when the decisive "road markers" for the much celebrated "linguistic turn" in the humanities are sought, German scholarship could just as easily be cited.[1] In the search for central figures in the German-speaking world, where language is given a primary role in the human sciences, the names of von Humboldt, Wittgenstein, Heidegger, and Gadamer immediately come to mind. The name of Martin Buber is not likely to surface very quickly, and remedying this tendency to ignore Buber in contemporary discussions of language, interpretation, and narrative is a central objective of this book.

Not only have Buber's writings on the host of issues that surround the "linguistic turn"—hermeneutics, referentiality, the "de-centering" of the self, narratology, conversation, and dialogue—been largely ignored by contemporary criticism but, until very recently, Buber scholarship has underemphasized Buber's writings on these issues.[2] Where critics of the 1970s started to revision the work of "existentialists"—Kierkegaard, Nietzsche, Heidegger—by looking at them from the perspective of their contributions to the turn to language, the process of recasting Buber's writings has just begun. This may appear all the more surprising if we note that Buber often referred to his work as a "philosophy of dialogue" and that in *I and Thou* he makes the distinction between the "I-Thou" and "I-It" relationships on the basis of language.

One reason why it has taken so long for contemporary critical theories of language and interpretation to be applied to Buber's writings can be found in the politics of Jewish Studies. The ruling methodological paradigm for the study of Judaism since its nineteenth-century beginnings in the *Wissenschaft des Judentums*, the "Science of Judaism," has been historical criticism. Translating, cataloguing, and dating Jewish literatures and determining their meaning by philological analyses and by establishing historical context have occupied and continue to occupy a great deal of the energy of scholars in Jewish Studies. Consonant with this methodological disposition, concerted (and certainly needed) efforts have been expended in translating Buber's German and Hebrew writings and in placing Buber in his historical and intellectual contexts.[3]

Recently, however, Jewish Studies has begun to take the "linguistic turn." Many scholars of Judaism no longer find the historical critical paradigm adequate. Not only has the claim to "objectivity" of historical criticism been challenged by contemporary historiography but hermeneutics has shown that historical criticism is radically deficient in helping us to understand and perform the crucial interpretative task of making texts of the past speak to the contemporary situation. In addition, narratology and semiotics have shown that explaining the way texts "mean" requires much more sophisticated linguistic analyses than nineteenth-century philology can provide. Because language and interpretation or "midrash" have always been of paramount importance to Judaism, the turn to literary paradigms is particularly apt for Jewish scholars. Scholars are finding fascinating points of contact between contemporary literary theories and older Jewish methods of interpretation. Scholars of Judaism are beginning to explore these points of contact not only in Jewish philosophy but in a large variety of Jewish texts and schools of interpretation from the biblical to the rabbinic to the mystical.[4] In the area of philosophy not only the writings of Buber but those of other continental Jewish philosophers such as Rosenzweig and Levinas are being reappraised for their relevance to contemporary critical theory.

Contemporary critical theorists in the humanities and "postmodern" philosophers usually cite epistemological reasons[5] to explain why a turn to linguistic categories is necessary. With a language focus one avoids the pitfalls of Idealism, Romanticism, and Foundationalism. Instead of the "mental forms" of the Idealists and the nonrational prelinguistic intuitions of the Romantics as determinative foundations of knowledge, we have language as a historically and physically bound human tool. This tool conditions all human signs and, therefore, all knowledge; yet because it is historically and physically bound, because it possesses no "noumenal qualities," it is intrinsically knowable. The move to language also moves the individual mind or "philosophical subject" out of the center of epistemological discussions and replaces the subject with concern for linguistic structures and properties that transcend any individual user of language.

Many Jewish philosophers who have taken the linguistic turn have found these epistemological arguments cogent, yet, in addition, they often cite certain historical events, most notably the Holocaust, as a major factor in their decision to eschew foundational philosophical models and approach the issues of Jewish existence through literary paradigms. The Holocaust both radicalizes epistemological concerns and brings up ethical and theological issues that make the turn to language necessary.

Jewish philosophical versions of the linguistic turn often fashion their apologies on the basis of a frustration with Kantian and Hegelian formulations of Jewish philosophy in the nineteenth and twentieth centuries. Kantian Jewish thought, in its presentation of God as moral will and humans as free moral agents, has no response to make to the total absence of a moral God at Auschwitz and to the sustained demonic activity of the Nazis and their collaborators.[6] Hegelian Jewish thought, in its presentation of God as rational mind and its description of "Modern Europe" as the perfection of humanity and the culmination of history, is equally baffled by the primitive and archaic forces

of hatred that were unleashed throughout Europe in the Second World War and
the utterly irrational and opaque quality that a God who "ruled" the earth during
the Holocaust takes on. The Holocaust represents the ultimate challenge to
ethical and rational formulations of Jewish theology. As Emil Fackenheim has
said, the Holocaust is a "reef" upon which rational thought founders. Try as it
may, philosophy cannot comprehend the immensity of the evil perpetrated
against the Jewish people in the Holocaust. Jewish philosophy cannot answer
the questions posed by the Holocaust, it can only ask the questions and tell the
stories. Irving Greenberg tells us that after Auschwitz Jewish thought must be
fragmentary, paradoxical, and dialectical: "After Auschwitz, there should be no
final solutions," be they political, philosophical, or theological.[7]

After Auschwitz, Jewish thought must be, in the words of Fackenheim,
"midrashic."[8] Midrash helps to lift up, reflect upon, and develop an understanding of the contradictions of Jewish temporal experience. Midrash interprets
narratively, it interprets by telling stories of events. Following Frank Kermode,
we could call midrash "narrative interpretation."[9] When Fackenheim summarizes the aims and literary forms of midrash, it becomes obvious why it is so apt
as a method for post-Holocaust Jewish thought.

> Midrashic thought, therefore, cannot resolve the contradictions in the root expe-
> riences of Judaism but only express them. This expression is (a) fully conscious
> of the contradictions expressed; (b) is fully deliberate in leaving them un-
> resolved; (c) for both reasons combined, is consciously fragmentary; and (d) is
> insistent that this fragmentariness is both ultimate for human thought and yet
> destined to an ultimate resolution. . . . Seeking adequate literary form, the
> Midrashic content can find it only in story, parable, and metaphor.[10]

One can see the affinity between post-Holocaust thinking and postmodern,
postfoundational philosophy. Both share a sense of the fragmentary quality of
knowing and both look to linguistic and aesthetic categories to express this
fragmentariness. The French philosopher, Jean-François Lyotard, in his *The
Post-Modern Condition,* places the narrative and plastic arts in the postmodern
vanguard and pleads: "Let us wage a war on totality; let us be witnesses to the
unpresentable."[11]

Yet as helpful and insightful as French poststructural philosophy is, I would
argue that thinking after, yet with, the Holocaust, thinking, as Greenberg starkly
puts it, "in the presence of the burning children,"[12] requires one to stop short of
certain assertions of French and French-influenced American poststructuralism. These are the assertions that writing—Derrida's *écriture*—is more important than human speaking, that the atemporal, synchronic dimension of language must be elevated above the historic or "diachronic," that words refer
only to other words and therefore lack a referential capacity, that texts are
labyrinths in which meaning, truth, and argument necessarily get lost, and
finally, that the "self" is an insubstantial fiction which is only further obscured
when brought to language.

Jewish thinking, though it must turn to language and narrative and interpretation after Auschwitz, must stop short of French poststructuralism because without a notion of the responsible speaking self, without a notion of the importance of time and history, without a notion of language as words that can refer to temporal historical reality, and without some notion of the substantial self there is no way to bring to language, to raise the questions of, to tell the story of, and interpret the suffering of the burning children.[13] If words only refer to other words, if language is hermetically sealed off from the world and temporal events, how can Holocaust testimonies and witnesses have any legitimacy or authority? Without a notion of language as "saying something about something to someone" how can words about Jewish suffering in the events of Nazi Europe said to a contemporary audience have any moral force?

At this point I would like to return to my distinction between French and German roots of the linguistic turn. Despite Nazi Germany and despite Heidegger's Nazism, I believe that Jewish thinkers making the linguistic turn after Auschwitz will be better served by German hermeneutics than by French deconstruction and postmodernism. For German hermeneutic thinking, and here I refer to both the *verstehen* tradition from Dilthey to Gadamer and to the Frankfurt School from Horkheimer to Habermas,[14] has both put language at the center of thinking and struggled to articulate meaningful notions of human history, temporality, subjectivity, argument, and conversation. With Gadamer one finds a recognition of the underlying *Sprachlichkeit,* or "linguisticality" of all human knowing, expressing, and acting. And with Gadamer one finds a recognition that linguistic expression can never capture human knowing, expressing, and acting whole but must be a constantly moving, incomplete process. Yet with Gadamer we also have a sense that the process of expressing and interpreting human signs is meaningful and does move toward the expression and interpretation of truth. And with Habermas we have the attempt to articulate those conditions of human dialogue that will limit distortions in human communication, maximize the expression of truth, and further human responsibility and emancipation.

Nathan Scott has voiced his dissatisfaction with French deconstruction on the basis of its inability to foster genuine dialogue. Deconstruction, he suggests, is so distrustful of the explicit meanings and references of words that it blocks the flow of conversation.

> . . . [T]he deconstructionist is not, in Wordsworth's phrase, "a man speaking to men," but, rather, one who sets out to construe only for the sake of deconstruing. . . . [Deconstruction] wants from the very beginning to dismantle, to root up, to eliminate. . . . Which means that, within the intellectual forum, it considers dialogue to be an antique sort of undertaking.[15]

Scott puts Gadamer at the head of a group of interpreters who take what he calls "dialogical approaches to the hermeneutical problem"[16] and in this group he includes not only other German figures such as Dilthey and Habermas but also the Russian literary critic Mikhail Bakhtin and the French phenomenologist/structuralist Paul Ricoeur.[17] Without altering the national allegiance of these latter two figures, I readily accept Scott's inclusion of Bakhtin and Ricoeur in the group of dialogical hermeneuts and use all of Scott's figures as "conversation partners" for my study of Buber's writings on interpretation and narrative. For if what we could call "dialogical hermeneutics" finds its roots in Germany with Dilthey, with Gadamer, and with Buber, it certainly has grown beyond Germany and includes not only European figures such as Bakhtin and Ricoeur but Americans such as Wayne Booth and David Tracy as well. "Dialogical hermeneutics" by its nature is open and continually developing, and I regard this book as an attempt to further the development of this hermeneutic approach by establishing Buber's proper place in it.

Part I (chapters 1–4) presents the development of Buber's hermeneutic method of interpretation from his early romantic period through his dialogical period to his biblical writings and late thoughts on language. Part II (chapters 5–8) turns from hermeneutic issues to more strictly narrative ones. The overall argument of Part II is that Buber's narratives provide privileged access to his philosophy of I-Thou and to his theology. Chapter 1 reviews the influence of Dilthey's "romantic hermeneutics" on Buber's early translations of Hasidic texts. Chapter 2 maps out a movement from Buber's romantic hermeneutic method to what I call his "dialogical hermeneutic method." By carefully analyzing Buber's aesthetics in *I and Thou,* I show that works of art, what Buber calls *geistige Wesenheiten,* are to be approached with the same attitude of "I-Thou" as persons and nature. The result is that the "I-Thou" relationship becomes the paradigm for the hermeneutic process. With this paradigm, I argue, Buber anticipated some of the most significant hermeneutic principles developed by Hans-Georg Gadamer in his *Wahrheit und Methode* (1960) (*Truth and Method*). I also attempt to address Scholem's highly influential critique of Buber's interpretation of Hasidism from a hermeneutic perspective.

In chapter 3 I focus on the Buber-Rosenzweig translation of and the interpretive writings on the Hebrew Bible. My first aim is to show that the Bible translation and the interpretations which result from it provide the best example of the application of Buber's dialogical hermeneutics. I also try to show that Buber's experience of translating the Bible led to important developments in his hermeneutic method. Although a strict application of the hermeneutics of the philosophy of I-Thou would suggest that techniques and methods destroy the immediate conversation between the interpreter and the text, in his biblical writings Buber appears to have become convinced that techniques and methods help to preserve a dialogical relation to the text.

In chapter 4 I attempt to place Buber in "dialogue" with contemporary hermeneutic theory and construct a general Buberian hermeneutic method for all texts. This method was never fully articulated by Buber but I use the full panoply of his writings plus a number of important contemporary hermeneutic theories to produce a hermeneutic method which can be broadly considered "Buberian." The focal "bridge" work here is Buber's late essay on language, "Das Wort, das gesprochen wird" (1960) ("The Word That Is Spoken").

In chapter 5, the first of the chapters exclusively devoted to narrative, I review a number of narratives in Buber's essay "Zwiesprache" (1929) ("Dialogue") and then introduce him as an interlocutor in current debates about narrative theory. The narratives about I-Thou encounters in "Dialogue" are distinguished by an emphasis on the middle and not the beginning or end of the plot. This, I argue, is so because for Buber it is the middle moment, the present moment, that is most important in life. I analyze Buber's focus on "the middle" and on the present moment in terms of the narrative theories of Frank Kermode and Paul Ricoeur.

In chapter 6 I focus on the collection of Buber's personal stories of I-Thou events, in his "Begegnung: Autobiographische Fragmente" (1960) ("Auto-biographical Fragments"). Here we see that the philosophy of I-Thou is as much dependent on a notion of the human self as it is on certain theological notions. I look at Buber's autobiography as an instance of literary and religious autobiography. Though his "Fragments" compares quite poorly with traditional autobiographies, it meets a number of the criteria of some of the more radical social theories of self and self-story. Buber's autobiography—fragmentary, event-oriented, and "Thou-focused" as it is—suggests that the self is ever-changing, relational, "dialogic." At the end of chapter 6 I address the issue of the poststructural, postmodern, "de-centered self." I try to show that Buber's notion of the self lies, in typical Buberian fashion, "between" modern and postmodern notions of the self.

In chapter 7 I am concerned with the ways in which the self encounters temporal dimensions that go beyond the immediate moment of I-Thou encounter. I am concerned with the way in which the contemporary Jew finds links to the Jewish "common memory" of the past and to hopes for the future. For Buber this is done through contact with the root narratives of Judaism located in the Bible. In reviewing Buber's narrative biblical theology, I show how this narrative theology is retold so that one of the burning issues of Buber's and our day, the "eclipse" of God caused by the Holocaust, is addressed. I argue that Buber's narrative theology does not "answer" theological questions philosophically but gives expression to suffering and develops a variety of responses to suffering that allow sufferers to persevere in faith and continue to work for the world's redemption.

In my concluding chapter I use Gary Comstock's distinction of "pure" and "impure" narrative theologians to discuss the "limits" of the use of narrative in Buber's theology. I argue that philosophical concepts do have a place in Buber's theology as they have a place in his philosophy of I-Thou. That place, however, is ancillary. Philosophy provides "bridges" between different narrative themes and aids to the hermeneutic dialogue between interpreters within and without specific language worlds.

In retelling biblical and Hasidic tales and in using the tale to address the modern situation, Martin Buber, famous modern heretic, found himself employing an extremely old Jewish means of theological expression. If we look at the entirety of Buber's narrative writings, what we have is a body of literature which represents a daring attempt to formulate a modern narrative Jewish theology.[18] The promise inherent in this narrative Jewish theology is truly great, for if this theology is fully explored and articulated it could provide the basis for an "aggadic" or narrative Judaism. This aggadic Judaism could reverse the traditional priority given to *halakhah* (law) over *aggadah* and provide a way back to tradition for those Jews who no longer subject all aspects of their lives to the dictates of Jewish law. If Buber's hermeneutics is seen in the context of contemporary hermeneutic studies in Judaism his work can be recognized as the beginning of what some have called the modern Jewish revival of the "midrashic imagination."[19]

I am indebted to a number of persons and institutions for support in the writing of this book. First I would like to acknowledge the influences of David Tracy and Paul Ricoeur of the University of Chicago and Paul Mendes-Flohr of the Hebrew University of Jerusalem. Tracy encouraged me in my first intuitions that there were resources in Buber's work to address issues of hermeneutics and narrative and Ricoeur made invaluable comments and suggestions for the project in its early stages. I was also aided at Chicago by Lou Silberman, Peter Homans, and Don Browning. I consulted with Paul Mendes-Flohr in 1985 at the Hebrew University when I received a Lakritz Grant to travel to the Buber Archives in Israel and in 1986 when I was at the University of Virginia as a Mellon Post-Doctoral fellow and Mendes-Flohr was at the University as a Bronfman Scholar in Jewish Thought. Mendes-Flohr provided me not only with crucial bibliographic references and invaluable insights into Buber's writings but with an example of the utmost care and reverence for the activity of scholarship. I would also like to acknowledge the intellectual influences of Nathan Scott, Jr., who helped arrange for my invitation to Virginia, and Larry Bouchard, who generously opened his home to me and whose knowledge of both literary theory and theology was extremely helpful to me. Maurice Fried-man and Mary Gerhart read Part I of the manuscript and provided me with pointed critical comments that helped me to correct and refine my arguments. I especially want to thank Peter Ochs, who did an extremely sensitive reading of the manuscript in its penultimate form and provided wonderful suggestions for the final draft.

I am thankful to Raphael Buber and to Margot Cohn of the Buber Archives of the Jewish National and University Library in Jerusalem for permission to use the archives and to quote from its materials. Margot Cohn was particularly helpful to me in trips I made to the archives in 1985 and 1987. I am grateful to the Mellon Foundation, the Memorial Foundation for Jewish Culture, the Amer-ican Academy of Religion, and the Lakritz Fellowship, which supported my research and writing from 1986 to 1988, and to Colgate University, which supported manuscript preparation. I wish to thank Blanche and Meredith Gardner for checking over my German translations and Norman Shore for checking my Hebrew translations. In addition, I would like to thank the editors at Indiana University Press. Last, but certainly not least, I wish to thank my wife,

Arlene Kanter, to whom this book is dedicated and who, more than anyone else, supported and encouraged me to finish this book (already!).

The Buber Estate and its agent, the Balkan Agency, has generously given me permission to quote from the following books: Martin Buber, "Die Geschichte von dem Rabbi und seinem Sohne," *Die Geschichten des Rabbi Nachman: Ihm nacherzählt von Martin Buber* (Frankfurt a.M.: Rütten und Loening, 1918), pp. 54–62. Martin Buber, "Der Werwolf," *Die Legende des Baal-Shem* (Frankfurt a.M.: Rütten und Loening, 1920), pp. 46–51. Martin Buber, "Der Spruch des Vaters," *Die Erzählungen der Chassidim* (Zurich: Manesse Verlag, 1949), p. 112. Martin Buber, "Original Remembrance," *Between Man and Man*, trans. R. G. Smith, Introduction by M. Friedman (New York: Macmillan Co., 1965), pp. 1–3.

Permission to reprint my own articles which were used in sections of chapters 1, 2, 6, and 4 has also been graciously granted by the following bodies: The Oxford Centre for Postgraduate Hebrew Studies to reprint my "A Hermeneutic Approach to the Buber-Scholem Controversy," *The Journal of Jewish Studies*, 38:1 (Spring 1987), 81–98; The President and Fellows of Harvard College to reprint my "Buber as Hermeneut: Relations to Dilthey and Gadamer," *Harvard Theological Review*, 81:2 (1988), 193–213, copyright 1988; The Society for Values in Higher Education and the University of Tennessee, Knoxville to reprint my "Buber's Autobiographical Fragments: Becoming Self Through the Other," *Soundings*, 73:2–3 (Summer/Fall 1990), 407–422; and *The Journal of Jewish Thought and Philosophy* to reprint my "Buber and Bakhtin: Towards a Dialogical Theory of Language and Interpretation," *The Journal of Jewish Thought and Philosophy*, 2:1 (1992).

Although I have generally used older editions of English translations of Buber's works, readers should be informed that many of these editions have been recently republished with new introductions by Humanities Press. I would, finally, like to mention that though I use gender neutral terms in my own prose, when I quote from or translate Buber's words I retain his use of male gendered terms such as "man" and "he" to refer to humanity in general. This does not represent my endorsement of this now outdated convention but rather my desire to remain faithful to Buber's texts.

I

Buber's Hermeneutics

I

ROMANTICISM, DILTHEY, AND BUBER'S EARLY HERMENEUTICS

> Oh love, how pitiful is art which does not
> seek the ultimate, which does not seek to
> solve the riddles of life or to dig into the
> most significant matters of the world.[1]
>
> Buber to Paula Winkler, April, 1900

The themes of German Neo-Romanticism at the beginning of the twentieth century—the salvational power of artistic creativity, the unifying properties of mysticism, and the expressive capacities of poetry and myth—are all present in Buber's early work[2] and provide the context for his early hermeneutic method. A number of scholars, among them Paul Mendes-Flohr, Grete Schaeder, and Maurice Friedman, have detailed the influence of Nietzsche, the New Romantic poets, and mysticism on Buber.[3] A somewhat overlooked influence, which we will attend to, is the romantic hermeneutic theory of Buber's teacher, Wilhelm Dilthey. The New German Romanticism affected both the subject matter and the style of Buber's hermeneutic method as he chose to work upon the texts of mystics and, in the specific case of Judaism, sought to aestheticize and remythicize the tales of the Hasidic tradition of the past.

The Romantic Influences

Nietzsche

In his "Autobiographical Fragments," Buber tells us that whereas Kant had a quieting and calming effect on his early philosophical searchings, Nietzsche had a fascinating and transforming effect on him. He tells us that Nietzsche "not only stirred me up but transported me into a sublime intoxication."[4] Buber became a "passionate Nietzschean" and, at the age of seventeen, he often carried *Thus Spake Zarathustra* with him to his Polish gymnasium and began to translate it into Polish.[5] In his "Nietzsche and Life Values" (1900), one of his first publications, Buber heaps lavish praise on Nietzsche. "Never before in our age have so rich and full words [*Worte*] been inscribed for the most painful

3

secret and for the wildest dream of the spiritual [*geistige*] man."[6] Buber, like
many intellectuals of his day, accepted Nietzsche's characterization of Western
urban and industrial civilization as spiritually and aesthetically anemic. The
crisis of the West was a crisis of *Kultur*.[7] Adopting Nietzsche's notion of the
human being as a creating being, Buber believed that through creative acts the
self and culture would be renewed.

In his "The Creators, the People and the Movement" (1902), Buber presents
his interpretation of the Nietzschean term "creator" and its significance for the
Jews of his day. "The creative ones," "*die Schaffenden*," are intellectuals and
artists and something more. They are less enamored of logic and more
attracted to mystery than are intellectuals and, unlike artists, they are not
limited by materials and concrete forms.[8] They "can create things which are
totally inner and beyond all language" forming "their work out of human souls,
out of peoples and cultures."[9] They are the "strong and multifarious ones"
through whom "new developments in spirit and action" are accomplished.[10]
Though the creative ones among the Jewish people have been suppressed or
have separated themselves from their community, they are its "secret kings,"
who must be reunited with the Jewish people if the struggle for national and
cultural renewal is to succeed.[11]

Grete Schaeder draws a parallel between Nietzsche's attitude to Germany
and Buber's attitude to the Jewish people. "Both struggled against the petrified
cultural values of the time and against an alienated tradition; both wished to
penetrate to the sources, to the hidden energies in the depths of the nation's
life."[12] Schaeder argues that from Nietzsche's *The Birth of Tragedy* Buber saw
"that the moribund myth of a people can be revived and become the symbol of
a national renaissance."[13] In a letter to his fiancée, Paula Winkler, in April 1900,
wherein Buber describes his hopes for a folk art of the Jewish people, we
clearly hear the Nietzschean themes to which Schaeder refers.

> What I seek is deep national ties, the release of the impulse of the folk-soul,
> the development of that which had not been developed . . . the flowing and the
> fermenting of the racial essence. To seize, with the hand, that which makes the
> immortally one blood certain, to pull out and create the forms which in real
> history remain unformed. The people whose folk-fate could not be completely
> expressed, this fate must be formed so that it does express itself.[14]

Buber's early involvement in Zionism and in Hasidic myth telling must be
seen, at least in part, as an outgrowth of Nietzsche's influence. Nietzsche's call
for cultural renewal and vitality, no doubt, affected Buber's primarily cultural
conception of Zionism.[15]

Neo-Romantic Poets

Moving from Poland back to Vienna, the city of his birth, for his university
studies, Buber quickly became caught up in the city's fin-de-siècle artistic
world. His Nietzschean concerns for creativity and art found a comfortable
home in Vienna, where, as Carl Schorske has shown, art had superseded both

religion and politics in importance for many intellectuals.[16] Buber chose to study subjects which were required fare for the avant-garde of his day: art, theater, and linguistics. But Buber not only studied art, he befriended artists and sought to become one. Hans Fischer-Barnicol tells us that Buber "appeared to want to become 'only' a poet, a member of the literati."[17] He struggled "through strict service to the word" to earn "the heritage" of the New Romanticism.[18]

Buber met Hugo von Hofmannsthal in Vienna and was profoundly influenced by him. In 1897, Buber wrote a review of Hofmannsthal's poetry in which he describes it as "so majestic that no on else today can match it."[19] In a later reminiscence of his Vienna days Buber tells how Hofmannsthal's poetry "penetrated into my reading and writing."[20] Buber also befriended the poet Richard Beer-Hofmann and was asked to write the introduction to his collected writings. In a remembrance of Stefan George, Buber writes that, at age eighteen, he discovered, in George's poem "The Day of Shepherds," that "in this, my time, a poet lives."[21]

Buber's correspondence of this period shows that he saw himself as an artist. The first letter (October 1897) of his published *Briefwechsel* refers to a number of poems which he sent to Richard Dehmel for his evaluation. In August 1900, Buber declares that he has found "an artistic way of his own."[22] In July 1901, he speaks of a "life or death" struggle to gather his "artistic initiative" and accomplish something. He juxtaposes the academic life with that of the artist and decidedly favors the latter.[23]

Buber spearheaded the fight of the "Democratic Faction" in the Fifth Zionist Conference (1901) against Theodor Herzl's purely political Zionism with a speech on Jewish art, "Von jüdischer Kunst." A full flowering of Zionism, Buber argues, will require uncovering the artistic "wells" of creativity which were covered over by ghetto culture.[24] National self-awareness and development require artistic self-awareness[25] and the flowering of artistic creativity in literature, theater, poetry, and music. As Buber developed his interests in Zionism he also championed the cause of the arts. Aside from his own poetry, he sought to encourage the "incomplete present" yet "great future"[26] of *"jüdische Kunst"* by writing reviews of Jewish artists' work and by editing books on Jewish art.[27]

Mysticism

Although Buber experimented with poetry, his unique contribution to the New Romanticism came not from his poetry but from his work in mysticism. If many intellectuals saw art as the vehicle for salvation, the source of artistic inspiration was often identified with an atheistic and aesthetic form of mysticism best articulated by Arthur Schopenhauer.[28] Schopenhauer used Kant's categories of space, time, and causality to argue that overly rational Westerners had allowed themselves to be locked into an individuated phenomenal world. Schopenhauer argued that one could experience the *noumenal* world of unity and harmony, one could avoid the pain of separation and isolation caused by living in the individuated world, by quieting the individual will and adopting an introspective attitude of mind. Nietzsche, of course, popularized these ideas of Schopenhauer's in his *The Birth of Tragedy* and developed his own Dionysian solution to the Western problems of alienation and isolation. But many of Buber's generation also turned toward the religions of the Orient for expressions of the unitary mystical experience which Schopenhauer spoke of.[29]

Buber was acquainted with the ideas of Schopenhauer through a course he took at the University of Leipzig in 1897 and through his early reading of Nietzsche's *The Birth of Tragedy*. Yet it appears that Buber began to take them most seriously when they were reintroduced to him in 1899 by his wife, Paula Winkler, and by Gustav Landauer, a member of a mystic society called the Neue Gemeinschaft.[30] In a talk which Buber gave to the Neue Gemeinschaft, Buber idealized the mystical experience of "a feeling of co-essentiality, of blissful, blessed fusion with all things in space and time."[31] Buber's dissertation (1904) investigated the problematic of individuation, and he went on to publish a number of books on mystical writings. Among these were his early Hasidic works and his *Ekstatische Konfessionen* (1921), a collection of mystical accounts from a variety of traditions and countries. The first line of Buber's introduction to *Ecstatic Confessions* begins with Schopenhauer's individuation problematic. "The commotion of our human life which lets in everything, . . . is closed to one thing: unity. . . . The commotion lets me have things and the ideas that go with them, only not unity of world or of I."[32] Buber goes on to say that only in mysticism, only in an ecstatic experience, does the "soul experience the unity of the I, and in this unity, the unity of I and world."[33] Making the important connection between mysticism and myth, Buber argues that the mystics use the language of myth to express their experiences.[34] Therefore, many of his authors present their ecstatic experiences in mythical form. Buber's authors on mysticism were immensely popular with artists and intellectuals. For example Robert Musil's *The Man Without Qualities*, a classic work of German Neo-Romanticism, contains almost three hundred references to Buber's *Ecstatic Confessions*. As Mendes-Flohr shows, it was through his mystical writings that Buber became an "honored member of the pantheon of New Romantic authors."[35]

Dilthey

Knowledge of the influence that Nietzsche, the New Romantic poets, and Schopenhauer's mysticism of "unification" had on Buber will help us greatly to understand his early hermeneutic approach to Hasidic texts. The work of Paul Mendes-Flohr, Grete Schaeder, and Maurice Friedman is of great assistance in this regard. Yet there is one other major influence on Buber's early hermeneutic method which has been given less attention—the hermeneutic theory of Wilhelm Dilthey.[36] Our review of the hermeneutic theory of Dilthey and of his predecessor Friedrich Schleiermacher will be illuminating not only for Buber's Hasidic writings, but also for his biblical translations and interpretations.

We know that Buber studied with Dilthey at the University of Berlin in the summer of 1898 and the fall of 1899 when Dilthey was lecturing on Schleiermacher and on his "new philosophy."[37] We also know that Buber attended Dilthey's lectures on and off in the years 1906–1911 when he lived near Berlin. Buber spoke of Dilthey as *"mein Lehrer"*[38] and, according to Grete Schaeder, regarded Dilthey as one of his "most congenial" teachers.[39] Dilthey seemed to have trusted Buber as his student, for he once asked him to edit one of his books. Given that Buber studied with Dilthey at the end of Dilthey's career, we can assume Buber was well acquainted with the writings that presented Dilthey's hermeneutical thinking.

To understand what I call, following Gadamer and Ricoeur, Dilthey's "romantic hermeneutic method," we need to first attend to the hermeneutic theory of the pioneer of modern hermeneutics and Dilthey's mentor, Friedrich Schleiermacher.[40] The liberal theologian Schleiermacher, who often directed his writings to artists and intellectuals, inaugurated modern hermeneutics in 1819 by attempting to free it from its traditional moorings in biblical scholarship. Where the preromantic hermeneutics of Spinoza and Chladenius had focused hermeneutic discussion on the misunderstanding of problematic biblical texts, Schleiermacher argued, first, that misunderstanding is not a sporadic phenomenon limited to difficult biblical texts—that "misunderstanding" is systematically present in the reading of all biblical texts—and second, that beyond the Bible, misunderstanding is present when we read any text. Schleiermacher's premise is that "misunderstanding emerges of itself and that understanding must be desired and sought *at every point.*"[41]

To counter systematic misunderstanding in the reading of all texts, Schleiermacher develops a two-staged hermeneutic method. The first stage, called "grammatical" interpretation, endeavors, through study of philology, grammar, and history, to discern the meaning of the words of a text as the author and original audience understood them. A crucial element of this hermeneutic stage involves investigation of the relation of the part to the whole: the relation of the word to the sentence, the sentence to the entire text, and the text to its particular genre. The second stage in Schleiermacher's hermeneutic schema, the stage for which he is most famous, is called "psychological" or "technical" interpretation. In this stage the interpreter is concerned with the author's intentions in writing the text. Here, one desires to discern, through "intuiting" and "divinizing," the "mind of the author." In the most direct experience of understanding, one knows what is in the mind of the person who writes. One not only perceives the author's intent and purpose in writing, one returns to the "inner origin" of the work.[42] Interpretation involves reconstructing the author's "individual unity" and perceiving "the train of thought" which produced the work.[43] If one is successful in both stages of Schleiermacher's hermeneutic method, one will be able not only to avoid misunderstanding but, as the famous formulation goes, to "understand the author better than he himself."

Many of the premises of Schleiermacher's hermeneutic method are evident in the interpretative theory of Dilthey. However, Dilthey attempts to spread the applicability of hermeneutics still further than does Schleiermacher. In his *Lebensphilosophie,* Dilthey suggests that hermeneutic theory can be applied not only to all texts but to the study of all human behavior and culture. Hermeneutics can be applied to the human "life-world" and to the study of history. Dilthey attempts to develop a hermeneutic method of investigation that covers all of the *Geisteswissenschaften,* the human sciences. This method is to bring to cultural and historical studies an element of objectivity that is characteristic of the natural sciences *(Naturwissenschaften).* Dilthey's distinction between the human and the natural sciences—and, indeed, his whole hermeneutic theory—is based upon a specific notion of experience, expression, and understanding. In brief, an individual has an experience which is expressed in a work and then understood by another individual who interprets the work.

Dilthey's Triad: Experience, Expression, Understanding

In an important summary statement about his work, Dilthey once said: "The basic thought that underlies my philosophy is that until now experience as a whole, entire and unfragmented, has never served as the ground of philosophizing."[44] Dilthey uses the word *Erlebnis* to speak about this "full, unmutilated experience," and he labors to distinguish it from *Erfahrung,* which he speaks of as "outer sensory experience." In his earliest formulation, Dilthey uses the term *Erlebnis* to refer to our inner, personal, and subjective experience. Following Schleiermacher, he uses the term *Gefühl* (feeling) to refer to the affective, nonrational, and totalistic quality of our lived experience. Yet later, Dilthey comes to stress the importance of the external social context within which *Erlebnis* occurs and to which *Erlebnis* is bound in "vital relationships."[45] *Erlebnis* is used to refer to the immediate, direct, prereflective experience of self, other, and human world. *Erlebnis* is also used to refer to that which is significant and lasting in an experience—"a yield or residue that acquires permanence, weight, and significance from out of the transcience of experiencing."[46] Thus, *Erlebnis* is experience that occurs within the socially constructed world and leads to the creation of value and meaning. *Erfahrung,* on the other hand, refers to "objectivating" and testing experience. It refers to sensory, empirical experience. When abstracted and quantified, it can be used to form causal laws.

On the basis of his distinction between lived and outer experience, Dilthey develops his well-known distinction between the human sciences[47] and the natural sciences. The human sciences use the processes of "understanding" *(verstehen)* to gain knowledge about human life, and the natural sciences attempt to "explain" *(erklären)* natural phenomena in terms of regular and universal laws.[48] *Erlebnis,* the lived experience of an individual, is so important to the interpretative work of the human sciences because, ultimately, it is what the interpreter wants to arrive at. Yet that which gives the interpreter access to another's lived experience is its "objectivation" or what Dilthey also calls its "life-expression" *(Lebensäusserung)*. Michael Ermarth explains that "expressions" are very important for Dilthey because they provide the only access to lived experience.[49]

Dilthey speaks of expressions as "occurring in the world of the senses; they are manifestations of mental content which they enable us to know."[50] Expressions are signs and symbols which "gather together" and "fix" lived experiences.[51] They include gestures, facial expressions, words, and more permanent forms of expression such as works of art, architecture, and written texts. The expression provides the vessel for lived experience and organizes, structures, and preserves it so that it can be understood.[52]

The goal of understanding is to arrive at the life-experience behind a life-expression. Dilthey, like Schleiermacher, postulates a first stage of analysis which requires attention to the details of language usage, historical context, and the dynamics of the part to the whole.[53] Dilthey, however, gave Schleiermacher's second stage of "psychological interpretation" far more specificity by explicating the notion of divinization with that of "empathy" *(Hineinversetzen)*. Dilthey speaks of understanding as "empathy with the mental life of others,"[54] "the process of recognizing a mental state from a sense-given sign by which it is expressed."[55] Here, understanding is conceived as the attempt to arrive at the mental state, the subjective, personal lived experience of the author, as he or she produced the work. Like Schleiermacher, Dilthey postulates a shared human ground, "an identity of mind,"[56] which allows the interpreter to empathize with the experiencing author. In Dilthey's empathic method, I allow the work to evoke an experience within myself—how I "enjoyed and suffered, desired and acted in similar situations."[57] I use the resources of my own life-experiences to picture the experience of the author and to put myself into his or her mood and frame of mind. After gaining the vantage point of the author, I then try to reconstruct the experience behind the work. This empathic notion of understanding, however, represents Dilthey's earliest formulation of the method of understanding.

In his more mature hermeneutic position, Dilthey presents the process of understanding in a more complex manner.[58] Dilthey becomes more interested in the life-experience of the author conceived as a lived experience in the human historical world. And Dilthey speaks of a movement from empathy to re-creation *(nachbilden)* and reliving *(nacherleben)*. In empathy, I aim to "retransform" an expression into the mental state of the author who produced it. But I go beyond empathy to re-creating and reliving when I seek not just a mental state but the sequence of events understood as events-in-the-human-historical-world. Here, I do not just go back in time to a discrete point but I move from that point forward with the author.

> Understanding [as mere empathy] moves in the reverse order to the sequence of events. But full empathy [empathy as re-creating or reliving] depends on understanding *moving with the order of events* so that it keeps step with the order of life. It is in this way that empathy or transposition expands. Re-experiencing follows the line of events.[59]

Thus, Dilthey suggests that in the most developed form of understanding, I relive and even re-create a sequence of historical events. I move with the order of events. In reexperiencing, Dilthey suggests, I discover aspects of historical reality which are sometimes not readily obvious. Reexperiencing allows me to see "continuity" in an experience which may appear fragmentary.

> The narrative of a novelist or historian which follows the historical course of events makes us re-experience it. It is the triumph of re-experiencing that it supplements the fragments of a course of events in such a way that we believe ourselves to be confronted by continuity.[60]

Dilthey asserts that this type of understanding requires what he calls "envisaging" or "visualization" *(Vergegenwärtigung)* and imagination.[61]

Although Dilthey does not say this directly, his comments suggest that in "following the lines of events," in discovering continuity in the fragmentary, in re-creating the past event, I not only reexperience the event as the author experienced it, I discover a continuity, I follow the line of events to a new conclusion that did not exist in the mind of the author.[62] This form of understanding requires a certain form of inspiration or "genius"[63] on the part of the interpreter which parallels that of the artist who produced the work. Dilthey often refers to the highest form of understanding as "interpretation"[64] or "explication." Explication, in its turn, properly works upon written texts. "As the life of the mind finds its complete, exhaustive and therefore objective comprehension in language, explication culminates in the interpretation of the written records of human existence."[65]

Buber's Early Hermeneutic Method

How did the variety of romantic influences affect Buber's hermeneutic approach to sacred texts? The influence is obvious if we listen to Buber's own description of his method of translating the stories from the *Shivḥei ha-Besht* ("In Praise of the Baal-Shem Tov") found in the preface to Buber's *Die Legende des Baal Schem* (1908).

> I have received it and told it anew. I have not transcribed it like some piece of literature; I have not elaborated it like some fabulous material. I have told it anew as one who was born later. I bear in me the blood and spirit of those who created it, and out of my blood and spirit it has become new. I stand in the chain of narrators, a link between links; I tell once again the old stories, and if they sound new, it is because the new already lay dormant in them when they were told for the first time.[66]

First, the Nietzschean influence is obvious as Buber attempts to revivify "old legends" of the Jewish people by telling them anew. Hasidism represents, for Buber, the hidden life of the Jewish people, the "moribund myth" waiting to be released. Buber's interest in Hasidic myth represents an attempt to find a cultural and artistic solution to the cultural malaise of the Jewish people. Buber, as storyteller and mythmaker, appears as the Nietzschean creative person taking on the future of his people's cultural life, finding within his own being, within his blood and spirit, a unity with his people, and attempting to pull his people forward into the present moment.

And too, Buber can be seen as the mythmaking poet, revealing a path of salvation through his art. When speaking of his early translations of the Hasidic tales, Buber uses an analogy from the arts, from painting, to discuss his method: "I had to tell the stories that I had taken from out of myself, as a true painter takes into himself the lines of the models and achieves the genuine images out of the memory formed of them."[67]

In a letter written to Paula Winkler in August 1900, Buber speaks of writing a book on the ancient Egyptian Satu-legends. He mentions a "way of creating" in which he uses the old legend as an outline and fills it out with his own imagination.

> These fine old sagas come to me as a unique coloring-book which is sketched in outline and waits to be drawn in. So sweetly and lovingly do they come to my hand. Never before have I felt so strongly the soul of the old Orient in me and the power to give life to its symbols.[68]

Buber also attempted to use this method in his early translations of Hasidic tales. He attempted to "feel the soul" of the Hasidic master and then to give fresh "color" to his tales and imbue their symbols with "new life." Buber, as modern Hasidic storyteller, finally finds proper outlet for his poetical strivings and artistic sensibilities. If Buber was not very successful as a poet, Buber as a Hasidic storyteller was quite successful. Indeed, it was as a storyteller that Buber won his place among New Romantic poets. Presenting Hasidic legends as the Jewish mythical representation of Jewish mysticism, Buber was able to educate Jew and non-Jew alike to the "oriental," mystical element in the Jewish past.

In the quotation taken from the preface to Buber's *Die Legende des Baal Schem*, we also see quite clearly the influence of Dilthey's hermeneutics on Buber's work on Hasidic texts. Buber is the romantic hermeneut who returned to the originative *Erlebnis* of the Hasidic master and, with empathy, divined the mental process of the master. In "My Way to Hasidism" (1918) Buber speaks of his earliest collection of Hasidic tales, *Die Geschichten des Rabbi Nachman* (1906), and tells us, "I experienced . . . my unity with the spirit of Rabbi Nahman." In writing of the Baal-Shem Tov Buber tells us "I realized my inborn binding with Hasidic truth . . . [and] sought to construct the inner process in the life of the master."[69]

And beyond empathy, Buber sought to reexperience, relive, and re-create the life-experience of the Hasidic master. In his essay "Hasidism and Modern Man" (1956), Buber says of his early method of translating the Hasidic tales that he felt "obliged to reconstruct the pure event," "the life-event," of Hasidic leaders.[70] In speaking of Nahman in his "My Way to Hasidism" Buber says, "I had found the true faithfulness: more adequately than the direct disciples, I received and completed the task, a later messenger in a foreign realm."[71] Buber is thus the romantic hermeneut who, returning to the originative experience, is able to follow a series of events and find in that series a continuity and bring to it a *new completion*. Buber is the genius, romantic hermeneut whose own powers of empathy and creativity allow him to understand the Hasidic masters *even better* than did the direct disciples.[72]

Buber spoke of himself as a "filter"[73] through which the tales of the past traveled on their path to the modern world. Using Dilthey's hermeneutic principles, Buber retold Hasidic tales in new ways. Buber built fragments of tales into more elaborate and complex tales. Using Dilthey's principles, Buber took old tales into his imagination and attempted to reimagine them, to discover new continuities and to complete the tales differently. In his forward to *The Tales of Rabbi Nachman*, Buber refers to his tales as a "re-creation"[74] through a "retelling." "I have not translated but retold them,"[75] he says. Here it is important to point out that Buber appears to have made a move from Dilthey's notions of re-creating and reliving to retelling. Buber understood Dilthey's use of the term *nachbilden,* to re-create, as an act of *nacherzählen,* to retell.

Because of this attempt to re-create the tales, I believe we must speak of Buber's Hasidic tales not primarily as translations but as interpretations. Here, I would like to draw upon a notion which Hans-Georg Gadamer has developed called "reproductive" or "performative interpretation."[76] Performative interpretation is something more like a musician or actor does than a literary critic or commentator does. The literary critic's interpretation of a piece of literature exists as a series of insights and arguments that properly remain outside the text. The interpretation of a musician or an actor, on the other hand, is performed or enacted through a new rendition of the piece of music or drama. Thus we speak of Itzhak Perlman's Violin Concerto of Beethoven or Olivier's Hamlet. This type of interpretation does not exist outside the original but is given in a new performance of the original. Similarly, Buber's Hasidic tales are performative interpretations in which he retells old tales in new ways. Buber interpreted Hasidic tales by becoming a modern Hasidic storyteller and reproducing the tales of the past. Buber's understanding of the tales is to be found not in a conceptual interpretation but in his new telling, his new "performance" of the tales. Indeed, Buber's performative interpretations of the Hasidic tales reveal, perhaps most clearly, the presuppositions of Buber's early hermeneutic method.

Romantic Hermeneutics Applied: The Tales of Rabbi Nahman

In writing of his Nahman tales to Samuel Horodezky in July 1906, Buber declares:

About the *sippurei ma'asiyot,* . . . in general it is not my goal to gather new facts, but rather solely to give a new interpretation of their coherence, a new synthetic presentation of Jewish mystics and their creations, so as to make these creations known to the European public in a form as artistically pure as possible.[77]

In comparing Buber's tales to the traditional texts on which they were based, one notices, from the outset, Buber's attempt to "clean up" the tales, to do away with *halakhic,* kabbalistic, and Yiddish references and writing style and to present a "charming" tale suitable for the cultured European public. Buber is very straightforward about the fact that his tales are "retellings" and not translations. Indeed, the full title of the German edition of the Nahman tales is *The Tales of Rabbi Nahman as Retold by Martin Buber.*

In addition to the presuppositions of Romanticism, Buber carried with him a further, very important assumption in undertaking the translation of the tales of Rabbi Nahman of Bratslav. This presupposition was that Nahman's disciples distorted the stories when writing them down: "The Tales have been preserved for us in the notes of a disciple, notes that have obviously deformed and distorted the original narrative beyond measure. As they lie before us, they appear confused, verbose, and ignoble in form."[78]

We know that the stories were published five years after Nahman's death and that he did not have a chance to edit them. We also know that Nathan Sternhartz, who recorded the tales, did not hear all of them firsthand and was told of them by other disciples.[79] There is, then, certainly room for distortion and for significant error in the 1815/16 Hebrew and Yiddish publication of the tales. The fact that the stories were distorted provided Buber with a justification to use the full scope of creative powers vouchsafed to him by the New Romanticism and Dilthey's hermeneutics. Buber felt he needed to retell the tales with "full freedom" to "re-create" the original tales.

Whether or not distortions of the magnitude which Buber assumes exist will never be known with certainty. From Buber's methodological point of view, however, and this is crucial, the question of textual authenticity was not the central hermeneutic problem that had to be faced. The central hermeneutic problem was framed in the well-known terms of romantic understanding—re-experiencing, re-creating, reliving—and not in the terms of textual authenticity and historical criticism. As Buber himself has said, "my presentation is no historical work. . . . The tapestry which my work is seen as is woven of elective strands."[80]

It is interesting to read Buber's text alongside the traditional text to see how he exercised his "elective" freedom to retell Nahman's tales. Buber's alterations, deletions, and additions to the original text can be seen by comparing the traditional Hebrew/Yiddish text to Buber's German text.[81]

Most of Buber's tales begin with temporal introductions, which give his tales something of the fairy-tale charm of the tales of the Grimm brothers: "In a distant land and at a distant time," "Many hundred years ago," "Once upon a time."[82] This is in contrast to the traditional tales, which use simple Hebrew beginnings: "Once there was a king," "This is a story about a rabbi," "Once there were two rich men," "There was a *Baal Tefilla*." Buber consistently ignores Hebrew and Yiddish style and adds artifice, imagery, and details to the tales, which are quite simple and sparse.

Nowhere is this more obvious than in "The Rabbi and His Son," where Buber uses two pages of elaboration to translate less than ten sentences. I present translations of the traditional Hebrew/German Nahman text first and compare it with translations of Buber's German retelling.[83]

The Translation of the Nahman text

This is a story about a rabbi who had no children. Finally, he had an only son. He brought him up and married him off. The son would sit in the attic and study in the manner of rich men and he studied and prayed always. But he used to feel within himself that something was lacking and yet he did not know what it was. The son had no true appetite for his study and prayer and so he spoke to two men, two youths. They advised him to go to a certain zaddik. And the son performed a commandment *(mitzvah)* that brought him to the aspect of the small light.

Parts of Buber's retelling

Once there was a rabbi, and he devoted his life to Torah. He used all his spirit to investigate it and with all his might he guarded the commandments so that they were observed in the most minute detail by the community. When, in his late years, an only son was born to him, it appeared to him as a reward and an assent from God. . . . and he vowed that his son, like him . . . would be a bitter enemy of those dreamers who surround the exalted word with illusion [i.e., the Hasidim]. . . .

. . . The son grew and became great in the knowledge of the holy books. He had a small room in his father's house where he liked to go and collect his senses and submerge himself in the secrets of the scripture. But his soul could not persevere with the books and his glance could not keep to the unending surface of the small stiff letters but slid again and again over the yellow billows of corn to the dark streak of the far-off pine forests. His soul slid out with his glance and cradled itself in the still air like a young bird. . . .

Nevertheless, he became learned; although wisdom streamed to him not out of the confusion of the words on the page before him but out of himself . . . it sprouted and embraced his soul. . . . Knowledge and holiness were joined to that deep and unfathomable transformation which is called the level of the small light and which from time to time appears in a single soul and then disappears with it. This was the level to which the youth was elevated without realizing it. . . .

> And though he believed, for the sake
> of the truth, that one should continue to
> study . . . when he merely approached
> the books it was as if he stepped into a
> void and an enigmatic need lay heavily
> upon him and he felt himself deserted in
> an abyss.

Here, we see how Buber adds not only imagery and descriptive material but also characterization to accentuate the difference between the rabbi and his son. The rabbi is a diligent *halakhist* and an opponent *(mitnagged)* of Hasidism. The son has an intense inward spiritual life and no patience with the demands of disciplined study and detailed observance of Jewish law. He also is attracted to the very Hasidim his father opposes.[84] Buber develops a contrast between the son as lover of nature and the father as a thoroughly scholarly and social figure in two very richly drawn sentences for which there is no basis in the Nahman texts.

> [The son's] glance could not keep to the unending surface of the small stiff letters but slid again and again over the yellow billows of corn to the dark streak of the far-off pine forests. His soul slid out with his glance and cradled itself in the still air like a young bird.[85]

These sentences reveal Buber's penchant for the literary ornate and show that Buber had no intention of trying to present the simple, direct, and "homey" style of the Hebrew or Yiddish texts. It also follows from Buber's aversion to *halakhah* and his interest in mysticism at this period in his life, that the son achieves the "level of the small light"[86] not through performing a *mitzvah*, a commandment (as in the traditional text), but through a mystical "unfathomable transformation."

The rest of the tale relates the son's journey with his father to find a zaddik, the holder of the "greater light," who could cure him of his sense of lack. The father, who does not believe in the power of the zaddik, then allows himself to be duped by the devil (in the guise of a merchant) into stopping his son from seeing the zaddik. And because of this the son dies. At the conclusion of the story we find out that the devil had blocked the son's access to the zaddik because if they had joined, the "lesser" and the "greater" lights would have joined and the messiah would have come. Buber's presentation of how the devil stops the son from meeting the zaddik is far more nuanced than the presentation in the traditional text, as this comparison shows.

The Nahman text:	*Buber's retelling:*
They set out and came to an inn to spend the night. They found a merchant there and they began to speak with him in the manner of merchants. They did not reveal to him that they were going	They traveled till evening and only sought out an inn upon the arrival of darkness. While they stopped to rest in the sitting room of the inn, a traveling merchant joined them and engaged

to see the zaddik, because the rabbi was embarrassed to say that he was going there. They spoke of worldly matters until the course of the conversation brought them to the subject of zaddikim and where they could be found. The merchant said to them that there was a zaddik there and there. So they began to speak about the zaddik to whom the rabbi and his son were going. The merchant answered them then with surprise, "But how superficial[87] he is! I am coming from him and when I was there he committed a sin." The father turned to his son and said: "See my son what this merchant says in his innocence? Did he not just come from the zaddik?" And they returned home.

them in conversation. The rabbi had resolved not to speak of his visit to the zaddik, for it was certain that it would bring him embarrassment. So they spoke about all sorts of worldly things, and the old man was astonished at how well-traveled and knowledgeable the stranger was in every sphere, and how cleverly and skillfully he knew how to guide the conversation. Soon the rabbi was like wax in his hands and the strange guest learned whatever he wished to know. While they spoke of this and that, the merchant led the conversation quickly and easily to the zaddikim and where they could be found. . . . The merchant mentioned that there lived, not far from there, a zaddik who aroused a lot of interest. . . . The youth shuddered, as if a shooting pain had awakened him from sleep, and he now heard his father ask the stranger if he knew this zaddik. "Truly I know him," replied the merchant with a frivolous yet scornful laugh. . . . "Never have I met a more worldly man than he. With my own eyes I have seen his sinful impulses," . . . The old man turned to his son and called out, "I suspected that it was as this man in his simplicity tells us. We shall return home."

Where the Nahman text presents the merchant quite innocently, Buber, without using "Samael," or "Satan," manages to tip the reader off to the merchant's strange, more than human qualities and his desire to subvert the rabbi and his son's attempt to find the zaddik. "The old man was astonished at how well-traveled and knowledgeable the stranger was in every sphere, and how cleverly and skillfully he knew how to guide the conversation. Soon the rabbi was like wax in his hands." The traditional text conveys the strange and evil power of the merchant somewhat awkwardly by adding a postscript to the tale.

That merchant was Samael himself who appeared in the guise of a merchant and led them astray. When he met the rabbi the second time, he teased him because he had heeded his word. But that is his way, as is known. May the Lord, blessed be He, save us!

Buber's additions and elaborations to this particular story, while staying fairly close to the original meaning, make the narrative flow more smoothly.

Throughout the other five tales of his collection, Buber makes changes and elaborations to clarify difficulties in the traditional texts. Take, for example, the story of "The *Hakham* and the *Tam*," "The Clever Man and the Simple Man."[88] Here, the unhappy life of a clever but unbelieving man is juxtaposed with the happy life of a simple, pious man.[89]

The *Hakham* is knowledgeable in many areas: in business, in medicine, in goldsmithing, yet he can gain no pleasure from his knowledge. At one point he makes a perfect ring for a nobleman and the nobleman does not like it. At another point, he prescribes the right medicine to a sick man and the sick man dies. The *Hakham* is distraught by these events but the traditional text does not explain exactly why. Buber, in the first case, adds lines that explain that the noble man was crude and ignorant of fine jewelry, and in the second example he explains that the relatives of the sick man "employed the remedy in an entirely perverted manner,"[90] and thus the man died. Buber emphasizes, at this point in the narrative, that the *Hakham*'s unhappiness is caused as much by the ignorance of his community as by his own arrogance.

At another point in the narrative Buber makes a slight change that makes the character portrait of the *Tam* more consistent. The *Tam* was known to wear the same pelt for all occasions. When situations required finer attire, he would put on the pelt and just imagine it to be a fancy suit. At one place in the tale the King sends for the *Tam* and provides him with new clothes. In the traditional text, the *Tam* is happy to finally have better attire. Yet in Buber's retelling, the *Tam* resists wearing the new clothes. "When the costly clothes were handed to him, however, he resisted them and would not allow them to be put on him for he wanted to appear before the King in his beloved, wonderously beautiful pelt."[91]

In this same story, however, Buber makes a more radical revision to the text when he omits the entire final section of the traditional tale. This section tells of how the devil captured the *Hakham* after he refused to believe in God, in a Baal-Shem, and in the devil himself and of how the Baal-Shem sets the *Hakham* free. Buber also omits discussion about devils in the tale "The King's Son and the Son of the Maid" and he does not explicitly use the term "Samael" in the tale of the "Rabbi and His Son." This pattern of deleting references to the devil and demons is definitely part of Buber's attempt to "modernize" the tales by deleting the superstitious and demonic references. It also stems from Buber's own philosophical aversion to the hypostatization of evil. Buber believed that as soon as evil became a separate power, a power to be addressed through magical means, human beings give up the responsibility for trying to overcome the evil that is within them through more effective rational means.[92]

However, according to a commentary of Adin Steinsaltz on the story of "The *Hakham* and the *Tam*" and on Nahman's other tales, Satan is crucial to these tales. Demons represent an important aspect of kabbalistic theosophy. Nahman explicitly employed demons in his tales and encouraged his followers to believe in them to repudiate Jewish Enlightenment *(Haskalah)* attempts to do away with superstitious and gnostic notions of evil in Kabbalah and Hasidism.[93] Thus, in doing away with demons in his retellings, Buber distorted some very important aspects of the tales. Buber, of course, has been severely criticized by Gershom Scholem[94] and others for these distortions. Although there are some very good hermeneutic reasons for the distortions,[95] in the next chapter we will see how Buber himself came to see his early tales and his romantic hermeneutic method as flawed. After the development of his philosophy of I and Thou, Buber altered his early hermeneutic method to correct the faults he perceived in it.[96] This led him to pay far more attention to the integrity of the original texts than he did in retelling the Nahman tales. Thus, although Buber's early translations of Hasidic tales can be understood as an outgrowth of the influences of German Neo-Romanticism and the hermeneutics of Wilhelm Dilthey, his later Hasidic tales and, we may add, his biblical writings cannot be properly understood as the product of romantic hermeneutics. These later writings result from what I will call a "dialogical hermeneutic method."

II

I AND THOU AND THE
DIALOGICAL HERMENEUTIC METHOD

Although Buber's early hermeneutic method of interpreting Hasidic texts is clarified by explicating its relationship to the "psychological" method of understanding first outlined by the "romantic" theologian Friedrich Schleiermacher and then further developed by Buber's teacher, Wilhelm Dilthey, Buber's later methodology cannot be defined in strictly romantic terms.[1] The development of the philosophy of I-Thou from 1916 to 1922 led to revisions in Buber's method of interpreting texts.[2] Buber became less interested in perceiving the mind or life-experience of the author behind the text and more interested in the integrity of the text itself. In addition, he developed a notion of interpretation as a dialogic relationship between the reader and the text. With this latter move Buber opened new ground for his hermeneutic theory and anticipated some of the hermeneutic developments usually associated with the contemporary philosopher of interpretation theory, Hans-Georg Gadamer.

In 1922, Buber wrote, in the introduction to *Der Grosse Maggid und seine Nachfolge* (1922), a new collection of tales of the Maggid of Mezritch and his successors, that he had changed his method of translation.

> I have learned to consider the task which is incumbent upon me to consist in giving the stories nothing more and nothing less than the form that is appropriate to them. I rewrite [*dichte*] no further. I add nothing new to the motifs which lie at hand. . . . This pure form opened to me late but in a definite clarity.[3]

Buber further explains, in the introduction to *The Tales of the Hasidim Vol. 1* (1946, Hebrew), that with the writing of *Der Grosse Maggid und seine Nachfolge,* "I rejected my [earlier] method of dealing with the transmitted material, on the grounds that it was too free."[4] He states that in the collections of tales published after *The Tales of Rabbi Nachman* and *The Legend of the Baal-Shem* he "considered it neither permissible nor desirable to expand the tales or to render them more colorful and diverse."[5] Buber tells us that, with regard to tales that related Hasidic teachings, he "tried to keep to the actual words of [the original] texts."[6]

This new respect for the integrity of the text can be seen in a comparison between Buber's early translation of "The Werewolf," one of the Baal-Shem legends, and a later translation which appeared after the publication of *I and Thou.*

<table>
<tr><td>

Buber's early translation

When death came over the old Rabbi Eliezer, the father of the child Israel, he surrendered to it, without a struggle, the soul which had become tired from many earthly years of wandering. . . . But his sad eyes still sought again and again the fair head of the boy. . . . He looked at him penetratingly: "My son the Adversary will confront you in the beginning, at the turning, and at the fulfillment; in the shadow of a dream and in the living flesh. He is the husk you must break.[7]

He is the abyss over which you must fly. There will be times when you will descend, like a bolt of lightning into his last concealment and he will disperse before your power like a thin cloud. And there will be times when he will surround you with a torrent of viscous darkness and you will stand alone on the reef in the middle of the ocean of his night. But know . . . that your soul is an ore that no one can crush and only God can melt. Therefore: Do not fear the Adversary, never fear anything."[8]

</td><td>

Buber's later translation

Israel was born to his parents in their old age and his father died when Israel was still a boy. When his father felt that death was near, he took his son in his arms and said to him: "I see that you will cause my light to shine out[9] and that it was not given to me to raise you. But, my beloved son, remember all your days that God is with you and you do not have to fear anything in the world."

These words remained engraved in Israel's heart.[10]

</td></tr>
</table>

It is no mere coincidence that Buber altered his hermeneutic approach to Hasidism about the same time that he was developing his dialogical I-Thou philosophy. Buber himself connects the "transformation" of his approach to Hasidism to the development of his philosophy of dialogue. "The realization . . . grew in me, that of human life as the possibility of dialogue with being. . . . At the same time, but in a special osmosis with it, my relationship to Hasidism was ever more basically transformed."[11]

Buber's quest for the "dialogue with being" turned his focus from the mind and creative experience of the Hasidic master to the truth about "Being" to which the Hasidic text points. In the development of the philosophy of I-Thou, Buber moved away from emphasis on the ineffable heightened experience *(Erlebnis)* of the individual and the quest for the mystical union that obliterates all distinctions to the dialogical relationship between an I and a Thou, represented, paradigmatically, by a meeting between two persons. The philosophy of I-Thou also brought with it a deeper appreciation for the every-day and historical world and for the interpersonal realm. In addition, it brought with it a change in Buber's view of language. Indeed, Buber uses his new view of language as the hallmark of his philosophy of I-Thou and the underpinning of his revised view of the interpretation of texts.

In his pre-dialogical period, Buber, like other neo-romantics, had despaired of the ability of language to express the deepest experience *(Erlebnis)* of mystical unity and the deepest reality. "Language . . . will never enter the realm of ecstasy . . . the realm of unity"; it cannot express "the ground of experience."[12] Among the important influences on Buber's change of heart regarding language was the intellectual challenge and new friendship of Franz Rosenzweig. In his "New Thinking," also called *Sprachdenken* ("Speech-Thinking"), Rosenzweig focused on the spoken word as a method through which German Idealism could be challenged and temporal existence made part of philosophy. "In the new thinking, the method of speech replaces the method of thinking maintained in all earlier philosophies."[13] Rivka Horwitz has used evidence from Buber's and Rosenzweig's correspondence and from Rosenzweig's notes on an early draft of *I and Thou* to argue that Rosenzweig was a crucial influence on Buber's changed view of language. Horwitz quotes a telling line from a letter from Rosenzweig to his wife on January 4, 1922, about an upcoming meeting with Buber: "Speech I will teach him in Frankfurt."[14]

I and Thou

By looking at the opening paragraphs of *I and Thou,* we can see that Buber heeded Rosenzweig's words on language.

> To man the world is twofold, in accordance with his twofold attitude.
> The attitude of man is twofold, in accordance with the twofold nature of the primary words which he speaks. . . .
> The one primary word is the combination *I-Thou.*
> The other primary word is the combination *I-It.* . . .
> . . . Primary words do not describe something that might exist independently of them, but being spoken they bring about existence.[15]

In addressing the subject of the primary word I-Thou Buber refers to the ontological power of language. Language "brings about existence," or, as Kaufmann puts it in his translation, language "establishes a mode of existence";[16] it establishes two types of worlds in which humans dwell. "When a primary word is spoken the speaker enters the word and takes his stand in it."[17] Buber uses the ontological power of language to criticize his old *Erlebnis* philosophy and propose his new philosophy of I-Thou. The primary word I-It establishes a world of discrete objects and discrete experiences. Speaking the word I-It, the individual probes his or her own experience; the individual uses the objects and persons of the world to reflect his or her own inner state or condition. The primary word I-Thou, on the other hand, "establishes relation." In speaking this word, the person discovers others, the uniqueness and concrete reality of others. And since the word I-Thou has a dialogical quality, the I is not lost in the other but is affirmed through it. The word I-Thou is the word of mutuality and reciprocity. It is an affirmation of the other and of the I at the same time.

That language is the primary tool of human communication, the tool of expression and reception of what is human, makes it an apt metaphor for the philosophy of I-Thou. In beginning with language, Buber marks his departure from his earlier philosophy of *Erlebnis* and mysticism, which was highly introspective and individualistic and despaired of the individual's ability to communicate his or her individual and mystical experience to another. But the recognition of language not only signals a movement away from mysticism and the philosophy of individual experience. When Buber comes to the task of interpreting texts after *I and Thou*, the notions of dialogue, reciprocity, and the value of otherness developed therein transform his method of interpretation.

What Buber's hermeneutic method after *I and Thou* requires is that the integrity, the otherness, the wholeness of the text be respected and not violated by radical refashioning. Buber's old romantic hermeneutic method may be described as a movement from the text to the interpreter's memory and imagi-nation (the psychic resources for empathy with the author) and back to the text to re-create it. After *I and Thou*, Buber becomes more interested in the text itself and in the dialogical relationship between it and the interpreter. The focus is the text and the truth about being it discloses instead of the mind of the author and the free, creative expression of the interpreter. The text becomes a Thou and interpretation a matter of an I-Thou relationship between the interpreter and the text. The psychological, romantic hermeneutic method, Buber himself recognizes, does not often produce a meeting of the reader with the author or with the text. Instead, it is a technique through which the reader uses the text to probe his or her own imaginative and creative faculties. Reading becomes another *Erlebnis*, a vehicle to inner experience, that ultimately excludes the text and the author. The romantic hermeneutic method assumes an impossible "identity" of the mind of the interpreter with that of the author or an impossible identity of the mind of the interpreter with what we may call the "collective mind" of the original audience.[18] It focuses too much attention on the reader's own experience as the basis of the empathy through which the author's experience is divined. It assumes that the reader has had such a vast range of experiences that he or she can readily empathize with the world of experiences represented by a text. This method fails to respect the strangeness, the other-ness, even the incommensurability of the world of the text and that of the interpreter. In turning to the reader's experience, the hermeneutics of Romanti-cism is often more monological than it is dialogical.

Because the I-Thou relationship is usually represented by a meeting between persons, and the word I-Thou is paradigmatically cast in terms of the spoken word between humans, it may not readily occur to readers of Buber that a work of art can be viewed as a Thou and that an individual can have an I-Thou relationship with it. However, we will see that this is possible, indeed, it is required by Buber's dialogical thought. The groundwork for this position is laid in the very section in *I and Thou* that follows Buber's opening remarks on language, the section which explores the I-Thou relation with *geistige Wesenheiten,* with works of art.

To map out the development of Buber's dialogical hermeneutic method we will first look at Buber's revised aesthetics in *I and Thou.* We will then attempt to highlight the unique aspects of Buber's dialogical hermeneutics by a comparison with the contemporary hermeneutic theory of Hans-Georg Gadamer. Finally, having articulated the presuppositions of Buber's interpretive methods, we use hermeneutic theory to approach the famous Buber-Scholem controversy over the proper interpretation of Hasidic texts.

Buber's Dialogic Aesthetics

In *I and Thou* we can clearly see the conceptual underpinnings of the new approach to Hasidism and a new hermeneutic philosophy. In the beginning of *I and Thou,* Buber develops a new view of the human relation to all creative works. Buber refers to creative works in his discussion of the three "spheres in which the word of relation arises."[19] These three spheres are nature, humanity, and *geistige Wesenheiten.* This latter term is translated as "spiritual beings" by Kaufmann and Smith, but a better translation is offered by Robert Wood—"forms of the spirit"—and Buber himself suggests "spirit in phenomenal forms."[20] In his more extended discussion of *geistige Wesenheiten* in *I and Thou,* it is clear that Buber associates the term with human creative activities—art, language, knowledge, and action—of which art is the "prime analogate."[21]

Paragraph thirteen, which explicates the term *geistige Wesenheiten,* begins: "This is the eternal source of art. . . ."[22] In this section Buber develops a notion of the origin and interpretation of art which is different from that of Dilthey. For Dilthey, the origin of the work of art is found in the lived experience, *Erlebnis,* of the artist, of which art is an expression.[23] For Buber, in *I and Thou,* art is presented as the expression, not of a human experience, but of a relationship between an individual and a suggestive artistic form, *Gestalt.*

> This is the eternal source of art: a man is faced by a form which desires to be made through him into a work. This form is no offspring of his soul, but is an appearance which steps up to it and demands of it the effective power. The man is concerned with an act of his being. If he carries it through, if he speaks the primary word out of his being to the form which appears, then the effective power streams out, and the work arises. . . . The relation in which I stand to it is real, for it affects me, as I affect it. To produce is to draw forth, to invent is to find, to shape is to discover.[24]

Thus, for Buber art is not "the offspring of the soul" of the artist, nor is it a record of the artist's past experience (as it is for Dilthey). Rather, art arises out of a response by the artist to the "call" of a form. It arises from an I-Thou relationship between the artist and the form. Art results from a discovery of something outside of the individual. It arises when the artist responds to an incipient form which desires concreteness, which "desires to be made into a work."

But whence does this form come? In *I and Thou* Buber suggests that it comes from the sphere of *Geist*, of spirit,[25] a sphere which Buber defines as that which lies "between I and Thou," and that which bestows the "power to enter into relationship."[26] Buber's notion of *Geist*, exploiting the multivalency of the German word and the variety of philosophic usages, seems to lie somewhere between a transcendent and divine reality and Dilthey's more empirical notion of *Geist* as comprised of cultural entities: language, art, religion, institutions.[27] We will not be too far from the text's usage, I believe, if we conceive of spirit as a transempirical reality, something, "in its own realm," which contains incipient forms which can gain concrete status if fashioned into works by humans with the attitude of I-Thou.[28]

Buber makes the crucial point, however, in *I and Thou*, that the production of a work of art, the fashioning into relief of the world, requires a "restriction" of "endless possibility."[29] In the language of *I-Thou*, the artist turns the limitless Thou into a thing, an object. The artist "leads the form across—into the world of *It*."[30] Thus the work can be carried about, categorized, and viewed by others. But it also can be brought to life again! Here we can see the grounds for a different hermeneutic in Buber's work. A form of spirit, which ostensibly is an It, can be brought to life again if the form is approached by a viewer with the attitude of I-Thou. I quote from two different places in *I and Thou*.

> The work produced is a thing among things, able to be experienced and described as a sum of qualities. But from time to time it can face the receptive beholder in its whole embodied form.

> . . . again and again that which has the status of object must blaze up into presentness and enter the elemental state from which it came, to be looked on and lived in the present by men.[31]

In these quotations we have the rudiments of Buber's transformed hermeneutic method. First we have the realization that a *geistige Wesenheit*, a work of art or form of spirit, although an *It*, can "blaze up into presentness," into the status of a Thou, again. The work of art which was produced by an I-Thou relationship between an artist and a sensed form can become a Thou again through a new I-Thou relationship. To properly interpret the work, the interpreter must take the attitude of a "receptive beholder" *(empfangend Schauender)*[32] who finds himself or herself "bodily confronted" by the work. Louis Hammer, in his remarks on the relevance of Buber to contemporary aesthetics, suggests that this attitude of receptiveness requires some restraint on the part of the interpreter. "The critic should exercise restraint . . . ; he must cause the work to step forward, not obstruct it by his own interpretive constructions."[33]

In his postscript to *I and Thou*, Buber illustrates the attitude of receptiveness which the interpreter must have by presenting us with a personal anecdote, an example of his own I-Thou encounter with an architectural "form of spirit"—a Doric pillar.

> Out of a church wall in Syracuse, in which it had once been immured, it first came to encounter me: mysterious primal mass represented in such a simple form that there was nothing individual to look at, nothing individual to enjoy. All that could be done was what I did: took my stand, stood fast, in face of this structure of spirit, this mass penetrated and given body by the mind and hand of man.[34]

Encountering a form of spirit as a Thou, we find ourselves encountered. The work addresses us, confronts us, says something that "enters [our] life."[35] The work, as Thou, has a "reality character."[36] It discloses a truth about form and our relation to it.[37] Encountering a work as a Thou one respects the integrity of the work. Hammer argues that Buber's notion of the interpretation of a work of art involves an encounter with "other being." To have interpreted "a work of art is to have reached out and encountered other being by giving oneself over to form within the spheres of sight or sound or human speech."[38] Here, we can begin to understand Buber's use of the curious term *"Wesenheit"* to refer to a work of art or form of spirit. To the extent that the work "blazes up" and becomes a Thou, it is capable of addressing another and appears as a *Wesen*, a being, addressing its viewer. Buber uses *Wesen* to refer to works of art in his later article on aesthetics, "Man and His Image-Work" (1955).[39]

It is obvious that with this notion of a work of art or form of spirit the intention or life-experience of the author behind the work will appear somewhat superfluous. The work itself "speaks and demands a response." And this response which the work calls for represents the second crucially important element in Buber's revised hermeneutic thinking. One cannot remain passive in facing a form of spirit, but must become active. In clarifying the I-Thou relationship with *geistige Wesenheiten*, Buber states:

> The You [Thou] encounters me. But I enter into a direct relationship to it. Thus the relationship is election and electing, passive and active at once.[40]

An I-Thou relationship with a form of spirit engages us in a conversation. Maurice Friedman states that the interpretations of these works "like the I-Thou relationships with nature are modified forms of dialogue."[41] Interpreting a form of spirit requires us to face the work as we face another being. We open our senses to it, to its particularities and to its total gestalt. We allow it to move us, to confront us, to speak to us. We try to perceive its special message and disclosure of reality. And we also respond to it. We present our reactions, we mirror-back our reading and look to see if the work confirms it.[42]

In "Dialogue" (1929), an essay written six years after *I and Thou*, Buber stresses the dialogical demand of works of art and the importance of the relationship between the work of art and the beholder.

> All art is from its origin essentially of the nature of dialogue. All music calls to an ear not the musician's own, all sculpture to an eye not the sculptor's, architec-

ture, in addition, calls to the step as it walks in the building. They all say, to him who receives them, something (not a "feeling" but a perceived mystery) that can be said only in this one language.[43]

Art calls out to the interpreter. It beckons the interpreter to respond. When the interpreter responds the work takes on life, it becomes a Thou and a dialogue is initiated. If the interpreter then gives concrete expression to this dialogue, the result is an "interpretation." In relation to Buber's work on Hasidism, Buber's mature Hasidic writings should be seen as the result of a series of fruitful dialogues with Hasidic texts.

Buber and the Hermeneutic Theory of Gadamer

In developing a notion of interpretation as a dialogue between the reader and a work of art or a text, Buber anticipated one of the most important hermeneutic principles that Hans-George Gadamer developed in his groundbreaking work *Truth and Method (Wahrheit und Methode),* first published in Germany in 1960. Interpreting a text, for Gadamer, is not a matter of empathy with the lived experience of an author, nor is it a matter of jumping out of the reader's historical period into a past one through the springboard of historical criticism. Interpretation arises, rather, out of a process of "conversation" between readers firmly planted in their cultural moment and a text which speaks in an alternative cultural mode. Although Gadamer comes out of the *verstehen* hermeneutic tradition, which originated with Schleiermacher and Dilthey, he is very critical of aspects of romantic hermeneutics.[44]

Gadamer shares the romantic conviction that the human sciences are qualitatively different from the natural sciences. He shares the romantic passion for the value of the task of understanding the products of human culture. Yet he does not share the romantic infatuation with "method" and is highly skeptical about the romantic attempt to establish a method for the human sciences that will bring them an atemporal "objectivity" that parallels the objectivity of the natural sciences. Gadamer argues that understanding is time-bound. The meaning of a text changes in accordance with the different temporal periods in which the interpreter stands. Gadamer also argues that technical methods, like the attitude of I-It, block, instead of open, avenues to understanding cultural products. He seeks a dialogical path to understanding much like that which Buber describes in *I and Thou.* A final disagreement which Gadamer has with the romantics is over the goal of understanding. In Gadamer's view, Schleiermacher and Dilthey attended far too much to the mind of the author and the "artistic thought"[45] that led to the work. In the attempt to recapture the aesthetic creativity of the artist, Schleiermacher and Dilthey miss the noetic dimension of art. Following Heidegger's interpretation of Greek aesthetics and ontology, Gadamer argues that the main import of art is the "truth" that it discloses about being. Understanding, for Gadamer, is "an encounter with something that asserts itself as truth."[46] By dwelling on the creativity of the author and the interpreter and developing technical methods to arrive at the original creative moment, romantic hermeneutics misses the truth-character of art.

To illustrate some of his constructive notions of interpretation, Gadamer suggests that a good model for the process which takes place between the interpreter and the text is provided by the dynamics of play.[47] In a game truly played, the players relinquish some of their control. The players are taken over by the game in such a way that they live in the challenges, the ups and downs, the back and forth movements of the game.

> Play obviously represents an order in which the to and fro motion of play follows of itself. It is part of play that the movement is not only without goal or purpose but also without effort. It happens, as it were, by itself. . . . The structure of play absorbs the player into itself, and thus takes from him the burden of the initiative.[48]

Gadamer asserts that the proper subject of play is not the player but "rather, the game itself." Thus "all playing is a being-played."[49] When one reads a good text attentively, one is similarly overtaken by it. The subject matter is neither the author nor the reader but, properly, it is the content of the text, the truth of the text, which enthralls, challenges, and educates the reader. Gadamer asserts that the interpreter must "subordinate" him- or herself to "the text's claim to dominate our minds."[50] And the text has this claim because, as Gadamer says, "it expresses itself like a 'Thou'"[!][51]

It remains something of a mystery why Gadamer does not so much as footnote Buber, who is responsible for developing and popularizing the notion of I-Thou.[52] Gadamer does not refer to Buber, but he uses the language of I-Thou to clarify the nature of text (or Gadamer generally uses the broader term "tradition") and the proper relationship that should be taken to it.

> But tradition is not simply a process that we learn to know and be in command of through experience; it is language, i.e., it expresses itself like a 'Thou.' A 'Thou' is not an object but stands in a relationship with us. . . . For tradition is a genuine partner in communication, with which we have fellowship as does the 'I' with a 'Thou.'[53]

Gadamer delineates three types of I-Thou relationships with people and he uses these to speak of parallel types of I-Thou relationships with texts. Two of these are not fully mutual and have the quality of what Buber calls the "I-It" relationship. In the first, we study a text as the scientist studies objects of nature, attempting to place it in categories which render it suitable for analysis. Here we are interested in the text only as an "instantiation of a general law."[54] Here the Thou is treated as a mute "object," and the I exercises a practiced neutrality, refusing to be affected by or involved in any way with the Thou.[55] This is typified, for Gadamer, by a social scientific approach to a tradition or text.

In the second type of I-Thou relationship with a tradition or text the I is concerned with the Thou not as a type but as a historically unique entity. Yet the relationship is fundamentally one of "self-relatedness." The interpreter is not really open to the otherness, the "strangeness,"[56] of the Thou and immediately seeks to understand the other in his or her own terms. Here, the goal is to "understand the other better than the other understands himself."[57] This is the approach, in Gadamer's view, of "historical consciousness," which is exemplified by romantic hermeneutics.

The third, authentic type of I-Thou relationship is based on an initial "separation" and "temporal distance,"[58] what Buber called "the primal setting at a distance,"[59] which guarantees "an acceptance of [the] otherness"[60] of the Thou and prepares the way for genuine relationship. Gadamer asserts that the crucial thing in an I-Thou relationship with a text is to "experience the 'Thou' truly as a 'Thou,' i.e., not to overlook his claim and to listen to what he has to say."[61] This requires a "fundamental sort of openness" which allows that the "criteria of our own knowledge" can be put into question by a traditional text.[62] Here the text is seen as a subject capable of "addressing" the interpreter as an involved, listening subject. Here the interpreter must approach the text with an attitude of ignorance (the Socratic *docta ignorantia*), or as Buber puts it, with an attitude of "receptiveness." Gadamer asserts that this attitude allows the "truth" of a text to be disclosed. Here, following Heidegger, Gadamer intends a notion of truth as *aletheia,* or disclosure. Truth "shines-forth," "radiates" from the work of art. Truth reveals itself in its being, it "presents itself" in the form of the work itself.[63]

However, like Buber, Gadamer does not expect that the interpreter, once addressed, will remain silent. The interpreter responds by being taken up into the back and forth movement of the subject matter of the text. The interpreter responds, Gadamer says, by engaging the text in "dialogue,"[64] by having a "conversation with the text."[65] In this conversation the interpreter confronts the text as an alternative "world" with an alternative "horizon" of meaning. This conversation involves a meeting of horizons, the horizon of the text and that of the interpreter. For Gadamer, it is crucial that we recognize that interpreters bring their own world, their own cultural presuppositions and cultural prejudgments, into the process of interpretation. Presuppositions provide the cultural tools—language, analytical techniques, literary and historical knowledge, traditions of study—through which the text is perceived and understood. In Gadamer's view, every text stands in a tradition of a series of interpretations which affect and limit the types of interpretations that a new interpreter can make.[66] The recognition of the importance of the role of the interpreter's prejudgments and the tradition of interpretation that preceded him, what Gadamer calls "effective historical consciousness"[67] is part of recognizing the time-bound quality of all interpretation.

Buber was certainly not as sensitive to the presuppositions which the interpreter brings to the hermeneutic task as was Gadamer. Like his romantic predecessors, Buber saw the interpreter, somewhat naïvely, as an individual devoid of cultural presuppositions. He viewed the interpreter as capable of a dialogue with a work of art on an immediate basis unencumbered by cultural presuppositions. Yet, like Gadamer, Buber did demand that the interpreter as "I" stand his or her own ground before the text as "Thou." One could say that demanding that the presuppositions of one's culture and tradition be given a positive role in hermeneutic activity is tantamount to the I demanding it be appreciated in its fullness in its dialogue with the text. In 1926, in an article on education, Buber articulated this principle with the term "inclusion" *(Umfassung)*.[68] "[The I], without forfeiting anything of the felt reality of his activity, at the same time lives through the common event from the standpoint of the other."[69]

For Gadamer the result of the meeting of world horizons when an understanding or interpretation is forged will be a "fusion of horizons,"[70] a fusion which will lead to a fundamental change not only in the interpreter's worldview but in his or her existential self. Gadamer, sounding particularly like Buber, asserts: "To reach an understanding with one's partner in a dialogue is not merely a matter of total self-expression and the successful assertion of one's own point of view, but a transformation into a communion, in which we do not remain what we were."[71]

Along with this transformation will come the application of the meaning of the text to the interpreter's own life and to the "present situation of the interpreter."[72] A great classic text, as a repository of truth, will always have something to say to the specific situation of the reader. Understanding, for Gadamer, is a process of mediating the universal to the particular, an "application of something universal to a particular situation."[73] Ultimately, the attempt to apply the message of a text to an actual historical life-situation concretizes the meaning of the text and assures that the interpreter heard the message of the text. As Gadamer puts it, it is application "that makes the interpreter the person to whom the text was originally addressed."[74]

Yet because understanding involves this act of application, because the present reader and his or her world is so important in the equation of the meaning of a text, every proper interpretation will entail a *different* understanding from the original understanding of the text's author or its first audience.

> The real meaning of a text, as it speaks to the interpreter, does not depend on the contingencies of the author and whom he originally wrote for. It certainly is not identical with them, for it is always partly determined also by the historical situation of the interpreter and hence by the totality of the objective course of history. . . . Not occasionally only, but always, the meaning of a text goes beyond its author. That is why understanding is not merely a reproductive but always a productive attitude as well. . . . It is enough to say that we understand in a different way, if we understand at all.[75]

We see Gadamer's principle of application at work in all of Buber's interpretations of Hasidism. Buber often insisted that his interpretation of Hasidism was ruled by his concern for its modern meaning. In his essay "Hasidism and Modern Man," Buber tells us that "Hasidism has its word to speak in the crisis of Western Man."[76] In "Replies to My Critics" Buber tells us that he chose to translate and interpret certain tales and not others because they suggested a way out of a modern dilemma. "I have chosen what I have chosen . . . because here is a way, one only to be sensed, but a way."[77] Whether or not we agree with Buber's analysis of the "contemporary situation" and his suggestion of a "neo-Hasidic" solution to it, it is important to recognize the hermeneutic principle which Buber supports in trying to articulate a contemporary meaning for Hasidism. That hermeneutic principle, as Gadamer articulates it, is: "The text . . . if it is to be understood properly . . . must be understood at every moment, in every particular situation, in a new and different way."[78]

The final element in Gadamer's theory of interpretation refers to the role of language. Gadamer asserts that the process of interpretation is intrinsically linguistic: the tradition, the text, the interpreter, the interpretation, all exist in and through language. "All interpretation takes place in the medium of a language."[79] Here, we must point out a crucial difference between Gadamer and Buber's hermeneutic theory as it is expressed in *I and Thou*. For though Buber asserts the primacy of language to the I-Thou relationship and though *I and Thou* begins by differentiating the I-Thou and I-It relationships with a discussion of different *Grundworte*, "basic words" that humans can speak, Buber's notion of language is broader than that which Gadamer uses. The term "language," for Buber, includes supra- or sublinguistic expression such as gesture, facial expression, the communicative capacity of animals, and even silence. Works of art "speak," but they do so "in their own language." Our relationship to works of art, Buber asserts, stands on the threshold of positive speech.

> The relation is wrapped in a cloud but reveals itself, it lacks but creates language. We hear no You [Thou] and yet feel addressed; we answer—creating, thinking, acting: with our being we speak the basic word, unable to say You [Thou] with our mouth.[80]

Given his assertions (at the beginning of *I and Thou*) about the ontological character of language, it is interesting that in *I and Thou* Buber uses painting, sculpture, music, and architecture as his primary examples of *geistige Wesenheiten* and not written texts. This is especially odd given that Buber regards speech as the most expressive tool for the I-Thou relationship.

> Of the three spheres, one, our life with men, is marked out. Here language is consummated as a sequence, in speech and counter-speech. Here alone does the word that is formed in language meet its response. . . . Here what confronts us has blossomed into the full reality of the *Thou*.[81]

Because it is through language that the full reality of the I-Thou relationship is found, one could argue that the highest form of art is not the plastic arts but the written arts. Perhaps in the "clouded" I-Thou relationship to art we have the vestiges of Buber's attraction to the ineffable and the mystical. Indeed, it must be said that the vestiges of mysticism can be found throughout *I and Thou*. For example, consider Buber's radical assertion that the I-Thou relationship represents a total fullness which obliterates all content[82] and that all means, all foreknowledge, all aims and desires are obstacles to the I-Thou relationship.[83] And consider, too, Buber's claim that one comes away from the I-Thou relationship with no "objective speech,"[84] no knowledge, and nothing which can be formulated conceptually. Indeed, as we have suggested, Buber's notion of "language" in *I and Thou* often means not positive language—German, English, Hebrew—but a large variety of communicative expressions. By "dialogue" Buber seems to mean, in *I and Thou,* existential encounter, meaningful exchange of selves, reciprocal revelation.

Many commentators have said that Buber uses the terms "word" and "language" in *I and Thou* metaphorically to refer to the variety of ways in which humans express themselves and relate to one another.[85] Linguistic terms such as "speech," "dialogue," "question," "response" convery qualities such as presence, dynamism, reciprocity, that are descriptive of the I-Thou relationship. The question of language raises the question of mediation: mediation between an I and a Thou and between the realm of I-Thou and that of I-It. In *I and Thou* Buber states that there can be no means to forge an I-Thou relationship and there can be no linguistic or conceptual means to relate the I-Thou event after it has occurred. In short, Buber establishes a radical disjunction between the realms of I-Thou and I-It. The only vehicles of mediation which Buber points to are works of art, which is a concrete expression of an I-Thou encounter with a form of spirit. This expression, when viewed with the attitude of I-Thou, can take on life again and speak as a Thou to its viewer. Yet there is no real theoretical provision for the viewer to move from his or her I-Thou encounter with a work of art to a linguistic or conceptual articulation, an "interpretation" of the work. It seems that for Buber the initial I-Thou relationship between the artist and the form of spirit occurs in an unmediated and prelinguistic sphere. And likewise, the relationship which the viewer or interpreter of the work has with the work arises out of the unmediated, prelinguistic sphere between the interpreter and the work of art. To be true to the hermeneutic philosophy of *I and Thou,* the most authentic form of interpretation of a work of art would have to be something like what Buber produced in his early performative retellings of the Hasidic tales: it would have to be another *geistige Wesenheit,* another work of art!

Because the I-Thou relationship with forms of spirit lies on the threshold of speech, this relationship often can be articulated in linguistic expression and thus we have Buber's Hasidic tales or his interpretations of the Bible. Yet it seems that, for Buber, the initial immediate I-Thou relationship with forms of spirit is prelinguistic. The issue of the linguisticality of the process of interpretation is related to the issue of the role of cultural presuppositions and past interpretations (what Gadamer called "effective history") in molding interpretation. Gadamer develops both of these notions with far more depth than does Buber. Interpretation takes place in and through language, culture, and tradition for Gadamer. For Buber, in *I and Thou,* interpretation arises out of the unmediated prelinguistic sphere of the between, the sphere between the interpreter and the work.

In sum we could say that in *I and Thou* Buber's reliance on the prelinguistic, unmediated encounter prohibits the full development of a theory of interpretation based on the written text and the written or spoken word of interpretation. For the development of such a mediated, language-bound hermeneutic we will have to wait for Buber's biblical writings and his late writings on language.[86]

A Hermeneutic Approach to the Buber-Scholem Controversy

I have tried to show how Martin Buber was related to the German *verstehen* hermeneutical school. As a student of Dilthey early in his career, Buber endeavored to re-create by imaginatively retelling Hasidic tales. After *I and Thou,* however, he developed a more dialogical approach to the interpretation of Hasidic texts. The relationship to Gadamer here is remarkable. If we take Gadamer's hermeneutic theory seriously, a defense for Buber's interpretation of Hasidism is in order. Gershom Scholem and others[87] have criticized Buber for not presenting a historically accurate picture of Hasidism and for not presenting the meaning of Hasidism for its original audience. Yet Buber, as he himself said, was not interested in Hasidism as a historical phenomenon.[88] Buber, like Gadamer, had little faith in the historical critical illusion of an "objective" presentation of a historical movement of the past.[89] Rather, he sought a new interpretation of Hasidism which would apply its meaning to the contemporary situation.

In the beginning of his famous critique "Martin Buber's Interpretation of Hasidism," Gershom Scholem states that many who have commented on Buber's writings on Hasidism "have not in the least been aware that Buber's work *is* an interpretation."[90] Yet Scholem is aware neither of the complexity of Buber's interpretative methodology nor of its development. Scholem uses the interpretative nature of Buber's work on Hasidism as grounds for criticism. Scholem's analysis suggests that Buber's presentation of Hasidism is interpretative and his is "objective." However, it can be argued that Scholem's work is also an interpretation of Hasidism. What we have is not Scholem's objective presentation and Buber's subjective interpretation, but, rather, a conflict of interpretations of Hasidism. The Buber-Scholem controversy will only be productively addressed by clarifying the underlying hermeneutic assumptions upon which Buber and Scholem operate. When the hermeneutic issues are articulated I believe the controversy can be clarified and new avenues for resolving it can be opened up.

Rudolf Bultmann has said that interpretation is partially a matter of posing questions to a text. He asserts that the questions an interpreter asks indicate the type of hermeneutic position he or she takes.[91] Let us begin to analyze the hermeneutic positions of Buber and Scholem by looking at the questions they ask of Hasidism.

Questions that appear in Scholem's various writings on Hasidism are: How is Hasidism connected to past forms of Judaism? What is new about it? Which

Hasidic texts can be considered authentic? What has Hasidism's impact on eighteenth-century Judaism? Buber, on the other hand, asks: What is the essential message of Hasidism? What is the significance of Hasidism for modernity? How can Hasidism be communicated to modern audiences? How can its mythical and epic essence be preserved? And how can Hasidism be a source for Jewish renewal?

It is obvious that Scholem and Buber ask qualitatively different types of questions of Hasidism. Buber asks questions of meaning and modern relevance and Scholem asks historical questions, questions which aim at placing Hasidism in the context of the history of Judaism. Buber once clearly articulated the hermeneutic differences between himself and Scholem and it is worth our while to quote him at length.

> There are two different ways in which a great tradition of religious faith can be rescued from the rubble of time and brought back into light. The first is by means of historical scholarship that seeks to be as comprehensive and exact as possible. The scholar takes this former tradition as an object of knowledge; he edits and interprets the texts of its teachings, investigates its origins and background, its phases of development, and the ramifications of its schools. The primary and controlling purpose of this type of investigation is to advance the state of historical knowledge about the body of religious faith in question. . . . The other, and essentially different, way of restoring a great buried heritage of faith to the light is to recapture a sense of the power that once gave it the capacity to take hold of and vitalize the life of diverse classes of people. Such an approach derives from the desire to convey to our own time the force of a former life of faith and to help our age renew its ruptured bond with the Absolute.[92]

Buber makes clear the different hermeneutic strategies that he and Scholem employ in their work on Hasidism. Buber looks at Hasidic texts with an eye toward their existential power and message for contemporary life and Scholem seeks their historical significance. We have already reviewed the presuppositions of Buber's hermeneutic approach. Let us now look more carefully at the presuppositions of Scholem's method.

Scholem and the Science of Judaism

Gershom Scholem's hermeneutic predecessors are the leaders of the nineteenth-century German Jewish movement called the Science of Judaism. Although Scholem was highly critical of the movement, he shared its overall aims and methods. Scholem's work can be seen as an attempt to correct the faults of the Science of Judaism and more adequately carry out its objectives.[93]

The goal of the scholars of the Science of Judaism was to trace and explain the postbiblical history of Judaism in its various manifestations through the means of critical scholarship. The early scholars of the Science of Judaism shared the assumptions and goals of historicism. They believed culture could be explained in terms of its historical antecedents and historical context. In investigating historical events they sought to know "whether or not something actually happened; whether it happened in the way it is told or in some other way."[94] They believed the requisite attitude to carry out their study was "a strictly scientific method of utter objectivity and detachment."[95] To this end they attempted "the suspension of all preconceptions . . . and religious belief systems" in undertaking their studies.[96]

In his programmatic essay "On Rabbinic Literature," Leopold Zunz divided the scholarship of the Science of Judaism into three areas: "ideational, philological, and historical." The ideational task involved tracing "the intellectual greatness"[97] of Judaism. It required an investigation of rabbinic theology and subsequent Jewish thought with an eye toward comparison with "the parallel learning embracing the world."[98] Zunz had studied philology with Friedrich Wolf and regarded philology as his chief method for, as he explains, "language is the first friend leading us unto the road to science. . . . It alone is capable of removing the veil of the past."[99] Philology was helpful in one of the primary tasks of the Science of Judaism, that of bibliography. A great deal of effort was expended to catalogue, date, and authenticate the vast quantity and variety of extant Jewish literature.

Aside from the ideational and philological tasks, the overall aim of Zunz's Science of Judaism was to present a picture of the history of Jewish culture throughout the ages so that Jews and non-Jews could see the riches of the Jewish people and understand the historical antecedents of the present Jewish situation. In this concern to paint a positive picture of the past of the Jews, however, one can detect the "nonobjective" ideological elements of the *Wissenschaft des Judentums.*

The Science of Judaism developed partially out of a response to frustration with the process of political emancipation, rising antisemitism, and a rash of Jewish conversions to Christianity in the first decades of the nineteenth century in Berlin. Advocates of the Science of Judaism sought to build Jewish self-respect and defend Judaism against antisemitic attacks. Their scholarship would show the Jews to have a noble heritage, a heritage in which reason and ethics were of paramount importance. The Science of Judaism was used to strengthen Jewish identity on the one hand and prove that the Jews were worthy of emancipation on the other. In addition, it was quickly embraced by leaders of Reform Judaism in Germany who were reformulating their religion in accordance with rational principles.

Zunz, who was a leading Reform preacher, argued that the Science of Judaism could provide information and criteria to "recognize and distinguish among the old and useful, the obsolete and harmful, the new and desirable"[100] aspects of Judaism. Thus the apologetic, political, and religious aspects of the Science of Judaism often compromised its avowed scientific neutrality.

In his article "The Science of Judaism—Then and Now," Scholem exhibits both his distaste for some of the problematic ideological elements of the Science of Judaism and his sympathies with its positive aims and methods.

> We cannot and must not forget that . . . nearly all of the creators and co-workers in the domains of Jewish historiography and Science of Judaism were theolo-

gians. The rabbinic share in both the positive and the problematic is enormous; it cannot be overestimated. These rabbis, who unlocked the sources, were the first to make possible precise inquiries and historical criticism. But at the same time, especially due to the influence of the nineteenth century, they brought with them a certain tendency . . . to water down Judaism and to spiritualize it.[101]

The destructive aspect of the Science of Judaism was its tendency to rationalize, to abstract, to "de-actualize" Judaism. Scholem was disturbed by what he calls the "de-Judaization" program of some scholars, most radically expressed in Moritz Steinschneider's statement: "We have only one task left: to give the remains of Judaism a decent burial."[102] What was constructive about the Science of Judaism was its precise inquiry and historical criticism, i.e., its scientific methodology, and its veiled sense of "the living peoplehood" and the "genius" of the Jewish people. Scholem took as his life's work the task of investigating the "life hidden in Judaism" through the scientific methodologies that the *Wissenschaft des Judentums* first developed. He suggests that the Science of Judaism of his day, carried out in the context of the secular Israeli and American universities, is no longer prey to the severe apologetic and political limitations which the founders suffered under. Scholem recognizes some ideological countercurrents in the contemporary period, yet he asserts that "the secularized view of Judaism opens up an enormously positive potentiality."[103] Scholem seems to think that the modern university scholar of the Science of Judaism can carry out the original tasks of understanding the "character and history" of Judaism and uncovering the most vital aspects of that history.

Scholem's Critique of Buber

If we look at Scholem's interpretation of Hasidism and his critique of Buber we can see some of the fruits of his interpretative methodology.[104] Scholem sought the hidden life of Judaism in the tradition of Jewish mysticism, which the rational founders of the Science of Judaism ignored, dismissed, or distorted. Through historical critical and philological methods Scholem dated and authenticated mystical texts and described the historical context and the development of various schools of Jewish mysticism. He single-handedly developed the academic study of Jewish mysticism and, perhaps more importantly, he displayed its proper place in the history of Judaism. When Scholem turned to his study of Hasidism he viewed it as a late and popular manifestation of Jewish mysticism.[105] It is from the perspective of mysticism and from the presuppositions of historical criticism that Scholem criticizes Buber's interpretation of Hasidism.

In "Martin Buber's Interpretation of Hasidism," Scholem begins his critique by stating that Buber's presentation of Hasidism militates against a proper historical understanding of Hasidism.

Buber combines facts and quotations to suit his purpose, namely, to present Hasidism as a spiritual phenomenon and not as a historical one. He has often said that he is not interested in history. . . . Buber omits a great deal of material which he does not even consider, although it may be of great significance for the understanding of Hasidism as a historical phenomenon.[106]

In Scholem's view, Buber is unreliable as a historian of Hasidism because he was too subjectively involved in it. Buber used Hasidism to express his own religious strivings. As his religious orientation changed, his interpretation of Hasidism changed. Thus Buber stressed the connection between Kabbalah and Hasidism in his early life but attempted to sever this connection as he came to oppose mysticism in his later life.[107] Scholem also criticizes Buber for failing to appreciate the magical and communal aspects of Hasidism, for stressing the importance of the legends over and above the theoretical litera- ture of Hasidism, and for misunderstanding the Hasidic attitude toward the profane sphere of the here and now.[108] He tells us that Buber read into Hasidism "his own philosophy of religious anarchism and existentialism, [which has] no roots in the texts themselves."[109] Therefore, in Scholem's view, there is a radical distance between Buber's interpretation of Hasidism and the actual historical phenomenon.

Scholem's careful scholarship and meticulous attention to texts have led many to accept his criticisms of Buber. Yet if we look at the Buber-Scholem controversy from a hermeneutic perspective new questions arise and the case no longer seems so clear-cut. First we must ask if it is appropriate to judge Buber's interpretation of Hasidism solely in the terms of the Science of Juda- ism, the terms of philology and historical criticism. As Scholem himself points out, Buber time and time again stated that he was not interested in historical issues. Coming out of the tradition of romantic hermeneutics, Buber was interested first in an intuitive communion with the Hasidic masters and later in an I-Thou dialogue with the narrative texts of Hasidism. From the perspective of Romanticism, Buber and Scholem operate on different epistemological and ontological levels: *Geisteswissenschaften* and *Naturwissenschaften*. They use different methods: *verstehen* and *erklären*.[110] To criticize Buber solely from the vantage point of historical studies is to criticize him from an alternative framework and to fail to respect the nature of Buber's project. As Gadamer has stated, "hermeneutics and historical study . . . are clearly not the same thing."[111]

A hermeneutic approach to Scholem's reading of Hasidism may lead us to ask why it is that he feels that his view of Hasidism is "objective" and Buber's is subjective and interpretative.[112] A host of historians, beginning with R. G. Collingwood in English historiography, Raymond Aron in French historiogra- phy, and Johann Droysen in the German *verstehen* tradition, admit that the historian must use his or her subjective capacities of imagination to recon- struct a historical phenomenon.[113] They assert that the historian's subjective preferences and intellectual background must influence his or her decisions in choosing to investigate certain historical events, in highlighting certain docu- ments over others, and in retelling the story of history in one way or another.[114] Most historians recognize that they cannot retrieve a past historical event as it actually happened. They retrieve only a facsimile, a possible version, an interpretation of the past. Given this, Scholem's presentation is also an interpretation of Hasidism.

Mediating the Dispute: The Hermeneutic Theory of Ricoeur

If we can establish that both Scholem's and Buber's writings on Hasidism are interpretative and that they begin from different hermeneutic presuppositions, must this lead us to simply assert the validity of each position without evaluating their strengths and weaknesses? In categorizing Scholem's perspective with the term "explanation" and Buber's with "understanding" are we necessarily creating a radical disjunction between the two positions? Is there any way to adjudicate the dispute between Buber and Scholem?

Although particular aspects of the Buber-Scholem controversy are unique, in general the controversy goes beyond Hasidism and two particular interpreters and can be found wherever historians and social scientists battle philosophers, theologians, and literary critics over the proper interpretation of cultural phenomena and texts. The controversy represents a focal question in all of contemporary hermeneutic theory: to what extent do methods of explanation and understanding represent epistemologically and even ontologically opposed approaches to the interpretation of culture? If we can see the Buber-Scholem controversy as an instance of this wider hermeneutic question, I believe steps toward a resolution of the controversy can be taken. In framing the controversy in terms of a larger debate on method, we will be able to take advantage of the work of a figure who has thought deeply about the estrangement of the social sciences and philosophy, the French philosopher Paul Ricoeur.

Ricoeur has shown, in addressing the issue of the radical separation between the methods of *verstehen* and *erklären*, that they need not be so estranged. Though the methods are certainly different they can be shown to complement each other in the task of interpretation. Ricoeur has argued that methods of explanation and understanding are not mutually exclusive.[115] For example, we can think of a human conversation as a model for human communication. When two people understand one another, statement builds on statement and creative dialogue rich with intuitive understanding ensues. Yet if one interlocutor suddenly does not understand the other, then free conversation is stopped and the partner is asked for explanations, reasons, exact information, analysis. After this is done the free and creative dialogue can continue. Thus, in conversation, explanation assists understanding. Similarly, when we read a literary text we find that an analysis of the structure of the plot, the style of the writing, and the period in which it was written assists us in understanding the meaning in front of the text, the meaning for our life and for our relationship to our world.

To apply this to the Buber-Scholem controversy we could say that Scholem's questions to Buber about the historical reality of Hasidism and the historical status of certain texts need not be regarded as irrelevant to Buber's hermeneutic task. Developing a "dialogue" with the texts which opens to an understanding of the "meaning" and modern significance of Hasidism can be aided by historical critical investigation. For example, Scholem's questions about the basis in the texts for Buber's interpretation of the relationship between the Hasidim and the mundane and physical activities of everyday life are certainly pertinent to Buber's hermeneutic aims. For if there is no basis in the texts, then Buber's interpretation results not from a serious dialogue with the texts but, rather, from a projection of his own views into the texts. Here, it is possible that Buber has lost sight of the "otherness" of the text which is so important to his dialogical theory. In this case it seems that Scholem's historical and philological approach can act as a much-needed corrective to Buber's interpretative method. To take this further, we could say that there is no reason why historical critical methodology must be antithetical to a dialogic or a Gadamerian hermeneutic approach.

In his essay "Explanation and Understanding," Ricoeur argues that "explanation *develops* understanding" and "understanding precedes, accompanies, closes, and thus *envelops* explanation."[116] Ricoeur argues that explanatory methods are especially important allies when we approach a phenomenon that is communicated not directly, as in the model of conversation, but indirectly, through textual form. Here, where texts are our only form of communication, we need forms of explanation to help us to decipher the cultural codes that the text assumes and with which it is written. "This exteriorization into material marks, and this inscription in the codes of discourse, make not only possible *but necessary the mediation of understanding by explanation.*"[117] Historical critical analysis can be of crucial importance in establishing the preunderstandings of the culture which produced a specific text. Without some information on these preunderstandings it is difficult to even begin a dialogue with a text.[118]

Thus, explanatory methods must not be seen as obstacles but, rather, as aids to understanding. Applying Ricoeur's argument to the Buber-Scholem controversy, we could say that the methodology of each alone is insufficient for an adequate interpretation of Hasidism, but if they were put together in a larger and more complex hermeneutic schema, with moments of explanation and understanding, a more adequate interpretation could be developed.

Scholem's historical approach lacks the resources to make Hasidism truly come alive for modern readers. Scholem criticizes the early scholars of the Science of Judaism for not being open to the lively and nonrational elements in the history of Judaism, yet when Scholem himself investigates these elements he does so in such a dry and distanced fashion that the spontaneous, nonrational aspects are deprived of vitality. Scholem cites apologetic, political, and theological prejudices as the true barriers to knowledge of the nonrational elements in the Science of Judaism but fails to see the detrimental effects of its underlying methodological approach. Not only do these methods seem to undermine a creative relationship to the nonrational elements of Judaism, they tend to fix them in the past and display them as antiquated phenomena of ages gone by. Using explanatory historical methods to the exclusion of others has the effect of further distancing many modern Jews from traditions in their past. As Yosef Yerushalmi suggests: "Those who are alienated from their past cannot be drawn into it by explanation alone; they require evocation as well."[119] Historical methodologies of explanation do not foster a dialogical interchange whereby the past can make a claim on the present as a source of meaning and truth.

Buber, in his attempt to understand and express the elemental spirit and present meaning of Hasidism, certainly brings Hasidism to life and attempts to engage it in questions of meaning that are relevant to contemporary audiences. With his dialogical hermeneutic approach Buber certainly paid more respect to the integrity of the original Hasidic texts than he did in his early method. Yet still, Buber's interpretation would have benefited from a more extensive exploration of the historical critical issues. Buber has allowed the legitimacy of his interpretation of Hasidism to be questioned by failing to address many of these issues.

I believe that Buber was hampered in this regard by the prejudice inherited from Dilthey against methods of *erklären*. Dilthey's distinction between *verstehen* and *erklären* appears in Buber's thought as the distinction between the I-Thou and the I-It. The I-Thou attitude can be correlated with understanding, and the I-It with explanation.[120] Buber argued in *I and Thou* that human culture should only be interpreted with the attitude of I-Thou. For Buber, interpreting Hasidism with the dialogical hermeneutic approach excluded historical critical methods. Historical critical methodology approaches texts and historical phenomena as objects to be analyzed and categorized. The text as "object" cannot "address" a reader as subject. Gadamer also attempts to exclude explanatory methods from the hermeneutic process. Using Aristotle's distinction between *phronesis* and *techne,* Gadamer argues that hermeneutics, as a form of *phronesis,* "must attain its true dignity and proper knowledge of itself by being liberated from history" and "the methodological ideal of the natural sciences."[121] He is particularly critical of what he considered to be Dilthey's hypocritical attempt to develop a "method" of *Verstädnis* which would bring the *Geisteswissenschaften* an "objectivity" parallel to that of the hard sciences. For Gadamer, the "truth" which the human sciences seek cannot be won by a "method," especially a method whose goal is an atemporal objectivity. Yet, as Ricoeur has shown, explanatory methods can be of help to the tasks of understanding, and I believe that they would have been a help to Martin Buber in his attempt to interpret Hasidism.

Both Scholem's and Buber's reading of Hasidism are interpretations. Although Scholem recognizes the interpretative nature of Buber's presentation of Hasidism, he never admits the interpretative quality of his own presentation of Hasidism. Although Scholem speaks of Buber's writings on Hasidism as interpretative, he did not appreciate the complexity of Buber's hermeneutic methods, nor was he aware of the development in Buber's hermeneutic method from the romantic to the dialogical. Scholem's own program of uncovering the vital living elements of the Jewish past would have benefited from

Buber's dialogical approach. On the other hand, Buber's philosophical hostility to explanatory methods of studying human culture prevented him from making full use of the historical critical methods which could have helped him establish the historical context and the original texts of the Hasidic masters. Had the text and context been secured, Buber's dialogical interpretation would have been more firmly rooted and a more authentic dialogue with the texts could have ensued.

A hermeneutic approach to the Buber-Scholem controversy over the proper interpretation of Hasidism allows us to identify the presuppositions that have led to the varying presentations of Hasidism. It also allows us to sketch a model for a more comprehensive hermeneutic schema and thus makes the tension between the two approaches productive. Buber and Scholem can complement and correct each other. In Ricoeur's language, a proper interpretation of Hasidism will result from an approach which allows explanatory methods to "develop" and dialogical interpretation to "envelop" the contemporary interpreter's attempt to understand the meaning of Hasidism for modern persons.[122]

Yet it appears that Buber was not impervious to the possibility of complementing a historical analysis with a dialogical one, for if we turn now from attention to Buber's interpretation of Hasidism to his interpretative writings on the Hebrew Bible we will notice a fascinating hermeneutic turn in Buber's method. Buber was far less averse to employing those historical critical methodologies that he eschewed in his Hasidic work in his biblical writings. Indeed Buber's use of *both* historical critical and dialogical methodologies makes his biblical writings extremely interesting and fertile as a resource for those contemporary theorists who are interested in bridging the gap between explanation and understanding approaches to the interpretation of texts.

III

BUBER'S BIBLICAL HERMENEUTICS

Where Scholem and many others have criticized Buber's interpretations of Hasidism for lacking sensitivity to historical critical issues and failing to meet the scientific standards of scholarship, Buber's writings on the Hebrew Bible have not drawn the same criticism.[1] Scholem states that Buber's biblical writings "present themselves as scientific analysis. . . . They are circumscribed by precise indications of sources and—compared to his other writings—a downright strikingly rich and seemingly ostentatious discussion of scholarly literature."[2] And at the same time that Buber's biblical writings adhere to the rigors of scientific scholarship, they lack none of the hermeneutic power of Buber's Hasidic writings. In writing about Buber's biblical works, Nahum Glatzer, Benyamin Uffenheimer, and Michael Fishbane all stress the fact that it is Buber's task to discern the existential meaning of the Bible and focus a message for the contemporary Jewish and human situation. Glatzer says that Buber explores the Bible in "an attempt to discern its relevance for the present day reader."[3] Uffenheimer tells us that Buber studies the Bible "to bring out those episodes capable of illuminating the paths of our generation in its perplexity."[4] And Fishbane sees Buber's writings as modern "midrash" which "transforms the text into sources of power for the renewal of personal and interpersonal life."[5]

Although Buber designates his Hasidic collection *Der Grosse Maggid und seine Nachfolge* (1922) as one of his first works of translation affected by the philosophy of dialogue, perhaps a more important work is the translation of the Hebrew Bible into German, which he began with Franz Rosenzweig in 1925. This work and the subsequent writings on biblical translation and interpretation not only incorporate the hermeneutic advancements over the romantic methods achieved in *I and Thou,* but also employ new elements not found in the dialogical hermeneutics. It is very clear from his remarks on the way in which the modern reader should read the biblical text that Buber sees his dialogical model as the proper paradigm. In the appendix to his translation, Buber describes the attitude which he hopes the reader will take toward the biblical text in ways which parallel his description of the attitude which the individual must take toward the "Thou." This is the attitude of the receptive beholder, the *"empfangend Schauender."*[6]

He, too, especially when he makes the subject truly important to him, can open himself to the Bible and let himself be struck by its rays wherever they happen to strike him; he can wait without preconception and without reservation surrender himself, let himself be tested; he can take up, with all powers take up and await what will happen to him, await whether or not a new uninhibitedness to the Bible sprouts up within him.[7]

That the receptive attitude of I-Thou and the concomitant hope for a dialogue with the biblical text are central elements in Buber's biblical hermeneutics is certain. Yet added to or inserted within the I-Thou paradigm is what might be considered the surprising use of a variety of technical operations and biblical critical methods. Buber appears to have become convinced that in order to ensure an I-Thou relationship between the reader and the Bible, technique and method need not be eschewed, as a strict dialogical hermeneutic approach such as that of Gadamer would suggest. Buber seems to be convinced that, in the case of the Hebrew Bible, it is precisely techniques and methods that ensure that the I-Thou relationship of the reader with the text is possible. Indeed, as we will see, Buber's biblical hermeneutics makes use of a method of interpretation that has affinities with Schleiermacher's first, "grammatical," stage of interpretation. Thus, what we find in Buber's biblical hermeneutics is a model for interpretation that employs both the paradigm of I-Thou and select techniques and methods of explanation, methods that are so important to Scholem and to our contemporary hermeneutic theorist, Paul Ricoeur. In his use of technical methods Buber even retrieves (the methodological) elements of romantic hermeneutics.

In addition to the issue of the role of historical criticism and methods of explanation, another hermeneutic issue addressed in Buber's biblical writings is that of language. In comparing Buber's hermeneutic philosophy to that of Gadamer in chapter 2, it became apparent that Buber's theory of interpretation, as we find it in *I and Thou,* is deficient in its articulation of the role of language in the interpretative process. The problem is that much of the process of the creation and the interpretation of the work of art takes place in a "clouded," prelinguistic realm. Yet if we look at Buber's biblical writings we find movement on this matter.[8] Buber not only addresses the biblical text itself as a *geistige Wesenheit,* a form of spirit, but he makes remarks about the word spoken by God to humanity, the written word of scripture, and the word of interpretation which, if pieced together, can be used to construct a linguistic continuum between the "word" of God, the written word, and the word of interpretation. This linguistic continuum establishes language as the medium through which the text is created and interpretation takes place.

We will now investigate Buber's translation of the Hebrew Bible and biblical hermeneutics with a special focus first on the technical devices used to create the Bible translation. These technical devices reveal that Buber was not averse to employing technique and that the aim of translation had definitely changed from creative retelling to an exacting struggle to present the peculiarities of a text in another language. Still, the Buber-Rosenzweig translation techniques and the translation itself, like all translations, must be considered interpretative. The translation is a first-level, elemental interpretation. The techniques provide hints from the text itself for an interpretation of the meaning of a biblical passage or book. And there are interpretative writings in which Buber follows, primarily, the hermeneutic hints suggested by these techniques. In Buber's larger studies, however, such as *Moses* and *The Prophetic Faith*, the translation techniques are augmented by historical critical methodology, creating a complex hermeneutic device.

In the next two sections of this chapter we briefly outline this complex hermeneutic method and place it in the context of contemporary biblical criticism. We then go on to explore Buber's sensitivities to the mediating power of language and outline what we call the "linguistic continuum" as it is found in his biblical writings. Finally we juxtapose Buber's biblical view of language with Gadamer's Greek view and argue that the former provides a better basis for contemporary hermeneutics.

The Translation and Its Techniques

In stark contrast to Buber's early Hasidic translations, in which Buber strays far from the written texts, the Buber-Rosenzweig German translation of the Hebrew Bible may be one of the most literal translations ever produced. In the biblical translation one sees immense respect for the integrity of the biblical text. Everett Fox points out that in the Buber-Rosenzweig translation "each man was taxed to the utmost *(especially Buber)* in the effort to restrain poetic enthusiasm in favor of strict adherence to an existing text."[9] Begun under the influence of the dialogical philosophy of *I and Thou* and the principles of translation which Rosenzweig developed in his translation of the poems of Judah Ha-Levi, Buber sought means to translate the semantics, the form, the rhythm, the rhetorical style, even the sentence structure of biblical Hebrew into German. Together with Rosenzweig he stretches the German language, making use of seldom-used or archaic words and exploiting the capacity of German to form neologisms to create a Hebrew-like German. After the death of Rosenzweig in 1930, having only completed the translation of Genesis through Isaiah, Buber continued to work on the translation alone, finishing the entire project in 1959.[10] We proceed by analyzing the overall philosophy for the translation and then look more carefully at the techniques that were used to produce it: colometric arrangements of lines of text, the choice of German words used to translate the Hebrew, and the leading-word principle.

The Buber-Rosenzweig Philosophy of Translation

The hermeneutic principles which Buber develops rather implicitly in *I and Thou* can be found in much more explicit form in Rosenzweig's epilogue to his translation of the poems of Judah Ha-Levi.[11] Here, Rosenzweig criticizes the "creative" translators of his day whose aim it was to make ancient literature "more understandable" by smoothing over perplexities in the text, altering odd stylistic devices, and transforming alien forms of expression into colloquial German.[12] Rosenzweig charges that, by putting the masterpieces of the past into "modern dress" and adapting them to modern German usage, the specific quality of the masterpiece, "its special tone," its "cast of mind" is lost. Rosenzweig suggests that the proper task of the translator is "not to adapt the foreign tongue to German, but German to the foreign tongue." The goal of translation should be to "reproduce an alien tone in all its alienness."[13] In preserving the uniqueness, the "otherness," of the foreign text, the translator allows the text to make a unique contribution to the language and culture in which it is translated.

Rosenzweig's philosophy of translation, which highlights the "otherness" of the text and attempts to encourage an encounter or "dialogue" with the text, fits very well with Buber's revised hermeneutic method and, in fact, helped Buber to articulate his postromantic hermeneutics. We see the tenets of this philosophy expressed in Buber's writings on the philosophy and techniques that were used in the Bible translation. In Buber's *Zu einer neuen Verdeutschung der Schrift,* "Toward a New German Translation of Scripture," he stresses the need for the biblical text to be approached as "unfamiliar," as "other."

> The "man of today" . . . must approach the scripture as if he had never seen it before; as if he had not had it presented to him in school and after that in the garb of "religious" and "scientific" certainties; as if he had not all his life experienced it through all kinds of illusory concepts and propositions which are based on those certainties; he must place himself anew before the book which has become new.[14]

Buber criticizes other translations of the Hebrew Bible—the Septuagint, the Latin of Jerome, the German of Martin Luther—for not proceeding from "the purpose of preserving the original character of the Bible."[15] Buber suggests that all these translations were executed with the desire of transmitting "a reliable foundation charter to a community," to the Jews of Hellenism, to the early Christian world, to the faithful of the Reformation. The translators often altered the "brittle form" of the Hebrew to make it more comprehensible to its target community.[16] Buber is particularly critical of these translations for transforming the concrete "sense and sensuality" of the Hebrew vocabulary into abstract philosophical and theological terminology. These translations stand like "palimpsests,"[17] writings which cover over the original Hebrew and prohibit access to it. Buber laments that the Hebrew has been "encrusted" not only by abstract theological terms and a desire to make the text amenable to certain communities, but also by aesthetic and literary concerns. In contrast to his early "romantic" and "aesthetic" translations of Hasidic tales, Buber tells us that in his Bible translation one will find no "aestheticizing."

> It would be a false, superfluous, questionable, late romantic unfelicitousness if the translation were inspired by aesthetic or literary reflections; or if the choice of word were determined totally or even partially by taste.[18]

Buber allows that the translation be dictated solely by "the demands of the [Hebrew] text."[19] The translation must "proceed with the purpose of preserving the original character of the book in choice of word, sentence structure, and rhythmic arrangement."[20] Buber stresses the import of the *"Von wo aus,"* that through which the biblical message arises. For Buber, the biblical "content" cannot be separated from the "form."[21]

Buber's translation is directed toward presenting the overall unity of the Bible. "The Bible demands to be read as *one* book."[22] Buber admits that there were various traditions and a variety of writers or schools that contributed to the writing of the Bible, but there was a final redaction of these writings and a canon was produced. Buber is thus primarily interested in translating the text "which has become a whole no matter out of how many and varied fragments it has grown."[23] To do this, however, he believes he must imitate the linguistic techniques through which the Bible became whole—techniques such as assonance, alliteration, repetition of cadence, and, most important, repetition of words or roots of words (what he called *Leitworte* or leading-words).[24]

Partially because of the extensive use of these linguistic techniques, which are properly heard and not read, Buber was convinced that the Hebrew Bible originated in speech and was originally spoken aloud. "Not only the Torah, Psalms, Proverbs are tongue-born and not feather-born, but also the Chronicles and the Law."[25] The Bible is the written "record of its spokenness *[Gesprochenheit]*,"[26] a written record of an originally spoken word. Buber reminds us that the traditional Jewish designation for the Hebrew Bible is *Mikra* or "Calling out." He argues that the masoretical pointing system was to facilitate, not primarily the chanting of the text, but its proper speaking.[27] The Bible is primarily a "Voice" and not a book, Buber declares.[28] We must learn not to read but to hear.[29] Buber demands that his translation be read aloud. "What originates in speech can only live on forever in speech; only through it [speech] can it [the Bible] be purely received and perceived."[30]

Colometric Arrangement of Lines

To return the Bible to speech, Buber employs a daring method of setting down the lines of text in his translation. He divides the lines of texts into "cola," "breath-units."[31] Buber describes the cola as "semantically complete speech units, each of which forms an easily articulable and easily recognizable rhythmically organized unit."[32] To form these cola he made extensive use of the masoretic diacritical marks but did not hesitate to vary from them when his own sense of the reading contradicted them. Thus, these units do not fully correspond to the traditional Jewish versification. Buber developed and executed the colometric method without Rosenzweig's help.[33] In Buber's attempt to follow and accentuate the stresses in speech, exclamations and commands are often given one line and unstressed legal and prose material receive longer lines. Buber used his colometric method to catch the living speech of the Bible, to relate the words as if they were meant to be spoken aloud. In reference to this method Buber tells us, "We want to reach the spoken word in the moment of its utterance."[34] Let us look at an example of the colometric method in the Buber-Rosenzweig translation and compare it to Everett Fox's English translation,[35] which was styled in the spirit of the Buber-Rosenzweig translation, and to the Revised Standard Version.

> Gott sprach: Licht werde! Licht ward.
> Gott sah das Licht: daß es gut war.
> Gott schied zwischen dem Licht und der Finsternis.
> Gott rief dem licht: Tag! und der Finsternis rief er: Nacht!

> God said: Let there be light! And there was light.
> God saw the light: that it was good.
> God separated the light from the darkness.
> God called the light: Day! and the darkness he called: Night!

> And God said, "Let there be Light"; and there was light. And God saw that the light was good; and God separated the light from the darkness. God called the light Day, and the darkness He called Night.

Notice how the Buber-Rosenzweig and the Fox texts, by arranging the verses in cola, break up the lines and facilitate breathing and direct the speaker's emphases. The Buber-Rosenzweig translation leads one to exclaim the naming of light, "Day," and the darkness, "Night," as the text suggests God did in creation. The cola give the verse a rhythmic, poetic quality that accentuates the formal character of the Hebrew in a way the prose presentation misses. The cola not only direct the vocalization of the text, but the accentuation also suggests certain textual meanings. For example, the active role of God in creation is indicated by placing his name at the beginning of every line.

Translating Hebrew Concreteness

Buber tells us that in preserving the "original character," the "otherness," even the "alienness" of the biblical text, the translator must not be afraid to use words that are odd, archaic, or totally new. Buber argues that the translator "must often reach beyond present vocabulary for unusual or even archaic words because the Hebrew has no well-attested synonym."[36] Buber's choice of German words to translate Hebrew terms was designed to capture the biblical Hebrew linguistic ambience, to capture the concrete and dynamic quality of the Hebrew word which had elsewhere been rendered into the static, abstract terminology of Greek and Western languages. Buber consciously tried to divorce Hebrew words from the Christian theological terminology in which they had been rendered in most Western translations. We now look at a number of representative words which Buber himself comments on in "Zu einer neuen Verdeutschung der Schrift."

Buber remarks that the Hebrew word *korban*, usually translated *Opfer*, "sacrifice," comes from the root *krv*, which means "near." "The purpose of an offering is to bring [the individual] near to [God]; it is not a sacrifice or an offering."[37] Therefore, Buber and Rosenzweig use the German expressions *Nahung, Danahung,* "approach," "approach there," for *korban.* For *olah,* the "burnt offering," *Höhung* or *Darhöhung* is used to catch the meaning of "going up" that *olah* connotes.

Buber points out that the Hebrew word *mizbeah,* usually translated in both English and German as "altar," comes from the root *zvh,* to slaughter. The locative *mem* at the beginning of the word makes the direct translation *Schlachtstatt,* "slaughter-site."[38] Buber believes that the modern Christian connotations of an "altar" at which one bows and prays is totally inappropriate for *mizbeah.* As Buber says, there are many instances of bowing in the Hebrew Bible, but never before a *mizbeah.*[39]

To preserve the assonance in the Hebrew expression *reah nihoah,* and drawing upon the root of *nihoah* (*noah*—soothe, satisfy), Buber constructs the German *Ruch des Geruhens,*[40] "scent of soothing." Similarly, the play on word-sound in the Hebrew *Urim v'Tummim* is preserved by the newly created German expression *die Lichtenden und die Schlichtenden,*[41] "the illuminating and the adjudicating."

The word *kodesh,* usually rendered by the static noun *das Heilige,* "Holy," is, in Buber's view, a dynamic concept representing a movement toward or a relationship with holiness. Thus Buber eschews the term *heilige Menschen,*[42] "holy people," and uses *Menschen der Heiligung,* "people of hallowing."[43] He employs not "holy offering" but *Darheiligung,* a "bringing the hallowing there."

To capture the dynamic notion of the word *ruah,* Buber employs the German *Braus,* "rushing,"[44] and makes compounds with *Geist*—*Geistbraus* (cf. Numbers 11:31)—or *Wind*—*Windbraus*—according to whether the Hebrew context dictates that *ruah* means the spirit which rushes from God or the wind which rushes from nature. Buber points out that the Hebrew often benefits from usages of *ruah* which fuse the meaning of wind with spirit. When this is the case Buber uses the term *Braus* separately, as in Genesis 1:2, *"Braus Gottes schwingend über dem Antlitz der Wasser."* "A rushing [wind/spirit] of God hovering over the face of the waters."

In every example cited above, it is obvious that the choice of words used to translate the Hebrew brings with it suggestions for the interpretation of textual meaning. The words *Nahung* and *Höhung* suggest that the meaning and purpose of Israelite sacrifice is not propitiation of God but a bringing near to God and spiritual elevation of Israel. The word *Braus* suggests that spirit is not something separate from but is part of and yet superior to humans and nature.[45]

Leitworte

The most lasting contribution of Buber to biblical scholarship has come from his astute sensitivity to the bibilical use of *Leitworte,* "leading-words." Buber argues that *Leitworte* give the biblical text rhythm and accentuate meaning. They are the defining attribute of biblical rhetoric. Buber delineates the term as "a word or word-root meaningfully repeated within a text, series of texts, or collection of texts."[46] His translation attempts to follow the biblical use of *Leitworte* by translating each Hebrew word or root consistently with one German word or root. In doing this Buber not only found that he was able to produce a more Hebrew-sounding German but he also found a key to the meaning of biblical passages and sections. Thus the leading-word technique became a principle for translation and, as with the other techniques, a principle of interpretation. Buber came to believe that it was through *Leitworte* that a unity of style and content could be found not only in the Torah, the first five books, but in the entire Tanakh. The leading word, in Buber's view, was the tool through which the last redactor forged a unity and established a canon for the Hebrew Bible.[47]

Because the use of *Leitworte* is so pervasive throughout the Hebrew Bible, examples can be found on every page. Take, for example, the Tower of Babel story in Genesis 11:1–9. The word *safah,* "language," is repeated four times. The phrase *kol ha'aretz,* "all the earth," is repeated five times, and the words and word stems *h'bah, banah, ir, patz* (come, build, city, scatter) occur three times each. Despite the fact that German and English style would suggest that one not repeat the same words over and over again, Buber translates the words of the Tower of Babel story directly into German as they appear in the Hebrew. The repetition and mirror arrangement of the *Leitworte* not only give the Babel tale a rhythm and unity of sound but also quickly bring the hearer to the central theme and meaning of the tale: There was one language over all the earth and the people said: "Come let us build a city, lest we be scattered." But precisely from the hubris of the thought that unity and domination could be built by human power alone, the people lost the unity and were scattered over all the earth.

A more elaborate example of how *Leitworte* can be used as hermeneutic keys to meaning is found in Buber's discussion of the central narratives about Jacob and Esau. In the Jacob-Esau narratives of Genesis 25–33 the leading words, as Buber reviews them, are *mirmah, "Trug,"* "deceit"; *bkhorah, "Erstgeburt,"* "first-born right"; *barakh, barakhah, "segnen, Segen,"* "to bless, blessing"; *panim, "Antlitz,"* "face." These words are theme words in the stories that revolve around getting the blessing of the first-born through deceit and being able to "face" the consequences of deceit and blessing.

When Esau first sells his birthright for a bowl of lentils, in Genesis 25:29–34, the word *bkhorah* appears four times, at the end of verses 31, 32, 33, 34, becoming something of a refrain and establishing the theme of this narrative. The sale of the birthright leads up to the moment when Isaac bestows the blessing of the firstborn on Jacob (Genesis 27:27–29). Buber points out that the words "to bless" and "blessing" are repeated no less than twenty-two times in Genesis 27. Blessing, indeed, is a key theme throughout the Jacob narratives. For it is not only that which is fought for but that through which reconciliation is sealed. When Jacob succeeds in wrestling with man/angel, *"ish"* (Genesis 32:27, 30), he receives a blessing from the man. And when Jacob and Esau are reconciled they are reconciled with a blessing (33:11). But though Jacob does eventually reconcile with his brother, he is not allowed to do so without going through a punishment for the deceit he employed to win the blessing. Because Jacob "took away the blessing" of the birthright (27:35) from his brother with deceit, *mirmah,* he is deceived, *rimah,* by Laban (29:25) into marrying Laban's firstborn daughter, *bkhirah* (29:26). Buber suggests, in his commentary on the use of this rare root, "*rmh,*" that by repeating it in these two different contexts, the biblical writer shows, without outright criticism of a forefather, that Jacob's theft of the birthright and blessing was a sin for which he had to pay.[48]

The leading word *panim,* "face," and its variant meanings of "in front of," "in the presence of," "in the grace of," "in the terror of," demarcates different aspects of Jacob's meetings with Isaac, with the angel/man, with God, and with Esau. Jacob says that it is God that brings him before the presence/face *(le-phanai)* (Genesis 27:20) of Issac [who cannot see] to receive his blessing. As soon as Jacob leaves Isaac's presence/face *(panae-Itzhak)* (27:30) with his blessing, Esau enters to find himself cheated and to reveal Jacob's deceit.

Before Jacob is to meet Esau his thoughts are revealed through multiple uses of the word *panim* (32:21–22):[49]

> For he said to himself:
> I will wipe (the anger from) his face *(phanav)*
> with the gift that goes ahead of my face; *(le-phanai)*
> afterward, when I see his face, *(phanav)*
> perhaps he will lift up my face! *(phanai)*
> The gift crossed over ahead of his face . . . *(al panav)*

Here the word "face," placed at the end of the cola, not only gives the verse rhythm and formal unity but exploits the multiple meanings of the word to accentuate Isaac's fear in "facing" the reality and consequences of his deceit. This is followed by the story of Jacob wrestling with the angel/man at the place Jacob names *Peniel,* "Face of God" (32:31). "For I have seen God, face to face *(panim el-panim),* and my life has been saved."

And then we have the reconciliation of Jacob and Esau (33:10), in which Jacob says:

> No, I pray!
> Pray, if I have found favor in your eyes,
> then take this gift from my hand.
> *For I have, after all, seen your face, as one sees the face of God,*
> and you have been gracious to me.[50]

The face of the angel/man, the face of God, the face of Esau are all linked by the repetition of the word *panim.* Jacob performed his deceit not in the dark but in full view of the face of God. This face is fierce in judgment and wrath; the sin must be atoned for through work [under Laban] and through a wrestling which leaves Jacob stricken in the thigh. Yet this face is also merciful and gracious and Jacob does receive the grace of blessing and reconciliation with Esau and can send Esau forth with a blessing. Jacob is constantly made aware that he lives his human drama simultaneously in the face of man and in the face of God and that, ultimately, he succeeds because "God has shown him favor."

In a number of Buber's interpretative essays on the Bible, the leading-word principle is used almost exclusively to develop an interpretation of a given section or theme or personality. This is particularly true in Buber's essays in *Die Schrift und ihre Verdeutschung* and in *Darkho shel Mikra*, which also includes essays that describe the philosophy and techniques of the translation. The *Leitwort* and the other translation techniques allow Buber to follow closely the peculiarities, the "sense and sensuality," of biblical Hebrew expression. Buber's attention to the specifics of Hebrew grammar, syntax, and semantics recalls the "grammatical" step in interpretation of Schleiermacher.[51] Buber's use of leading-words to plot out the threads of unity throughout individual sections and the whole Hebrew Bible recalls Schleiermacher's attention to the relationship of parts of a text to the whole as a key to meaning. Yet in Buber's major interpretative books on the Bible—*Kingship of God, Moses, The Prophetic Faith*, and *Der Gesalbte*[52]—Buber does not use only the hints of the *Leitworte* to develop his interpretations. In these studies he combines leading-word analysis with historical critical methodologies and the dialogical hermeneutic method to create a complex method for biblical interpretation.

The Complex Biblical Hermeneutic Method

The translation of the Hebrew Bible into German and the interpretations based on the *Leitwort* and other translation techniques can be considered as "literal" interpretations, *pshat* readings, of the Hebrew Bible. Yet Buber does not stop at this first level. Building upon the translation techniques and employing the variety of critical methods of modern biblical scholarship, the second step of Buber's biblical hermeneutic involves a reconstruction of the primal narrative which relates events of meeting between God and his people. Buber starts from the premise that Judaism is a religion based upon historical events. God is a God of history who acts in history. In Buber's own formulation, Judaism is based upon events of meeting and dialogue between God and Israel. "Israel [is] touched in all its generations by the shuddering awe of a history experienced as dialogue."[53] It is the central task of the Bible to capture these events of dialogue and preserve them.

Having established the principle of the primacy of the events of meeting between God and humanity and the narratives which preserve them, Buber sets out to find the biblical narratives closest to the primal events—"to penetrate to that original nucleus of the saga which was almost contemporary with the initial event."[54] Buber endeavors to trace out a tale of events of meetings which stretches from Abraham through Moses to the writing prophets. He also attempts to map the "narrative system of faith"[55] and the depiction of God and human beings that this faith entails. This yields a biblical theology which Buber calls the "Kingship of God" and a peculiar type of faith which Buber calls the "Prophetic Faith." Although this biblical theology is constructed through *Leit-wort* analysis and narrative reconstruction, it must also be seen as the result of a dialogue of Buber with the Bible and an attempt to apply the message of the text to the contemporary Jewish and human situation.

In the introduction to *Kingship of God,* Buber tells us that his aim is to "establish anew, upon the basis of critical research, the thesis of an early direct-theocratic tendency in Israel."[56] The "critical research" which Buber depends upon is philology, historical documents, and comparative analysis of kingship systems of the ancient Near East. Buber tells us that "the historical bias" of texts—their historical context, their audience, their original pur-poses—is "fundamentally decisive"[57] to his method of analysis. He does not believe one can clearly isolate and date sources J, E, P but he does believe that there are "trends of literature," "manners of manipulating traditional material," and that knowledge of these "traditions" can be very helpful in interpreting the Bible.[58]

In his later books, *Moses* and *The Prophetic Faith,* Buber further outlines his use of historical criticism. He tells us his aim is to unearth the "tradition which we may regard legitimately as being near to the historical events."[59] His goal is to "penetrate beneath the layers of different redactions of tradition and their tendencies,"[60] to "separate the early from the late here, and then to advance, as far as possible, from the reworking of tradition to what may be presumed to be tradition, orally preserved."[61] To these historical critical methodologies Buber adds the literary methodology of the leading-word so that, he believes, he is able to "treat . . . the Hebrew text in its formal constituents more seriously"[62] than most other historical critics.

A good example of the way in which Buber complements historical criticism with the leading-word technique is found in *Kingship of God.* The entire book is dedicated to proving the historicity of the Gideon passage in Judges 8:23, "I will not rule over you, neither shall my son rule over you: the Lord shall rule over you."[63] Protestant biblical scholars Karl Budde, Hugo Gressman, and Julius Wellhausen had suggested that this saying of Gideon's is "too lofty" for the period of the Judges; it does not correspond with the development of Israelite faith, which at that time had not arrived at the point of conceptualizing such a potent God that could supplant the need for human rulership. What actually happened with Gideon, these critics argue, is that he did accept the offer to be king and that this is confirmed by the statement of one of Gideon's son's, Abimelekh (Judges 9:2). Abimelekh, who, in an effort to usurp the power of his brothers who were ruling after their father, Gideon, says: "Which serves you better, that seventy men rule over you, all sons of Jerubbaal [Gideon], or that a single man rule over you? [i.e., me, Abimelekh]."[64]

Buber uses the leading-word technique to show that the theologies of Judges 8:23 and 9:2 cannot be so easily severed. In both of these passages a Hebrew word, *mashal* (the German, *"walten,"* "to rule"), which occurs only two times elsewhere in the book of Judges, occurs many times here (three times in 8:23, two times in 9:2). This repetition not only prohibits the attempt to disconnect the passages but also provides a way to harmonize their seemingly contradictory meanings. Buber notes that the root *malakh,* "to be king," is not used here, but, instead, *mashal* is used, which signifies the "factual possession of power" and not the dominion of a "ruler's office." Thus, Abimelekh is acknowledging that Gideon and his seventy sons had practical power but never assumed the office of king. Gideon and his sons ruled, i.e., exercised power, yet all the while knowing full well that God was ultimate king. Buber complements this leading-word analysis with a comparative historical analysis reviewing the kingship systems of Babylon, Egypt, and South Arabia to show that the germ of a notion of an "immediate, unmetaphorical, unlimitedly real theocracy" suggested by Gideon existed at his time and was not necessarily developed after him.[65]

In *Moses* and *The Prophetic Faith* Buber continues to use his leading-word and historical critical method to establish that the roots of the tradition of the "Kingship of God" can be found back at Sinai, and even before that, with the fathers: Abraham, Isaac, and Jacob. Having established the antiquity of this tradition and the central events of dialogue upon which it is based, he then attempts to map out its development and transformation into the faith of the prophets, ending with the Babylonian prophets of the Exile.

Buber's Biblical Hermeneutics and Contemporary Biblical Criticism

Given the recent interest in literary analysis and interpretation theory in academic circles in general and Jewish Studies in particular, Buber's exegetical writings are receiving increasing attention. Edward Greenstein has shown that Buber's leading-word analysis continues to have relevance to contemporary biblical criticism. In reviewing five books which employ literary analyses of the Bible, Greenstein shows how all employ Buber's leading-word technique.[66] Michael Fishbane[67] and Harold Bloom[68] have also focused on Buber's literary sensibilities. Yet, though there has been a tendency to concentrate on his literary techniques alone, Buber's adept ability to combine literary and historical analysis also deserves attention. For it seems that we have arrived at a time in biblical studies where many are realizing that one type of method—be it source criticism, form criticism, tradition criticism, or literary criticism—is not adequate to the complex task of interpreting the Bible. There is a movement away from the use of one methodological approach or one kind of method toward the use of a plurality of methods—methods which have often been opposed to one another and considered mutually exclusive by their original progenitors.

Important Jewish and Christian interpreters have argued that the turn toward the literary dimension of the Bible is not hindered but aided by historical scholarship. Meir Sternberg has stated that compositional issues, dating of texts, and historical studies of the ancient Near East "prove indispensable to literary study as such."[69] David Tracy has argued that, more than any other means, it is historical critical method that establishes a distance between modern readers and the biblical text and thus "preserves the otherness of the text," and allows for a true dialogue with the modern reader.[70] In his use of both historical critical and literary tools, Buber remains an overlooked resource for this most recent movement to use a plurality of methods in interpreting the Bible.

Yet the uniqueness and significance of Buber's biblical hermeneutics do not rest solely on the preliminary question of how many and which methods to employ in interpreting the Bible. What is more important is the end to which Buber puts his methods. And this end was nothing less than the restoration of the role of the Hebrew Bible in the intellectual, religious, and practical life of the Jewish people. Though Buber uses historical biblical criticism, his work represents a passionate desire to rescue the biblical text from antiquarian studies and biblical scientists. With Buber, the study of the Bible is fundamentally not about picayune philological or historical analysis; it is not an exercise in taking the text apart and revealing its different sources, it is not about drawing parallels between Israelite faith and the faiths of the nations among which the Israelites lived, and it is not essentially about revealing the literary modes and techniques used in the Hebrew Bible. Although Buber uses all of the tools of modern biblical criticism, he does so always with an eye toward articulating the uniqueness and coherence of biblical faith and the meaning of that faith for contemporary readers. Through this task the Bible is rescued from its isolation in the hands of the critics and made relevant to the intellectual and spiritual life of the Jewish people.

To accomplish this goal of opening the biblical text to modern Jewry, Buber's first task was to bring his readers to the Hebrew text itself. His German translation, filled with neologisms, odd sentence structures, and rhetorical styles which are dissonant to the German ear, is perhaps most properly understood as an invitation to the reader to take up the Hebrew text itself. Buber's translation is an interpretation of the *pshat*, the plain meaning of the text. It is an interpretation that stays so close to the text that it reveals the text's problem areas and its blemishes but also its concrete forms of expression and uniquely Hebrew forms of rhetorical power.

The translation of the Hebrew Bible is aimed at presenting the text as *sepher kodesh*, "sacred text." The translation aims to present the text, in Buber's interpretation of the word *"kadosh,"* as distinct and unique.[71] It aims to present the biblical text as "other," even alien, so that readers can have fresh encounters with the text, encounters which, like all I-Thou encounters, will have transforming affects on them.

> He must place himself anew before the book which has become new, withhold nothing, and allow what happens between it and himself to happen. He does not

know which saying, which image from this source will seize and remold him,
from where the spirit will rush in and penetrate him in order to embody itself
anew in his life; but he is open.[72]

And reading the Bible, for Buber, cannot only be an occasion for personal
transformation, it must also result in an application of the message of the Bible
to what Gadamer refers to as the "present situation."[73] Although it is obvious
that, in Buber's own case, he derived great personal solace and satisfaction
from his reading of the Bible, Buber's interpretive writings were always aimed
at addressing the contemporary situation of the Jew and the modern world. For
example, one could argue (as I do in chapter 7) that Buber's narrative biblical
theology ends with the Babylonian Exile and not with the establishment of the
Monarchy because Buber thought that the situation of exile better expressed
the Holocaust experience of the European Jews of his day.

In his interpretive role, Buber saw himself in the tradition of the prophets
who used the narratives of the events of their tradition to address the issues of
their day. The prophet, the *navi,* for Buber was *"Künder,"* "announcer" of the
word. The prophet was the "interpreter who explains words handed down."[74]
Buber stresses that the prophet is not primarily a prognosticator of the future
but a perceptive reader of the present. The prophet "utters his words directing
them into an actual and definite situation."[75] Thus, Buber views the prophet as
something of a hermeneut, an interpreter, who applies the biblical word to the
current situation of Israel. In his biblical interpretations Buber himself tried to
take on the role of prophetic hermeneut addressing Israel in its situation of
crisis. In less elevated, more contemporary language, we could say that Buber
was a hermeneutical theologian, an interpreter who used the texts of his
tradition to speak to his contemporary situation.

Buber's Biblical Hermeneutics and Language

It should be obvious that Buber's biblical writings require an immense
sensitivity to the intricacies and subtleties of the Hebrew and German languages. The translation was founded on a paradoxical premise. On the one
hand Buber believed that the Hebrew text was "fundamentally untranslat-
able."[76] Hebrew sound-pattern, rhythm, rhetoric, sentence structure, and
semantics cannot be replaced by German equivalents. Although "analytical
science" may think it can dissolve a language into semantic components and
concepts and then find equivalent expressions in other languages and other
times, the semantics of language are tied to sounds and syntax whose equivalents often cannot be found.[77] On the other hand Buber shared a "faith in the
reception and transmission [of language] which transcends time."[78] Buber
shared Rosenzweig's belief, articulated in the epilogue to his translation of the
poems of Judah ha-Levi, that a translation molded to the rhetorical, rhythmic,
and semantic patterns of another language could become a classic work of

literature in its own right and make a genuine contribution to its own linguistic culture no matter how different the language and culture of the original text. The Bible translation grew out of the faith of both Rosenzweig and Buber in the existence of "one language of the spirit."[79] When the translator "again and again pushes to its limits the language into which he is translating," Buber says, he can, at moments, touch what Goethe called "that simple universal language."[80]

The primary goal of returning the Bible to its "spokenness," grew out of not only a belief that the Bible was itself originally a spoken and not a written document, but also the Jewish and biblical belief in the divine origins and ontological power of the spoken word. In his "Biblical Humanism,"[81] Buber remarks that the first sentences of the Bible teach us that all being owes its existence to the spoken word of God. "All being of things that are comes from having been spoken, from the being spoken of the primary word: 'He Himself spoke and it was.' "[82] In God's "speech-acts" there is creation, and to the extent that we use language properly we can also participate more fully in that creation.

The desire to return the Bible to its spokenness also resulted from the belief that the speech of the Bible holds within it something of the original dialogic events that occurred between God and humanity. At the core of the Hebrew Bible is not the mystery of divine speech alone but, primarily, that of divine-human speech. Buber's biblical writings represent a concern to address the direct dialogue, the "immediacy" between God and human beings.[83] At the core of the Bible are events of dialogue between God and his intermediary, the prophet, the *navi*, "who bears the word of message from heaven to earth and the word of petition from earth to heaven."[84]

Buber's remarks on the spoken word of God and humanity, the written word of scripture, and the word of interpretation in his biblical writings, reflect a deepening of his appreciation of the power of language. His comments on the various modes of language can be used to establish what I call a "linguistic continuum" among the spoken word, the written word, and the word of interpretation. This continuum strengthens Buber's notion of interpretation and can be used as an answer to a Gadamerian critique of the underdeveloped notion of language in Buber's dialogical hermeneutic as we find it in *I and Thou*. Although Buber himself never explicitly articulated this linguistic continuum, we now attempt to construct it not only to clarify Buber's biblical hermeneutics but also to prepare for the next chapter, in which a general Buberian hermeneutic theory is sketched.

The Spoken Word of God

Buber's remarks on the Prophet Jeremiah in *The Prophetic Faith* include an extended discussion of his view of the "Word" of God in the Bible. He states that the "contact between godhead and manhood . . . is not bound up with the rite but with the word."[85] By this he means the "word spoken" by God.[86] Buber writes of a number of types of divine speech. The primal word is prelinguistic. It "breaks into the whole order of the word world . . . it suddenly descends into the human situation, unexpected and unwilled by man." It is "free and fresh like the lightning."[87] This word is not spoken in the language of human beings; rather, it comes as a "*Happening*, the 'fire,' the 'hammer' that 'smashes the rock.'"[88] It is that which befalls the Jewish people; it is history itself.[89] In "The Dialogue Between Heaven and Earth," Buber says, in the spirit of Psalm 19:2, that "everything, being and becoming, nature and history, is essentially a divine pronouncement *(Aussprache)*."[90] It is the central task of the prophet to translate this prelinguistic "Word" of God into human language. "Before the word is spoken by him [the prophet] in human language it is spoken to him in another language, from which he has to translate it into human language."[91] Like Hermes, the messenger of the Gods from whose name we get the word "hermeneutics," the prophet must become a hermeneut; he "represents the Lord, he enunciates the message and commands in His name."[92]

Yet God does not only "speak" in events. There are times when he speaks the language of humanity and listens to that language.[93] "Over against [the prelinguistic event] stands the . . . actual divine speech to man."[94] Here the need for anthropomorphism is given. "In order to speak to man, God must become a person."[95] God, as "person," as "Thou," addresses the human being as "Thou" in human language.[96] And, having been addressed, this person then answers God in human language. "This human person not only adopts the word, he also answers, lamenting, complaining to God Himself, disputing with Him about justice, humbling himself before Him, praying."[97] Thus we see Abraham and Moses arguing, pleading, speaking directly with God. Buber notes that the book of Jeremiah displays the speech between God and the prophet in an explicit "dialogic form" and the Psalmist "reports to the world words of personal reply, of personal granting, as spoken immediately to him."[98] In the move from the "prelinguistic" language of events to the language which humans speak we are moved into the recognition of the linguisticality of all religious expression.

The Written Word

In his "Biblical Humanism," Buber is explicit about the language in which the speech between God and humanity is inscribed. In the *Tanakh*, the Hebrew Bible, we hear "The voice of the Unconditional resounding in Hebrew."[99] In the Hebrew Bible we hear the "voice of God, resounding in human idiom and captured in human letters."[100] Hebrew, the sacred tongue, not only provides the vessel for the spoken dialogue between human persons and God, but also is the language of inscribing that dialogue.[101] Hebrew captures the dialogue in "human letters" and is the language of the sacred text. In his book on Moses, when Buber discusses the transference of the law given at Sinai to the tablets, he refers to the miracle of writing, its marvelous capacity to preserve and act as a testimony to the great events of dialogue between God and humanity.

There is one means of placing a more comprehensive, clearer, verbally dependable witness upon the stone. That is the wondrous means of writing, which for early Israel was still surrounded by the mystery of its origin, by the breath of God, who makes a gift of it to men. By means of it one can embody in the stone what has been revealed to one; so that it is no longer simply an event, the making of the covenant, but also, word by word, it continues to serve as evidence of a revelation, of the law of the King.[102]

The written word of the Bible stands as testimony for the generations to the founding events of dialogue that occurred long ago erasing the span of time and making those events present.

And the tables remain as "tables of testimony" or "tables of making present" whose function it is to make present unto the generations of Israel forever what had once become word.[103]

The written word, as testimony to the generations and to the spoken Word between God and humanity, holds within it the powerful dialogic events and the message of those events which occurred to the Chosen People.

The Word of Interpretation

Yet in order for the dialogue and the message embedded in the biblical text to be re-heard the text must be approached with a certain type of attitude, it must be read as "sacred text," as a "Thou." For the person of today, reading the Bible is a matter of standing "before the biblical Word in order to hearken to or to take offense at it . . . [to] confront . . . his life with the Word."[104] If the Bible is translated somewhat literally by Buber to heighten the encounter with the text as "Thou," he still maintains that the goal of interpreting it cannot be to merely elucidate the *pshat* or "literal" meaning of the text. The Bible cannot be treated as "absolute, sufficing, immutable."[105] As a Thou it demands a response from us; it demands dialogue. The frozen script, in order to release its message, must be rescued from the written word and returned to the spoken through dialogue. The reader's dialogue with scripture connects the written word with the living word given in the book. "Some, like myself, will not let the biblical word usurp the place of the voice; they will not acknowledge the word, as that voice's absolute, sufficing, immutably valid expression."[106] If not engaged in living dialogue by a reader, the Bible is not met, it is not alive: "without the rousing, and renovating life of the word, even the book does not live."[107] Although Buber does not articulate it thus, we could say that the voice of God between humans and God retains its oral status, its living quality, through interpretation. Through interpretation the word takes on life and addresses the reader in his or her situation. By interpreting, the reader "lets himself be addressed by the voice that speaks to him in the Hebrew language"[108] and responds with his life. And as in any form of I-Thou relationship, one cannot leave a true encounter with the biblical text without being existentially affected. "Whenever we truly read it, our self-understanding is renewed and deepened."[109]

Thus, what we find in Buber's writings on the Bible is an extension of the principles of interpretation of works of art developed in *I and Thou* to the sacred text, the Hebrew Bible. Like the work of art the Bible can be regarded as a Thou and the process of interpretation phrased as a "dialogue" with the text. Although Buber uses art as an example of *geistige Wesenheiten* in *I and Thou*, the Bible may have provided a better example. For in the Bible, even more than in art, we find a "phenomenal form" that can address an individual as a Thou addresses another person. Here, with the biblical text, we understand how something that is not truly "living" can question its reader and demand a response. With the *Mikra* we understand how one can have a "dialogue" or "conversation" with a text as one has with a person. We also have the recognition of writing as a form of mediation of the original I-Thou event. Indeed, Buber seems to be more open to the whole question of mediation of the I-Thou event in his biblical writings than he is in *I and Thou*. For together with Rosenzweig he develops "means," techniques of biblical translation, which are fashioned to preserve the dialogical quality of the biblical text. Buber openly employs academic methods of scholarly interpretation of the Bible such as historical criticism and philology and he also argues for the validity of a certain kind of language to capture primal dialogic events—the language of narrative. And though Buber himself speaks out against theology in *I and Thou* as a form of expression which destroys the immediacy of the I-Thou relationship to God, he tries to develop a biblical theology in his writings on scripture (see chapter 7). These moves toward forms of mediation and toward the acceptance of the mediative power of language are further elaborated in Buber's late writings on aesthetics and philosophical anthropology. Extended analysis of these writings will allow us to sketch, in the following chapter, a general Buberian theory of interpretation. Before we move to this general theory, however, I would like to suggest that Buber's biblical linguistic continuum offers an alternative basis on which to erect a hermeneutic system other than the Greek philosophical foundation offered by Gadamer.

Buber's Biblical Linguistics: An Alternative to Gadamer's Greek Basis for Hermeneutics

Buber specifically attempts to differentiate the biblical and Jewish view of language from the Greek *logos*. For the Greeks, logos "possesses eternal being."[110] For the Hebrew, "the Word" is dynamic and connected to a divine being and human beings that speak. Buber juxtaposes the beginning of the Greek-influenced Gospel of John with the Hebrew Bible.

> The Greek logos *is;* it possesses eternal being. Although the prologue of the hellenizing Gospel of John begins, like the Hebrew Bible, with "In the beginning," it immediately continues with the totally un-Hebraic *"was the Word."* In the beginning of the Bible's account of creation . . . there is no "word" that is not spoken; the only being of a word resides in its being spoken.[111]

The Hebrew word of God is not an abstract and timeless monument to eternal truth but the vessel of God's instruction, command, plea, and response to a people in need. The word which is uttered by this people is "outcry" and "appeal," not "formal elocution."[112] The biblical word arises out of concrete situations and events. It is fundamentally different from the word of the Greeks, which is "removed from the block of actual spokenness, sculpted with the artful chisel of thought, rhetoric, and poetry . . . [and] valid only when it becomes pure form."[113] Buber argues that even in Plato's Socratic dialogues, where we would expect spontaneity and true give and take, there is an "element of immutability in communication."[114] Plato's dialogues have been too "worked over and hammered into shape"[115] to retain any of the quality of the original dialogue.[116]

Buber's point is that the drive to formal perfection in the Greek word removes it from the concrete situation from which humans speak and reduces the dynamism and dialogical quality of language. The "detached and formally perfected"[117] word ever striving for the universal and eternal "tends [toward the] monological."[118] The perfected form "attains fulfillment by itself," whereas the biblical cry, emerging directly from human suffering, demands a response and requires the answering word of another to complete it.

> Whosoever is addressed by the tragic chorus—men or Gods—is, ultimately, not addressed at all; its foreboding song attains fulfillment by itself. But the psalmodic chorus, which has prayed: "Save us for Thy mercy's sake!" (Ps. 6:5), then listens in the stillness to hear whether its prayer has been granted. Untransfigured and unsubdued, the biblical word preserves the dialogical character of living reality.[119]

Greek notions of language as the servant and representation of the logos have led to Western humanist notions of language as "form" or "formation," *Gebild* or *Bildung*,[120] the "power of giving shape." Language, as *Gebild*, is used to form the person and the polis "as perfectly as possible." To be formed as perfect is to be self-enclosed and independent.[121] Language, as *Gebild*, is the secret domain of "Truth" and mastery of it gives the power to dominate. To these Western humanist notions of language as form and formation Buber juxtaposes the language of "biblical humanism."

> The law of Biblical humanism must be different. It conceives language as an event *(Geschehen)*, an event in mutuality. . . . Its intent is not the person who is shut up within himself, but the open one; not the form, but the relation; not mastery of the secret, but immediacy in facing it; not the thinker and master of the word, but its listener and executor.[122]

Here Buber shows how central principles of his dialogical hermeneutics—mutuality, openness, listening, and relationship—find a ground and support in biblical notions of language. Although Gadamer shares many of Buber's dialogical principles, he has sought to ground his hermeneutics in Greek philosophy and Western Humanism. In *Truth and Method* Gadamer employs

Plato's dialectic, Aristotle's *phronesis,* Heidegger's *aletheia,* and the Humanist's *Bildung* and tries to make these notions serviceable for his hermeneutics by stripping out the static metaphysics present in them. What Buber offers is an alternative, biblical linguistic foundation for hermeneutics that, from the beginning, situates the word in a concrete living and dynamic context and naturally gives rise to an open and moving hermeneutic system where the give and take of dialogue is of paramount value.

IV

CONSTRUCTING A BUBERIAN HERMENEUTIC THEORY

We have now completed a review of Buber's hermeneutic methods of translating and interpreting the Hasidic tales and the Bible. We have mapped out a development from the early empathic method, to the dialogic method developed in *I and Thou,* to the inclusion of technical methods and historical methods of explanation in Buber's biblical writings. Although an important series of linguistic notions such as "speech," "language," "word," "dialogue," and "conversation" are introduced in *I and Thou,* these notions are most fully developed in Buber's biblical hermeneutics and latter writings. In a very rich yet often overlooked essay, "Das Wort, das gesprochen wird" [1960] ("The Word That Is Spoken"), which was first published five years before Buber's death, Buber sketches a dialogical theory of language which deserves to be included among major contemporary statements on language and interpretation.[1]

In his biblical writings, Buber ties the origins of language and the spoken word to the divine word and concentrates on the dialogue between God and humans. Yet, in "The Word That Is Spoken," Buber carries his biblical views of language outside of the context of the Bible and shows how a theory of language based on dialogue can provide a hermeneutic theory for secular as well as sacred literature. This essay, taken together with some other late writings, can be used to develop a Buberian general theory of textual interpretation. The linguistic and dialogical qualities of this theory can only be properly appreciated when placed in the context of other dialogical theories, such as those of Mikhail Bakhtin, Hans-George Gadamer, Paul Ricoeur, Jürgen Habermas, Wayne Booth, and David Tracy.

Toward a Dialogical Theory of Language and Interpretation

In responding to a charge that he failed to take language seriously enough, that he attempted to "overcome" the necessity for linguistic expression, Buber answered, in his "Replies to My Critics" (1963):

There is nothing that lies so far from me as wanting to "overcome the linguistic expression"; nothing helps me so much to understand man and his existence as does speech, and even beyond the human its most sensuous concreteness mediates to me daily new and surprising insights.[2]

Buber asserts the importance of first spoken and then written language as the source of understanding humanity and the mediating tool of insight and truth. In "The Word That Is Spoken," which is included in Buber's *Werke* under the rubric of philosophical anthropology, Buber shows that he has moved from a focus on the prelinguistic, immediate relationship between person and world and person and person in *I and Thou* to further develop the linguistic notions which were first introduced therein. For example, Buber asserts, in "The Word That Is Spoken," that "a precommunicative stage of language is unthinkable."[3] Buber includes this essay on language with other essays on the subject of philosophical anthropology because he wants to argue that language is part and parcel of what it means to be human. "The mystery of the coming-to-be of language and that of the coming-to-be of man are one,"[4] he says. The language which is primary to Buber, however, is not language as it stands separated from human speakers but language as it is spoken by human beings that speak.

Against Heidegger, Buber insists that it is not "language that speaks,"[5] but, rather, human beings that do so: "Man, he alone, speaks."[6] In his "Biblical Humanism," Buber says: "There is no 'word' that is not spoken; the only being of a word resides in its being spoken."[7] Buber does not find "the house of being," in language, but, instead, designates the human being as the essential dwelling place of language. This unbreakable connection between language and human beings is characteristic of Buber's abiding humanism.

Buber's humanistic interpretation of language separates him not only from Heidegger but also from poststructuralist theorists like Jacques Derrida, who, in his *De la Grammatologie* (1967), presents language as a closed self-referential system which can be analyzed separately from human speakers and from external references to the world. Buber's theory of language, in fact, is directly opposed to Derrida's, for where Derrida, through a radical interpretation of Saussure, attempts to establish the priority of writing *(écriture)* over speech, of *langue* over *parole,* of sign over reference,[8] Buber, without trying to do away with the other elements in the polarities, attempts to establish the primacy of speech over writing and reference over sign. Here, Buber is joined by that influential Russian literary theorist and critic Mikhail Bakhtin (1895–1975),[9] who was once quoted as saying that Buber "is the greatest philosopher of the twentieth century, and perhaps . . . the sole philosopher on the scene."[10] Like Buber, Bakhtin asserts that writing "is constructed . . . on concrete social speech"[11] and that the "referential and expressive" must be put before "linguistic markers"[12] in priority. It does not appear that Buber was aware of the work of Bakhtin before or at the time of the writing of "The Word That Is Spoken"[13] but he certainly would have benefited from Bakhtin's work.[14] Given that Bakhtin dedicated considerably more time and effort to his theory of language than did Buber, we will use Bakhtin's theory to further amplify that of Buber.

Buber and Bakhtin

Our discussion of relations between Buber and Bakhtin on issues of language and interpretation will benefit from a review of common starting points and shared problematics. After the Bolshevik Revolution, Bakhtin joined a circle of intellectuals that regularly read Kant and Hermann Cohen, the Jewish Marburg neo-Kantian.[15] Bakhtin was attracted not only to neo-Kantian Idealism but to religion, particularly to Orthodox Christianity, as a way of providing a "spiritual basis for socialism"[16] and authentic communal relations. As a student in Vienna and Germany, Buber was also trained in neo-Kantian thought and, as we well know, was also attracted to religion as a basis for his idea of community or *gemeinschaft.*[17]

Both Buber and Bakhtin struggled to find religious, existential, and linguistic solutions to problems of Idealist subjectivism and abstract universalism. Bakhtin, like Buber, was dissatisfied with neoromantic solutions to the problematics of neo-Kantianism because these solutions were based on a more pronounced subjectivism than that which we find in Kant and the neo-Kantians. Bakhtin tried to get beyond the problematics of Idealism and Romanticism by developing what Katerina Clark and Michael Holquist have called an "existential philology" of human dialogue.[18] With concrete human dialogue at center Bakhtin was able to bridge the gap he saw in Idealism between the self and others, the self and the social world.[19] Dialogue provided Bakhtin with a principle of particularity and pluralism that allowed him to battle not only the abstract and monolithic quality of Kantian universalism, but the monolithic, indeed totalitarian, aspects of Soviet cultural life. Buber, similarly, saw "dialogue" as a key to overcoming neo-Kantian and neoromantic subjectivism and as a way of introducing particularity and "otherness" into the reign of the universal that Kant had ushered in.[20] It was, then, the notion of "dialogue," for Bakhtin and for Buber, that provided solutions to shared problematics inherited from neo-Kantian Idealism and from Neo-Romanticism.

It is important to note, however, that Bakhtin and Buber's notions of dialogue are not identical. For Buber dialogue is a very special form of communication—communication that employs facial expression, body language, and silence along with positive speech—in an effort to move persons into the realm of the I-Thou relationship. We could use Kantian language and call this realm "noumenal" and we could call Buber's dialogic language "noumenal speech," although Buber was more comfortable with ontological designations. Thus, he refers to dialogue as the language of "Being" and "essence" and he speaks of I-Thou as the realm of "ontology." The ontology of dialogue, it is crucial to note, undergirds relationships not only in the human world but in the natural world of plants, animals, and rocks as well.

For Bakhtin, on the other hand, dialogue is limited to the human world. Dialogue is the language of human conversation, the language of "provocation, interrogation, polemics and taunt" between two partners.[21] Like Buber, Bakhtin believes that only dialogue brings us to "the genuine life of the personality."[22] Like Buber, Bakhtin believes that dialogue contains the secret life of a commu-

nity. But Bakhtin's notion of dialogue is closer to the commonsense usage. It is
what we say to another in everyday conversation; in Kantian terminology, it is
"phenomenal speech." Following Kant's emphasis on the "phenomenal" world
and the dialogue of social life, Bakhtin moved further away from philosophical
and religious categories and more toward linguistic and sociological categories than did Buber. Buber certainly shared Bakhtin's interest in the everyday in
language and in society but he continued to look for the extraordinary in the
ordinary, the unsaid divine Word in the human word, and the spiritual center of
the *Zwischenmenschliche* of the social world.

This distinction between Buber's and Bakhtin's notions of "dialogue,"
however, as necessary as it is to make, should not be taken as absolute.[23]
Bakhtin never gave up on his philosophical interests and had great appreciation for the "ontological" and religious dimensions of human dialogue, selfhood, and community. One could say that Bakhtin never abandoned this
dimension but saw it along with and as a part of all linguistic and social
utterance and structure. Buber took more and more interest in positive language, in social and political structures, and in the phenomenal realm of the
"It" in his later work. Without ever abandoning the separation between the
I-Thou and the I-It realms, Buber continually sought ways to bring the two
realms together and to see the Thou through, in, and with the It. Thus we could
say that, at their limits, Bakhtin's and Buber's notions of "dialogue" are not far
apart.

With these remarks as a preface, let us now review Buber's mature statement
on language, "The Word That Is Spoken." Here, Buber talks most explicitly
about spoken and written language and here the affinities between Buber and
Bakhtin are most apparent.

The Word That Is Spoken
In "The Word That Is Spoken," Buber designates three modalities of language
as it pertains to the spoken word: present continuance *(präsenter Bestand)*,
potential possession *(potentialer Besitz)*, and actual occurrence *(Begebnis)*.
These terms form the basis of a Buberian theory of language, text, and interpretation.

Present continuance is "the totality of that which can be spoken in a
particular realm of language in a particular segment of time, regarded from the
point of view of the person who is able to say what is to be said."[24] Although
present continuance is the presupposition for all speech and writing, it is not
an atemporal code that can be objectified and analyzed separate from speech
like Saussure's *langue.* Buber warns against the objectification of the present
continuance of language. "Every attempt to understand and to explain the
present continuance of a language as accessible detached from the context of
its actual speakers, must lead us astray."[25] The present continuance of language properly exists for the temporal speech-situation or what Buber calls
"the being-with-one-another of living men."[26] This term has some affinities with
Bakhtin's notion of "heteroglossia." Buber would have been able to articulate a
much richer notion of *präsenter Bestand* had he made use of Bakhtin's term.

Heteroglossia is used to designate the wide-ranging variety of linguistic systems and contexts which surround and support the spoken word. Bakhtin explains "heteroglossia" as

> a diversity of social speech types and a diversity of individual voices. . . . social dialects, characteristic group behavior, professional jargons, generic languages, languages of generations and age groups, tendentious languages, languages of the authorities, of various circles and of passing fashions, languages that serve the specific sociopolitical purposes of the day, even of the hour.[27]

By his second term, "potential possession," Buber means that linguistic expression which has already been uttered or written down. Potential possession, however, has a "decisive limitation," for it, too, is conceived in relation to the spoken word. Potential possession represents those written words which can "still today be lifted by a living speaker into the sphere of the living word."[28]

The Primacy of the Spoken Word

The "actual occurrence" of language is its use in human dialogue, its *Gesprochenheit,* "spokenness," or "being spoken."[29] By addressing language as system and language as written, only in relation to the spoken word, Buber aims to establish what he calls "the priority of the spoken word."[30] Buber quotes Goethe: "Wie das Wort so wichtig dort war, weil es ein gesprochen Wort war" ("How important the word was there, because it was a spoken word"). The spoken word is privileged for Buber because it is from human dialogue that language draws its ontological power. Language as spoken between persons is language which derives from and helps to facilitate the sphere of "the between," the sphere of the I-Thou relationship.

> The word that is spoken is found . . . in the oscillating sphere between the persons, the sphere that I call 'the between' and that we can never allow to be contained without a remainder in the two participants.[31]

A description of the dialogical character of the spoken word much like Buber's is also found in the writings of Bakhtin.

> The word in living conversation is directly, blatantly, oriented toward a future answer-word: it provokes an answer, anticipates it and structures itself in the answer's direction. Forming itself in an atmosphere of the already spoken, the word is at the same time determined by that which has not yet been said but which is needed and in fact anticipated by the answering word. Such is the situation in any living dialogue.[32]

The language of "the between," the language of true dialogue, bestows something extra on each individual partner's linguistic universe. Buber claims that the word that is spoken has a *sui generis* quality to it. There is an element of originality in language when it is spoken. Buber designates this quality of originality as the "otherness" of the speaking partner which brings with it something unpredictable. Speech contains a "moment of surprise"[33] where language is used in different ways, where a large variety of uses of vocabulary, composition, pronunciation, and rhythms of speech are heard. Buber refers to that extra element which dialogue gives to language as an element of semantic "tension." In fact, he refers to all language as a "system of tensions." This tension results from the fact that every speaker understands and uses language differently. And for Buber, it is precisely these differences and the semantic tensions they produce that make conversation "fruitful." In conversation we learn about "the ambiguity of the word," its polysemy, what Buber calls its "aura."[34]

Bakhtin also calls human dialogue, a "tension-filled interaction,"[35] and asserts that this dialogue is the proper context for determining a word's semantic horizon. "The word is born in a dialogue as a living rejoinder within it; the word is shaped in a dialogic interaction."[36] Bakhtin, too, points to dialogue as the source of language's creativity or fruitfulness. In dialogue "languages become implicated in each other and mutually animate each other."[37] The "dialogized process," the process of conversation between peoples, provides the context out of which the word "breaks into its own meaning."[38] In conversation the polysemy of a word, its different usage by different speakers, constantly comes up against the univocality of the word—the struggle for shared meaning. The tension within which the spoken word is suspended is the tension between the "heteroglot voices" of different speakers' usage and the social need for univocal "authoritative" definitions. The word exists within the tension of centrifugal forces of language, which give language semantic diversity and threaten to pull it apart toward chaos, and centripetal forces, which strive for univocal meaning and absolute definitions, for what Bakhtin calls a "unitary language."

> Unitary language constitutes the theoretical expression of the historical process of linguistic unification and centralization, an expression of the centripetal forces of language. A unitary language is not something given but is always, in essence, posited—and at every moment of its linguistic life it is opposed to the realities of heteroglossia. But at the same time it makes its real presence felt as a force for overcoming this heteroglossia, imposing specific limits to it, guaranteeing a certain maximum of mutual understanding and crystallizing into a real, although still relative, unity—the unity of the reigning conversational [everyday] and literary language, "correct language."[39]

Although Bakhtin, partially in reaction to the centralization and totalitarianism of Soviet society, tends to focus on the value which the heteroglot voices give to language, Buber finds something essential to humanity in the struggle for shared meaning. "It is the communal nature of the logos as at once 'word' and 'meaning' which makes man man, and it is this which proclaims itself from of old in the communalizing of the spoken word that again and again comes into being."[40] Within the communal struggle to determine a word's meaning each human being gives voice to his or her unique usage at the same time that he or she submits this use to negotiation for a shared agreement on meaning. Language, as tool of communication between human beings, only "remains operative" as a tool if a balance is reached between the individual and shared usages of words.

Having delineated the most important aspects of the spoken word for Buber and Bakhtin, we can make some more general observations about this word. Although the spoken word lives in the present moment, Buber argues that it need not be limited to that moment and the immediate linguistic resources of the partners in speech. The spoken word "is served by" the given linguistic system or context (present continuance) and the past usages of a language (potential possession). Buber asserts that the spoken word draws from "the gushing and streaming waters" of continuance. He is also adamant that by the "spoken word" he does not mean language that is manufactured or created anew like the univocal technical terminology of the sciences. The spoken word is "the great old word" weighted down by the history of its uses and fraught with the ambiguity of its past uses, yet, still, given new and clarified meaning by the living speaker who utters it.[41] For Bakhtin, the spoken word, too, arises out of the variety of linguistic contexts provided by the present heteroglossia of linguistic matrixes and also the genres of the history of literature.[42]

Buber initially focuses on the single "word" that is spoken to delineate the fruitfulness of language, but, following the analyses of Edward Sapir and J. G. Hamann, he asserts that one must move to the larger unit, the sentence, if one is to more fully understand the nature of interhuman speech. With the sentence, the full referential power of language is realized. With the sentence, we not only have pronouns and names that designate human agents and verbs that reveal their intentions and actions, but we also have the ability to "manifest" and "apprehend" a human event in the interhuman realm, what Buber calls "an actual situation between two or more men who are bound together through a particular being-directed-to-each-other."[43] Whereas single words refer to things, sentences refer to human situations, and Buber asserts: "not things but situations are primary."[44] Thus, the true power of spoken words is their capacity to address and bring human beings into a situation of human encounter.

Buber's issue of the relationship between the sentence and the situation is addressed by Bakhtin in his discussion of the relationship between the "utterance" and the "extraverbal situation." Bakhtin can be seen in clear opposition to the contemporary tendency in linguistics to divorce utterance and situation, sense and reference. He argues that utterance and the situation to which it refers cannot be analyzed separately, they are part and parcel of one another.

> In no instance is the extraverbal situation only an external cause of the utterance; it does not work from the outside like a mechanical force. On the contrary, *the situation enters into the utterance as a necessary constitutive element* of its semantic structure.[45]

The Text and Its Interpretation

After establishing the primacy of the spoken word and mapping out its sources and powers, Buber describes genuine literary and poetic texts as the written expression of this spoken word. Like the spoken word, the written word is certainly not divorced from the given linguistic context (present continuance) or the past expressions (potential possession) of language. Buber, in fact, designates present continuance as a source upon which the author must draw. And in his late essay on aesthetics, *Der Mensch und sein Gebild* (1955),[46] "Man and His Image-Work," he refers to the value of past expressions. He asserts that all artists must seek "the assistance of all past generations that have elaborated our seeing-relation and our hearing-relation into a world."[47] However, the primary source of literary art is the author's own experiences with the spoken word of dialogue. It is from here that authors and poets draw their "creative force." "The author . . . receives his creative force in fief from his partner in dialogue. Were there no more genuine dialogue, there would also be no more poetry."[48]

In Buber's biblical writings he delineates biblical prose—narrative—as the most appropriate genre to capture the spoken word.[49] Yet in "The Word That Is Spoken" he asserts that poetry represents the spoken word of dialogue. Poetry represents "the truth of the word that is spoken," "in its highest form."[50] The successful poem, for Buber, is an extension of the spoken word, a "witness to genuine dialogue."[51]

Bakhtin, too, locates the creative source of writing in the spoken word. Yet he does not choose poetry as the privileged genre for relating human dialogue. In Bakhtin's view, poetry is too formalized and structured to capture all the cacophonous voices of speech. Like Buber in his biblical writings, Bakhtin asserts that it is prose that best captures these voices. Most specifically, for Bakhtin, it is the modern prose of the novel which re-presents human heterophony.[52] "For the prose writer [the novel] is a focal point for heteroglot voices . . . every prose discourse . . . cannot fail to be oriented toward the 'already uttered.' "[53]

In a statement reminiscent of Buber's view that art is created out of a dialogue of the artist with suggestive artistic forms *(geistige Wesenheiten)*, Bakhtin asserts that the novel arises out of a dialogue between the author and the variety of voices and languages provided to him or her by the linguistic context. "All authorial intentions are orchestrated, refracted, at given angles through the heteroglot languages available in a given era."[54]

Having articulated a path in language from the spoken to the written word, Buber moves to complete the linguistic continuum by discussing the word of interpretation. The written word (for Buber, the poem) is never satisfied to remain as a monument to a past dialogue. It, in itself, calls out for dialogue, for a continuance of the conversation which the poem represents and extends over time. The poem itself is nothing other than a call to the other, a call to the Thou. "The poem is spokenness, spokenness to the Thou"[55]—it calls out for renewal of dialogue. Here we see the need for interpretation. The poem calls out to a Thou, to a reader, to an interpreter who, in responding to the written letter, "lifts" the written words anew "into the sphere of the living word."[56] In the poem, the spoken word of dialogue transcends time, it gains "permanency." But through its reception by a reader, the poem, "wins its life ever anew."[57]

Bakhtin, too, saw the process of interpretation as a continuation of dialogue, the plurality of dialogues brought into focus by writing. To ensure that a proper dialogue between interpreter and text occurs Bakhtin stresses that a certain condition must be maintained. That condition is respect for otherness, for "alterity," for what Bakhtin calls "exotopy"[58] and Buber calls "over-against-ness."[59] Bakhtin, like Buber, criticizes romantic hermeneutics for describing the goal of understanding in terms of empathic unity of the reader with the author.

> The mistaken tendency [is] to reduce everything to a single consciousness, to dissolve in it the other's consciousness (that one understands). . . . Understanding cannot be understood as empathy and setting of the self in another place (loss of one's place). . . . Understanding [is] the transformation of the other into a "self-other."[60]

Understanding requires, in the words of Bakhtin's important interpreter, Tzvetan Todorov, that the " 'I' and 'Thou' are radically distinct."[61] It requires a "dialogics of culture"[62] in which the tension between the text and its interpreter is sustained. The horizon of the text and that of the reader are never "fused," as Gadamer would wish, but are held in vibrating tension like the bold patches of color that jut up against one another in the paintings of Mark Rothko. Bakhtin, in his struggle to open our ears to "a dialogical context [which] knows no limit,"[63] is far less interested in the final task which a Gadamerian hermeneutic requires—the task of forging common understanding of the meaning and truth of a text. Here Buber, in his search for vibrant dialogue, may be more like Bakhtin than Gadamer.

It is crucial to realize that interpretation, for Buber, does not end with the dialogue between the reader and the text. What is suggested by Buber's final movement back to the spoken word of interpretation, back to dialogue, is that the interpretation of a text is a matter of dialogue not only between the reader and the text but also between the reader and fellow interpreters. The "sphere of the living word" into which the interpreter lifts the poem is the sphere of public dialogue.

In his essay "What Is Common to All" [1956] Buber refers to the "living word" as "speech between men," "common logos,"[64] "communal speaking."[65] He also refers to the sphere of the living word as the "communal guarding of meaning."[66] In pointing us to the stage of communal dialogue Buber directs the process of interpretation away from the intersubjective I-Thou relationship between an individual reader and the text toward the testing waters of public dialogue. Buber shows that the question of interpretation cannot be merely a matter of individual response but must be a public and communal matter.[67]

Dialogical hermeneutics requires, however, that the move to a community of interpreters does not close down hermeneutic options. Bakhtin, in particular, struggles to open our ears to a large variety of interpretations of a text. Like the Midrash, which says that there are seventy faces to every verse of scripture,[68] and the Talmud, which seeks to preserve the most farfetched and unpractical of interpretations, Bakhtin argues that the "dialogical context" of interpretation must remain open.

> There is no first or last discourse, and the dialogical context knows no limits (it disappears into an unlimited past and in our unlimited future). Even *past* meanings, that is those that have arisen in the dialogue of past centuries, can never be stable (completed once and for all, finished), they will always change (renewing themselves) in the course of the dialogue's subsequent development, and yet to come. At every moment of the dialogue, there are immense and unlimited masses of forgotten meanings, but, in some subsequent moments, as the dialogue moves forward, they will return to memory and live in renewed form (in a new context). Nothing is absolutely dead: every meaning will celebrate its rebirth. [This is] the problem of the *great temporality*.[69]

Bakhtin's reference to the "great temporality" of the interpretative dialogue suggests that interpretation is not limited to the immediate community of interpreters but, properly, runs back to the interpreters and interpretations of the past and stretches toward the interpretations of tomorrow.

To summarize, then, the dialogical hermeneutics of Buber and Bakhtin begin from the fundamental linguistic reality of human dialogue. The world's great literatures give expression to this dialogue and the process of interpretation is a matter of engaging the literature in a conversation first with the reader and then with a community of readers which extends from the present to the past to the future.

There are, to be sure, important differences between Buber and Bakhtin on language and interpretation. Buber, as religious hermeneut, gave extensive attention to the ontological and theological dimensions of language and litera-ture. Buber was fascinated by the style and power of the sacred texts of the Hebrew Bible and of Hasidism. These ontological and theological concerns were brought to Buber's discussion of "secular" poetry and literature. Bakhtin, as literary critic and theorist, writing in the intellectual climate of Soviet socialist realism, wrote on secular literatures and was most sensitive to the relationship between the genres and craft of literature and social life. Buber and Bakhtin differ considerably on the Bible. For Bakhtin the Bible represents rigidity and absolute authority—the opposite of heteroglossia—and for Buber it is the first record of the most rich and spontaneous dialogues that ever existed, the dialogues between God and His Chosen People. Other differences which we find between Buber and Bakhtin can be located in Bakhtin's far richer sensitivity to the varieties of types of speech that exist in a given culture. Bakhtin attends to vocational, social, and class distinctions in language that Buber's theory misses. And Bakhtin has an appreciation for parody, irony, the picaresque, and the "carnival" in language and literature that extends well beyond the quaint sense of humor which we find in Buber's Hasidic tales.

Yet despite the important differences between Buber, the Jewish hermeneut, and Bakhtin, the Russian literary critic, I have tried to underscore the common insight into the importance of human dialogue for speaking, writing, and interpreting. This insight preserves the referential character of language and texts, the reference to the speech which expresses the suffering, acting, and meeting of persons in the world. This insight preserves a vital link between language and living, speaking persons that much of contemporary linguistics severs. Buber and Bakhtin draw a "hermeneutic circle" which connects human speech, written texts, and interpreters of texts and yields a hermeneutics that is at once dialogic and humanistic.

Conclusions: A Buberian Textual Hermeneutic

In 1924, in a *Festgabe* for the publisher Anton Kippenberg, Buber wrote some brief remarks on a mythical book, the *Ar Vif* of the Bretons, which include rich hermeneutic reflections.

> The Bretons believe in the demonic book. It has different names, one in each region. In that of Quimper it is called *Ar Vif*, that is, The Living.
>
> It is a gigantic book. When it stands upright, it has the height of a man. The pages are red, the letters are black. But he who goes up to it and opens it sees nothing except red. The black signs become visible only when one has fought with the *Vif* and overpowered it.
>
> For this book lives. And it will not let itself be questioned. Only he who conquers it tears it from its mystery. . . . I think that every real book is *Ar Vif*.[70]

Here Buber uses as a paradigm for all books the animate, gigantic *Ar Vif*, whose letters are hidden from naïve seekers and whom readers must battle and subdue if they are to reach understanding. Having traversed the full range of Buber's writings on the translation and interpretation of sacred and secular texts which culminate in the linguistic continuum present in "The Word That Is Spoken," we are now prepared to outline Buber's strategies for "conquering" texts. Drawing from a variety of Buber's hermeneutic writings we will try to sketch a general interpretative method. To the extent that Buber's writings are used to develop this hermeneutic method it may be considered "Buberian." Yet given that Buber never articulated a systematic hermeneutic method for all texts and given that the proposed model is supplemented with the work of contemporary theorists who have thought more about hermeneutic theory than did Buber, the model cannot be strictly attributed to Buber but, more properly, is a product of my own construction.

To sketch this Buberian hermeneutic theory I will use, as a framework, a little known and quite brief paper written by Buber for the New York Public Library, "Advice to Frequenters of Libraries" (1944).[71] In this article, Buber begins by describing the type of attitude which must be taken toward reading a book. He then directs the reader to take note of the particular elements that go into the composition of the book and finally to turn to his or her own life and to other fellow readers.

Initially, Buber suggests, one should look at the book as a whole, as a "unit conceived and shaped as a totality."[72] Buber speaks of the attitude one must have in reading as a "sense of wonder" and "astonishment."

> Be sure not to look for anything in particular, but rather enter without any preconceived notions into the realm the book opens before you. Let it astonish you. Do not let yourself be irritated if its manner differs from what you are accustomed to, or even from what you consider correct.[73]

Buber, quite clearly, is describing the attitude of I-Thou which one needs to take toward a text—a precritical, impressionistic, meditative attitude that allows the text as living *Wesen* to speak to the reader, to challenge the reader, to disclose different aspects of reality that the reader is not aware of. In this very first stage of interpretation the reader is relatively passive. It is a stage in which the reader only develops "hunches" as to the meaning and significance of the text. The attentive reader of a good book is "amazed," "baffled," not only because the message of the book first appears hidden like the black letters hidden within the red pages of *Ar Vif*, but also because as the initial passive strategy, the I-Thou attitude of "receptive waiting," allows the letters, words, sentences to appear, the coalescing message presents an alternative world, a foreign linguistic horizon, a decidedly other, even alien, "Thou" to the reader.

From a Gadamerian perspective we may say that Buber is naïve when he asks the interpreter to read "without any preconceived notions," yet Gadamer, too, suggests there is an initial, passive stage in the hermeneutical process where interpreters are not yet concerned to make their prejudgments, their cultural presuppositions, conscious. Very soon, however, as one reads, the challenge which any text of the status of what Buber calls *Ar Vif* or what David Tracy calls a classic[74] breaks through the initial, passive attitude of the reader and calls for a response, calls for dialogue. Here the reader becomes caught up in a conversation with characters, with notions and concepts, symbols and metaphors, and with the threads connecting the plot. The experience of reading lifts the reader into another world, in which, Buber says, the "intellect," "the aesthetic sense," and "the whole soul" are engaged.[75]

Reading a book, like meeting any Thou, is the experience of otherness, of alterity and difference, which makes readers aware simultaneously of another and of themselves. "When one says You [Thou], the I and the word pair I-You [Thou] is said, too."[76] Because saying "Thou" requires saying "I" the reader is brought to a realization of who he or she is as reader. Buber says that the I-Thou relationship is not "ontologically complete" for the I unless the I *becomes conscious* of how it is constituted as a distinct "I" through the other. The I-Thou relationship, properly, does not occur unconsciously but requires a high degree of awareness.[77] The shock of otherness should reveal to the reader not only a different linguistic horizon but the reader's own linguistic horizon. Here, though Buber himself did not articulate it thus, the logic of I-Thou necessitates Gadamer's position—that the readers cannot remain in the initial state of the fantasy of presuppositionlessness. They must bring to consciousness their presuppositions and those of the cultural traditions from which they speak and interpret. The reader's activity, the reader's response, must include, then, a dialogue with his or her own language and culture. The question "Who is this text?" elicits the question "Who am I?".

This latter question should reveal to the reader what Gadamer considers the positive as well as the negative function of cultural prejudgments. On the one hand cultural prejudgments provide the tools, the analytical categories, the background knowledge we need to read and understand anything at all. On the other hand, prejudgments can cloud our relation to a text as the English word *prejudice* suggests. These prejudices can distort the reader's reception of the text and must be made conscious to the reader.

Buber addresses this issue somewhat obliquely with his existentialist notions of "Being" and "Seeming." To have a genuine I-Thou relationship, Buber asserts, one needs to "proceed from what one really is" and not from "what one wishes to seem."[78] With the term "Seeming," Buber recognizes that our own illusions about ourselves cloud our relations to the "Thou." Yet Gadamer suggests that clouding prejudgments belong not only to the realm of "Seeming" but to our very being, to fundamental ways in which we see the world, others, texts. Gadamer, however, believes that the negative aspects of prejudgments, connoted by the English term *prejudices,* can be overcome by the goodwill and self-reflection of the interpreter brought on by the dialogue between the interpreter and the alternative horizon of the text. Thus, in Gadamer's view, the interpreter who "seeks to be aware of [his/her] prejudgments and to control [his/her] own preunderstanding" is generally successful.[79]

Other hermeneutic theorists, however, are not so trusting of the conscientiousness of interpreters and see prejudices and biases as more difficult to uproot and eradicate. The leading representative of this position has been the recent heir to the Frankfurt School of critical theory, Jürgen Habermas. Habermas argues that prejudices are often so deeply rooted and thoroughly intertwined with the reader's thinking patterns that they have to be addressed with sophisticated analytical tools and critical theories. Habermas uses the works of Marx and Freud to argue that prejudices are "ideologies" that "systematically distort"[80] an interpreter's ability to read texts. All thought, all language, all traditions, mask social violence and psychological repressions that prohibit the full liberation of peoples and cloud over their ability to discern. To unmask the ideological character of an interpreter's language requires theories on the model of psychoanalysis or Marxian ideology critique. Only systematic critique can eradicate systematic distortions and allow for the "communicative competence" and the "ideal speaking situation" upon which true dialogue is built.[81]

As we will see in our discussion of Buber's biblical theology, Buber was well aware of the anti-Jewish ideologies of certain Protestant biblical scholars and, without an explicit theory, he systematically attacked these ideologies to open up new possibilities for reading the Hebrew text. In the prefaces to his Hasidic and biblical writings Buber was very careful to present the presuppositions and underlying philosophy of his interpretations. These introductions reveal that Buber was sensitive to the need of the interpreter to make his or her pre-suppositions and prejudgments conscious.[82] We also see sensitivity to the problem of ideology in Buber's writings on problems of the centralization of social and political institutions in his essays on religious socialism[83] and also in his radical critique of the I-It mentality in religion, in society, and in everyday life.[84] Yet Buber's strategy in addressing these "ideologies" was not to embrace critical theories on the model of Marxism or psychoanalysis, but to argue for the power of his alternative attitude of I-Thou. Thus, a hermeneutic method in the spirit of Buber's thought would face the problem of prejudgments in a manner closer to that of Gadamer than that of Habermas.

After interpreters bring their own prejudgments to consciousness and ex-ercise a distanced eye upon themselves and their culture, distance must be taken between the interpreter and the text. Buber does not use the term "distance" in "Advice to Frequenters of Libraries," but rather "pauses." Buber asserts that one must "allow pauses," "pauses for reflection, for deliberating on what you have read, for looking at the author, for re-concentrating your thoughts."[85] Here, we suggest, though Buber does not say it directly, is the place for precise analysis and explanation of the text. The warrants for this move to criticism can be found in Buber's use of literary techniques and historical critical methodologies in his studies of the Bible and in his discus-sion of productive value of "distance" in his article "Distance and Relation" (1950). Buber's biblical hermeneutics suggest the need for literary critical techniques to reveal the peculiarities of grammar, syntax, rhythm, and rhetoric of a text. We have already mentioned that, methodologically, the techniques used to translate the Bible are reminiscent of the "grammatical" method and part/whole analysis that Schleiermacher developed. Logically, however, a large variety of explanatory literary critical methods, including structural, semiotic, and even deconstructive analyses,[86] could be used to fulfill the task of illuminating the structures and forms used to produce a literary text.[87]

In "Distance and Relation" Buber provides further support for the use of explanatory methods to analyze the text by addressing the necessity of distance for any proper I-Thou relation. "One cannot stand in a relation to something that is not perceived as contrasted and existing for itself."[88] Distance allows for the other to be seen as "separate" and "independent," and is the "precondition" for relation. Buber does not explicitly say how the distance is to be ensured in relation to texts, but others, such as David Tracy, have argued that it is precisely methods of explanation like historical criticism that set a text apart from the reader's world and allow for the distancing that is needed to develop a genuine relationship to a text.[89]

Ricoeur has spoken of the need for "critical distance"[90] in interpretation and he attempts to elaborate what he calls a "positive and productive notion of distanciation."[91] He begins by showing how the text itself must be understood as a product of "distanciation" from the author and from the original audience[92] and then argues that to "understand" this product, this text, we must subject it to a series of explanatory exercises which reveal those procedures which produced it. Although these explanatory measures may seem to contradict the initial attitude of I-Thou, as Buber showed in his biblical interpretations and as we argued in chapter 2, there is no need to see these explanatory analyses as detrimental to the process of understanding the text as a Thou. What Buber says of the value of the "pause" may be said of methods of explanation: "If the relationship [to the text] is a true one, it will only be enhanced by pauses."[93]

After subjecting a text to explanatory analyses a Buberian hermeneutic, in a fourth step, directs the interpreter's attention toward the author of the book. This must be understood not (as Buber puts it in "Man and His Image-Work" and in "The Word That Is Spoken") out of romantic concern for the "inner life of the artist"[94] or for the author as "the subject of a biography,"[95] but, rather, as a concern with the author as the figure out of whose dialogue with other human beings and with language the work was produced. Reflection on the author as the human being that produced the work is the beginning of the final stage of interpretation, which includes the requirement to turn from text to life and from the written word to the word that is spoken and the word of interpretation. The figure of the author is important to the interpreter, not as a determinant of the text's meaning but, rather, as a warning never to cut the written text from the spoken word and the spoken word from the human being who speaks.

At the same time that Buber struggles to articulate the ontological power of language, he never allows that language and text be cut off from human beings. The imagined human author who hovers over the text implores me, as interpreter, to respect this book as a product of a dialogue of a human being with a form of spirit and not to do violence to it. The resistance to turning completely to the text and the dialogical relationship between interpreter and text stems from an ethical imperative well put by Bakhtin. "A living human being cannot be turned into the voiceless object of some secondhand, finalizing cognitive process."[96] This imperative is, perhaps, best expressed by Emmanuel Levinas in his notion of the "face of another." It is the face of one's fellow human being, more than anything else, that presents me with the reality of otherness, of alterity. The face, more than a text (which finally is not alive and which, however hard I try, can still slip into the status of mirror to my soul), "puts a stop to the irresistible imperialism of the same and the I."[97] The face of the author (or perhaps we should say, following the title of one of Levinas's articles, "the trace of the other"[98] as author) hovers over the text and prohibits the interpreter from severing the text from the concrete life of dialogue and the human suffering and joy out of which the text arose. For our Buberian hermeneutic method the author represents both the struggle against the abstract hypostatization of linguistic categories above the human realm and the call to return the "crystallized" dialogue of the written text to the spoken word.

In moving to develop an interpretation of the meaning of the text and apply it to one's life with other human beings the interpreter arrives at the moment in

the interpretive process which Gadamer calls "application."[99] Ricoeur suggests
that through this process of application the text becomes "the mediation by
which we understand ourselves."[100] Buber addresses this principle in his
discussion of the humanistic requirement of interpretation. Humanism requires that one turn from language and text to the human person.

> Humanism moves from the mystery of language to the mystery of the human
> person. The reality of language must become operative in a man's spirit. The
> truth of language must prove itself in the person's existence.[101]

Here, in this quotation, we see the "existential" aspect of the hermeneutic stage
of application. Interpreting a text must involve assimilation of the text's meaning into the personal life of the interpreter. Application should bring along with
it a reorienting of the interpreter's life and reorienting of the interpreter's
perception of the world.

Yet for Buber the application of the message of the text cannot stop with the
interpreter's life. Buber's conception of the self as self-in-relation pushes the
interpreter out into the world. Application of the meaning of the text entails
dialogue with fellow human beings. As we saw in "The Word That Is Spoken,"
the interpretation of a text is only completed when the interpreter brings the
word of interpretation into the sphere of public dialogue. Buber's "advice" to
interpreters of books is that when you interpret a text you must "turn
wholeheartedly to your neighbors."[102] Buber admonishes: do not sit privately
with your interpretation but "testify it in your communication with other
men."[103] Here, it must be not only testified to but also tested for truth and
adequacy.

In his assertion of the importance of the "common world" and the "common
logos" of public dialogue to the process of interpretation, Buber joins hands
with a number of contemporary theorists who have developed what Nathan
Scott, Jr., has called "dialogical approaches to the hermeneutical problem."[104]
This group includes Gadamer, Bakhtin, Ricoeur, and Habermas. Scott may
have also included in this group others such as literary critic Wayne Booth and
theologian David Tracy.[105] What the principle of dialogue means as a common
theme in hermeneutic theory is first and foremost respect for the validity of
different voices in the interpretative process. An openness to a variety of
interpretations is dictated, in Habermas's terms, by the requirements of "the
presupposition of symmetry whereby each participant has the same chance to
give rise to communications and to open them, as well as to perpetuate them
through conversation, questions, and answers."[106] Initial openness is required,
in Buber's terms, by the demands of respect of the I for all others as "Thous."[107]

As Scott explains, the principle of dialogue is apt for our current situation of
cultural and methodological pluralism. This principle offers a nonhierarchical,
egalitarian model for the relationship between the reader and the text and
between different interpretations of the text which is based on a "morality of
mutual respect."[108] This principle challenges attempts to establish "any kind of
'totalistic' or absolute doctrine of truth 'with the big T'" which would auto-

cratically determine the "validity of any given text."[109] In this sense, to borrow a phrase from the poststructural theorists whom Scott deliberately excludes from his group,[110] dialogical hermeneutics opposes traditional Western "logocentrism." Scott's group of dialogical interpreters, however, does not include poststructuralist and deconstructionist interpreters, because the dialogical group struggles, on the one hand, to articulate the meanings and references of texts which transcend the mere inner-linguistic play of signifiers so important to the deconstructionists, and on the other hand, to establish criteria by which the truth references of texts and the truth claims of different interpretations can be judged. The criteria established are not derived from absolutist metaphysics but, rather, from philosophies of pragmatism and consensual notions of truth. Thus, in Scott's terms, judgments as to the truth reference of texts are made in accordance with "rightness of fit with . . . the *Lebenswelt*."[111] Conflicts in interpretations are settled through an "adjudicating discourse."[112]

David Tracy and most of the other theorists of dialogical hermeneutics stress that the interpretations made by individual interpreters and the consensus won by pragmatic and dialogic criteria are not "absolutely," but relatively adequate. Interpretations are serious attempts to determine truth forged by historically and temporally limited human beings.

> Relative adequacy is just that: relative, not absolute adequacy. If one demands certainty one is assured of failure. We can never possess absolute certainty. But we can achieve a good—that is, a relatively adequate—interpretation: relative to the power of disclosure and concealment of the text, relative to the skills and attentiveness of the interpreter, relative to the kind of conversation possible for the interpreter in a particular culture at a particular time.[113]

For each theorist, the way in which the relative adequacy of an interpretation is reached is somewhat different. Gadamer suggests that a "supporting consensus" on the best possible interpretation of a text is won through a "discipline of questioning"[114] inherent in all genuine conversation. For him, an interpretation which a community of inquirers can consent to cannot be "proved" as a statement of fact but must be won through "persuasion" or "oration" and through the rhetoric of conversation.[115] David Tracy, however, has argued that an interpretation is a "claim"[116] which one must defend not only through the rhetoric of conversation but also with argument. "Argument . . . is not a replacement for exploratory conversation. Rather, argument is a vital moment within conversation that occasionally is needed if the conversation itself is to move forward."[117] Tracy includes, among the types of argument valid for making an interpretive claim, "topical arguments [to] analyze all substantive claims [and] formal arguments [to] analyze claims to consistency."[118] Habermas has suggested even more formalized rational criteria for his "ideal speaking situation" which all but exclude the more spontaneous and intuitive rhetorical skills of human dialogue that are so important to Gadamer.

Wayne Booth offers three criteria: "vitality, justice, and understanding" to help "winnow" out the weaker and spurious interpretations.[119] Booth warns, however, that the overarching requirement of a vital pluralism in interpretation may very well preclude the possibility of arriving at a consensus on the "true" or "most relatively adequate" interpretation. Realizing the complex nature of any time-tested text and the elaborate relationships between author, text, and reader, Booth argues that we must expect and accept the fact that no one interpretation will bring about his desired goal of "critical understanding" of a text. Different interpreters will focus on different aspects of the text and different elements of the author-text-reader relationship. These interpretations are rightly "not reducible to each other."[120] The goal of arriving at a single interpretation that is "true" for a particular community of inquiry may be not only elusive but, finally, stifling to the basic enterprise of a hermeneutics based on what Booth (joining in our chorus of interpreters) calls "conversation and dialogue."[121]

Certainly Buber, in his struggle for a "common logos" which shapes what he called a "common world," desires not a logos that leads to one monistic world, but a logos which opens our ears to the variety of worlds which humans inhabit and which texts open us to. Dialogical hermeneutics requires that we listen to a variety of interpretations and that we converse on the validity, adequacy, even "truth" of different interpretations in an effort to critically refine, separate, and judge their merits. Though we will easily be able to discount some interpretations as incoherent, silly, ideologically distorted, or inadequate to the complexity of a text, many interpretations will meet the most rigorous of hermeneutic criteria yet still conflict in fundamental ways. Here, the community of interlocutors will have to accept the differences and conflicts of interpretations in the same way that two persons engaged in dialogue often have to accept their differences and conflicts. If, as the rabbis say, a great text has "seventy faces," we should expect that it will take more than one interpretation to reflect the variety of countenances that a text exhibits.

Summarizing the Four Hermeneutic Steps

We can summarize our Buberian general hermeneutic method with four steps.[122] The first step calls for treating the text as a Thou and with the passive attitude of receptive waiting. This quickly moves the reader to a more active give-and-take dialogue. The interpreter moves into the second stage of interpretation when the otherness of the text brings to consciousness the interpreter's own individual and cultural presuppositions and the interpreter wins a distance on these presuppositions which allows him or her to see the world of the text more clearly. The third stage of interpretation begins when the interpreter exercises critical distance and employs methods of explanation to analyze the structure and rhetoric of the text. The fourth stage is gained as the interpreter reflects on the author, who serves as a reminder to reconnect the text to life. The application of the message of the text to the interpreter's life entails sharing the interpretation of the message with a community of inquiry which will challenge and refine the interpretation through a common dialogue.

II

Buber's Narrative Theology

V

NARRATIVE AND THE PHILOSOPHY OF I AND THOU

That a text can be a Thou, that a text can put us in touch with the fertile area which Buber calls the *Zwischenmenschliche,* "the between," means that texts, when properly interpreted, can open us to other worlds, to ourselves, even to a glimpse of the eternal Thou. But what kind of texts are Thous? Hypothetically any particular text and any genre has the possibility of appearing to a reader as a Thou. And although Buber, in "The Word That Is Spoken," pointed to poetry as the privileged written genre, if we look at Buber's work as a whole we see a decided partiality toward narrative expression. As we mentioned in our discussion of Buber's biblical hermeneutics in chapter 3, Buber argues that narrative is most adequate to the task of expressing I-Thou events of meeting and dialogue between God and his people. Volumes 2 and 3 of the three volumes of Buber's *Werke* are largely devoted to the translation and interpretation of biblical and Hasidic narratives. And in the first, philosophical volume, we often find narratives employed to begin a philosophical discussion or to illustrate a philosophical point.[1]

Why is it that Buber was drawn to narrative expression? What are the connections between the world, the selves, the truths which texts disclose, and narrative? How is it that narratives disclose these selves and truths? What is the connection between hermeneutics and narrative? What is the connection between narrative and Judaism? How does Buber's use of narrative fit in with contemporary developments in narrative theory and narrative theology? The second part of this book is devoted to exploring questions about connections between narrative and Buber's philosophy of I-Thou. We will begin our exploration of these questions by looking at an important essay which was published six years after *I and Thou.* This essay, "Zwiesprache," or "Dialogue," includes some wonderful narrative illustrations of Buber's own I-Thou meetings and it will be used to launch us into a discussion of important issues in the relationships between narrative, Buber's thought, and contemporary narrative theory. After reviewing the narratives in the essay "Dialogue," we will look at some leading theories on the nature and powers of narrative and then return to Buber to analyze his narratives with more theoretical sophistication.

The Narratives in "Dialogue"

It may be said that Buber's essay "Dialogue," written in 1929, revolves around a series of narratives about Buber's I-Thou encounters. Indeed, Buber tells us in the foreword to the English publication of the essay that "Dialogue" was written out of "the desire to clarify . . . [and] illustrate"[2] the dialogical principle expressed in *I and Thou.* Buber provides us with a clue as to why clarification of the philosophy of I-Thou would lead him to narrative expression. At one point in the essay he tells us that his thought "cannot be conveyed in ideas to a reader; but we may represent it by examples."[3] He then switches from conceptual analysis to the language of story and provides a concrete life instance of the thought he is trying to express. Thus, Buber suggests that the advantage of narrative over conceptual philosophical expression lies in its ability to communicate concrete life examples of a philosophical notion to readers. We will begin with Buber's hint and explore the efficacy of narrative in terms of its ability to provide illustration of the philosophy of I-Thou.

Yet extended reflection on the power of narrative and analysis of the structure of the particular narratives which Buber writes reveal that the power of narrative (and the peculiar power of Buber's narratives) goes well beyond illustration of certain ideas. Buber's narratives give his ideas concrete expression and reveal the existential ground and temporal elements out of which the philosophy of I-Thou grows. The massive amount of recent work in narrative theory by linguists, literary critics, psychologists, philosophers, and theologians has brought to light aspects of narrative of which Buber was certainly not consciously aware. Still, as we analyze what Buber said about the nature of narrative, and, more important, as we analyze the unique type of narratives which Buber wrote, we find that Buber has an immense amount to contribute to contemporary debates on narrative theory.

In the following review of three narratives in Buber's essay "Dialogue," I will talk about a variety of reasons why narrative is a particularly apt form of expression for Buber and his philosophy of I and Thou. I find it most striking that in Buber's narratives, unlike most stories, and in opposition to some leading theories of narrative, it is the middle of the narrative that is most important and not the end. There are good reasons for this unique focal point in Buber's narratives, and we will explore why it is that Buber's "sense of a narrative middle" is so productive for his work.

My first narrative for analysis is the story which appears in the beginning of "Dialogue" under the heading "Silence Which Is Communication." In this story, Buber claims that communication, and particularly the deep communication of I-Thou dialogue, can occur without speech or gesture; it can occur in silence. Buber's story is not about the tender, silent communication which occurs between "lovers resting in one another," nor is it about the "mystical shared silence" of two holy men meeting. Rather, it is a story about two men who meet in the course of a day's travel and in a silent moment are moved from foreignness and isolation to intimacy. Buber presents us with the setting for the story.

> Imagine two men sitting beside one another in any kind of solitude of the world.
> . . . They are not in one another's confidence, the one knows nothing of the
> other's career, early that morning they got to know one another in the course of
> their travels.[4]

Through this barest of settings, given in a quick, almost thoughtless manner, we struggle to fill in the gaps. Who are these men? What do they look like? Are they traveling by train? What did they learn about each other in the morning? Is Buber one of the men? Even this is not stated. This lack of information reinforces the strangeness and solitude of the two men involved. We do not receive specific information because the two men themselves care little about the details of each other's lives. They are content to remain strange, content to remain in their solitude. Most important, we do not receive background information; Buber wants to stress that such information is not a necessary precondition for an I-Thou encounter.

Buber gives us only those elements of a character sketch necessary for an understanding of the dynamics of the I-Thou event. We are told that one of the men is receptive, calm, open—"his being seems to say that it is too little to be ready, one must also really be there." The other man is an opposite type. He is tense, closed, reserved—"a man who holds himself in reserve, withholds himself."[5] Through some childhood trauma this man has been closed off from the world and others. "A childhood's spell is laid on him . . . [he is] entrenched [in] the impenetrable inability to communicate himself."[6]

Then suddenly, as the men sit beside each other "not speaking with one another, not looking at one another, not having once turned to one another," something happens. Buber relates:

> Let us imagine that this is one of the hours which succeeds in bursting asunder
> the seven iron bands about our heart—imperceptibly the spell is lifted.[7]

Our closed and reserved man, through a special grace, is suddenly able to open himself, and this the other man feels though no word is said or gesture made.

> But even now the man does not speak a word, does not stir a finger. Yet he does
> something. The lifting of the spell has happened to him—no matter from where
> —without his doing. But this is what he does now: he releases in himself a
> reserve over which only he himself has power. Unreservedly communication
> streams from him, and the silence bears it to his neighbor. Indeed it was
> intended for him and he receives it unreservedly as he receives all genuine
> destiny that meets him.[8]

What is said in this stream of communication? What did the neighbor receive from his silent traveling partner? He received not words, not a piece of knowledge, but a moment of intimacy, a moment of "unreserve." Here we see the dialogue, "the Word," which transpires in the I-Thou relationship as a special kind of event. Buber ends the story with the proclamation, "where unreserve has ruled, even wordlessly, between men, the word of dialogue has happened sacramentally."[9]

In the next section of the essay, titled "Opinions and the Factual," Buber follows this somewhat odd and mysterious story with a more comprehensible, autobiographical account. This next story is told to make it clear that I-Thou encounters occur not in moments of wild ecstacy or in flights of fancy but in "factual events," "thoroughly dovetailed into the common human world and the concrete time-sequence."[10] Where in the previous story Buber attempts to show us that the dialogue of I-Thou can be consummated in pure silence, here he seeks to illustrate a movement in I-Thou, a movement from discussion and argument to deep understanding and friendship. He refers to this movement as a "genuine change from communication to communion."[11] The example is taken from an event in Buber's own life.

On Easter, 1914, a few months before the outbreak of the First World War, Buber met with a group of concerned public figures from various European nations who joined to "establish a supranational authority," a kind of European United Nations. In a discussion of the membership of a larger group which was to be formed to carry out the objectives of the original group, one man, a former clergyman, objected that the large number of Jews nominated to the board was not proportionate to the small number of Jews in Europe. Buber felt this statement to be "tainted in its justice," and thus he rose to respond. But the reply turned somehow from a discussion of Jewish representation on this multinational board to a discussion of the exclusive and special relationship the Jews had to Jesus.

> Obstinate Jew that I am, I protested against the protest [of the former clergyman]. I no longer know how from that I came to speak of Jesus and to say that we Jews knew him from within, in the impulses and stirrings of his Jewish being, in a way that remains inaccessible to the peoples submissive to him. "In a way that remains inaccessible to you"—so I directly addressed the former clergyman.[12]

At this date, Easter, amidst the tension of a conference which sees the impending catastrophe of war, we can well imagine the potential for violent argument between Buber and the former clergyman. Yet, then "something happened," the moment of grace, of "turning." "He stood up, I too stood, we looked into the heart of one another's eyes. 'It is gone,' he said, and before everyone we gave one another the kiss of brotherhood."[13] In this moment, as Buber puts it, "communication was transformed to communion," a heated discussion led to a bond of friendship.

> The discussion of the situation between Jews and Christians has been transformed into a bond between the Christian and the Jew. In this transformation dialogue was fulfilled. Opinions were gone; in a bodily way the factual took place.[14]

The third and final narrative which we will look at relates the experience of an I-Thou encounter between a boy (Buber in his youth) and a horse. This story reverses the common structure of the narratives in "Dialogue," because it begins from a description of an I-Thou experience and moves to a turning point which marks the fall of the I-Thou relation to the relation of objectification and manipulation, the relation of I-It. In this story, Buber wishes to show that in an I-Thou experience an I meets a Thou in its separateness and uniqueness. There is not a merger of the two into a mystical oneness, but, rather, two meet and communicate what is special to themselves. An I meets a Thou as "something that is absolutely not himself and at the same time something with which he nevertheless communicates."[15]

Buber's story about the simple experience of an eleven-year-old boy stroking the neck of a "dapple grey" horse on his grandfather's farm conveys well the experience of "the other" approaching and communicating.

> When I stroked the mighty mane, sometimes marvelously smooth-combed, at other times just as astonishingly wild, and felt the life beneath my hand, it was as though the element of vitality itself bordered on my skin, something that was not I, was certainly not akin to me, palpably the other, not just another, really the Other itself; and yet it let me approach, confided itself to me, placed itself elementary in the relation of *Thou* and *Thou* with me. The horse, even when I had not begun by pouring oats for him into the manger, very gently raised his massive head, ears flicking, then snorted quietly, as a conspirator gives a signal meant to be recognizable only by his fellow-conspirator; and I was approved.[16]

This passage, with its rhythmic cadence, its rich detailed description, its repetition of key phonemes, words, and phrases, its long sentences which finally pause and end, "and I was approved,"[17] relates the experience of I-Thou with a powerful immediacy that pure philosophical language could not manage.

The second part of the story shows just how fragile the I-Thou relation is, for merely by becoming conscious of the objective dynamics of the experience, by taking one step back and observing ourselves in it, the delicate balance of I and Thou, the magic spontaneity of communication, is destroyed and the relation of I-Thou reverts back to the more common relation of I-It. The story turns when the child in the tale performs one such act of objectification.

> But once—I do not know what came over the child, at any rate it was childlike enough—it struck me about the stroking, what fun it gave me, and suddenly I became conscious of my hand. The game went on as before, but something had changed, it was no longer the same. . . . And the next day, after giving him a rich feed, when I stroked my friend's head he did not raise his head. A few years later, when I thought back to the incident, I no longer supposed that the animal had noticed my defection. But at the time, I considered myself judged.[18]

Note here how Buber subtly indicates that a moment of "objectification," of distancing, of I-It, has occurred by switching from the first to the third person.

Instead of saying, "I do not know what came over me," Buber says, "I do not know what came over *the child.*" As the horse becomes a distant and no longer a close speaking "other," the relationship to the self is also distanced and objectified.

Narrative as Philosophical Method

Our brief account of three narratives in "Dialogue" has shown that Buber's anecdotes illustrate well central themes of his philosophy of I-Thou. By show-ing that I-Thou can occur in silence, that I-Thou often spontaneously results from conflict, that I-Thou is founded on a meeting of separate and unique creatures of God and by revealing the crucial role of "otherness" in one I-Thou relationship, the narratives in "Dialogue" help to clarify aspects of the philoso-phy of I-Thou. Maurice Friedman states, in the introduction to the 1965 collec-tion of essays in which "Dialogue" appeared, that the narrative material in "Dialogue" is one of the elements that makes the essay the best introduction to Buber's thought.[19] We might well ask why it is that these narratives are able to so clarify Buber's philosophy of I-Thou. We could look for the answer to this question in the content of the narratives themselves. The stories provide colorful illustrations for Buber's philosophy. The autobiographical information that the stories provide sheds light on the origin and meaning of Buber's thought. Yet beyond illustration and the particularities of the stories, there is something about the structure of Buber's thought that makes it especially well-suited to narrative expression. The overall thrust away from philosophical concept to existential experience and encounters, the focus on individual characters and the transformation of character through event, the search for the moment of change from the ordinary to the extraordinary, the focus on human relationship, these central themes of the philosophy of I-Thou make narrative more than just a convenient technique for illustration. Buber's philosophy is concerned with inherently narrative themes.

Narrative, through its formal qualities alone, makes certain essential philo-sophical points for Buber. Narrative shows us that important interpersonal events do not occur within an atemporal, ahistorical context. Important events are both preceded and followed by ordinary real-life events. They are em-bedded in our common time-sequence. In Buber's simple anecdotes he shows us that the imaginary and the fantastic are mixed with the real. Through story, Buber illustrates that if we do truly seek the fantastic we can find it by looking deeply into the details of the real.

Detail is the storyteller's art. Details which the storyteller's sensibility notices are crucial to the event which is about to occur. Buber tells us, theoretically, that detail is crucial to the I-Thou event. But it is only when we read in his story, "When I stroked the mighty mane, sometimes marvelously smooth-combed, at other times just as astonishingly wild, and felt the life beneath my hand," it is only then that we see that every detail is part and parcel of the I-Thou experience.

Narratives not only show us details but, more important for Buber, *narratives show us the relationship between details.* In a narrative we see how this detail leads to this detail which eventually leads to an important encounter. The plot of narrative connects one event to the next and reveals the significance of the connection. Narrative, in its capacity to draw and reveal relationships between event and event, person and person, is peculiarly apt to reveal the dimension of "the between" which is so important to Buber.

As we explore, more deeply, the reasons why Buber is attracted to narrative expression we will find that narrative is far more than a device to "illustrate" or clarify concepts from the philosophy of I-Thou. Buber moves to narrative because narratives say things that concepts cannot. Narratives capture, express, "hold" the complex mix of I and Thou and world that cannot be clearly summed up in a philosophical concept. The complex of relationship cannot be dissolved into or neatly transferred to a concept. Only story can hold within it the web of relationships within which I-Thou occurs. The move from philosophy to story is a natural one for Buber because it is a movement to the origins of his thought—a movement to the medium which most adequately relates the encounters which lie at the base of his thought.

Narrative Theory

We have suggested some reasons why it is that Buber turned to narrative expression to express his thought. Yet to systematically and more thoroughly plumb the depths of narrative we will need to avail ourselves of some more refined theories of the power and function of narrative in human culture.[20] Given the vast extent of recent work in this area, our discussion could go on interminably. Therefore, we will concentrate on the work of two important theorists, the literary critic Frank Kermode and the philosopher Paul Ricoeur. We concentrate on these two figures because they are both sensitive to the connection between narrative and temporal events and therefore can address the connection between Buber's narrative and I-Thou events, and also because the theories of Kermode and Ricoeur have a wide scope and are intended to comprehend a range of narrative genres and a range of contemporary narrative theories.

Kermode's Literary Theory

Frank Kermode's two books on narrative theory, *The Sense of an Ending* (1966) and *The Genesis of Secrecy* (1979), reveal the outlines of a central tension in the contemporary study of narrative: the tension between theorists who see in narrative provisions for organization and explanation that give life a sense of a tidy ending and those that find in narrative an opacity, a darkness, a secrecy which is expressed but never dissipated. These two positions, each eloquently argued for by Kermode at different periods in his work, delineate the boundaries of one of the most important debates in contemporary narrative theory. Does the power of narrative stem from its ability to give us order, or from its ability to put us in touch with chaos? Or is the value of narrative to be found in its ability to bring us to the combination of order and chaos found in the mix of language and reality? We will begin to explore these questions by reviewing the two books in which Kermode presents his narrative theory.

The Sense of an Ending

In his *The Sense of an Ending*, Frank Kermode locates the power of narrative in its ability to help humans to "make sense" of the world. A narrative, for Kermode, is a configuration of temporal episodes into a meaningful pattern. In narratives we project "endings" which give structure, direction, meaning to the chaos of experience. Narrative is a privileged form of "sense-giving" because of its mimetic function, its plot structure,, and its peculiar epistemological status.

Through its plasticity of form—its ability to relate fact and fancy, concept and metaphor, naïveté and paradox, individual personality and social group—narrative has the capacity to be highly mimetic. Narrative is able to remain faithful to the "putrid soup" of reality. Yet narrative not only captures life, it organizes life, it places human events and human temporal experience of time in a "unitary system."

Through the plot structure of narrative, through the beginning, middle, and end, human time is organized and given form. Narrative not only organizes time, it gives time meaning. It transforms our ordinary experience of time as a mere succession of passing moments to a time that is grounded in a past and an origin and directed to a future and an end. "Within this [plot] organization that which was conceived as simply successive becomes charged with past and future."[21]

Kermode stresses the import of the ending of the narrative for giving meaning and ultimacy to all moments in time. The plot "presupposes and requires that the end will bestow upon the whole duration and meaning."[22] The end of the narrative provides the central point of the story. Each moment is "charged with meaning derived from its relation to the end." The narrative which provides the master plot through which beginning and middle find their fulfillment in the end is the biblical narrative. The Bible provides the model for narrative as a "unitary system" that gives place and meaning to all human events by showing its relation to ultimate beginning (creation) and ultimate end (redemption/salvation).[23]

Pre-Moderns, with their biblical narratives and myths, believed that their unities and meanings were true. The peoples of the past believed that they were merely imitating "natural laws" in their sacred narrative systems. The modern West, however, changed this by substituting the modern novel for sacred narrative. Narrative fiction still fills the meaning-giving function of sacred narrative but it does so in a peculiarly modern way. Modern narrative fiction, as narrative, declares that we must have order and project an end to give time on earth meaning. Yet as fiction, as "the consciously false,"[24] modern narrative shows us that order and meaning are artificial creations of humanity. At the same time it captures and orders reality, narrative fiction reveals that this order is contrived and artificial. Kermode argues that, unlike religious cultures, modern cultures possess no "supreme fiction,"[25] no religious myths, that make pretenses to revealing absolute reality.

The Genesis of Secrecy

As convinced as Kermode was in his early work that the purpose of narrative was to give humans a sense of an ending, in his more recent work he has become convinced that narratives do the opposite: narratives generate secrecy, opacity, darkness. What is interesting about this turnaround is that Kermode again turns to biblical literature for his models and prooftexts. However, where his early model for narrative came from the overarching biblical narrative that runs from Genesis to Apocalypse, the model in *The Genesis of Secrecy* comes from the much shorter parables of Jesus. Kermode believes, however, that these brief parables "reflect pretty well all the possibilities of narrative at large."[26]

Kermode notes the intricate connection between parables and "enigma" and thus, at once, associates all narratives with the enigmatic, the dark, the opaque. Kermode does not totally deny his earlier point, that narrative involves sense-making and the giving of ends, but he relegates these functions to the simple, "manifest" level of a narrative. When we look at narratives more closely and analyze the small details of plots, we often find inconsistencies, elements that do not "fit in" to the overall plot, elements that defy or even subvert the meaning or point of the story, which we receive in and through its ending. Here, Kermode sounds very much like Derrida, Paul De Man, and the host of deconstructive narrative theorists who show us the multiple ways in which narratives deny their readers a sense of order, theme, and harmonious ending.

To "deconstruct" Jesus' parables Kermode, in chapter 2 of *The Genesis of Secrecy*, takes us through the large variety of interpretations that have been given to the same parables. Through this exercise Kermode tries to show how "not very reasonable narratives are" and how "susceptible" they are to conflicting presentations of their meaning. If the same parable generates a variety of conflicting interpretations, in what sense can we say that a parable gives a unitary "sense of an ending"? For every reader of a narrative there is, in effect, a different ending. Narrative coherence, to the extent that it exists, is imposed on narrative from the outside by "supra-literary forces"[27] such as a community or "guild" of interpreters.[28] Like the radical philosophers of history Michel Foucault and Haydin White, Kermode asserts that the attempt to narrow and freeze the meaning of a narrative meaning is often done for reasons that have more to do with power and authority than literature and truth.[29]

In chapter 3 Kermode shows us how a single simple detail can upset the manifest sense of a narrative and reveal the underlying dark domain of secrecy. Moving from parables to more extended narratives, Kermode compares the Boy in the Shirt who pops up at the moment of Jesus' arrest in verse 14:51 of Mark's gospel to the Man in the Macintosh in Joyce's *Ulysses*. In both cases these figures are anomalies that do not fit into the overall plots. Of the Man in the

Macintosh, Bloom says what the reader thinks: "Where the deuce did he pop out of?" The man is a stranger whom nobody knows. He appears five times in the text and each time his character changes a bit making his identity thorough-ly enigmatic. The Boy in the Shirt is perhaps even more enigmatic because he is only mentioned once in Mark's gospel and does not appear in Matthew or Luke.[30] The verse raises a host of unanswerable questions. Who was the boy? What kind of shirt was it? a light summer garment? a death shroud? Why did he not flee with the disciples? What is the significance of his nakedness?

Faced with enigmatic details in narratives readers have two options. One is to declare the detail insignificant and ignore it and the other is to use it as a key to an underlying secret meaning hidden within the manifest meaning of the plot. Enigmatic details such as the Man in the Macintosh and the Boy in the Shirt can upset the plain reading of a text because they affect the relationship of the part to the whole.[31] Kermode gives us examples of elaborate reinterpreta-tions of the meaning of *Ulysses* and the Gospel narrative based on the figures of the Man in the Macintosh and the Boy in the Shirt.[32]

All skilled authors place enigmas in their narratives to ensure the interest of their readers. Kermode quotes Joyce: "I've put in so many enigmas and puzzles that it will keep the professors busy for centuries over what I meant, and that's the only way of ensuring one's immortality."[33] Kermode elevates (or deni-grates) this statement of Joyce's to the status of a theory by suggesting that the essence of narrative is to be found in its enigmatic passages. These give narrative its life, its "hermeneutical potential."[34] Yet, Kermode does not allow the opacity of narrative to totally overthrow its manifest clarity, its sense of an ending. He does not, as he himself admits, go as far as the deconstructionists. For the enigmas of a narrative appear as enigmas only in relation to the coherence that the manifest plot provides. The narrative rationality of the plot, its sense of an ending, provides the background against which the enigmas appear in relief.

The fundamental difference between Kermode's early and later theory is that, in the former, he locates the power of narrative in its order-giving capacities and, in the latter, he locates the power of narrative in its darkness, its secrets. Kermode does not totally overturn his earlier work, however, for though he rhetorically stresses the enigmatic and dark side of narrative, he finally asserts the value of tension between obscurity and clarity, order and disorder, with which we began this review of narrative theories. Kermode retrieves his earlier work in his later by pointing to a "double function" for narrative. Kermode tells us that narratives "proclaim a truth as a herald does, and at the same time conceal truth like an oracle."[35] Kermode uses an at once felicitous and ambiguous expression to describe narratives. Narrative, he says, is a "radiant obscurity."[36] From the very darkness of their enigmas narratives bespeak a "momentary radiance."[37] Yet what is this radiance about? What is illuminated dimly by narratives? To what do they refer? The world? language? God? This Kermode does not clearly say.

For some answers to these questions about the truth and reference of narratives let us now turn to the philosopher Paul Ricoeur.

Ricoeur's Philosophical Theory of Narrative

As the title of Paul Ricoeur's three-volume *Time and Narrative*[38] suggests, Ricoeur locates the power of narrative in its relationship to time. Human beings are fascinated by narratives because they articulate, organize, and allow us to reorganize our temporal experience. Ricoeur specifically employs the term "narrative," *récit*, because he wants a term inclusive of both fiction and nonfiction.[39] He wants to argue that *all* narratives—nonfictional and fictional—work upon our temporal experience. Ricoeur speaks of a healthy circle between time and narrative. "Time becomes human to the extent that it is organized after the manner of a narrative; narrative, in turn, is meaningful to the extent that it portrays the features of temporal experience."[40] That Ricoeur designates time as the ultimate referent and "truth" of narratives aligns him with Kermode's earlier work[41] and pits him against the trend in contemporary narrative theory—in philosophy of history, historiography, and narratology—to "de-chronologize" narrative, to reduce it to laws and atemporal structures.[42] Ricoeur relies on the Aristotelian notion of *mimesis* to make his claim for the inextricable link between narrative and time. Also, like Buber and Bakhtin (ch. 4), and basing himself on the linguistics of Emile Benveniste and not Saussure,[43] Ricoeur looks to the larger unit of the sentence and not just individual words to establish referentiality: "language is oriented beyond itself; it says something *about* something."[44]

The purpose of Ricoeur's three-volume work is to show how central concerns about time in Western philosophy can be addressed by thinking about and with narratives. Ricoeur attempts to address the philosophical problematic or "aporias" of time by correlating dimensions of narrative with the thoughts of Aristotle, Augustine, Kant, Hegel, Husserl, and Heidegger on time. Ricoeur's analysis is far too complex to cover briefly. Therefore, we will lift up those elements of his discussion which are most pertinent to our concerns about Buber's narratives by summarizing Ricoeur's view of the referential quality of narrative and reviewing correlations between narrative and Heidegger's phenomenology of time in *Being and Time.*

The Temporal Reference of Historical and Fictional Narrative

Ricoeur's narrative theory is based on the Aristotelian notion of mimesis. This notion suggests that narrative is not a mere "copy or identical replica"[45] of human action but a creative representation of that action,[46] an "elaboration of an articulated significance of some action."[47] Ricoeur recognizes that once human action takes place it is impossible to recapture exactly "as it happened." As Ricoeur remarks, "Real events recede to the level of the *Ding an Sich.*"[48] He also recognizes that language is limited by its own structures and genres in relating the complexities, paradoxes, and chaos of much of human activity. Still, he holds that human action and temporal experience stand behind narrative and provide the circumstances, events, characters, and dramas that provide the fundamental material and psychological impetus for narrating. In recognizing the difficulties in capturing human temporal experience, Ricoeur does not move to the poststructural position that the task is impossible; instead, he makes the rather bold claim that it takes the two broad types of narrative, fiction and nonfiction, to do the job.

What Ricouer tries to argue is that history and fiction approach the ultimate referent of human time somewhat differently. History relies on documents, archives, and objective reports. It attempts to "articulate its reference claims in compliance with rules of evidence common to the whole body of science."[49] Where fiction can explore the present and even propose future scenarios, history is wed to the past. Even if it cannot bring us directly to the past, the past remains the primary referent of history.[50]

Yet it is precisely because history is limited to the past and to strict claims to scientific truth and to "conventional descriptions of the world" that it often misses something of the essence and core of human action. Fiction, no less than history, shares a "realistic intention." Yet, through its suspension of positivistic descriptions of the world, "the world of fiction ultimately redirects us to the core of the actual world of action."[51] Because fiction writers are spared the obligation of faithfulness to historical sequence, they can often bring us to deeper levels of human temporal experience. "Freed from linear aspects of time—[fiction] can explore the hierarchical levels that form the depth of temporal experience."[52] Fiction writers have at their disposal a variety of strategies to express different types of human temporal experience.[53] They can cut up sequence, transpose tenses, and distort the given tropes and rhetorical devices in an effort to relate the more radical types of human experience. Ricoeur suggests that fiction often has to include within it the "discordant" in order to better relate chaotic aspects of human temporal experience.

However, Ricoeur argues that in order to relate the most significant and complex aspects of human temporal experience, both fiction and history will have to be employed together. This, he suggests, is the power of epic: it combines history with fiction. "By fusing . . . with history fiction carries history back to [its] origin in the epic."[54] When history and fiction are "interwoven," as, for example, it often is in attempts to recapture a powerful modern event like the Holocaust, then narrative attains the heights of its mimetic capacities.[55]

Philosophy and Time

If Ricoeur succeeds in convincing us that human temporal experience is the proper referent of narrative and that both narrative modes are required to relate this temporal experience, we might still want to know more about what Ricoeur means by the term "temporal experience." Indeed, as Ricoeur explores the history of presentations of time in Western philosophy we find that there is anything but agreement about what time or "temporal experience" is. Augustine, in chapter 11 of his *Confessions,* has given classic expression to the dilemma of speaking about time: "What, then, is time? I know well enough what it is, provided nobody asks me; but if I am asked what it is and try to explain it I am baffled."[56]

Augustine is struck by the fact that on the one hand humans recognize and speak of a past, present, and future, yet, on the other hand, they directly experience only a fleeting moment. He asks the obvious human question: How can time exist if the past is no longer, if the future is not yet, and the present is not always? Augustine's solution is that time does not exist in physical extension; rather, it exists in the mind as three qualities of consciousness: the present of things past [memory], the present of things present [attention], and the present of things future [expectation]. But Augustine's solution is highly problematic because it relegates time solely to the sphere of the individual soul and human mind and neglects the public, external, and cosmological aspects of time that clocks and calendars aim to capture. Ricoeur juxtaposes Augustine with Aristotle and an "entire cosmological tradition according to which time surrounds us, envelops us, and dominates us, without the soul having the power to produce it."[57] In his search for a notion of time that respects both the psychological and the cosmological aspects Ricoeur brings us to Heidegger's phenomenological analysis. In Heidegger's analysis of the relationship between Being and Time there is an attempt to speak of the human experience of time as it is embedded in the world. Heidegger's existential analytic of *Dasein* aims at articulating the temporality of Being-in-the-world.

This temporality (as Augustine suggests with his notions of the present of things present, the present of things past, and the present of things future) is experienced by humans as a series of levels or dimensions of our experience of the present moment. Heidegger speaks of these dimensions with the terms "within-time-ness" *(Innerzeitigkeit)*, "historicality" *(Geschichtlichkeit)*, and "temporality" *(Zeitlichkeit)* proper. In the first temporal level we are mainly conscious of the present moment, "the now," in the second level our present moment is filled with memories and is given depth by the past, and in the third level the present is put in tension with the future and the powerful realization of our mortality. As Ricoeur analyzes Heidegger's phenomenology of each of the levels of human temporal experience he shows how narrative gives these temporal dimensions linguistic expression. Indeed, it is through Ricoeur's brilliant correlation of features of narratives and the existential aspects of time that his thesis about the interrelationship between time and narrative attains some of its deepest perceptions. Let us now follow Ricoeur in his correlation of aspects of narrative with Heidegger's temporal dimensions of "within-time-ness," "historicality," and "temporality."

Within-time-ness describes the time in which we actually live and act.[58] It is opposed to the mathematical notion of time as "a neutral series of abstract instants," a linear series that can be precisely and mechanically measured in abstract units. Within-time-ness describes the time which we are concerned to use or waste. It is the time in which we are bored and the time we try to stretch to get things done.

> Within-time-ness describes time as it is measured in human terms—after, later,
> earlier, since, till, while. It is time that is not measured by clocks, but time that is
> "reckoned" by human beings. This time finds its proper measurement in the unit
> of the day. . . . A day is the most natural of measures. "Dasein," Heidegger says,
> "historizes *from day to day.*" But a day is not an abstract measure; it is a
> magnitude which corresponds to our concern and to the world into which we are
> thrown.[59]

Within-time-ness is not the internal time-consciousness of the individual but
datable "public time." It is the time in which people act and suffer, act and
suffer amongst themselves. Within-time-ness is defined by the primacy of the
"now," the primacy of the present moment which confronts individuals with its
trials and demands.

Ricoeur argues that the time in which narratives occur is precisely the
existential time (between psychological and cosmological time) that is described by Heidegger's analysis of within-time-ness. Heroes of narratives "reck-
on *with* time, they have or do not have time *for* this or that. Their time can be
gained or lost."[60] Characters of narratives act and suffer with others in the
public time that is shared. Characters of narratives struggle with the challenges
presented by the present moment, the "now" of living.

Beyond giving expression to the existential dimension of time described by
Heidegger's notion of within-time-ness, Ricoeur argues that narratives move us
into a deeper temporal dimension which Heidegger calls "historicality."
Heidegger speaks of historicality, in its genuine and authentic form, under the
rubric of "repetition." Repetition works through the faculty of memory. It
involves an "alternative to the representation of time as moving from the past
forward into the future, according to the well-known metaphor of the arrow of
time."[61] In repetition, time moves backward. We move back into the past
through individual and collective memory to find resources for the present and
future. Repetition is that human mental activity in which the valuable and
essential elements of individual and communal history are preserved.

In repetition individuals find their fate and communities their destiny.
"[Repetition] means the retrieval of our most basic potentialities inherited from
our past in the form of personal fate and collective destiny."[62] Repetition
involves a process of drawing from oneself the seeds of one's fate. It is a
process of actively choosing what is initially given to us in inherited cultural
and biological potential.[63]

Ricoeur suggests that the mechanism through which repetition occurs is to
be found in narrative plots. Repetition occurs in the construction of plots (what
Ricoeur calls "emplotment" by authors), and in their apprehension and re-
apprehension by readers. In constructing a plot the author *already knows* the
major plot theme and the ending. The author constructs the events of the plot
in relation to the end. The author forges connections and establishes a logic
that makes the events of a story "followable."[64] Like Kermode, Ricoeur stresses
that it is the end of the story, the "conclusion," which "furnishes the point of
view from which the story can be perceived as forming a whole."[65] The author

works backward from his or her ending so that the events of the story will appear necessarily to lead to it. This working backward for the sake of the ending parallels the backward movement of time for the sake of the anticipated future engendered in Heidegger's repetition.

The reader who rereads or retells personal and traditional narratives already knows the story's ending and rereads the story to apprehend this known ending. In repeating a known story the reader sees the seeds of the end already in the beginning. The rereading or retelling engenders something of the process of reversing the common order of time. "We learn also to read time itself backward, as the recapitulating of the initial conditions of a course of action in its terminal consequences."[66]

As we repeat the well-known personal or collective narrative, we "grasp together" the strands of our past, confirm our sense of identity, and become prepared to accept our personal fate and collective destiny. Thus, having faced the past through narrative repetition of it, we have taken one giant step toward the future. Ricoeur states the irony that the "concept of repetition [of the past] succeeds at once in preserving the primacy of the future."[67]

> The cardinal function of the concept of repetition is . . . to recover the primacy of anticipatory resoluteness at the very heart of what is abolished, over and done with, what is no longer. Repetition, thus, opens potentialities that went unnoticed, were aborted, or were repressed in the past. It opens up the past again in the direction of coming-towards.[68]

Repetition, then, brings us to the doorstep of the third temporal dimension, the present of things future. And the end, the future of all life, is death. In the future, in death, narrative brings us to the deepest dimension of time, what Heidegger refers to as "temporality." Death holds the underlying truth about time because death is the truth of time passing, it is the ultimate sign of our becoming, our ever-changing, growing, and deteriorating status as living beings. The connection between time and death, as Ricoeur puts it, is the "oscillation of an existence torn between the sense of its mortality and the silent presence and the immensity of the time enveloping all things."[69] Facing death with "resoluteness" is having learned the Heideggerian truth of "being-toward-death."

Kermode says, in *The Sense of an Ending,* that the ending of a narrative fascinates readers and tellers most because "the End is a figure for their own deaths."[70] Kermode suggests that narrative endings provide "cathartic discharge" of our fear of death. Ricoeur takes this one Heideggerian step further by suggesting that narratives bring us to Heidegger's goal of "anticipatory resoluteness."[71] Through contemplating narrative ends we come face to face with the reality of death and learn to face death neither with fear nor with the illusory release that catharsis can provide, but with stoic resolve. And with this resolve we can truly face the future and the end it holds for us. In Heideggerian language, we could say that narrative makes *Dasein* "*authentically* futural." Through narrative, *Dasein,* which was originally thrown into existence without direction and identity, gains identity and the proper orientation toward its end. The sense of an ending which the plot gives to the reader's life prepares the reader to refigure her or his own sense of time and face death resolutely.

The Heideggerian dimensions of time which narrative gives expression to are certainly not obvious to most readers. To use Kermode's language, we could say that these truths constitute the underlying secrets, the opaque depths, the latent sense of narratives. Ricoeur says that the levels of time which Heidegger's phenomenology identifies are only "intended obliquely through the temporal armature of narrative."[72] This "oblique intentionality" of narrative, however, does not mean that the expression of time can be transposed to phenomenological discourse. "Temporality cannot be spoken of in the direct discourse of phenomenology but rather *requires* the indirect discourse of narration."[73] Here, we again see the circle which Ricoeur establishes between time and narrative. This circle means that the exploration and expression of human time cannot be primarily an analytical or phenomenological process. It means that telling time is telling stories.

Buber and the Sense of a Middle

We have now finished a review of two comprehensive theories of the nature and powers of narrative. A common theme in both of these theories is time and the organization which narrative gives to time. The question of the mimetic or referential capacity of narrative—its ability to point outside of itself to the world and to action—is also a central issue. Ricoeur argues for Kermode's early position that narratives are mimetic; yet Kermode, in *The Genesis of Secrecy*, turns away from this position and toward the deconstructionist view that narratives are self-enclosed systems. This self-enclosed quality of narratives contributes to their darkness and opacity, for there is no point outside of the narrative that can be used to determine its meaning. The tension between meaning and order on the one hand and disorder and secrecy on the other is another polarity which can be identified in both of our theories. In Kermode it shows up in the dynamic relationship between the secret opacity of narratives on the one hand and the desire of humans to assign meaning to them on the other. In Ricoeur's theory the tension appears in the relationship between the often discordant quality of human temporal experience and what he considers to be the concordant nature of plots which give order to human experience through their endings.

Let us now reexamine Buber's three narratives in "Dialogue" with reference to the narrative theories of Kermode and Ricoeur. To begin with we can say that Buber, like Ricoeur, has mimetic expectations from narrative. Buber expects that he will be able to capture and express something of the power and nature of the I-Thou encounter in the tales he tells about these encounters. Buber expects that narratives will be able to express the intricate set of relationships between persons and between person and world that is part of the I-Thou encounter. An appreciation for the importance of relationships is indeed one element that a Buberian perspective can contribute to discussions of narrative. The relationship between events that one finds in a narrative of an I-Thou encounter is of a different order than the causal relations that the historian is after. Causal relationships belong to the I-It and not the I-Thou realm. The relationships in Buber's narrative also take on a more fundamental role than just contributing toward the steps that lead to the narrative point or theme received at the narrative's end. The relationships that narrative discloses are not a chain of causes and effects each of which builds in one direction toward the end but a concatenation of details, events, persons whose relations are mutually determined and must be considered as a whole.

Perhaps the most interesting aspect of Buber narratives is that the attempt to relate the I-Thou encounter requires Buber to alter the traditional ending-based plot structure. Each story in "Dialogue" consists of two parts, with a turning point in the middle. The first part outlines an ordinary human experience, and through the breakthrough, the "turn," this experience is transformed into a special and unique experience. This plot structure is different from the model which Kermode, in *The Sense of an Ending*, and Ricoeur, in *Time and Narrative*, present as paradigmatic to narrative. In these two theories the end of a narrative plot is most important because it is the ending that bestows order on the narrative and, correlatively, on our temporal experience.[74] In Buber's dialogical narratives, however, it is the *middle* of the plot that is most central and not the end. The middle of the story relates the event of I-Thou as it breaks in upon the ordinary span of time, the time of beginning and end, which the narrative establishes.

Both Ricoeur and Kermode have used the Aristotelian notion of *peripeteia* to talk about the middle of a plot.[75] The *peripeteia* is a peculiar, unexpected "reversal"[76] in the plot, a "falsification" of that which we expected,[77] that makes us doubt that the story will come out all right. In the end, however, the *peripeteia* is "redeemed" and our expectation is reconfirmed. Kermode refers to the *peripeteia* as "a falsification of expectation, so that the end comes as expected, but not in the manner expected."[78] Buber's middle, however, is more than a *peripeteia*, because it is the focal point of the plot. It is in the middle that the "theme," the "point," of the story is to be found. In short, we could say that the middle functions in Buber's plots as the end does in Kermode's and Ricoeur's model.

Buber's focus on the middle in his narratives is consistent with his focus on the present moment of existence, the moment of the middle between the past and the future. As the present moment is the time in which I-Thou events occur, it is the middle of Buber's plots that is emphasized over and above the beginning (the past) and the end (the future). The middle represents the time of the everyday in which we live, act, suffer, work, and love. The middle represents the time when we are in direct contact with other humans. It can be said that birth and death are essentially individual matters. The first breath is something that each infant must take himself or herself, and no one can die for another person. But life lived in the middle is life lived in contact with and dependent on others. Life transpires in the "between," between beginning and end, between birth and death. We cannot know our birth nor can we truly know what our death entails. We do, in actuality, live in the middle, *in medias res.* Buber presents the reality and possibilities of this middle in his I-Thou narratives. For Buber, it is in this full moment that we are put in contact with our origins and with our future. Here, we anticipate the unity of present time and eternity. Here, we are to find our eternity. Here, in the "eternal middle" and not in the end, we are to find our way. As Buber says in *I and Thou:* "For this finding is not the end, but only the eternal middle, of the way."[79]

If we were to use a Heideggerian analysis of Buber's narratives we could certainly say that the notion of "within-time-ness," with its aspects of present-ness, publicness, and everydayness, well characterizes the temporal dimension of Buber's middles. Yet, as Ricoeur tried to show, the entire thrust of *Being and Time* is toward the primacy of the future. "Being-toward-death" and, correlatively, narrative ending, not narrative middle, are most important for Ricoeur's analysis of Heidegger. In the Heideggerian scheme, within-time-ness is the most superficial temporal dimension. Historicality has depth and meaning because, through repetition of the past, a way to the future is opened. Yet, as we learn from Augustine, the past and future are really only dimensions of the present. Awareness of the deeper temporal dimensions is awareness of the present of things past and future. The middle, the present, is the only route to the past and the future. It is the genius of Buber's narratives to make this point by altering traditional narrative structure. When the primacy of the present becomes an "eternal middle" then all temporal dimensions are opened to us.

The German intellectual historian Walter Sokell has tried to point to the underlying "Christian structure" of Heidegger's thought.[80] Sokell has compared Heidegger's notion of non-Being with Christian sin and Being with salvation. Although I find this analysis to be an oversimplification I have come to believe that there is something to Sokell's suggestion that Heidegger's thought shares important structural similarities with Christianity. I believe these similarities are related to an emphasis on the future and death. In *The Sense of an Ending,* you will remember, it is Christian Apocalypse that provides the original model for Kermode's analysis of plots. In making his case, Kermode says something about Christianity which sheds particular light on the subject at hand.

> Death and election are individual matters and became so early enough in the story. The disconfirmation of the primary eschatological predictions threw the emphasis on personal death as well as on to the sacraments; it has been said that Christianity of all the great religions is the most anxious, is the one which has laid the most emphasis on the terror of death.[81]

Could it be that the underlying connection between Heidegger and Christianity is the mutual focus on the future and on Being-toward-Death? Could it be that Heidegger's obsession with the end and death is routed in the primal

Christian anxiety about death and the Christian focus on Apocalypse and the end as the moment of salvation?[82] And, to take this point one step further, can we find the reasons for the focus on the middle in Buber's plot in his connection to his Jewish heritage? Certainly, there was Jewish apocalyptic writing and most certainly there was and is Jewish messianism. But we do have a decided emphasis on this life in Israelite religion. The focus on the land and the people of Israel as the locus for religious life, the polemic against the Egyptian preoccupation with the afterlife, all this had the effect of focusing attention on this world and the present. Much of biblical Jewish messianic hope was focused on the coming of an earthly prince who would purify the time of the present and establish a kingdom on earth, an "eternal middle" and not an entirely new time at the end of time. Jacob Neusner has tried to show that the temporal dimension most important to rabbinic Judaism was the time "between time and eternity," the everyday time of "home and hearth."[83] So much of *halakhah* is directed toward the behaviors, the problems, the sanctification of everyday life that one can quite easily argue that a focus on the middle, on the present life, is a prevailing concern of Rabbinic Judaism.[84] The Hasidism of the Baal Shem Tov, in Buber *and* in Scholem's view, specifically addressed itself to "neutralizing" messianic concerns.[85] We could say, then, that Buber's focus on the present and his "sense of a middle" are supported by a central emphasis in Judaism.

Buber's "sense of the middle," however, may not only be a result of his Judaism. Kermode has pointed out that as the notion of a divinely determined beginning and ending became less convincing to Western cultural elites, the attention of many writers gradually was drawn to the middle, to the present. Kermode argues that the movement from Apocalypse to Elizabethan tragedy involves a movement to endless *peripeteia,* to endless crisis, endless transition without end or resolution.[86] This sense of endless crisis has certainly been carried into our contemporary world and contemporary fiction. The sense of interminable crisis has spawned the production of the radical fiction of writers like Robbe-Grillet and Samuel Beckett where the middle of the plot is enlarged to subvert the sense of beginning and end.

What makes the novels of Robbe-Grillet and Beckett peculiarly modern or even postmodern is an additional move to empty the middle of a sense of crisis. The plot is deprived of narrative tension and narrative movement in an attempt to frustrate the meaning-giving function of narratives. Beckett's novel *Molly* goes on page after page without divisions or chapter titles that would give clues to beginnings and ends. Of Beckett's narrators, the critic Ted Estess has observed, "They increasingly can't begin or end a story."[87] "They drone on endlessly, day after day, blackening the pages with words until their time passes."[88] Estess suggests that Beckett does this in an attempt to "admit chaos" into his art,[89] the chaos which the modern person experiences in daily life. Kermode notes that in Robbe-Grillet's *La Jalousie* we find an endless middle.[90] "The narrator is 'explicitly unconcerned with chronology,' perceiving only that here and now in which memory, fantasy, anticipation . . . may intrude, though without sharp differentiation."[91] Some of these attributes are also to be found in the existentialist literature of Sartre and Camus.

If we look at Buber's I-Thou narratives there are some similarities to the modern "anti-novel." Like the authors of these novels, Buber alters the traditional narrative pattern in an effort to bring the experience of everyday life to expression. We could say, too, that the I-Thou narratives "admit chaos" into the plot, so that the shattering and transforming power of the I-Thou event is revealed. Yet Buber's narratives, in their tone, are decidedly different from the "anti-novels." Kermode speaks of the middle of the anti-novel as a "discontinuous, unorganized middle."[92] Buber's middle functions, in reverse, to give order and meaning to the plot. In the middle of the story the I-Thou event breaks in upon and transforms the ordinary into the extraordinary, transforms passing time into significant time, transforms the persons involved into beings who are "no longer the same as they were when they entered" into relationship. If the middles in the anti-novel and in Buber's narratives do different things, they still do show us that narratives are not always focused on endings. In fact, the possibility that middles could be the focus of plots led Kermode, in *The Genesis of Secrecy*, to alter his model for plots. Kermode adopts Dilthey's notion of "impression-point" as the focal point of a plot.

> One may perceive in a life some moment that gives sense and structure to the whole, and it need not come at the end of a life. . . . A work of art [Dilthey] believed, would have this same impression-point, around which the whole gestalt must be articulated.[93]

Buber's middle could very well be described as the "impression-point" of his plots around which the whole tale is organized. There are also other parts of Kermode's theory in *The Genesis of Secrecy* that might illuminate other aspects of Buber's narratives in "Dialogue." If we return to analyze Buber's stories in "Dialogue" more closely we can find a number of elements that make the meaning of the stories a lot less clear. For example, let us look again at the first story we reviewed, the story of the two silent men. Buber uses this story to "clarify" the point that dialogue can occur in silence. Yet the story raises so many unanswered questions that one could easily challenge Buber on the extent to which his point about silent dialogue is "clarified." When we introduced the tale in the beginning of this chapter we raised some obvious questions. Who are these men? What do they look like? What did they learn about one another in their morning travels? If we assume that Buber was one of the men in the story this would make Buber both the narrator and a character in the story. But if Buber was one of the characters, one of the silent partners in the tale, and the other man said nothing to him about his inner life ("They are not in one another's confidence"), how did Buber, as narrator, know about the partner's childhood ("a childhood's spell is laid on . . .")? And what does the narrator mean when he says, "This is one of the hours which succeeds in bursting asunder the seven iron bands about our heart—imperceptibly, the spell is lifted"? Clearly, this is not a straightforward account of an encounter Buber had. For if the two men were silent there is no way that Buber could know about the other man's psychological "reserve," his "childhood spell," and the "imperceptible" lifting of the spell.

Buber, in a sense, "cheats" in his tale by playing the part of both narrator and character. As narrator, he is able to set background: "Imagine two men sitting beside one another. . . ." As narrator he is able to increase the narrative tension he needs to make the middle turning appear as a sudden dramatic transformation. He employs the very popular narrative technique of describing elements of his characters' psychologies and past lives that each other are unaware of, and this has the effect of polarizing the psychological makeup of his characters. Yet, by leading us to assume that Buber himself is the open, receptive character, the characteristically Buberian man who "receives all genuine destiny that meets him"; by leading us to assume that the open character is the same person, the same Martin Buber who encountered the horse and the clergymen in the other tales in "Dialogue," Buber attempts to add to the "believability" of his stories. He adopts a confessional, autobiographical tone which suggests that this *really* happened to him and therefore we should believe that the dimension of the I-Thou relationship described is "real" and can happen to us.

Buber depends upon the "trust" of his reader that he is a "reliable narrator."[94] Buber expects the reader to accept the denouement, the middle "impression point" of his plot. ("But even now the man does not speak a word. . . . Yet he does something. . . . Unreservedly communication streams from him, and the silence bears it to his neighbor.") Yet if the bond of trust between the reader and narrator is at all questioned, if the narrator is regarded as an "unreliable narrator,"[95] then the tale may very well fail to "clarify" Buber's philosophy of I-Thou. Indeed, a careful examination of the details of the story and the narrative techniques employed may serve to obfuscate Buber's philosophy of I-Thou. One must say that even with the most naïve of readings this tale leaves the reader not totally sure about what Buber means about "silent dialogue."

And if we look at the other two stories we could certainly also raise questions about them. In considering the story "Opinions and the Factual" (which tells about the Easter peace conference) we might well ask how it came to be that a conference with Christians and "former clergymen" would schedule a meeting on Easter! And we really might want to know how it was that Buber "came to speak about Jesus" at this conference. In the very famous story about the horse we may want to know more about what Buber did to objectify and alienate the horse. Or we might ask what the difference is between seeing the horse as "other" (a requisite element of I-Thou) and seeing the horse as "object" (a characteristic of I-It). This tale, of course, raises the question of how a person can have a dialogue with a horse. Is Buber projecting his own voice onto the horse, or is the horse really "speaking" to him? This is perhaps the most fundamental question that we ask of all I-Thou meetings. Do we really meet the other, and hear their voice, or is it just a reflection of something within us that we meet? Is there any way that the tales of I-Thou dialogue can authenticate or verify that the voice that I hear really is that of the other?[96]

These examples of curious details in Buber's stories should be enough to provide evidence for Kermode's point that narratives can be opaque at the very instance that an author uses them to gain clarity. We may guess that Buber himself was aware of the opacity of his tales and that it is for this reason that the tales are given titles and are preceded and followed by statements that give us the "meaning" Buber wants us to take away from the tale.[97] Certainly there is within Buber's narratives enough lacunae to give them a discordant character. But does this invalidate the use of narrative as a form of expression for Buber's philosophy of I-Thou? Does my "deconstruction" of Buber's tales render them meaningless? Does the fact of narrative ambiguity discount narrative as a philosophical method for Buber? The answer to this, I think, is decidedly no! Buber's narratives clarify his philosophy in the very fact of their unclarity. What the I-Thou narratives do is to present that mix of order and disorder, of illumination and doubt, of abiding question and surprise that is at the heart of the I-Thou encounter. It is precisely in their ambiguity, their obscurity, their openness to a variety of interpretations, that the tales shed light on I-Thou. In this sense Kermode's phrase for "radiant obscurity" is particularly apt. A simple and absolutely "clear" tale with all relevant background and foreground in-formation about an I-Thou event would fail to capture the mystery and element of surprise that is involved in an encounter. We could return to Ricoeur's language and say that an I-Thou narrative needs a healthy element of dis-cordance to relate the upsetting and transforming nature of I-Thou. An I-Thou tale, then, is rightfully a "discordant concordance."

What the discordant concordance of Buber's narratives can teach us not only about the philosophy of I-Thou but about all narratives is their incessant need for interpretation. The mysterious discordant concordance of any good philosophy like any good narrative draws its readers into the interpretative process. As Kermode has said, it is precisely the ambiguity, the questions and lacunae in a narrative that gives it its "hermeneutical potential." Here is the link between narrative and interpretation. All narratives which struggle to express human encounter with world and person immediately call forth questions and interpretations. To speak in narrative is to speak as clearly and directly as possible about the *Zwischenmenschliche.* To speak in narrative is first to pull you to the window and to point to the world of encounter and to ask you what you see and then to open the window to the interpretive process which begins in reading and ends in the reader's own   life meetings.

Ricoeur addresses this issue of the relationship between a text and the life of the reader with his notion of "refiguration." As readers confront the author's attempt to "configure" human temporal experience in narratives, they are led to "refigure" their own sense of time. This refiguration has the practical result of altering not only the reader's relation to the world but the reader's actions in the world.

> It is only in reading that the dynamism of configuration completes its course. And it is beyond reading, in effective action, instructed by the works handed down, that the configuring of the text is transformed into refiguration.[98]

For Ricoeur, the "refiguring of time" culminates in an "intersection" between the world of the text and the world of the reader, a "fusion of horizons," in Gadamer's terms. This fusion means that the reader sees him- or herself in terms of the narrative plot. There is an intersection or "interpolation" between the narrative of the reader's life and the narrative read. When this happens the reader finds his/her own being-in-the-world reorganized and enlarged.

> To understand these [narrative] texts is to interpolate among the predicates of our situation all those meanings that, from a simple environment *(Umwelt)*, make a world *(Welt)*. Indeed we owe a large part of the enlarging of our horizon of existence to poetic [narrative] works.[99]

Buber's narratives in his essay "Dialogue," with their vibrant middles, their questions, and their lacunae, are structured not only to draw the reader to interpret but to push the reader toward Ricoeur's notion of "refiguration" or what we called (in chapter 4 of this book) the "fourth stage" of hermeneutics: the application of the narrative to the interpretation of the reader's own life. The most important questions that Buber would have his readers ask of his tales are: How do these narratives shed light on my own experiences of meeting? What of these tales can I take into my own encounters with others and the world? How does the present tense that the narratives of "Dialogue" open up include my present? The opacity, the middles, the empty spaces in Buber's narratives have a crucial function; by building in space for questions, middles, and lacunae in his tales Buber provides his readers with the space to insert themselves.

VI

"AUTOBIOGRAPHICAL FRAGMENTS": BECOMING SELF THROUGH THE OTHER

In the preceding chapter we focused on correlations between elements in narrative plot and dimensions of time. Unlike many plots which focus on the end, Buber's plots are focused on the middle and this brings his readers to the present moment and its potentialities for encounter. In following Ricoeur's (and Aristotle's)[1] commitment to plot and time we have arrived at some important insights into the nature of narrative and into Buber's narratives in particular. Yet our focus on the correlation between plot and time has led us to overlook another very important element of narrative. Narratives are concerned not only with temporal events and incidents but also with human selves and personalities. Narratives are concerned with the human "character."[2] In the oft quoted words of Henry James, "What is [narrative] incident but the illustration of character?" In James's view narratives give us not human temporal events but the varieties of human characters.[3]

The arguments over whether plot or character is more "primary" to narrative can be, as Kermode suggests, somewhat "absurd" given that the two elements are intricately related and mutually enrich each other.[4] Yet it is probably true that certain tales and tragedies are more involved in exploring aspects of human events and therefore more plot-centered and other works are involved with the exploration of human character. It may very well be that one distinguishing mark of the modern novel is a preoccupation with the idiosyncracies of the human character that premodern narratives lacked. Ian Watt has argued that the "novel is the form of literature which most fully reflects the individualist . . . reorientation" of the modern world.[5]

If we do not want to go as far as James in his assertion that the primary concern of narrative is characterization, it seems safe to say that there is one particular narrative genre where the expression of a human character is more important than human events; that genre is autobiography. Most critics agree that the expression of character, in particular, the character or "self" of the author, is the preoccupation of autobiography. In the introduction to his fine collection of contemporary criticism on autobiography, James Olney reminds us that the term "autobiography" comes from the Greek meaning "self-life-writing"; he then goes on to argue that the modern study of autobiography was initiated by the realization that autobiography is "at once a discovery, a creation, and an imitation of the self" of the author.[6] This position seems to be born out by the wide variety of critics included in Olney's collection. For almost all of these critics make the connection between autobiography and self. Thus, William Howarth compares autobiography to a "self-portrait."[7] Jean Starobinski refers to autobiography as a "self-interpretation."[8] And Georges Gusdorf speaks of autobiography as a "means to self-knowledge."[9] Even the most radical poststructural theorists, who cast doubt on the ability of autobiography to express the self, highlight the fact that it is the self as discovered, as created, as de-centered, even as mystified or lost, that is the central concern of autobiography. The autobiographer usually writes with the sentiments of Stendhal, who declared, in the beginning of his autobiography, "It's high time I got to know myself."[10]

Given that autobiography and self are interconnected, it could be argued that cultural and authorial conceptions of the self have an important influence on the construction of autobiographies. Indeed, Georges Gusdorf and Karl Weintraub have tried to show that the very existence of autobiography depends upon a notion of the individual as unique and separate from others, a notion of the individual which is indigenous to the West and unique in world history. To use Gusdorf's language, one of the "conditions and limits" of modern autobiography is a notion of the "singularity" of the individual self.[11]

In this chapter I will both examine and test the limits of the modern genre of autobiography by analyzing the autobiography of Martin Buber under the rubrics established by current autobiographical theory. Because Buber's autobiography does not neatly conform to the established rubrics and to the traditional limits and conditions of autobiography, I will suggest that Buber's autobiography represents a novel autobiographic strategy and that it presents a unique form for the genre. This form is predicted on a notion of self as relational which Buber developed in his philosophy of I-Thou. This notion of self, in its turn, is based on certain theological presuppositions that properly make Buber's autobiography a religious autobiography.

The "Autobiographical Fragments"

When we look at the autobiography of Martin Buber, suggestively titled *Autobiographische Fragmente* (1960), we are confronted with a work which appears unique when compared with many autobiographies. Buber was commissioned to write an autobiography for *The Philosophy of Martin Buber*, Volume 12 of the Library of Living Philosophers Series, which was edited by Paul Schilpp and Maurice Friedman. Buber was asked, as are all the other philosophers in the series, to write an intellectual autobiography that would trace the important intellectual forces that affected the formation of his thought. What Buber produced was neither a continuous narrative about his intellectual development, nor a search for his self, but twenty autobiographical anecdotes which relate important events, meetings and "mismeetings," which occurred in his life. A number of the anecdotes which were included were written by Buber at earlier times in his life and were published previously as parts of other essays. Some of the anecdotes from the essay "Dialogue," which we reviewed in the last chapter, are included in the autobiography and the reader can get a fair idea of the type of "fragments" that appear in the auto-biography by glancing back at Buber's story "The Horse."[12] Buber himself describes the autobiography in this way:

> It cannot be a question here of recounting my personal life (I do not possess the kind of memory necessary for grasping great temporal continuities as such), but solely of rendering an account of some moments that my backward glance lets rise to the surface, moments that have exercised a decisive influence on the nature and direction of my thinking.[13]

In the first anecdote, titled "My Mother," Buber briefly describes the divorce of his parents and his subsequent move at age three to Lvov in Galicia to be raised by his paternal grandparents. Out of his realization that his mother would "never come back," Buber tells us, he developed the notion of *Vergegnung*, "mismeeting or miscounter"—the "failure of a real meeting between men."[14] The autobiography then goes on to review a series of meetings and mismeetings that had a determinative role in Buber's life. Among these are encounters with a school headmaster, Buber's famous I-Thou meeting with the horse, a mismeeting with a very disturbed young student which altered Buber's view of religion, and important encounters with Zionist leader Theodor Herzl and philosopher Paul Natorp.

The form which we outlined for the anecdotes in "Dialogue" holds for most of the narratives in the autobiography. The anecdotes usually begin with a brief description of the setting of the meeting, then build to a crescendo in the middle where Buber describes the particularities of the meeting or mismeeting, and then end with an enigmatic statement about the personal or intellectual message Buber received from the encounter.

What makes the work unique as an autobiography is that there are no prose or narrative connecting links between the anecdotes. Each is a self-contained unit. Also, the anecdotes seldom focus on matters of personal feeling, self search, or self definition. Rather, the focus of the autobiography is on life events and significant meetings with others, on what Buber calls "I-Thou relationships."

Buber's Autobiography and Traditional Autobiographical Theory

When Buber's autobiography is analyzed with an older, standard auto-biographical theory, such as that provided in Roy Pascal's *Design and Truth in Autobiography,* one may question whether the "Fragments" can really be called an autobiography at all. Pascal defined autobiography as follows:

> The reconstruction of the movement of a life, or part of a life, in the actual circumstances in which it was lived. Its center of interest is the self, not the outside world. . . . Autobiography is a shaping of the past. It imposes a pattern on a life, constructs out of it a coherent story.[15]

Although we do get some sense for the existential circumstances in which important events of Buber's life occurred, there is not enough written in his anecdotes to establish the context more fully. Certainly, we do not have a sense of the overarching movement of Buber's life from one stage to the next. The movement seems to occur within each anecdote itself, a movement based around Buber's meeting or mismeeting in the story. The center of interest in the "Fragments" also does not seem to be Buber's self. We quoted Buber in the opening paragraph of his autobiography as saying that his autobiography is not a "recounting of his personal life." Indeed, we learn little about Buber's personal life and very little about those intimately connected to him. (The "Fragments" hardly mention his wife and children.) In a revealing letter on the subject of autobiography Buber tells Maurice Friedman that he has no real interest in himself.

> You must understand, the thought that I should say "This is what I am" disturbs me. I do not have this kind of relationship to myself. Will you understand what I mean when I say that I am not interested in myself?[16]

Finally, the fragmentary nature of the autobiography does not give us a sense of a coherent story. Many crucial events and periods of Buber's life are omitted. Anecdotes often follow one another without apparent connection. The autobiography presents no real unifying theme.

Given any of the many theories that highlight the autobiographical task of presenting a history of the self and articulating a life theme, Buber's autobiography appears lacking. Buber fails in constructing what Olney, in his early work, called an autobiographical "monument of the self,"[17] a self-narrative with beginning, middle, end, and unifying theme.

Yet before we cast Buber's "Autobiographical Fragments" aside as an unsuccessful work of autobiography, I believe we will benefit from analyzing some underlying assumptions about the self and its presentation within autobiography. I take Weintraub very seriously when he says in "Autobiography and Historical Consciousness": "The manner in which men conceive of the nature of the self largely determines the form and process of autobiographic writing."[18] And to take this further I would suggest that conceptions of self affect autobiographical theory as well as autobiographical literature. The assumed notion of self that has had such a determinative effect on autobiographers and theoreticians is what Gusdorf calls the "singular" self and what Weintraub calls "individuality."

Self-assumptions and Self-story

The self as singular is a self that conceives of itself as "opposed to others." It "exists outside of others," and even against others. It is not a self that defines itself "with others in an interdependent existence that asserts its rhythms everywhere in the community."[19] Gusdorf argues that the notion of the individual as singular required the breakdown of the "mythic framework" and the

establishment of historical consciousness. Historical consciousness establishes the new, the idiosyncratic, the individual as a value over against the
repetition of traditionally given paradigms taken from the past.[20] Gusdorf dates
the origin of the modern notion of the self (and concomitantly the birth of
modern autobiography) to the Copernican Revolution in the sixteenth century.[21]

> The curiosity of the individual about himself the wonder that he feels about the
> mystery of his own destiny is thus tied to the Copernican Revolution: at the
> moment it enters into history, humanity, which previously aligned its develop-
> ment to the great cosmic cycles, finds itself engaged in an autonomous adven-
> ture. . . . Henceforth man knows himself a responsible agent.[22]

Gusdorf points to Montaigne as the first writer who "assumes the task of
bringing out the most hidden aspects of individual being."[23] Weintraub also
cites historical consciousness as a prime factor in the rise of the notion of the
self, which he refers to as "individuality," yet he argues that this notion gained
true expression in the nineteenth century after historians Johann Gottfried von
Herder and Justus Möser.[24] For Weintraub, the first person to tell this individual
story was Goethe. "It was he who first wrote his own life as the history of an
individuality."[25]

Although Gusdorf and Weintraub look to science and literature for the roots
of modern notions of the self, we could also look to modern philosophy. With
Descartes, we have the turn to the individual cogito for philosophy's first
principle and the basis of all knowledge. Kant's apriori principles and categories are also found in the individual mind, and his struggle for the autonomous
moral self is fundamental to modern conceptions of the individual. Other
important contributions to the singular self come from Locke's theory of natural
rights and individual liberties.

Whether the source of the singular self be a matter of historical consciousness, philosophy, or literature, *that* the modern West has engendered a revolu-
tionary notion of the self seems certain.[26] Gusdorf's particular use of the term
"singular" self illuminates in two ways the conception of the self implicit in
much modern Western autobiography. On the one hand the self is single in that
it is unique and distinct from others, and on the other hand the self is single in
that it is "one," integral, unified across time. The former meaning supplies the
condition for the possibility of writing an autobiography; that is, it assures that
there is a distinct subject to write about. And the latter meaning suggests
certain limits to the form which autobiography has taken. Autobiography
strives for a unity which mimics the assumed unity of self.

The assumption of a separate self, or what I would like to call a
"monumental self," has fostered the creation of monumental autobiographies—literary artifacts which present the history of the self in the form of the
epic or romantic novel. The self is divided into chapters: childhood, youth,
adulthood, professional fulfillment, and the unifying narrative theme comes to
represent the author's raison d'être, her purpose in life, her true self. This

autobiographical pattern has been labeled "teleological" or "oratorical" by Howarth.[27]

The assumption of most autobiography is that the self exists as an essence compressed within the individual and personal life is a matter of uncovering, unfolding, or finding adequate expression for this inner essence. As Weintraub puts it, the task of life is "translating potentiality into actuality."[28] The unfolding may be relatively uncomplicated and, in this case, the autobiographer merely tells the tale of his or her achievements. On the other hand, this unfolding may be very difficult and blocked by life's circumstances. In this case the auto-biographer leads his reader on a search which is often unfulfilled. Yet even with this later type of autobiography, which Howarth calls "poetic,"[29] the assumption is that the self exists as separate, it just is hidden from the author and reader.

The development of this Western notion of a separate self, which follows a path from the dawn of historical consciousness to philosophical notions of the autonomous self, to romantic notions of individuality, to existential notions of the lonely and creative person, culminates in modern depth and humanistic psychologies.[30] Autobiography, as the "literary form in which an individuality could best account for itself,"[31] has celebrated and furthered the popularity of notions of the self as singular. The virtual explosion in the writing of auto-biographies (six thousand American titles alone were located in a 1961 study)[32] in recent decades bears witness that this notion has captured the cultural imagination of the West. One critic has labeled the most exaggerated and grotesque manifestations of the singular self as "The Culture of Narcis-sism," and a variety of social critics have tried to outline the destructive effects of this apolitical, overindividualistic cultural ethos on public, social, and political life.[33]

Buber's Relational Self and Fragmentary Autobiographical Form

Martin Buber responded to the development of cultural notions of the single self by developing a radically relational conception of the self. Buber de-veloped a notion of self that is, in some ways, a throwback to the premodern *Gemeinschaft* world. His self is the mirror image of Gusdorf's singular self. It is not "opposed to others," nor does it "exist outside of others." Indeed, it defines itself "with others."[34] In the opening paragraphs of *I and Thou,* Buber states: "When one says You [Thou], The I of the word-pair I-You [Thou] is said, too."[35] The self is thus intrinsically related to another. The self, in Buber's view, only grows to selfhood through relation to another. "Man becomes an I through a You [Thou]."[36] In his later essay "Distance and Relation" Buber articulates more thoroughly his relational view of the self.

> For the inmost growth of the self is not accomplished, as people like to suppose today, in man's relation to himself, but in the relation between the one and the other, between men, that is, pre-eminently in the mutuality of the making present—in the making present of another self and in the knowledge that one is

made present in his own self by the other—together with the mutuality of acceptance, of affirmation and confirmation.[37]

Buber speaks of the development of a sense of self as "becoming a self with me."[38] Humans are "confirmed" as selves by other humans, they require mutual confirmation to be.

> The human person needs confirmation because man as man needs it. . . . secretly and bashfully he watches for a Yes which allows him to be and which can come to him only from one human person to another. It is from one man to another that the heavenly bread of self-being is passed.[39]

Michael Theunissen has carefully argued, in his study of "The Other" in modern existential and phenomenological thought, that for Buber, "personal subjectivity does not possess its substantial fullness beyond the relationship to the Other."[40] Because an individual becomes an "I" through another, through a "Thou," because the self is recognized and confirmed only by and through the other, to ask the question of individual identity is to ask the question of relationship to others. *With this relational view of the self Buber could not write a traditional monumental autobiography. The story of the I must be the story of relationships to others and to the world.* For Buber, there is never merely a "single one." To cast the individual in these Kierkegaardian terms is to deny the self its full reality. For Buber, the individual must not be seen in isolation from others, for it "can and may have to do essentially with another."[41]

Buber originally shied away from writing an autobiography. He tells us that he lacked the proper memory for such an endeavor. He also says he has no interest in his self. Yet, perhaps his reluctance had something to do with a frustration about the genre. When pushed to write his autobiography he responded in the spirit of Rousseau, who declared: "For what I have to say I need to invent a language." Buber created an autobiographical form in which the self is shown not as separate, but in its relationships with others and with the world. We do not receive an abundance of information about Buber's intimate feelings; these feelings are not essential to the constitution of the self. The self grows and is expressed in the "between," between an I and a Thou. The story of the self is not the story of one's emotional life; it is the story of one's interaction with others and with the world.

If we were to introduce Buber to the discussion about character and plot with which we began this chapter we could say that the character, the self, which Buber's autobiography portrays is one that is highly dependent upon the "plot dimension" in narrative. Buber's self is known in the embeddedness of its actions in temporal events that the plot dimension reveals. Buber's autobiography is a fine example of Kermode's point that plot and characterization cannot be separated. It is in and through relational actions in the world, it is in and through what Kermode calls "the complex of human relations" which plot captures,[42] that the self is told.

The series of self-enclosed anecdotes in Buber's autobiography reveals the self to be confirmed anew in each relational event. Every I-Thou event requires a reorganization of the self. Every I-Thou event carries a "Word," a "judgment,"[43] a message that reorients the self and dictates a "turning," redirecting of the self. The anecdotes in Buber's autobiography present the self as a moving entity constantly being transformed and created by significant life meetings. Karl Weintraub has said that the hallmark of life is that it is process,[44] yet Weintraub seems to believe that this process is crystallized through one major event of crisis. "At such a crisis point lives undergo a wrenching: personal matter in diffused suspension is catalyzed to take on clarified form. . . ."[45]

Buber believes that there is not one cataclysmic crisis around which the self coalesces but that every I-Thou event carries the potential for the reorganization of the self. If we look at Buber's autobiography we certainly do not find one, but a number of major crisis events. Indeed, Buber asserts in his writings that we are "addressed" and can be transformed at each and every moment but we construct an "armor" around us to protect us from the constant change that true listening would entail.[46]

In 1957 Buber made a forward-looking statement on individual development to a neo-Freudian audience when he suggested that: "In certain crises of later childhood I feel that more decisive formation is going on than in infancy."[47] Here, I believe, Buber is not only trying to combat the determinism of infancy in Freudianism but he is also suggesting that there can be a number of determinative crisis points in a life. This viewpoint was to be proposed by Erik Erikson[48] and has been adopted by a number of developmental psychologists. Bertram Cohler argues that there are at least three "transformative" periods in life (movement to late childhood, to adolescence, and to midlife), but he warns that the path of the movement through these crises cannot be easily charted and, more significantly, individual reactions to these crises cannot be predicted.

> As a result both of recent findings from longitudinal studies and increased appreciation of the significance of larger historical factors in determining particular lives, it has become clear that lives are much less ordered and predictable than formerly recognized.[49]

The anecdotes in Buber's autobiography present well the sense of a self in constant process, redefining itself through the experience of relational crisis events. The recent work of Theunissen[50] in German philosophy and the work of Charles Brice[51] in psychology has shown the novelty of Buber's notion of self in the history of these respective disciplines.[52] Yet these works in philosophy and psychology have not pointed out the novel implications this notion of self has for the writing of autobiography. Buber's autobiography is one of the few that take seriously the relational and process qualities of the self and try to develop an autobiographical form that reflects these qualities.

The Postmodern Self, Autobiographical Theory, and Buber

Some recent autobiographical theorists have moved away from the rather narrow guidelines established by older commentators like Pascal. Many of these theorists recognize that representing the self in narrative is not as simple as it may seem. A number of theorists have discarded the naïve belief in the historical accuracy of autobiography and have come to see that autobiography is often more a reflection of the self of the author at the time of the writing than an accurate presentation of the history of the self at a succession of moments in the past.[53] In the introductory article to his collection on autobiographical theory, Olney asserts that a number of philosophers and psychologists have come together to assert the "idea of a self that defines itself from moment to moment amid the buzz and confusion of the external world."[54] Olney speaks of the self as "open-ended and incomplete; it is always in process or, more precisely, is itself a process."[55] Using a French poststructural approach to autobiography, Louis Renza has argued that because the self is never completely given, autobiography must be recognized as an "endless prelude . . . a purely fragmentary, incomplete literary project."[56] Renza follows the path of the postmodern positions of Lacan, Derrida, Barthes, Foucault, Rorty, who call into question the modern notions of the singular self in ways that are far more radical than those of Buber.

Given the poststructural view that language is closed off from external references, that words only refer to other words, the easy connection between the self of the author and the self portrayed in an autobiography is no longer regarded as tenable. Autobiography is not an expression of the self of the author, it is the presentation of a character that lives only in the words of the text. Writing the self in autobiography accomplishes exactly the opposite of what the older theory presupposed. The self that is written is not the self that is found, crystallized, monumentalized and immortalized; it is the self that is lost in literary types and tropes. The self that is written is the self that is forced into the necessarily contrived and artificial metaphors of self, sketches of character, and turns of plot that the genres of literature provide. Foucault, who is famous for announcing the postmodern "death of man," tells us that committing the self to writing is inserting the self into an "opening where the writing subject endlessly disappears."[57] Foucault argues that where an older conception of narrative or epic "guaranteed the immortality of a hero. . . . Writing is now linked to sacrifice . . . it is a voluntary obliteration of the self."[58] In the words of Roland Barthes, writing represents not the eternal life but the "death of the author." "The voice loses its origin, the author enters into his own death, writing begins."[59] Thus, with the postmodern we have gone beyond the notion of the singular self expressed in the monumental autobiography to the self that isappears and dies in language. Autobiography, for postmodernism, has the contradictory effect of obliterating the very self it tries to capture.

Where do Buber's views of the self and autobiography fit with these post-modern, post-self positions? Certainly Buber's social or relational self is not a self that disappears. The self found in the space and language opened by the I-Thou relation is a living, becoming self. As we tried to show in chapter 4, Buber does not accept the view that language is self-enclosed and self-referential. The language of I-Thou dialogue refers to that which is unique in each of the interlocutors. In I-Thou relationship self-growth, self-recognition, and self-confirmation occur. And in the "Autobiographical Fragments" the relational self is expressed and not lost. If Buber does not accept the notion of the singular self and the value of monumental autobiographies, he does not go so far as to say that the self has no substance and cannot be said. Buber's position lies, characteristically, between the modern and postmodern views of self and autobiography. Yet situating Buber thus should not be cause to regard his thought as an intermediate stage on the way from the modern to the more current and therefore more "correct" position. Indeed, as Calvin Schrag has argued in his fine study *Communicative Praxis and the Space of Subjectivity*, if we are to have a modicum of sociality and communication between human beings, if we are to be able to make any ethical judgment about human behavior, we must be able to hold individuals accountable for their words and actions. If civilization is to persist we must be able to assume that "discourse and action are *about* something, *by* someone, and *for* someone."[60] Even the contemporary masters of suspicion on the self recognize the necessity of some notion of the self. In the same article in which we quoted Foucault proclaiming the disappearance of the self, Foucault also states that the "subject should not be entirely abandoned."[61] Schrag quotes Derrida making a similar point:

> The subject is absolutely indispensable. I don't destroy the subject; I situate it. That is to say, I believe that at a certain level both of experience and of philosophical and scientific discourse one cannot get along without the notion of subject.[62]

To provide that needed "notion of the subject" which takes the postmodern critique of the modern self seriously yet refuses to accept the extreme postmodern position on the self's death, Schrag suggests that we look for a "decentered and transfigured intersubject, co-emerging with other subjects."[63] Sounding much like Martin Buber, Schrag calls for a notion of self that is to be found neither solely within the single individual nor without the individual in social and professional roles. Schrag's self is also not to be located solely in language or solely in action but is embedded in the intersection of the individual and society, language, and action. The self is to be found in an intricate "web of delivered discourse, social practices, professional requirements, and the daily decisions of everyday life."[64] Schrag argues that the self can only be appropriately seen in its "ineradicable situationality." This is a "holistic space," which he calls "the space of communicative competence" or "communicative praxis."[65]

Though Schrag does not refer to Buber, his self exists in the space which sounds very much like Buber's *"Zwischenmenschliche,"* the space between the I and the Thou. Schrag's description of the self is full of Buberian terminology.

> The conversational space of the "I" in discourse is coinhabited by the "you." In the dialogic transaction, which is if not a privileged surely a frequent posture of discourse, the "I" and the "you" slide back and forth within a common space. In the saying of "I," in submitting my thesis or contention in the form of "I believe . . ." or "I maintain . . .," the indexical posture of "I" is dialectically bonded with the posture of "you" as the one being addressed. . . . I am able to say "I" only because of an acknowledgment of you as my interlocutor within the dynamics of the dialogic encounter. The "I" and the "you" are as it were coconstituted, sharing a common, intersubjective space."[66]

What Schrag shows is that the Buberian position on the self is not a step away from modern notions and toward postmodern ones but, indeed, a highly promising theory of the self that provides a way out of the nihilistic postmodern view of the self which is destructive to the notions of self agency and individual responsibility that are a requirement for human communication and sociality. Because I am constituted in and through the other person in the social context I am in radical need of others and of society. I must respect and be responsible for the other if I am to be at all. It is crucial to recognize that the social self is not the self bestowed by social roles. The relational self is also not a self that the I shares jointly with the Thou. In both of these descriptions the I would be robbed of agency and responsibility. Rather, as I grow in relation I become more me and you more you. As I grow I become more enmeshed in concentric circles of relation that grow out of the dyadic relation and toward greater involvement and responsibility in family, community, and public life.

Buber calls the ever widening series of human groups to which the individual is bound in responsibility the "manifold We,"[67] or, borrowing from Heraclitus, the "common world."[68] Schrag, also referring to Heraclitus, calls this public space in which the individual is embedded *"ethos."*[69] This *ethos* or "dwelling place" is both a linguistically and an ethically charged realm. For as I grow in it I become more and more sensitive to the linguistic and behavioral speech of others as a rhetorics of demand, a call to me to respond to the needs of the other. Schrag argues that the moral life of the relational self cannot be "guided by theories of the moral subject"[70] but is led by the sensitivity of the self to the call of the other and the ability of the self to perform "a fitting response."[71] Buber has articulated the moral life of the relational self in similar terms and he gives us some beautiful images to picture what he, and (I think also) Schrag, means.

> Genuine responsibility occurs only where there is real responding. Responding to what? To what happens to one, to what is to be seen and heard and felt. . . . We respond to the moment, but at the same time we respond on its behalf, we answer for it. A newly-created concrete reality has been laid in our arms; we answer for it. A dog has looked at you, you answer for its glance, a child has

clutched your hand, you answer for its touch, a host of men moves about you, you answer for their need.[72]

We can see that Schrag provides us with a notion of self, much like Buber's, that restores a space for responsible subjectivity in the postmodern situation. Yet for all his postmodern sensitivities to the linguistic contexts and situationality of the self, Schrag does not provide us with a concrete linguistic portrait of this self in its situation. For that we need a narrative. In Buber's "Autobiographical Fragments" we have narratives of the social self. As he does in the above quotation (which ends with bare outlines of narratives), Buber, in his autobiographical anecdotes, provides concrete images and examples of the relational and situated self. In his autobiography Martin Buber has come up with a novel autobiographical strategy which respects the relational and process nature of the self and presents it in the form of individual anecdotes about meetings with others in the "common world."

Buber's Autobiography as Religious Autobiography

An analysis of Buber's autobiography would not be complete unless the relationship to the religious element is discussed.[73] Buber did speak of his autobiographic stories as "pure examples," "paradigms" for the "life of dialogue."[74] Because the life of dialogue is intricately involved with the life of faith[75] I believe we can regard Buber's autobiography as a model for the religious life and as a species of religious autobiography. The presuppositions about the process and relational character of the self are tied to certain religious notions about the human relationship to God. Ultimately, Buber's focus on the "other" as the vehicle to the self is motivated by his religious belief that one finds, through each true meeting with another, the sure foundation of the self, the eternal other, God.

> The extended lines of relations meet in the eternal Thou. Every particular Thou is a glimpse through to the eternal Thou.[76]

The eternal Thou assures that the fleeting, transitory, particular I-Thou event has an ontological basis and that new I-Thou events will occur again. As Paul Mendes-Flohr has argued, the eternal Thou, for Buber, is "The perduring ground of each discrete I-Thou encounter."[77] God, as radically other and the ultimate ground of human existence, enforces the value of otherness. The eternal Thou, as other and ground, enforces the principle of "the dependence of man on that which exists independently of him."[78] The eternal Thou, as the Thou who calls the individual out to relationship with other humans and with world and is known through these relationships, serves as a warning about the pitfalls of hubris and narcissism. The eternal other demands that the self find itself not in itself but in and through the other in genuine relationships. "The genuineness and adequacy of the self cannot stand the test in self-commerce, but only in communication with the whole of otherness."[79]

If we look at Buber's "Autobiographical Fragments" as an instance of Western religious autobiography then, again, Buber's "Fragments" appear unique. The uniqueness here is both stylistic and conceptual. Given that Judaism has not generated a long autobiographical tradition,[80] most of the Western religious autobiographies are Christian. The Christian root narrative of an individual man who dies and is resurrected and Christian concerns for individual salvation through spiritual rebirth have spawned a rich autobiographical and confessional tradition from Saint Paul to Augustine to Teresa of Avila to Luther and Wesley. Certainly, Christianity must be seen as another important source of modern Western notions of the singular individual and Western paradigms for autobiography. The classic Christian tale follows the pattern of the well known hymn, "I once was lost but now I'm found, was blind but now I see."[81] Christian autobiography is the story of the sinner who finds salvation in Christ. Christian autobiography is often presented as a gift, a prayer, or, to use our phrase, a "monument" to Christ. Christian autobiographies are Christian monuments to the monumental Christian self. The beginning of these self-narratives tells of sinfulness, the middle speaks of conversion, and the end tells of new life and peace in Christ. The theme of the story is "How I became a Christian," or in Augustine's words, "How a prodigal became a saint."

Buber's "Autobiographical Fragments" differs from the Christian paradigm in a number of important respects. First, the fragmentary quality of the autobiography defeats the sense of closure and neat end that the Christian autobiography provides. Buber's autobiography is structured to open the religious life to encounters with others in the world. There is not one central conversion experience but a series of "turnings" which constantly reorient the self and lead to a sense of endless process. Buber's "Fragments" presents a peculiarly Buberian message for the religious life: Seek God in and through meetings with others and the world. Seek the other as unique and different, as "other," for behind the other as human partner stands the eternal and transcendent other, the eternal Thou, God.[82]

Much of the recent excitement about autobiography in religious studies has centered on the ways in which autobiography represents a challenge to the universalizing and abstracting tendencies of theology by grounding the religious life in a particular person, place, and time. Thus in her work on autobiography and Augustine, Janet Varner Gunn argues that "there is always a place from which the autobiographer adumbrates his or her perspective on the self" and that the "act of autobiography is finally to be understood as moving more deeply into time and not beyond it."[83] Sallie McFague echoes Gunn in her assertion that the self in autobiography "is incarnated in details and concrete events."[84]

Yet one may ask if Augustine's *Confessions* is really the right place to look for an autobiography that grounds theology in time and place.[85] For Augustine's

Confessions seems to fall too neatly into the traditional Christian story of the sinner born again into the life of Christ. The particularities of Augustine's time and place seem most important as occasions for sin which Christ saved him from. The sins of idleness, pride, sex, and Manichaean heresy are important only insofar as they bring Augustine to realize his sinfulness and move him toward the truth and grace and eternal life in Christ. The temporal world is important only as a portal to the eternal world. Augustine's autobiography must be classed as a "monumental autobiography" (structured like the Psalm he analyzes in Book XI) which gives the self a unified theme and sense of an ending. Augustine's relationships to other people appear somewhat shallow. Others (including Augustine's mother) are important not in and of themselves, but only insofar as they impede or encourage Augustine's relationship to Christ.

If the benefits of autobiography come from the ways in which it grounds theology in the concrete, then Buber's autobiography would provide Gunn with a much better example than Augustine. For with Buber, time, place, world, and other persons are taken far more seriously. As he has said, "real relationship to God cannot be achieved on earth if real relationships to the world and to mankind are lacking."[86] In Buber's "Autobiographical Fragments" the religious life is shown to be fulfilled only in and through relationship to the particular. In Buber's autobiography one sees the value of what McFague calls "detail and concrete events" for the life of faith. In his autobiography Buber shows that it is precisely in concrete events, in what Buber calls "factual" events "thoroughly dovetailed into the common human world and concrete time-sequence,"[87] that the religious self is constituted and God glimpsed. In Buber's autobiography he shows that "God speaks . . . within the limits [of] and under the conditions of a particular biographical [and] historical situation."[88]

Buber's Autobiography and Judaism

Since we contrasted Buber's autobiography with Christian religious auto-biographies we may want to ask about connections between Buber's auto-biography and his Judaism. Is Buber's autobiography different from Christian religious autobiography because of Buber's Judaism? Are there connections between the social self and Judaism? Are there connections between Buber's emphasis on "otherness" and on the value of time and place to the religious life and Judaism? Despite the lack of overt references to Judaism, is Buber's autobiography "Jewish" in any significant and interesting ways?

It is certainly interesting that Judaism lacks a longstanding tradition of religious autobiography.[89] Where we find autobiography in confessional litera-ture almost from the beginning in Christianity, there is almost none of this type of literature in the rabbinic tradition. David Roskies argues that "the rabbis never treated the individual as worthy of memorialization."[90] It very well may be that the theological doctrine that the individual is only saved in and through the community and the general "collective focus"[91] in Judaism discouraged con-fessional and autobiographic writing. Richard Rubenstein has given a number of reasons why Judaism "has not proven to be a particularly fertile ground for the expression of personal religious testimonies." Among these reasons are the emphasis on the "aspirations of the group rather than the individual," the stress on conformity to paradigms of behavior established by Jewish law and the resultant discouragement of spontaneous individuality, and, finally, the lack of narrative traditions which tell of "dramatic rebirth experiences" in which the old self dies and is reborn anew.[92]

We could speculate that Buber's initial hesitation in writing an autobiography had its roots in the traditional Jewish aversion to religious autobiography. Buber's Judaism would, then, be another factor in the development of his novel model for autobiography. There are undoubtedly connections between Buber's Jewish roots and the extent to which the social and communal dimension is stressed in his view of the self. Indeed, I would argue that along with certain personal and psychological insights into the importance of human relations for the development of the self were certain Jewish theological dispositions about the centrality of human relations and community to the religious life. We see Buber's appreciation for this theological disposition throughout his writings on Judaism. In the first of his early "Three Addresses on Judaism" (1911), Buber tells us that the only way for an individual Jew to gain a sense of "ground" and "destiny,"[93] a sense of "harmony and secure growth," is through a "relationship to the people," Israel.[94] The main point of Buber's later essay on Hasidic ethics, "Love of God and Love of Neighbor" (1943), is that "true love of God begins with the love of men."[95] Buber argues that for Hasidism, "One cannot, . . . have to do essentially with God if one does not have to do essentially with men."[96]

What I find very interesting is that in the work of the three major figures of modern Jewish existentialism and phenomenology—in the writings of Buber, Rosenzweig, and Levinas—we find social and relational notions of the self.[97] I would argue that this social and relational definition of self and the concomitant concerns for social and communal life constitute the common element in the thought of these figures that makes their thought uniquely Jewish and separates it from the philosophy of non-Jewish existentialists and phenomenologists. I have noted that Michael Theunissen has shown that Buber's concern for "the other" separates him from Husserl,[98] Heidegger, and Sartre. I would like to suggest that Rosenzweig and Levinas also have this appreciation for the other and that it is the Judaism of these three figures that gives them this appreciation.[99]

The sense of the "other" in Judaism derives from the import of developing a relation to the utterly other, the unseen and transcendent God. This respect for otherness also means that the other-than-me, the world and others, is of ultimate value. Yet there is an additional element to this appreciation for otherness that comes from Judaism. This is the Jewish sense of being different, being the "other" in relation to the mainstream of Christian societies. Living for centuries as the outsider, as pariah, the Jew has come to appreciate the value of otherness.[100] In order to live with themselves and love themselves Jews had to live with and love their otherness and thus Jews have come to appreciate the value of otherness.

And what of the issue of autobiography and the religious import of the particular moment in time and place? What role has Judaism to play here? Certainly Judaism has stressed, more than most religions, the importance of particularity. The Chosen People, the Land of Israel, the Exodus from Egypt as a historical event, the Jewish notion of the Messiah as a human being who will come in time and lead his people and the world to peace, *halakhah,* which attempts to address the everyday problems of life lived in the here and now— these are just some elements of Judaism that reveal its sense that it is only through the particular event, time, place, person, and community that goals of universal goodness and value are won. Given the Jewish sensitivity for the value of particularity I would suggest that Buber chose an autobiographical form that was calculated to show the self as embedded in particular relations to others in time and place and to reveal God to be glimpsed only through these embedded relations.

VII

NARRATIVE BIBLICAL THEOLOGY: RESPONDING TO THE ECLIPSE OF GOD

> We Jews are a community based on a common memory. A common memory has kept us together and enabled us to survive. This does not mean that we based our life on any one particular past, even on the loftiest of pasts; it simply means that one generation passed on to the next a memory which gained in scope—for new destiny and new emotional life were constantly accruing to it—and which realized itself in a new way we can call organic. This expanding memory was more than a spiritual motif; it was a power which sustained, fed, and quickened Jewish existence itself.
>
> Buber, "Why We Should Study
> Jewish Sources"

Buber's autobiography shows that the self can be known only as it relates to that which is other than it. To find its depth and destiny the self must be embedded in ever widening circles of responsibile relationship to other persons, to family, community, and world. The autobiographical anecdote makes these points by disclosing the space of contact between the self and other in the present moment of encounter. But appreciation for otherness eventually brings the self into contact with that which is other than the present moment. Appreciation for ever widening circles of relationship pushes one's temporal frame of reference out from the present back to the past and toward the future. Buber writes, "I begin to realize that in inquiring about my own origin and goal I am inquiring about something other than myself."[1] The genuine knowledge of and relationship to friends, family, community, and world necessarily entail knowledge of a friend's past, a family history, and a community's traditions. If selves and communities grow through significant I-Thou events, then a history of those events is obviously important. And relationship to others as full human beings involves relationship not only to others in their past but also to others in their hopes for the future. Buber tells us that in the I-Thou relation the I imagines the other's future potential and "induces the process of [the other's] inmost self-becoming."[2] Similarly, concern for family, community, and world must involve concern for their futures.

The lesson of the embeddedness of genuine life in the particular and concrete which narrative teaches brings one quite naturally out of the blinding light of the immediate I-Thou encounter into the histories and futures of selves and institutions. What narrative teaches is that every self, family, community, and society is known through its particular story. Even God has a story and is known only through the particularities of that story.

For Buber, exploration of the larger Jewish cultural past and future came, on the one hand, through his work in Zionism and, on the other, through his writings on the Hebrew Bible (and these concerns were not unrelated).[3] What Buber finds in the Bible is an "otherness" and a larger context than the philosophy of I-Thou, limited to the present moment and the present world, can articulate. What he finds in the Bible is a sense of tradition and a way back, for him, to Jewish tradition. The tradition which Buber finds, however, is not the tradition most important to his rabbinic predecessors; it is not the tradition of *halakhah;* it is also not the tradition of ritual life celebrated by Rosenzweig. Rather, it is the tradition of myth and story, a tradition which Buber believes is found throughout the history of the Jewish people and can be traced from biblical saga to rabbinic *aggadot* and midrash, through Kabbalah, to Hasidism.[4]

Buber's biblical writings reveal him to be, despite his own statements to the contrary,[5] a Jewish theologian. Buber's theology, as we find it in his biblical writings, is certainly not a systematic theology; it is not an attempt to articulate a biblical faith in systematic conceptual form. Rather, it is a hermeneutic theology, or perhaps a better term, which Buber himself used, is a "narrated theology."[6] For Buber has said, "The Bible does not present us with theological statements about this intention and this meaning; it presents us with a story only, but this story is theology; biblical theology is narrated theology."[7] In his attention to the narrative portions of Genesis, Exodus, Judges, Samuel, the Writing Prophets, Job, and the Psalms, Buber constructs a narrative biblical theology.[8] This theology speaks of a God who is active in the foundational events of history, what Fackenheim, using the work of Buber, called "root-experiences" and "epoch-making events."[9]

If we take Buber's biblical writings as a whole, a three-step method of biblical theology can be discerned. The first step involves the translation of the Bible into German. This project, which Buber began in 1925 with Franz Rosenzweig, used a variety of novel translation techniques, which we reviewed in chapter 3. Building upon the translation techniques and employing the variety of critical methods of modern biblical scholarship, the second step of Buber's biblical hermeneutic involves a reconstruction of the primal narrative which relates events of meeting between God and his people. This yields a narrative biblical theology, which is then used to respond to the contemporary Jewish situation.

There is no question that we hear themes from Buber's philosophy of I-Thou in his biblical theology. Buber dwells upon the moments in the Bible of heightened encounter, events of meeting and dialogue "between God and man" and "between man and man." Buber's utterly free God of the wilderness who manifests himself as he wishes is like the "moment" God who is glimpsed in the I-Thou relationship. Buber's animus against the priesthood and the institutions of worship, his animus against the monarchy, and his failure to truly address the role of *halakhah* in Israelite faith all could be traced back to Buber's aversion to religious and political institutions and the I-It relations that characterize them.

Yet Buber's biblical theology cannot be seen simply as a biblical exemplification and justification for the I-Thou philosophy. The biblical theology resulted from a true I-Thou encounter between Buber and the biblical text which transformed Buber the man and Buber the thinker. When Buber spoke of the underpinnings of his biblical theology he mentioned not his philosophy of I-Thou but Jewish theological concepts articulated in the theology of Franz Rosenzweig. These were the notions of creation, revelation, and redemption.[10] What Buber's encounter with the *Mikra,* the Bible, did for him and what he hoped it would do for modern readers was to introduce a sense of 'tense' and 'tension' into the present of everyday life. When we are conscious of the significance of the creation of the world in the past and the redemption of the world in the future our present moment becomes charged by awareness of the past and future.

What the Hebrew Bible does to the middle moment in which we live is to stretch it out and give it a depth that reaches back to ancestors and forward to descendants. One of Buber's central concerns, in his biblical writings, is to extend boundaries of the Jew's personal memory to include the past of the Jewish people. For Buber, Judaism is based on a "common memory,"[11] a "memory of generations," which is preserved in narratives.[12] Biblical narratives, which Buber refers to as "the immediate and single way of articulating . . . 'knowledge' about events,"[13] hold the first, most precious episodes of this common memory.[14] The Jewish common memory is forged through the retelling of biblical stories symbolized by the ritualized retelling of the Passover story by parent to child throughout the generations. By "telling the story of God's leading," Buber suggests, Jews from all generations can "experience [the] historic deed as occurring to themselves."[15] And thus, what is part of the common memory becomes part of the personal memory of every Jew.[16]

As one reads through Buber's major books on the Bible, *Kingship of God, Moses, The Prophetic Faith, Darkho shel Mikra,* one is struck by the apologetic tone which one of the great modern Jewish iconoclasts takes toward the Bible. Buber, as we have tried to show in chapter 3, accepts the central insight of biblical criticism—that the Bible is the product of multiple human authorship and not the Torah of God given whole to Moses.[17] Yet despite his acceptance of the presuppositions of modern biblical criticism, Buber expends enormous scholarly energy trying to establish a unity of style, story, and theology in the

Hebrew Bible. Against attempts to portray Abraham, Isaac, and Jacob as legendary figures Buber argues for their historicity.[18] Against attempts to fragment Hebrew theology and show that Israel had different Gods in different historical periods—a tribal deity, a mountain God, a royal deity, and, finally, a universal God—Buber uses every historical and literary critical tool available to him to argue that the God of the Fathers is the very same God of Moses and that this God is also the God of the Kings and Prophets. We already reviewed Buber's attempts to use *Leitworte,* "leading words," to establish a stylistic unity in the Bible. Given these elaborate attempts we might well ask why it is that Buber was so consumed by issues of historicity of major biblical figures, narrative unity, and the continuity of the faith from Abraham to the prophets.

On one level Buber's apologetic tone can be explained by an attempt to overcome the antisemitic Marcionite tendencies of much of the German biblical scholarship of Buber's day.[19] Buber, like other Jewish biblical scholars of his time, M. D. Cassuto and Yezekiel Kaufmann, sought to disclose the complexity, the grandeur, the particular and universal message of the Hebrew Bible for modern Jews and non-Jews. Yet I would also submit that Buber's concern was for the viability of what he calls the Jewish "common memory." It is this common memory that holds the key to a sense of otherness in the Jewish present. This common memory preserves certain events which are at the foundation of Jewish identity and faith. This common memory can help the sometimes fragmented social self endure the stresses and strains of constant movement and redefinition. This common memory gives the present its depth and holds the key to its future. As Buber writes, Judaism "cannot establish a new continuity unless the age old bond of memory is revived."[20] Thus, I would argue that Buber is concerned with the integrity of the biblical narrative traditions out of concern for the integrity of the common Jewish memory through which a Jewish sense of past and future is forged. Without it Jews are only creatures of the "meaningless drift"[21] of the modern world.

This discussion of Buber's "apologetic tone" in his biblical writings should alert us to the fact that Buber was very much concerned with the third stage in Ricoeur's narrative schema—the stage of appropriating the meaning of the biblical text for himself and for the contemporary reader. As Uffenheimer puts it, Buber approached the Bible not as a "philologian [or] historian seeking the historical, objective truth . . . [but] as a thinker . . . seeking in the Bible his own truth and the truth of his generation."[22] Buber and Rosenzweig's translation of the Bible was calculated to make the biblical text seem foreign, distant and "other," to contemporary Jewish readers. But the establishment of distance and otherness was never to be ultimate. Rather, what Buber and Rosenzweig desired in setting the Bible at a distance was the "lesson that distance alone can teach."[23]

In his article "Distance and Relation," Buber argues that it is a primal setting-at-a-distance that allows for relationship and intimacy. "One can enter into relation only with being which has been set at a distance."[24] What Buber clearly found in the Bible and what he hoped others would find was the deepest expression of life lived in the "awful and splendid"[25] perils and promises of the middle. To see this we only need realize that, for Buber, the middle point between creation and redemption, which the Bible describes, is not fixed to the time and place in which the Torah was revealed but is "movable and circling." The middle point of the Bible is waiting for the reader who opens the text and finds his or her present moment addressed.

> But the Jewish Bible does not set a past event as a midpoint between origin and goal. It interposes a movable, circling midpoint which cannot be pinned to any set time, for it is the moment when I, the reader, the hearer, the man, catch through the words of the Bible, the voice which from earliest beginnings has been speaking in the direction of the goal. The midpoint is this mortal yet immortal moment of mine. Creation is the origin, redemption the goal. But revelation is not a fixed, dated point poised between the two. The revelation at Sinai is not this midpoint itself, but the perceiving of it, and such perception is possible at any time.[26]

Thus, Buber is concerned with a movement from distance to intimate relation with the biblical text wherein my present, my middle, my personal narrative is "interposed" into the middle of the biblical narrative. When this happens all is different. The community Israel, "A community of the dead, living, and yet unborn," becomes my community and "the ground of my I." Suddenly the personal "I" finds contact with the generations as it "is fitted as a link into the great chain."[27] Personal memory is extended back and the future is given a goal. "The past of his people is his personal memory, the future of his people his personal task."[28]

But even though intimacy with the Bible brings an "awareness of origin and goal"[29] it is important to see that the extended temporality that the biblical narrative bestows upon readers does not eclipse the centrality of the present moment and the sense of the middle in which we live. Rather, we come to see all of human history, and particularly Jewish history, as lived in the middle. Buber tells us that "The Jewish Bible is the historical document of a world swinging between creation and redemption."[30] Because the Messiah has not yet come, because redemption for all has not yet come, we live in the middle: waiting, hoping, working. But the waiting is made easier by the fact that both the beginning and the end, creation and redemption, are not abstract and distant realities but part of the middle in which we live.

> Revelation is, as it were, focused in the middle, creation in the beginning, and redemption in the end. But the living truth is that they actually coincide, that "God every day renews the work of the Beginning," but also every day anticipates the work of the end. . . . If I did not feel creation as well as redemption happening to myself, I could never understand what creation and redemption are.[31]

An I-Thou relation to the biblical text allows Buber's Jewish reader to find expression for the deepest longings of his or her soul. Because the Hebrew Bible is not primarily a book of systematic theology, not a book of doctrines, and not, primarily, a manual for ritual; because the Bible is not primarily concerned with "religion," but with "stories of encounters" between "a group of people and the Lord of the world"[32] and the struggle for union "between the spirit and everyday life,"[33] the Bible can address the needs of the spiritually searching contemporary Jew. Because the Bible is essentially narrative and not doctrine it opens itself to a variety of interpretations that leaves space for contemporary Jews to find their struggles and "perplexities" illuminated. Contrary to Erich Auerbach's view, the Hebrew narrative is not a monolithic structure that imposes itself on its reader and demands allegiance to one interpretation and one world-view.[34] As the Jewish midrashic tradition shows, the Bible is open to a multiplicity of meanings.[35] One wonders if Auerbach really read the biblical text, for the most cursory of readings reveals countless contradictions, lacunae, and unexplained details that belie any attempt to forge univocal readings. Buber's reading of the biblical narratives underscores the openness of the text. And his position seems to be that in the openness of biblical narrative, in what contemporary critical theory calls the "indeterminacy of meaning," there is room for the contemporary Jew. Certainly, Buber felt that in the biblical text his own longings and secret hopes were expressed.

Buber's Narrative Biblical Theology

Let us pose a very simple definition. *Narrative biblical theology involves a retelling of narratives of the Bible in such a way that the central issues of the contemporary situation are expressed and addressed.*[36] This definition immediately brings forth a question. How can the Bible, a text from a radically different era, address our situation today? The answer is found in the Bible's respect for time. Even if the biblical text is radically other than our own culture it can still address our contemporary temporal reality because it shares in (indeed is the root of) our Western cultural commitment to time and historical events. Buber has put this point in this way: "The essence of time, which is closely allied to the essence of our spirit . . . time, which distinguishes between past, present and future, . . . in the Bible, reaches its most concrete expression."[37] Buber argued again and again that it is events, "unplanned, unexpected events which transformed the historical situation of the community," that lie at the root of the biblical narratives and biblical faith.[38]

Certainly, Buber is not the first to point out that the Bible is preoccupied with historical events. Indeed, commentators have been pointing out for centuries that Israelite faith is distinguished by its concern for the religious significance of history.[39] Yet it is easy to lose the hermeneutic significance of this fact in the scholarly debates which try to prove the existence or non-existence of "anti-historical" "pagan," and "mythological" elements in Israelite religion. The hermeneutic significance of the biblical preoccupation with time—with the past, present, and future of mankind and with the significance of human actions and historical events—is that because biblical narrative takes temporality seriously we, who also take time seriously, can regard the Bible as a source to express and address our own temporal situation.

I would note that the terms "express" and "address" used here and in our definition of narrative biblical theology are carefully chosen. For when biblical stories are retold for the contemporary situation, definitive "answers" are not provided. Rather, the human questions, contradictions, sufferings, and joys come to language, are given voice, and receive a series of replies. Through the retelling of biblical narratives human temporal experience enters the sphere of dialogue through which that experience receives responses. These responses facilitate thinking about the ultimately unanswerable questions of life and give individuals and communities the strength to persevere in faith and hope.

Biblical Super-mimesis

We may begin to explore the resources in biblical narrative for the expression of human temporal experience by looking at Buber's views of the nature of narrative biblical expression. What Buber's approach to biblical narrative can give us in our contemporary situation, first, is a fresh look at an often over-looked model of freedom in applying diverse and varied narrative modes to the mimetic expression of our temporal reality. Given the Israelite concern for the significance of historical events, what we find in the biblical narrative is a preoccupation with narrative as the receptacle of events. What is very interesting in terms of contemporary discussions of narrative mimesis is that we find, in the Bible, a large variety of narrative forms and strategies to capture and preserve historical events and human action. Indeed, Harold Bloom has aptly characterized biblical narrative as "super-mimetic."[40] Methodologically, biblical narrative is fascinating not only in its scope and variety but in its free mixing of chronicle and legend, hymn and poetry. Biblical narrative, with its interweaving of fictive and nonfictive modes, is perhaps the best example we have of what Ricoeur, in volume three of *Time and Narrative,* calls "epic." In its creative interweaving of narrative forms, biblical narrative represents a tremendous resource for our contemporary attempts to capture our own temporal experience.

In the first chapter of his book *Moses,* Buber attempts to delineate the unique type of historical remembrance in the biblical narratives of Moses with the term "saga." Buber is quick to note that "saga"[41] is "basically different in character" from what modern historians call "history."[42] We must be clear that saga does not aim to record "what really happened."[43] And we know that many events recorded "can never have come about in the historical world as we know it."[44] Yet biblical saga does start from historical events and aims to "preserve . . . historical memories."[45] Biblical saga does not, like history, seek "what the consequences show to be [the] 'historical event' but . . . that which roused the emotions of the men undergoing the experience."[46] Biblical saga aims at representing the inner emotions of those who experienced a great event; it aims at preserving the awe, the wonder, the belief component of the experience of the event. It represents what Buber calls "historical wonder."[47]

Buber argues that sagas about events often take lyric and musical form. This is so because human enthusiasm "naturally expresses itself in rhythm."[48] The rhythmic form of song has a structural rigidity that resists alterations and therefore has the effect of preserving "unchanged for all time the memory of the awe-inspiring things that had come about."[49] The set rhythmic form is also more easily memorized and aids in the process of forging an individual and collective memory of the founding events of biblical belief. Thus, Buber speaks of biblical saga alternatively as "poetizing memory," and "poetizing belief."[50]

Buber is also sensitive to the wonderful interweaving of narrative modalities in the Bible. The events which Deborah tells are made more vivid by "parallel accounts" where "prose is found side-by-side with poetry" and "loosely ca-denced versions accompany the more strictly versified form."[51] Buber argues that the different forms of narrative—saga, song, chronicle—reflect the per-spectives of different social and class groups. Saga and song spring from the populace and chronicle issues from the court. The Bible attains to the heights of "super-mimesis" when "historical saga," "historical song," and "historical record" or chronicle (the precursor to our "scientific writing of history")[52] exist alongside one another.[53]

In its use of highly varied narrative modalities the Bible is able to capture an extremely wide range of human temporal experiences. Buber shows how biblical narrative is successful in representing not only human political and social life but the rare limit experiences of the human encounter with the divine. In our attempts to express the diverse character of our own temporal experience we could certainly learn much from the "super-mimetic" capacities of biblical narrative.[54]

The Meaning of Time

Biblical narrators not only sought to capture and preserve the significant moments of their temporal experience, they also struggled to understand the significance and meaning of that experience. Buber recognizes that the com-mon memory which biblical narrative attempts to forge is constantly shaped and reshaped. Buber speaks of it as a "molding memory," *bildnerisches Gedächtnis;*[55] it is an "organic and organically creative memory."[56] The ele-ments of poetry and song which are introduced to preserve a historical event can also alter some of the characteristics of the original experience they aim to capture. Poetry and belief may alter the event to better serve the dictates of form, style, and faith. Buber asserts that narrative may even "transform the experience [of the historical event]."[57] An essentially hermeneutic element, an element of interpreting, even "molding," thus arrives simultaneously with the attempt to preserve the event. Here, an important element of creative imagina-tion enters into the mimetic enterprise of memory. As Michael Fishbane shows, in his magisterial study of interpretive techniques within the Bible, biblical narrators interpreted and reinterpreted events as they told and retold them; this, to better address the issues of their contemporary situation.[58] What we may call "interpretative retelling" also occurs in Buber's attempts to retell the narratives of Moses, Israelite kingship, and aspects of prophecy. Buber sought to retell the biblical story in such a way that his own situation, his own narrative, and the narratives of his fellow Jews would be addressed.

Buber's interpretive retelling of the biblical story to address the contemporary situation involved an assessment of the problematics of the situation. For Buber, the essential issue which he and his generation faced was what he called the "eclipse of God"—the absence of a spiritual and ethical dimension in modern, everyday social and political life. We see this problem formulated differently throughout his work. At the beginning of Buber's work the problem is presented in terms of the alienation of the individual, and the solution in the search for unity and direction in mystical oneness with God. In *I and Thou* Buber speaks of the "progressive augmentation of the world of It" and the hope given by the I-Thou relationship where the eternal Thou is glimpsed. In his Hasidic writings, Buber bemoans the separation of the spirit in religious institutions and juxtaposes this with the joyful Hasidic "hallowing of the everyday." In his political and Zionist writings he speaks of the perils of the amoral and antirelational social structures of capitalism and state socialism and idealizes the *Gemeinschaft* community of the Israeli kibbutz. In all of these writings the issue is similar: the spiritual dimension has been lost, how can it be regained?

In his biblical writings Buber allows himself to be openly theological. The problem for the contemporary Jew, indeed for all persons, is the hiddenness, the silence, the "eclipse of God." How does the person who once was in dialogue with God cope with God's silence? Note the way this question is formulated. In his biblical writings Buber is not primarily addressing the person who has never had faith and who seeks some access to faith; this person was addressed in *I and Thou.* The person whom Buber is primarily concerned with in his biblical writings is the one "who, after tasting nearness, must experience distance."[59] It is crucial to recognize the way in which the contemporary problem is formulated in Buber's biblical writings because it is through his biblical writings that Buber addressed the most critical issue of our day, the absence of God caused by the Holocaust.[60] Buber responded to the Holocaust not as a person outside of faith trying to figure out whether or not God had died or ever existed, but as a person who had deep faith and trust in God, a person who was confident that he had heard God's voice before, and now had to cope with His silence and hiddenness.

Perhaps because of the distance the foreign text creates, Buber, in his biblical writings, allows his deepest longings, his most intimate wishes and fears to surface. What he found in the Bible was a space to express those wishes and fears without expecting that the problems surrounding them would be solved by the Bible. In this sense, in the space for deep expression granted to Buber by the biblical text, much of Buber's biblical theology must be seen more as a form of catharsis and even therapy than as a search for philosophical and theological solutions. I will address this issue again soon, but first let us look at Buber's retelling of biblical narratives and see how it is that the Bible gives expression to the deep longings of the contemporary Jewish soul.

The Narratives of God in Relation

In "The Man of Today and the Jewish Bible" Buber summarizes what is for him the central "theme" of biblical narrative.

> The theme of the Bible is the encounter between a group of people and the Lord of the world in the course of history, the sequence of events occurring on earth. Either openly or by implication, the stories are reports of encounters. The songs lament the denial of the grace of encounter, plead that it may be repeated, or give thanks because it has been vouchsafed. The prophecies summon man who has gone astray to turn, to return to the region where the encounter took place, promising him that the torn bond shall once more be made whole.[61]

Thus, the God of the Hebrew Bible is a God of encounter with humans, in particular, with Israel, and the central issue that the biblical narrative deals with is the issue of Buber's modern person: how shall the "torn bond" with God "be made whole." Buber addresses this issue through close readings of biblical narratives that disclose the dialectic of God's nearness and farness, his distance from and relation with his people. These narratives show the divine-human relation to be far more fragile than a modern secular or "religious" reader of the Bible might expect. Buber's narrative theology gives expression and consolation to the contemporary soul by showing that biblical persons often experienced the bond with God as torn and their trust in the relationship challenged yet still managed to cling to faith in the relationship.

Buber sets up his exploration of the rift in divine-human relationship with a variety of narratives of divine-human intimacy. When Buber retells the narrative of Abraham, Isaac, and Jacob it is the caring relationship with God that they have which preoccupies him.

> God takes Abraham from his house and from his land, brings him to a land, which he wants to "show" him and "leading him through all the land of Canaan" (Josh. 24:3), He promises to be "his shield." So too God journeys with Jacob in all his journeyings, and finally even goes down with him into Egypt. The deity of the patriarchal tales too is a deity that leads. And the one who is led is devoted to Him in faith, "goes" at the sound of His call.[62]

Buber describes YHVH as the "One-Who-goes along, the Leader-God" who goes down to Egypt with Joseph and his family, Israel, and, with Moses, "brings them up again."[63] The intimacy of God and Moses is revealed at the burning bush where God calls Moses by name and reveals His name to Moses. The simple openness of Moses to God is seen in his answer to the call: "Moshe, Moshe." Moses answers, "Here I am" (Ex. 3:4).[64] God reveals himself to be at once the same God of Moses' ancestry and part of Moses' family. "I am the God of your father/ the God of Avraham/ the God of Yitzhak/ the God of Yaakov" (3:6).[65] God then reveals his closeness to the larger family, the people of Israel, by referring to them with an expression which Buber tells us becomes one of the crucial *Leitworte* of the entire Bible, the expression *ammi,* "my people." "I have seen, yes, seen the affliction of [*ammi*] my people that is in Egypt" (3:7). This God is a God that is concerned about his people, a God who "sees the affliction" and oppression, hears the cry and "knows the suffering" of his people (3:7-9).

When Moses fears he is not up to the mission God sets for him, God reassures him. "I will be there with you" (Ex. 3:12). When God reveals His name to Moses he receives an even deeper assurance. *"Ehyeh Asher Ehyeh,"* Buber explains that God's name cannot be translated with the abstract statement of "pure existence," "I am that I am," but the verbal structure of the Hebrew suggests "happening, coming into being, being there, being present."[66] Therefore the first word of God's name, *Ehyeh,* means " 'I shall be present' not merely, as previously and subsequently, 'with you, with your mouth,' but absolutely, 'I shall be present.' "[67] The second and third words should be translated: "As which I shall be present." YHVH will be present but only as He wishes to be, in the form and way in which He, the unconjurable and unlimited God, desires. In revealing His name, YHVH lets Moses know that though the way in which He will appear in the future must remain unknown to humanity, He will be with Moses and Israel in the present moment of the middle.

That YHVH is, indeed, with His people is known through the Exodus, where "YHVH goes before them,/ by day in a column of cloud,/ to lead them the way" (Ex. 13:21),[68] and where, like a protective mother, he "bears them upon eagles' wings" (Ex. 19:4).[69] The Song of Moses exalts that YHVH, as king, not only saves Israel but will "reign in time and eternity" (Ex. 15:18). Buber stresses the reign of this king in time more than in eternity. YHVH is "the One in the midst of the human world."[70]

Buber develops a philological interpretation of the word "king," *melekh,* based on the semitic root *malk,* that serves to present this king as peculiarly accessible to humanity. The Israelite *melekh* is "leader,"[71] "accompanying God"[72] "helper," "counsellor."[73] This king desires a "theo-political" kingdom spoken of at Sinai as a *mamlekhet kohanim,* a kingdom of priests, a *goy kadosh,* a holy nation (Ex. 19:6). In Buber's interpretation of these terms, the word *kohen* does not refer to priest as functionary for a separate religious sphere but as "a secular court office,"[74] or as a companion and assistant to the king.[75] *Mamlekhet kohanim* is "composed of those of [YHVH's] companions who are at his immediate disposal, his immediate retinue."[76] *Kadosh* refers to the power of YHVH which is distinct to Him and separate from the "common realm" of earth. A *goy kadosh* is a nation charged and appointed by God's holiness to be holy, to be distinct and separate. That God requires the whole nation to be holy means that the people must be dedicated to Him "with all its substance and all its functions, with legal forms and institutions."[77]

In the covenant which YHVH offers the nomadic desert community of Israel Buber finds his ideal formulation of the relationship between God and humanity. This relationship is relevant to the modern egalitarian spirit and a helpful model to overcome the modern rift between the religious and sociopolitical realms. There is not an elaborate hierarchy established within the nomadic community of Israel. All are priests, all "stand in the identical direct and immediate relationship of retainers" to God.[78] And God is not removed from but is "fundamental . . . to public life."[79] There is no separate religious sphere, no separate political sphere—only one theopolitical rulership. This theocracy is "immediate, unmetaphorical, unlimited."[80] There is no separate priesthood and no king of Israel; YHVH alone is their king. Maximum freedom is granted to the people yet order is preserved and anarchy prohibited by the just rule of God given through the law at Sinai.[81]

The faith relationship between God and Israel which develops out of the "tribe-forging and nation-forging migrations"[82] of the nomadic period is a relationship based most fundamentally on trust and not belief. Buber describes this relationship in his study of *Two Types of Faith*. Trust "depends upon a state of contact"[83] between God and His people. Buber defines faith, *Emunah*, as "a perseverance in trust in the guiding and covenanting Lord."[84] This faith includes in it not only the passive sense of trust but also the active elements of "fidelity" and "loyalty."[85] Faith as trust plus fidelity is something that one earns over time and is built on a "memory" of a dialogic event.[86]

It is crucial to see that for Buber faith is not simply a noetic matter. Faith is not an intellectual affirmation to a set of beliefs or dogmas but a "confidence which embraces and determines the whole of life."[87] Mendes-Flohr uses John Hick's notion of "experiencing as" to suggest that Buber's notion of faith involves a "distinctive way of experiencing" the world.[88] Buber says that one "stands in" faith or " 'finds himself' in the relationship of faith."[89] And thus faith happens to one's "entire being."[90]

Distance and Repair

However trusting and loyal God is to Israel, the terms of the covenantal faith should make clear that God's attitude toward His people is not that of Carl Rogers's "unconditional positive regard." God's attitude is at once all accepting and all demanding, both saving and commanding. The divine human relation, as defined by the covenant, "is dialogic, promising and demanding at the same time."[91] Thus, when the people fail to meet their obligations the relationship can be put in jeopardy and extreme "distance" between God and Israel can occur.

As Buber uses the term "distance" to describe both a precondition for dialogue and an impediment to dialogue, perhaps a word on different types of "distance" is needed. In "Distance and Relation," Buber speaks of *Urdistanz,* or the primal setting-at-a-distance, which is a requirement for dialogue. Buber argues that if there is no separation between beings, if there is only amorphous enmeshment, there can be no boundaries delineating the different beings, and therefore there can be no dialogue. *Urdistanz* establishes the basic boundaries of difference that allow dialogue between human and human and between human and God to begin. *Urdistanz* between God and humans is crucial, not only because there is such a fundamental quality of difference between the two beings but because God's infinite light could so easily obliterate a human being. As the Exodus text says, "No man shall see me and live" (33:20). Yet there is another type of distance that obstructs or blocks dialogue. This is the closed-off distance of silence, what the Bible refers to as "the hiding of the face."[92] Here there is a radical distancing, a turning away that prohibits any word from being uttered or heard.

One such moment of obstructing distancing in the relationship between God and the Jewish people occurs with the sin of the "molten calf." Given his concern for rifts in the relationship between YHVH and Israel and the ways biblical faith copes with these problems, Buber is fascinated by the exchange between God and Moses and with Moses' defense of the people, Israel, when the sin of the "molten calf" is committed.[93]

That the relationship is in jeopardy is signaled in parashah *Ki Tisah* (Exodus 30:11–34:35) when YHVH refers to Israel as the people of Moses, *amkha,* and not as His people, *ammi,* and even distances Himself from His role in the Exodus. "YHVH said to Moshe: Go, down! for your people/ whom you brought up from the land of Egypt/ has wrought ruin!" (Ex. 32:7). The relationship is shown to be in true danger when YHVH expresses His desire to destroy the people and make a new nation for Moses (32:10). But here Moses reveals the depths of his commitment, loyalty, and relationship to his community and we have one of the clearest examples of a self bound to its community in responsibility. For when offered the opportunity to rid himself of his connection to his community, when offered a "dictator's dream—the cloning of an entire nation from himself,"[94] Moses immediately refuses. "He does not want to be saved alone, he and the people are one."[95] Moses launches into a defense which Buber calls a "massive fortress" unique in all literature.[96]

At the "first level" of this defense Moses attempts to reconnect God to his people and to the Exodus linguistically by using the possessive, "your people." "For what reason,/ O YHVH,/ should your anger rage against your people/ whom you brought out of the land of Egypt" (32:11). In the defense Moses then asks God to "remember" His promise to this people through Abraham, Isaac, and Jacob. "In the same way that I have remained loyal to the people, you must remain loyal," suggests Moses.

Buber marvels at the "chutzpa" and "daring super-logic"[97] of Moses, who not only unceasingly pushes to reinstate the intimate relationship of God with Israel but seeks ever deeper intimacy. When Moses succeeds in "soothing" (32:11) YHVH's wrath, YHVH offers to send a messenger to help Moses and the people, but the wary YHVH still refuses to be present "in your midst" as before. "I will send a messenger before you/ . . . But: I will not go up in your midst" (33:2-3). Moses does not accept this but first implores YHVH for further intimacy, "Pray let me know your ways" (33:13), and, second, demands that YHVH Himself lead the people.

> See,
> This nation is indeed your people!
> . . . If your presence does not go,

> do not bring us up from here!
> For wherein, after all, is it to be known
> that I have found favor in your eyes,
> I and your people?
> Is it not (precisely) in that you go with us,
> and that we are distinct, I and your people,
> from every people that is on the face of the soil?
> (Ex. 32:13–16)

Note the repetition of the *Leitwort* "your people," three times—as if to force a rapprochement between the people and God. Moses argues that the relationship between God and Israel is so important because if Israel is not in intimate contact with God it will lose its identity, it will no longer be "distinct."

After YHVH agrees to the first request, to reveal His "glory," Moses is not satisfied and immediately returns to the second request. "Quickly Moshe did homage, . . . and said . . ./Pray let my Lord go among us!" (34:8-9). The relentless Moses apparently gains this, too, but only on YHVH's covenantal terms. "Here, I cut a covenant . . ./Here I am driving out before you/the Amorite, the Canaanite . . ." (Ex. 34:10-11). I will go "before you" and be in your midst as you wish, God tells Moses, but only *if* you and Israel obey the covenantal terms.

The Prophetic Faith

If the greatest of all Jewish leaders, Moses, succeeds in repairing the rift between God and Israel, the repair is only temporary and problems in the relationship occur again and again in the narratives that follow. Buber's ideal "nomadic faith," characterized by the Kingship of God, is predominant in the period of the Judges. Charismatic leaders—Joshua, Deborah, Gideon, Samson—lead the people in the mission of the conquest of Canaan inspired and counseled by YHVH as *melekh.* The nomadic, kingship faith survives with Samuel and the early period of David's rule, but then is eclipsed by the institutions of the monarchy and the priesthood. Statecraft becomes divorced from concern with the spirit and from God's control, and religious life is set apart in an elaborate cult and in set sacred locations such as the temple in Jerusalem. Henceforth, the Kingship of God, the "unlimited recognition of the factual and contemporary kingship of God over the whole of national existence,"[98] is left in the hands of the writing prophets as a vision to be further refined, a symbol motivating criticism of the monarchy and the people, and a hope for a future reconstituted rulership of God.[99]

The prophets Buber dwells upon first in his explication of what he calls "the prophetic faith" are Amos, Hosea, and Isaiah. These prophets of the same generation all play upon narrative themes in the common memory of Israel which emphasize different aspects of YHVH as king and of his relationship to his people. These prophets each attempt to make as clear as possible God's nature and His demands and the negative consequences of disobedience. In

Amos we find the metaphor of God as righteousness. The God of Amos is a God
(as related in the narrative of Amos's vision, ch. 7) with a "plumb line" (7:7).
This is a God of stern judgment in the face of sin, a God concerned with the
plight of the poor and the needy and with justice within and among all the
nations of the world. In Hosea we find the needed complement to God's stern
judgment, his loving mercy. As Hosea shows, it is God's mercy that allows
Israel to remain God's people, *ammi* (3:27), in the face of their sin. And with
Isaiah the metaphor for God given in Isaiah's early vision is holiness.

> Holy, Holy, Holy!
> The Lord of Hosts!
> His radiating glory fills all the earth! (6:3)

Buber states that with these three prophets—Amos, Hosea, and Isaiah—and
their corresponding conceptions of God as righteous, loving, and holy, the
essential revelation of the name, "YHVH," given to Moses "has been unfold-
ed."[100] These prophets help to articulate the nature of the God who led the
patriarchs and was with their descendants through their wanderings and conquest of Canaan. They reiterate the central themes of the nomadic ideal and the
Kingship of God and underscore ethical obligations and spiritual aspects of
the covenantal relationship. Buber translates the Hebrew *navi* ("prophet") with
the German *Künder*, "announcer." "The essential task of the prophets of Israel
was not to foretell an already determined future, but to confront Israel, at each
given moment, with the alternative that corresponded to the situation."[101] The
primary role of the prophet is not to prognosticate about the future but to
announce the judgment of God and in so doing use the future to force a
decision to alter human actions in the present.

> [A]s he [the prophet] time and again announces the judgement, at the same time
> he calls out of the ever more weighty actuality of the moment to turn to God; and
> all the time that it is still possible to come to political decisions.[102]

However, the prophets do also express a concern for the future and Buber
regards what he calls the prophetic "turning to the future" as a new element in
the prophetic faith of Amos, Hosea, and Isaiah. The turning to the future results
from a disillusionment with the status quo—with the monarchy and the people—and a sense that the present situation is radically broken and that the
relationship between Israel and God is in an extended state of separation.
There is a recognition that there will have to be some kind of winnowing of the
people so that the old, ideal relationship between God and the people can be
reestablished. Here, Buber finds the seeds of what eventually develops into
messianism and here Buber begins to develop the position that overcoming the
despair of separation from God's presence requires some notion of hope and
the future. If suffering is to have an answer the sufferer must have a notion of
the future.

In Buber's view messianism begins with hope for a restoration of the
"nomadic ideal." It is thus based on the common memory of the past. Thus, we

have Amos's prophecy of a destruction in which not the total house of Jacob but "sinners . . . shall perish" (9:9) After this the "fallen booth of David" (9:11), the booth of the nomad shepherd, will be restored. In Hosea, YHVH speaks of a future time in which the people forsaken by Him (*Lo-ammi,* "not my people") become once again His people whom He will lead. "I will say to *Lo-ammi,* 'You are my people' " (2:25). With Isaiah's prophecy of Immanuel (7:14-17; 8:5-10), the notion of the restoration of the past ideal is most clearly expressed. Immanuel, the boy from the house of David, is to come as king of the remnant of Israel, an "Anointed" who will establish a "real, political kingship, or rather a theo-political one."[103]

Buber stresses that the prophetic hope does not involve "eschatology" or "a conception of the 'last things.' "[104] This hope has a "concrete historical core" and "does not belong to the margin of history where it vanishes into the realms of the timeless."[105] Similarly, the prophetic Messiah is not "more than human," he is not derived from "ancient Eastern mythology" but "grows out of history."[106] This Messiah is YHVH's "vice-regent," a human being like the charismatic leaders of the past. He, like the best of the kings, will help set up the "divine order of human community" in the historical realm through "human forces and human responsibility."[107] The coming of the Messiah depends on the "human vital decision" to turn back to God. Isaiah's prophecy is not a "prediction but an offer."[108] If you decide in this present moment for God then the Messiah will come. Human decision is crucial here. "There is something essential that must come from man."[109] Thus the "prophetic view" of the key to the coming of the Messiah and a better future is human action in the present conditioned and interlaced with the hope given through the common memory of the past.

Addressing the Holocaust—The God of Sufferers

Though Buber stresses those aspects of biblical narrative that address issues of divine-human separation, up until this point Buber's interpretive retelling of biblical narratives has not really addressed the radical situation of separation between God and Jew caused by the Holocaust. Indeed, Buber's interpretation of the role of human decision in the coming of the Messiah and the renewed relation with God is inapplicable to the Holocaust where there were millions of innocent victims whose personal decisions could have no effect on their Nazi murderers and, seemingly, no effect on their felt separation from God. As Rubenstein, Fackenheim, and Greenberg have argued, the theological problem of the Holocaust is not one of Jewish disobedience and failure of will but one of divine apathy and absence.[110]

It is in the last chapter of Buber's summary statement on the biblical narrative,[111] *The Prophetic Faith,* published first in Hebrew in 1942, that Buber begins to address the issue of the Holocaust.[112] In this chapter, titled "The God of the Sufferers," Buber addresses "questions of the righteousness of collective punishment"[113] and the "question of innocent suffering." He speaks of a different kind of Messiah from that which we saw in the prophetic faith of Amos, Hosea, and First Isaiah; he refers to the "suffering Messiah" of Deutero-Isaiah. This Messiah is not from the house of David, he is "despised and rejected of man; a man of pains, and acquainted with sickness" (53:3). In the last page of the chapter and the last page of the book, Buber refers to the suffering Messiah as a figure that "appears from generation to generation and goes from martyrdom and death to martyrdom and death,"[114] in the history of Judaism. He refers to "unity of the personal servant and the [collective] servant Israel"[115] and thus presents this Messiah not as an individual but as a collective body, the community Israel. Buber also refers to the boundedness of "the mystery of suffering and the promise of the God of sufferers" as the hope of the people throughout the wandering and exile of the generations.

The words of this last page of *The Prophetic Faith*, I maintain, cannot be read outside of a connection to the great suffering and death of European Jewry. They can only be properly understood as a response to the Shoah which was still raging at the time of the publication of *The Prophetic Faith*.[116] How else can we explain the fact the Buber ends the book which summarizes "the completion" of the "teaching" of the Bible[117] with the distance from God and the suffering represented by the Babylonian exile? I would suggest that Buber's interpretative retelling of biblical narrative in *The Prophetic Faith* ended with exile, suffering, and the radical separation of God and humanity to give expression to the radical separation or "eclipse of God" caused by the Holocaust. I find further support for my view in the fact that in one of the very few places in his published works where Buber addresses the theological problems of the Holocaust directly, in the last section of the essay "The Dialogue Between Heaven and Earth" (1952), Buber uses Job, Deutero-Isaiah, and the Psalms, the very sources that make up the last chapter of *The Prophetic Faith*, to develop a response to the Holocaust. Job, the suffering servant, the psalmist, through these biblical figures Buber articulated the suffering of his generation. And through Job's tenacious enduring faith, through the servant's willingness to suffer, and through the entire history of a biblical faith that, despite periods of harsh distance from God, always presented Israel as able to reestablish a relationship with God, Buber tried to articulate hope for his generation.

It must be stated again that Buber's response to the Holocaust begins from what Fackenheim has called the "stance of faith."[118] This is why the metaphor of the "eclipse of God" is used by Buber. An eclipse suggests only that God's image is hidden; He still exists and can be trusted to reappear. Because of this starting point Buber may leave behind Holocaust survivors who no longer regard faith in the Jewish God of History as possible or "secular" Jews who have never had a "faith experience." These groups of Jews may regard Ruben-stein's "death of God," Greenberg's "dialectical faith," or Fackenheim's 614th commandment for Jewish survival as more adequate responses to the Holocaust.[119] Yet as Buber and countless other religious thinkers have shown, the "faith experience" is such a complex and ambiguous phenomenon that it is well-nigh impossible to make a neat distinction between those who have had the experience and those who have not.[120] And since no Jewish thinker and no Jewish community has come up with a Holocaust theology that has won consensus in the larger Jewish community we need all the theological resources we can find. Jews and non-Jews, be they "faithful" or "secular," may want to take note of what Martin Buber has to say about the Holocaust. For although Buber's response to the Holocaust is often overlooked[121] as either superficial or inadequate I believe that it can be shown that Buber's thoughts on the Holocaust remain a profound resource for post-Holocaust theological reflection. In reviewing Buber's chapter "The God of the Sufferers," with special attention to his retelling of the story of Job, we will begin to see Buber's biblical response to the Holocaust.

God of Sufferers

With the Babylonian exile the "One-Who-goes along, the Leader-God" ceases to be with Israel directly and immediately. God " 'Leaves his house.' He withdraws to heaven. . . . He wants to be recognized as 'God from afar' (Jer. 23:23), filling heaven and earth, perceiving all yet remaining above all."[122] In this move of extreme distancing, the God revealed and seen by Abraham, by Moses, and by the prophets becomes a God "that hides himself."[123] Buber suggests that with the Exile and the hiding of God, "a mysterious connection is opened" "between God and suffering."[124]

The "rise into prominence of suffering" as a religiously important category is the central theme of the book of Job, a work of narrative theology which Buber dates to the period of the exile. Job asks "the question of the generation,"[125] the question "which has persisted ever since." "Why do we suffer what we suffer?"[126] Buber makes clear that, for Job, God's existence and God's power are not in question. "That everything comes from God is beyond doubt and question; the question is, How are these sufferings compatible with his Godhead?"[127]

The book of Job begins with evidence of Job's righteousness and his relationship to God. Job "was whole *(tam)* and upright and one who feared God." Then Job is wronged by God's willingness to put Job in Satan's hands. As Satan takes away the righteous Job's possessions and family members, Job's first search is for vindication of his righteousness and an explanation from God for His evil actions. Job first asks the intellectual questions of theodicy, and his "friends" further pique his search by providing him with the stock theological answer that his peril is punishment for his sins. This inadequate answer leads Job to cry out in his innocence and against the God who treats him unjustly. In the "Dialogue Between Heaven and Earth," Buber points the survivors of Auschwitz to Job's angry cry as an expression of their "own cry."[128] Job, Buber says, "not only laments but he charges that the 'cruel' God (30:21) 'has removed his right' from him (27:2) and thus that the judge of all the earth acts against justice."[129]

Yet underneath questions of justice and injustice, underneath questions of theodicy and expressions of anger, Buber shows, there lies the much more basic and primary question of the status of the trust relation with God. What Job, in his deepening suffering, wants, and what many Holocaust victims wanted, is not an intellectual answer to the question of theodicy but some evidence of God's presence in their suffering. The most fundamental issue that the victim of sustained violence and hatred faces is not whether evil exists— that question has already been answered in the affirmative—but whether there are any sources of life that can be trusted despite the evil. The most fundamental search then of Job as a man of faith is for contact with the "Power in which his being originates."[130]

> [Job first] declares that he wants to reason with the deity (13:3); he knows he will carry his point (v. 18). In the last instance, however, he merely means by this that God will again become present to him. "Oh that I knew where I might find Him!" (23:3). Job struggles against the remoteness of God, against the deity Who rages and *is silent*, rages and "hides His face," that is to say, against the deity Who has changed for him from a near-by person into a sinister power.[131]

What becomes most difficult for Job, what becomes the "source of his abysmal despair,"[132] is not the intellectual issue of theodicy but "this hiding, the eclipse of the divine light."[133] God's "answer" to Job does not come in the intellectual realm. Indeed, God frustrates the intellectual question. "Thou canst not understand the secret of anything or being in the world, how much less the secret of man's fate."[134] The answer comes in the appearance of God to Job again. "The abyss is bridged the moment [Job] 'sees' [42:5], is permitted to see again."[135] This is why when God appears and speaks out of the "tempest" (38:1) Job ceases to pose his questions and "repents in dust and ashes" (42:6). Buber sums up God's "answer" in this way.

> The true answer that Job receives is God's appearance only, only this, that distance turns into nearness, that "his eye sees Him" (42:5), that he knows[136] Him again. Nothing is explained, nothing adjusted; wrong has not become right, nor cruelty kindness. Nothing has happened but that man hears God's address.[137]

What Job learns is that though previously he recognized God as "the near and intimate" now "he only experiences Him through suffering and contradiction, but even in this way he does experience God."[138] Experiencing God again, Job, despite all the evil that has happened, "cannot dismiss Him"[139] and the ultimate vindication in divine justice which he does not now understand.

What the book of Job makes clear again is that a sense of expanded temporality, of both past and future is crucial to overcoming the despair of God's absence. What gives Job hope and underlies his faith is the fact that Job had previous faith and thus a memory of a trusting relationship to God. We know this from the opening line of the book. "And Job feared God."[140] With this memory he could endure the absence of God in the present moment of his suffering and upon this memory he could base his hope for a renewal of the relationship in the future. When Job "sees God *again*" God immediately refers him to the past when there was "communication between Creator and creature."[141] This, as if to say, "I was with you in the past, I gave you life, good and full life. You knew me as just, why do you doubt me now?" Seeing God again, and not only seeing but speaking with God and therefore renewing their relationship, Job finds a response to his suffering that gives him hope.

If Job's answer to his suffering is based on his "experience" of God, in what way can this be an answer to the suffering of Holocaust victims and survivors? In what way can this be an answer to those who say they have not had an "experience" of God such as Job had? Here, as I would interpret Buber's discussion of Job in *The Prophetic Faith,* it seems that we are led back from the caesura of the event of the Holocaust to God's presence in the beginning, in creation, and forward to God's unceasing presence in the continual creation of life where, as Buber notes, the prayerbook tells us "God every day renews the work of the Beginning."[142] The God that reveals himself to Job is the God "who laid the foundations of the earth," the God who "shut up the seas . . . , made the cloud . . . , commanded the day to break . . . , surveyed the expanses of the earth" (Job 38:4-18).[143] This is the God whose "glory," the psalmist says, is declared by the heavens and earth. This is the God glimpsed through what Buber calls, in *I and Thou,* the sphere of nature. This is the God who gives life and whose justice Buber calls a "distributing, giving justice."[144]

Was this approach to God through creation and nature utterly cut off by the Holocaust? I do not think so. As Victor Frankl has shown, even concentration camp inmates could perceive and, in the briefest of moments, did take pleasure in the beauty of nature.[145] Many of those who survived and lived, despite the fact that they, as Buber says, "have not got over what happened and will not get over it,"[146] many of them have found some solace and joy in the life within them and around them. And those of us who had no direct experience of the Holocaust, we who feel the pulse of created life within us, we who have seen the lives of our children so full with life, certainly we cannot deny the gift of life, which remains God's gift, despite all.[147] This God of creation who continually creates, this God of nature who, after all, must be the same God of history of whom the Bible speaks, does not absolve God from his obligations to human history. Buber admits the Holocaust has caused, for this Jewish God of history, an "estrangement . . . too cruel," a "hiddenness too deep."[148] But God's presence in life is a beginning and a sign of hope which prohibits us from turning our lives over to blind fate or giving up on heaven and on earth in despair. As Buber suggests, this God of continual creation, this "Lord of Being," is a presence that still sparks our desire to work for redemption of this world and will not let us give up hope for a renewal of "God's utterance in history."[149]

> Do we stand overcome before the hidden face of God like the tragic hero of the Greeks before faceless fate? No, rather even now we contend, we too, with God, even with Him, the Lord of Being, whom we once, we here, chose for our Lord. We do not put up with earthly being; we struggle for its redemption, and struggling we appeal to the help of our Lord, who is again and still a hiding one.

In such a state we await His voice, whether it comes out of the storm or out of a stillness that follows it. Though His coming appearance resemble[s] no earlier one, we shall recognize again our cruel and merciful Lord.[150]

Waiting for the God of History: The Faith of the Psalmist

If the person of faith "in the time in which there is an Auschwitz"[151] must wait for God's voice of justice and presence in history, how is this waiting to be accomplished? If Job's God of creation alone does not provide the requisite resource for patience, are there other resources in the Hebrew Bible to assist the distraught soul in a time of the "eclipse of God?" The Hebrew Bible, of course, has an immense resource for consolation and hope for the sufferer and this is found in the Psalms.[152] Buber recognized and availed himself of this resource from the time that he was a young boy, deprived of his mother when his parents divorced. He once wrote to Franz Rosenzweig, "For me the Psalms have maintained the bodily relationship which they always had for my mother-less childhood."[153]

In the last chapter of *The Prophetic Faith*, Buber points out similarities between aspects of the book of Job and Psalm 73, and in "The Dialogue Between Heaven and Earth" he uses Psalm 82 to express the injustice of the Holocaust. Buber's remarks on these psalms are expanded and included, along with interpretations of Psalms 12, 14, and 1, in the first half of his *Good and Evil*, published in 1952. This book too must be seen in the context of the tragedy of the Holocaust and also in the context of the failure of Buber's efforts to bring out a bi-national Arab-Israeli state in Palestine.[154] That Buber continued to experience failure in the late years of his life, the failure of the "German-Jewish synthesis," the failure of Christian and Jewish dialogue, the failure of his *Ihud* ("unity") party in Israel,[155] yet continued to speak as a man of hope and faith must, at least in part, be attributed to his "bodily relation" to the Psalms which he interpreted in *Good and Evil*.

In the five psalms that Buber interprets he sees the struggle of the suffering victim to cope with the victory of injustice in the world. Buber is not afraid to put this in the starkest of theological terms: wrong conquers right, evil wins out over good in the world continually. Buber knows that these five Psalms were written by different authors, but because the texts share a "basic view and attitude,"[156] because the Psalms possess what contemporary critical theory calls an "intertextuality" wherein the narrators can be viewed as speaking to one another, Buber constructs a kind of dialogue on the problem of evil among the psalmists. And though the answers which result from this hypothetical "dialogue" are ultimately unsatisfying, in the expression of the struggle, in the half-answers which are continually shown to be not quite adequate, fellow-sufferers who read the Psalms can find their suffering consoled, their strength of faith renewed, and their basic trust in God rewarded.

A theme which Buber stresses often in his interpretation of the Psalms is the role which falsehood plays in evil. In Psalm 12 the narrator sees the world as ruled by an entire "generation of the lie."[157] Through the "smooth tongue" of the lie, what we might call in our day "propaganda," the rulers have gained supremacy and control of the world. Lying has become a "form of life" and has led to the "disintegration of human speech."[158] Lying as a way of life has destroyed goodwill between persons and undermined human loyalty and reliability.[159] In the face of the generation of the lie the psalmist is consoled by the existence of God's words of truth and promise of trusting relation which cuts through the lies. The psalmist is consoled by his knowledge of the "human truth . . . of being devoted to truth."[160]

But the sufferer quickly becomes distraught when victory upon victory goes to the wicked and lies persist and truth is still not heard. The sufferer then turns to Psalm 14 for another answer. Here, it is the answer of "suffering servant" that is presented. The sufferer is isolated and abandoned by others precisely because all are evil and God has chosen just a few, a scattered suffering righteous remnant, who shall rise to proclaim justice.

But this solution, too, seems inadequate as the suffering of even the remnant persists, and in Psalm 82 the theme of deception and illusion is given another, deeper interpretation. The world is not ruled merely by lies of men but by a more troublesome form of bad, a quasi-divine force, something which is better labeled "Evil" than a lie. The psalmist imagines that God, frustrated with human sinfulness, gave the rulership of earth not to man but to angels. But the angels, with their quasi-divine powers, instead of righting the situation, made things even worse. It seems there is nothing that a human being can do to break the spell of injustice perpetrated by evil judges with the powers of angels. The psalmist, realizing that the power of God is required for a solution, expresses his anger and despair with a cry that is intended to wake God from His apathy and slumber. "Arise, O God, judge the earth!" (82:8).

In Psalm 73 the sufferer comes to a difficult conclusion: the way of the wicked is the way of the world and being with God in this life means "being separated from Him."[161] The secret to living a life with meaning lies, then, in one's attitude toward the suffering in life and one's attitude toward the distance from God which is the lot of humanity. Buber's interpretation is based on the first verse of Psalm 73: "Surely God is good to Israel: To the pure in heart." When one's attitude toward suffering is changed, when the attitude of the heart is altered, then the sufferer experiences God's goodness even if his or her suffering is not altered.

> One who is pure in heart, one who becomes pure in heart . . . experiences that God is good to him. But this does not mean that God rewards him with His goodness. It means rather, that God's goodness is revealed to him who is pure in heart: he experiences this goodness.[162]

Living in the proper "state of the heart" means living "in the truth." As the fifth psalm which Buber interprets, Psalm 1, suggests, living with a pure heart means "walking in the way of God."[163] In this way the outer aspects of life may not go well but this cannot be "confused with the illusion that God is not good to him."[164] Walking in the truth is walking as near to God as humans get. And this nearness contains a "happiness which is not obvious to all eyes,"[165] a "secret happiness hidden by the hands of life itself, which balances and outbalances all unhappiness."[166] In the face of this secret truth and secret happiness all lies, injustices, and evil appear as the unreal, the illusory, that which will "peter out."[167] This happiness is not what the philosopher calls the intrinsic reward of the virtuous life or the "self-enjoyment of the moral man."[168] Rather, it can more properly be understood from the vantage point of faith. For the happiness of the psalmist is the happiness of renewed contact with God based not on a knowledge of what is good but on the "renewal" of "man's intercourse with God"[169] and on a renewal of the trust that lives in faith.

Buber makes it clear that the answer to human suffering that arises from the dialogue among the psalmists is not complete and may not answer the dilemma of theodicy which the philosopher sees. The psalmist's answer does not totally cover the "abyss opened by the question" of evil.[170] The question remains, yet the person of faith also remains a person of faith through the reading of the Psalms. This is a process that the psychotherapist may understand better than the philosopher. In giving expression to pain, in presenting models for endurance and trust in the face of pain, the Psalms console and renew the basic trust of the sufferer. This is a form of consolation born out of the intersection between what Buber calls the "story"[171] of a psalmist's "experience of life" and what we may call the story of the reader's life experience. It is a form of consolation that results not from merely acknowledging that a person in the past, known through the texts of the common memory of the Jews, was able to preserve his trusting relation with God in the face of a severe sense of separation, but from a meeting of life experiences. Gadamer describes this with his notion of the "fusion of horizons" of the text and the reader, and Ricoeur discusses this same process with his notion of "refiguration."

This is, again, the fourth stage of interpretation which we outlined at the end of chapter four. Buber speaks of it as "existential exegesis."[172] He describes it, quite simply, in beginning his discussion of one of the Psalms. "The deeper my experience of life, the more thoroughly do I understand this Psalm."[173] What this means, I take it, is that Buber has come to see his experience in and through the psalmist's narrative. Here we can see the movement of a narrative from the common memory of Judaism to the interpreter's personal memory. It is an interpretive experience that happens in and through a life experience. In the morning I read the Psalm and it appears as a beautiful but strange and austere expression of an unhappy man. In the afternoon I lose a life-long friend and suddenly the psalmist's words ring through my head again as if they were my own. It is an experience described by one of the psalmists as "deep calls to deep" (Ps. 42:6).[174]

From psalmist to psalmist, to Buber, to us as readers, "deep calls to deep." And if in the depth of this call, echoing through the common memory of Jews that is written in the narratives of the tradition, some say they hear the faint voice of the God who calls himself "YHVH," the God who is present with His people, perhaps, even we, who are so hardened to hearing, can respond as the psalmist once did: *"Hodu Adonai ki tov ki l'olam ḥasdo."* "Give thanks unto the Lord, for He is good, for His mercy endures forever" (Ps. 106:1).

VIII

CONCLUSION: BUBER AND
THE NARRATIVE THEOLOGIANS

In his "Two Types of Narrative Theology" Gary Comstock distinguishes between what he calls "pure" and "impure" narrative theologians.[1] The pure narrative theologian is a storyteller alone who eschews all forms of objectifying and explanatory discourse be it philosophical or social scientific. Theology is a matter of telling and retelling stories. For Christians the root stories are found in the Gospels and for Jews the root narratives are found in the Torah. Christianity, in the view of George Lindbeck, is a "cultural-linguistic system," a special kind of "language-game" which can only be understood from within the system by "playing the game," i.e., by telling the stories of the tradition and enacting them through rituals. Christianity keeps its root narratives intact and fresh through its doctrines.[2] Judaism, as well, can be seen as a linguistic system based on root narratives which are preserved and made current through narrative interpretation, or "midrash." Theology for the narrative purist is thus a process of continuous storytelling that can only be enacted within a specific tradition.

The impure narrative theologian sees narrative as the primal language of his or her biblical faith yet is not afraid to use the discourse of philosophy or social science, which is external to this faith, to further articulate themes and interpret root narratives. Philosophy provides analytical tools and concepts that help to tease out and connect themes and push contradictions in stories so they can be clearly seen and more systematically considered. Philosophy can also help to justify the bases of narrative theology and judge the adequacy of narrative theological responses to religious issues.[3] Social science helps to establish historical context, disclose "systematic distortions" caused by bias and prejudice, and give psychological and sociological insights into the meaning of ancient narratives.

Given this helpful distinction between pure and impure narrative theologians we might well want to know where Buber stands vis-à-vis it? Is Buber to be considered a pure or an impure narrative theologian? By way of answering this question I would like to review a narrative that I regard as a summary of all of Buber's thought. Let us return to the essay "Dialogue," the essay we reviewed in chapter 5, and look at the story which opens the essay. The story is about a dream, a dream which Buber calls "the dream of the double cry." The reader will, I hope, bear with me as I quote fairly extensively from this story and use it, in somewhat of a round-about fashion, to address the pure or impure status of Buber's narrative theology.

> Through all sorts of changes the same dream, sometimes after an interval of several years, recurs to me. I name it the dream of the double cry. Its context is always much the same, a "primitive" world meagerly equipped. I find myself in a vast cave . . . or in a mud building. . . . The dream begins in very different ways, but always with something extraordinary happening to me, for instance, with a small animal resembling a lion cub . . . tearing the flesh from my arm and being forced only with an effort to loose its hold. The strange thing is that this first part of the dream-story . . . always unrolls at a furious pace as though it did not matter. Then suddenly the pace abates: I stand there and cry out. . . . Each time it is the same cry, inarticulate but in strict rhythm, rising and falling, swelling to a fullness which my throat could not endure were I awake, long and slow, quiet, quite slow and very long, a cry that is a song. When it ends my heart stops beating. But then somewhere far away, another cry moves toward me, another which is the same, the same cry uttered or sung by another voice. Yet it is not the same cry, certainly no "echo" of my cry but rather its true rejoinder. . . . Each time the voice is new. But now, as the reply ends, in the first moment after its dying fall, a certitude, true dream certitude comes to me that *now it has happened.*[4]

Now it has happened. What has happened? Deep calls to Deep. The word of simultaneous hope and despair is uttered, sung, called out. The cry of the I for its Thou rings out over and over again and is finally answered, not, mind you, an answer that is a repetition of the first cry, but "its true rejoinder"—a rejoinder that is an answer because it is not a mere echo of the voice of the "I" but a different cry, the cry of the other, of another. Here we have in capsule a portrait, a metaphor, a narrative description of Buber's philosophy of I-Thou. Here we have something of the expression of the primal urge for dialogue, the "inborn-Thou," rising up in that most primal of human locales, the dream. This dream of the double cry is set forth at the beginning of an essay whose task, as Buber tells us, is to "clarify" his philosophy as he presented it in *I and Thou.* This tale repeats the central themes of the philosophy of I-Thou—the need for dialogue, the search for mutuality, the value of otherness—in narrative form. It is a kind of "narrative interpretation" of the I-Thou philosophy. And very interestingly, after Buber tells the tale, he repeats it, he interprets it by retelling it.

> After this manner the dream has recurred each time—till once, the last time, now two years ago. At first it was as usual (it was the dream with the animal), my cry died away, again my heart stood still. But then there was quiet. There came no answering call. I listened, I heard no sound. For I *awaited* the response for the first time; . . . Awaited, it failed to come. But now something happened with me. . . . I exposed myself to the distance, open to all sensation and perception. And then, not from a distance but from the air round about me, noiselessly, came the answer. Really it did not come; it was there. . . . It exceeded the earlier rejoinder

in an unknown perfection. . . . When I had reached an end of receiving it, I felt again, that certainly, pealing out more than ever, that *now it has happened.*[5]

Now it has happened again, and in a manner more perfect than the earlier rejoinder. What happened that made the rejoinder more perfect? The dream starts out on a rather negative note, the "I" cries out and awaits a response which does not come. In fact, the very waiting for it is the thing that prevents the rejoinder from coming. And then, through remaining with this silence and in being exposed "to the distance," suddenly the rejoinder not only comes but exceeds the earlier expression.

The most obvious interpretation of Buber's telling of the dream of the double cry is that in the second go-round Buber let himself go, opened himself further to the moment of encounter. In the second tale the immediacy of the I-Thou encounter is heightened by Buber's openness. As Buber says, he heard the rejoinder "with every pore of my body."[6] The second tale makes the rejoinder a part of the everyday natural order of things. "Really it did not come, it was there." What all of this would suggest for an attempt to place Buber's narrative theology in Comstock's continuum is that Buber is a purist. Buber's second telling brings further insights into the first by re-telling it. We are entered into the dreamland of myth and story and continue in it seeking primal urges and primal expression. The themes of the narratives themselves reinforce the value of immediate expression, the flow of sensation and attention to that which is simply given.

One would have to admit that there is much about Buber's narrative render-ings of I-Thou and narrative biblical theology that places him in the camp of the "pure" narrative theologians. Indeed, in chapter 7, I suggested that Buber's response to the Holocaust eschewed philosophic argumentation on the prob-lem of theodicy and presented a narrative response to suffering. Yet even given my own presentation of Buber's narrative biblical theology I would offer that the logic of Buber's hermeneutics as presented in part one demands that we consider him as an "impure" narrative theologian.[7] If we return to the dream of the double cry a different interpretation than the ostensible and obvious one can be suggested. I would base this alternative reading on the importance of the moment of distancing in which Buber awaits the rejoining response in the second tale.

Although Buber seems to argue that it was the expectation, the waiting for the response, that prohibited the response from coming, I would like to suggest that it was precisely this waiting, this break from the immediacy, that made the response, when it finally came, more perfect than the earlier one. I would suggest that what Buber thought about in his moment of frustration and distance and waiting were certain fundamental principles, even concepts, articulated in his book *I and Thou.* The principles of dialogue, such as mutuality, receptivity, and the value of otherness, certainly help to bring out I-Thou relations. These principles and the formal philosophy of I-Thou may really not be enough to convey what is at stake in the I-Thou relationship. To give readers concrete examples of I-Thou relationships, to most adequately describe the I-Thou meeting, to bring readers into the I-Thou sphere, we will need narrative. That has been the argument of this book. Yet narrative alone is not enough. What good would the narratives in the essay "Dialogue" be without the philosophical sections in *I and Thou?* What I find most powerful in Buber's essay "Dialogue" is the artful interspersing of philosophical analysis with narrative expression.

The view of Buber as narrative purist parallels a view of Buber as concerned with the I-Thou sphere to the exclusion of I-It. It is a view that is based on Buber's idealization of the immediate, unthought I-Thou relationship between infant and parent and between the "primitives" and their environment.[8] There are nostalgic and mystical aspects of this idealization that may be a holdover from Buber's romantic mysticism. Certainly, there are places in Buber's writings where a radical gulf is established between I-Thou and I-It and any objectifying language is excluded from the I-Thou dialogue. Yet Buber also talks of the I-It as the "chrysalis" out of which the I-Thou flies like a butterfly.[9] And he shows how in Hasidism the "It" world can be hallowed over and over again. And thus we come to see the relationship between I-Thou and I-It not as a dichotomy but as an oscillating dialectic.

In a very real way, what we are rehearsing here is our discussion about the use of methods of understanding and methods of explanation in chapter two. There I used Ricoeur's hermeneutics to argue that the explanatory methods of the social scientist, methods that the "impure" narrative theologian employs, do not impede but assist our understanding of Hasidic narratives. And as I pointed to Buber's use of historical criticism and techniques of translation to better understand and interpret the biblical text in chapter three, I would now argue again that explanations can further our understanding of religious narratives. Using Buber's biblical hermeneutics as a warrant, I would suggest that, for him, narrative discourse can be supplemented with social scientific discourse without doing injury to its message. The second and the third stages of the hermeneutic process as presented in chapter four are dependent upon moments of objectification and methods of explanation and critical analysis of a text. My argument there was that these methods can clarify the ways in which our own preconceptions prejudice or distort our readings of texts and can give us additional tools of textual analysis that result in richer interpretations of texts.

In his essay "Distance and Relation," Buber suggests that a fundamental moment of distancing is needed to properly allow for an I-Thou relationship to occur. Buber also seems to suggest that the highest form of I-Thou relation can be achieved only when the partners have some "knowledge" of the dynamics of human relationships. The I-Thou relationship, he says, is "complete only when the other knows that he is made present by me in his self and when this knowledge induces the process of his inmost self-becoming."[10] Here "knowledge," which Buber tells us in *I and Thou* is the culmination of I-It expression, is an essential ingredient in the "complete" I-Thou relationship! I would like to draw a parallel between the recognition of the value of distance and knowledge in the essay "Distance and Relation," the period of waiting before the "perfect" rejoinder given in the second rendering of the dream of the double cry, and the "pause" which Buber spoke of in his "Advice to Frequenters of Libraries" (which I pointed to in my attempt to develop a Buberian hermeneutic in chapter 4). In every one of these cases there seems to be a recognition on Buber's part of the need not only for the language of immediacy, which we could call narrative language, but for the language of mediacy, which we could call social science or philosophy.

A telling remark which specifically addresses the utility of philosophical language is found in Buber's book *Good and Evil.* In the process of analyzing mythic narratives about good and evil in the Bible Buber speaks to the need for concepts.

> We are dealing here, as Plato knew, with truths such as can be communicated adequately to the generality of mankind only in the form of myths. . . . Everything conceptual in this connection is merely an aid, a useful bridge between myth and reality. [But] its construction is indispensable. . . . [We] need the bridge.[11]

Buber's position here on the primacy of mythic narrative language for the expression of good and evil is clear: conceptual language of philosophy is not the primary vehicle of expression for the topic of good and evil, it is a secondary aid to narrative expression.[12] Yet, as Buber says, concepts provide an "indispensable" bridge, a bridge to "reality" that we simply need to have.

In a reply to a question about the role of reason in his thought published in *Philosophical Interrogations* (1964), Buber says "the 'corrective' office of reason is incontestable, and it can be summoned at any moment to set right an 'error' in my sense perception—more precisely, its incongruity with what is common to my fellow men."[13] I do not think that Buber is drawing some sort of ontological connection between reason and conceptual thought and that which is "really real" here. He has far too much invested in narrative and poetic languages to cut them off from participation in "reality." Reason functions as a "corrective" to adjust our individual narrative to a consensus which is built on the meeting of many narrative descriptions of the world. Concepts allow us a way out of the more restricted "language-games" of particularized narratives into a wider sphere for dialogue. With conceptual language we can move into what Buber, borrowing from Heraclitus, called the "common world."[14] Here we come not to put our narratives and their "original concreteness"[15] down but to share them, to test them, to examine them with others who may never have heard them. Here we come not to put down our particular narratives and join as a "team hitched to the great wagon" but to battle in a "strenuous tug of war for a wager."[16]

This "wager" is the faith in a "common logos," a logos "which does not attain its fullness in us but rather between us."[17] This common logos is not a common language of reason but a communicative space in which people who speak "many tongues"[18] and in different language-games can hope to be heard in their differences. To enter into this common logos people do not have to plunge their narratives into a solvent bath of pure reason which would strip them of all particularities. Buber was clear that the search for a common world did not require speakers to adopt some common Esperanto. When Buber was once asked to dispense with the particularities of his Jewish narrative tradition and use only a "universal" language, he answered: "In order to speak to the world what I have heard I am not bound to step into the street. I may remain in the door of my ancestral house: here too the word that is uttered does not go astray."[19]

Yet at the same time that Buber asserts the importance of the particularity of Jewish narrative expression he recognizes that stubborn attempts to remain solely within the bounds of one's ancestral expression can be symptomatic of a "flight from the common cosmos into a special sphere"[20] that closes one off from that which is truly "other." Here, one could develop a Buberian critique of the "pure" narrative theologians who hermetically seal their discourse up in their own language-games.[21] Buber's common cosmos is suggestive of a space where narrative discourses mix with what Bakhtin has called the different "heteroglot" voices of a culture and where concepts are utilized as bridges between cultures so that people can "genuinely think with one another,"[22] in what we may call a "dialogic of cultures."[23] This notion of a "dialogic of cultures" as the ultimate end of Buber's hermeneutic and narrative theology radicalizes the hermeneutic dialogue required by the fourth stage of interpretation as we presented it in chapter 4. Interpreters whose I-Thou encounters with a traditional narrative yield particular interpretations must not only bring their interpretations to their particular communities of inquiry but they must bring their interpretations to "common" communities outside their home communities for a final stage of hermeneutic dialogue.

And what is the proper outcome of this dialogical and hermeneutic speaking and thinking together of peoples? For Buber it is nothing less than the renewal of the earth and the upbuilding of peace.

> Hearkening to the human voice, where it speaks forth unfalsified, and replying to it, this above all is needed today. The busy noise of the hour must no longer drown out the *vox humana,* the essence of the human which has become a voice. This voice must not only be listened to, it must be answered and led out of the lonely monologue into the awakening dialogue of the peoples. Peoples must engage in talk with one another through their truly human men [and women] if the great peace is to appear and the devastated life of the earth to renew itself.[24]

This quotation from Martin Buber makes clear the redemptive, indeed, messianic, dimension of his hermeneutic and narrative theology. For Buber, we do not, finally, tell and interpret the stories of our common memory to find our collective "I" but to awaken the tellings of others. Our telling is a cry, a search, not for ourselves but for the "Other." What we seek is not a repetition of our own story but the rejoining voice of another's story, a different story. If the search for the other is first the search for the stories of my mother, my father, then my friend, then my people, it cannot end here in my own home and culture. The search for the other, the search for the Thou, must be carried to the unfamiliar, the foreign and the strange.

Buber's philosophy suggests that as the distance between the I and Thou is increased the possible depth and power of the I-Thou meeting is also increased. The search for the Thou must therefore be carried to the cosmopolitan street where we meet those whose stories are radically different from our own. Here, in the street, not in home and not in synagogue, must we seek the other. If we review Buber's I-Thou narratives—personal, Hasidic, biblical—we will find that many take place in the street, on the shtetl dirt road, on the desert path, on the city promenade. On the way, outside of home, between ventures, while attempting to meet a simple obligation, the ultimate obligation to meet the other and speak to him or her with the attitude of I-Thou, the stories of I-Thou occur. Here, in the street of meeting, the contest for a glimpse of the eternal Thou takes place. Here, in the street of meeting, the difficult struggle to hear the Thou, the voice of the Other, as it speaks in stories that are different from our own must occur.

Why must the dialogue with the other occur? The imperative is at once ethical and redemptive. For in listening to the human voice of the other and responding with our human voice we touch that which is human. In touching the human we close the gap that separates peoples. In closing the gap we repair the tear in human relations. And in repairing the tear in the sphere of the human we repair the tear in the world. This is the act of *Tikkun Olam*, repair of world. This repairing of world is the transformation of world, and this transformation is the world's redemption.

NOTES

Preface. The Linguistic Turn in Jewish Philosophy

1. The distinction I am making between "French" and "German" speaking worlds is meant as a heuristic device. I do not mean to establish any kind of "intrinsic" national "roots" or "traits" for these different hermeneutic strategies and, as the reader will see, the distinction is drawn rather loosely, for I will eventually include a Frenchman, a Russian, and a number of Americans under a rubric I will finally call "dialogic" and not "German" hermeneutics.

2. Laurence Silberstein's *Martin Buber's Social and Religious Thought* (New York: New York University Press, 1989) is the first book-length treatment of Buber which views him in the context of critical theories of language and interpretation. My study differs from this book in that I rely more on German hermeneutics and Silberstein uses French-inspired poststructural theories. I also concentrate specifically on analyzing Buber's methods of interpretation and style of narration in his Hasidic, biblical, and autobiographical writings and Silberstein ranges more broadly through Buber's writings to establish Buber, in the words of Richard Rorty, as a "postfoundational," "edifying thinker" in contemporary social and religious thought. Another much shorter attempt to place Buber in the "postfoundational," "postmodern" camp is Alan Udoff's "Introduction to New Edition" in Buber's *The Knowledge of Man,* ed. M. Friedman (Atlantic Highlands: Humanities Press, 1988).

3. An additional reason why Buber's writings on interpretation have been ignored is that many contemporary Jewish philosophers have been trained in the Anglo-American analytic tradition and have not found Buber's sensitivities to issues of text, interpretation, and narrative particularly interesting.

4. Biblical studies are the most advanced in applications of linguistic paradigms. See the work of Edward Greenstein, Robert Alter, James Kugel, Michael Fishbane, Meir Sternberg, Adele Berlin, and Alan Cooper. In rabbinics see the recent work of José Faur, Daniel Boyarin, Stephen Fraude, Richard Sarason, David Stern, and Martin Jaffee. In Kabbalah see the work of Moshe Idel, Eliot Wolfson, Naomi Janowitz, and Ithamar Grunewald. In philosophy and theology see the recent and forthcoming work of Peter Ochs, Susan Shapiro, Yudit Greenberg, Jacob Meskin, Robert Gibbs, Bernard Zelechow, Adi Ophir, Edith Wyschogrod, and Susan Handelman, as well as Silberstein and Udoff. We could add to this already substantial list the unique religious psychology of Mordechai Rotenberg and the Holocaust criticism of James Young. For a collection of representative articles by many of these scholars see my forthcoming edited work *Contemporary Critical Jewish Hermeneutics,* New York University Press.

5. For a fine series of succinct summaries of issues and terms in postmodern epistemology and literary theory see Frank Lentricchia and Thomas McLaughlin, eds., *Critical Terms for Literary Study* (Chicago: University of Chicago Press, 1990). My analysis follows in the line of argumentation presented by W. J. T. Mitchell on "Representation" and John Carlos Rowe on "Structure." For a discussion of postmodern epistemology that is more sensitive to the influence of computers and artificial intelligence see Jean-François Lyotard, *The Post-Modern Condition* (Minneapolis: University of Minnesota Press, 1984). For a critical response to postmodernism see Jürgen Habermas, *The Philosophical Discourse of Modernity,* trans. F. Lawrence (Cambridge: MIT Press, 1987).

6. For an analysis of the ways in which Kantian and Enlightenment thought failed to

prevent, indeed, even encouraged Nazism see Berel Lang, *Act and Idea in the Nazi Genocide* (Chicago: University of Chicago Press, 1990), ch. 7.

7. Greenberg, "Cloud of Smoke, Pillar of Fire: Judaism, Christianity, and Modernity After the Holocaust," in E. Fleischner, ed., *Auschwitz: Beginning of a New Era?* (New York: KTAV, 1977), p.26.

8. I am not certain that Greenberg and Fackenheim would feel comfortable with my attempts to include them in a group of Jewish thinkers who have taken the "linguistic turn." They have not, to my knowledge, embraced thinkers usually associated with the turn to language. And some aspects of their work, for example Fackenheim's allegiance to Hegel and Greenberg's allegiance to certain theological formulations of Jewish orthodoxy, may suggest that they do not belong in the group I have described. Yet, the aspects of their work that I have pointed to not only argue for their inclusion in my grouping but also help to articulate reasons for why the turn to language is so important for Jewish thought. For an article by Greenberg in which the category of narrative is crucial see his "Judaism and History: Historical Events and Religious Change," in S. Kazan and N. Stampfer, eds., *Perspectives in Jewish Learning,* Vol. 1 (Chicago: Spertus College Press, 1977). And see the commentary on this article by Michael Goldberg, *Theology and Narrative* (Nashville: Abingdon, 1981), pp.168–73. For more by Fackenheim on midrash and narrative as a response to the Holocaust, see "Midrashic Existence After the Holocaust," in his *The Jewish Return into History* (New York: Schocken, 1978), ch. 16, and *To Mend the World* (New York: Schocken, 1982), pt. IV, chs. 8–9, where Fackenheim points to narrative testimony of survivors as a source of post-Holocaust theology.

9. Kermode, *The Genesis of Secrecy* (Cambridge, MA: Harvard University Press, 1979), p.xi.

10. Fackenheim, *God's Presence in History* (New York: Harper, 1970), p.20.

11. Lyotard, *The Post-Modern Condition,* p.82. For a more extended discussion of Lyotard's thoughts on the affect of the Holocaust on language and philosophy see his "Discussions, or Phrasing 'after Auschwitz,' " in A. Benjamin, ed., *The Lyotard Reader* (Oxford: Basil Blackwell, 1989), pp.360–92.

12. Greenberg, "Cloud of Smoke," p.23.

13. James Young, in his *Writing and Rewriting the Holocaust* (Bloomington: Indiana University Press, 1988), admits that there could be "unacceptable consequences" of the application of certain poststructural theories to the Holocaust. "If Holocaust narrative is nothing but a system of signs merely referring to other signs, then where are the events themselves?" (p.3). Young believes, however, that we cannot turn back from the insights that poststructuralism has given us and that these theories can be used to analyze Holocaust literature productively if the more radical aspects of the theory are "carefully constrained." Young's strategy is certainly an admirable one and one that yields a positive result. However, I am not certain he has confronted the issue of referentiality head-on; to do so would require that he engage in some theoretical acrobatics that more extensive use of the work of Gadamer and Ricoeur (see below) could help him to avoid. For a masterful work of post-Holocaust philosophy which begins with Hegel, Heidegger, and Levinas and also manages to make use of the insights of French postmodernism see Edith Wyschogrod, *Spirit in Ashes: Hegel, Heidegger, and Man-Made Mass Death* (New Haven: Yale University Press, 1985).

14. Although the "*verstehen* School" would eschew explanatory methodologies in certain moments of the hermeneutic dialogue that the Frankfurt School would embrace, both schools agree on the importance of the principle of dialogue in interpretation and both share concerns for meaningful notions of history and subjectivity.

15. Scott, "The House of Intellect in an Age of Carnival: Some Hermeneutical Reflections," *Journal of the American Academy of Religion,* 55:1 (Spring 1987), 8–9.

16. *Ibid.,* p.13.

17. Ricoeur's work is particularly compelling as he has been involved in bridging the

phenomenologist's concern with time and meaning and the structuralist's and post-structuralist's concerns with language and text. Indeed, I regard Ricoeur's work as exemplary and use his theories of language, interpretation, and narrative throughout this book to articulate and refine Buber's positions.

18. See my "A Narrative Jewish Theology," *Judaism,* 37:2 (Spring 1988), 210–17.

19. Paul Mendes-Flohr, "Buber and Post-Traditional Judaism," *European Judaism,* 12:2 (Winter 1978), 6.

1. Romanticism, Dilthey, and Buber's Early Hermeneutics

1. Martin Buber, *Briefwechsel aus sieben Jahrzehnten,* Vol. I, ed. G. Schaeder (Heidelberg: Lambert Schneider, 1972), letter no.10, p.155. This and other translations from Buber's correspondence are my own.

2. By Buber's "early work" we mean all his publications up until *I and Thou* (1923). For a detailed analysis of the movement from Buber's early romantic and mystical thought to the philosophy of I and Thou see Paul Mendes-Flohr, *Von der Mystik zum Dialog: Martin Bubers geistige Entwicklung bis hin zu "Ich und Du"* (Köningstein/Ts.: Jüdischer Verlag bei Anthenäum, 1978) or the English version, *From Mysticism to Dialogue* (Detroit: Wayne State University Press, 1989). Mendes-Flohr designates 1916 as the year in which Buber began to move toward his dialogical philosophy (see ch.5). See also Maurice Friedman, *Martin Buber's Life and Work: The Early Years, 1878–1923* (New York: Dutton, 1981), pts.5, 8. And Rivka Horwitz, *Buber's Way to I and Thou* (Heidelberg: Lambert Schneider, 1978).

3. Paul Mendes-Flohr "Orientalism, the Ostjuden and Jewish Self-Affirmation," in J. Frankel, ed., *Studies in Contemporary Jewry,* Vol. I (Bloomington: Indiana University Press, 1984). Grete Schaeder, *The Hebrew Humanism of Martin Buber,* trans. N. Jacobs (Detroit: Wayne State University Press, 1973). Friedman, *Buber: Early Years,* pt. 1. See also Laurence Silberstein, *Martin Buber's Social and Religious Thought* (New York: New York University Press, 1989), ch.1. Here, Silberstein specifically focuses on the import of Nietzsche's notion of alienation for Buber.

4. Martin Buber, "Autobiographical Fragments," in P. Schilpp and M. Friedman, eds., *The Philosophy of Martin Buber* (La Salle, IL: Open Court, 1967), p.11.

5. Friedman, *Buber: Early Years,* pp.26, 29. Mendes-Flohr, *Von der Mystik zum Dialog,* p.88 n.2.

6. Martin Buber, "Ein Wort über Nietzsche und die Lebenswerte," *Die Kunst im Leben,* I/2, xii (1900), p.13. The translations from this article are my own. Buber, who was an overly sensitive and melancholic young man, seemed to be energized by Nietzsche's exaltation of the will to power, the hidden powers of the self, and the *"Übermensch."* Buber speaks of himself when he declares that the reader of Nietzsche finds in him "the release of the most secret treasures of his individuality which are transformed into active energy." Buber, "Nietzsche und die Lebenswerte," p.13.

7. See Mendes-Flohr, *Von der Mystik zum Dialog,* pp.9–10.

8. Martin Buber, *"Die Schaffenden, das Volk und die Bewegung"* [1902] in Buber, *Die Jüdische Bewegung: Gesammelte Aufsätze und Ansprachen,* I (Berlin: Jüdischer Verlag, 1920), p.67. The translations from this article are my own.

9. *Ibid.*

10. *Ibid.,* p.68.

11. *Ibid.,* p.76.

12. Schaeder, *Hebrew Humanism,* p.34.

13. *Ibid.*

14. Buber, *Briefwechsel* I, letter no.10, p.155. Knowing the eventual use of doctrines of the "folk-soul" in Nazi ideology, one cannot read Buber's discussion of the Jewish "folk-soul" without a slight shudder. George Mosse has detailed the popularity and uses of folkish notions for Jews at the turn of the century in his *Germans and Jews* (New York: Fertig, 1970).

15. Friedman, *Buber's Life: Early Years,* pt.2.

16. Carl Schorske explains that "By the 1890's the heroes of the upper middle class were no longer political leaders, but actors, artists and critics. . . . The life of art became a substitute for the life of action. Indeed, . . . art became almost a religion, the source of meaning and the food for the soul." *Fin-de-Siècle Vienna: Politics and Culture* (New York: Knopf, 1980), pp.8–9.

Grete Schaeder discusses how the poets Hugo Von Hofmannsthal and Stefan George saw themselves as both prophets and myth-makers. For George and his circle poetry was to lead the way to cultural rejuvenation. Hofmannsthal suggested in his 1907 address *"Der Dichter und diese Zeit"* that the poet had tapped the sources of salvation and that the "man with a [poetical] book in his hand has supplanted the kneeling worshipper of the past." Schaeder, *Hebrew Humanism,* pp.68–69.

17. Hans Fischer-Barnicol, " '. . . und Poet dazu.' *Die Einheit von Denken und Dichten bei Martin Buber," Bulletin des Leo Baeck Instituts,* IX:33 (Tel Aviv: Bitaon, 1966), p.11. As quoted in Friedman, *Buber's Life: Early Years,* p.16.

18. "Reminiscence," in Martin Buber, *A Believing Humanism,* trans. Maurice Friedman (New York: Simon and Schuster, 1967), p.30. This book is a translation of Buber's *Nachlese* (Heidelberg: Lambert Schneider, 1965).

19. This statement comes from four essays which Buber wrote in Polish for the "Weekly Review of Social Life, Literature, and Fine Arts of Warsaw" (June and July 1897). William Johnston translated them and they appeared in "Martin Buber's Literary Debut: On Viennese Literature," *The German Quarterly,* 47:4 (Nov. 1974), p.561.

20. "Reminiscence," p.30.

21. Martin Buber, "Über Stefan George," *Die Literarisch Welt* (July 13, 1928).

22. Buber, *Briefwechsel* I, letter no.12, p.156.

23. *Ibid.,* no.15, p.159.

24. Martin Buber, *"Von jüdischer Kunst"* [1901], in Buber, *Die jüdische Bewegung* I, p.57.

25. *Ibid.,* p.59.

26. *Ibid.,* p.60.

27. Martin Buber, *Jüdische Künstler* (Berlin: Jüdischer Verlag, 1903).

28. Arthur Schopenhauer, *The World as Will and Representation* (New York: Dover, 1966).

29. See Paul Mendes-Flohr, "Orientalism."

30. Mendes-Flohr has shown that the ideology of the group followed the program of Schopenhauer's thought fairly closely. Mendes-Flohr, "Editor's Introduction," to Martin Buber, *Ecstatic Confessions,* trans. E. Cameron (San Francisco: Harper and Row, 1985), p.xvi.

31. Paul Flohr and Bernard Susser, *"Alte und neue Gemeinschaft:* An Unpublished Buber Manuscript," *AJS Review,* 1 (1976), p.53.

32. *Ecstatic Confessions,* p.1.

33. *Ibid.,* p.2.

34. *Ibid.,* p.10.

35. Mendes-Flohr, "Orientalism," p.109. Mendes-Flohr shows how writers such as Kafka and Rilke and intellectuals such as Walther Rathenau, Georg Lukacs, Ernst Bloch, and Gustav Landauer were profoundly affected by Buber's early mystical Hasidic tales (pp.116ff). See also B.J. Morse, *Martin Buber's Baalschem and Rilke's Ninth Duino Elegy* (unpublished manuscript, Buber Archive, Ms. 258).

36. I am not saying that the influence of Dilthey on Buber has been overlooked, but that the specific influence of Dilthey's hermeneutic writings on Buber's hermeneutics has not been fully investigated. Mendes-Flohr does mention that Buber's "concept of translation as an act of emphatic retelling seems to be influenced by the doctrines of Wilhelm Dilthey." Mendes-Flohr, "Orientalism," p.135 n.93.; cf. p.111. Mendes-Flohr also refers, briefly, to Dilthey's hermeneutical influence in Mendes-Flohr, "Martin Bu-

ber's Reception Among the Jews," *Modern Judaism* 6:2 (May 1986), 120 and in his *Nachwort* to the republication of Buber's *Die Geschichten des Rabbi Nachman* (Heidelberg: Lambert Schneider, 1989). For Dilthey's influence on Buber's *Erlebnis* oriented concept of mysticism see Mendes-Flohr, *Von der Mystik Zum Dialog,* pp.13, 77ff. For Dilthey's influence on Buber's orientation toward the human historical world and life-philosophy see Schaeder, *Hebrew Humanism,* pp.41–46. For an elaboration of the implications of Dilthey's notion of the human sciences *(Geisteswissenschaften)* on Buber's philosophical anthropology see Maurice Friedman, "Philosophical Anthropology and Dialogue," unpublished lecture, and *The Confirmation of Otherness* (New York: Pilgrim Press, 1983).

37. A copy of Buber's registration at the University of Berlin in the Buber Archives shows his course with Dilthey on Schleiermacher in the Fall of 1899. Martin Buber Archive, Ms.Varia.350,4. See Ulrich Herrmann, *Bibliographie Wilhelm Dilthey* (Weinheim: Beltz, 1969), pp.120–22, for a record of Dilthey's other lectures at the University of Berlin at the time Buber was there. Dilthey's important essay "The Development of Hermeneutics" was published shortly after the Fall of 1899. This essay appears in Dilthey's works as "Die Entstehung der Hermenutik" [1900], *Gesammelte Schriften,* Vol. 5 *Die geistige Welt I.,* ed. G. Misch (Stuttgart: Teubner, 1957). Hereafter *Gesammelte Schriften* will be referred to as *G.S.*

38. Martin Buber, "Das Problem des Menschen," *Werke* I (Heidelberg: Lambert Schneider, 1962), p.317; see also *Werke* II (1964) p.14. Paul Mendes-Flohr reports that Buber's friends Nathan Rotenstreich and Ernst Simon both told him that they often heard Buber speak about his indebtedness to Dilthey. Mendes-Flohr, *Von der Mystik,* p.49 n.40.

39. Schaeder, *Hebrew Humanism,* p.41.

40. My presentation of Schleiermacher's hermeneutics follows the lines of Gadamer's view of him in Hans-Georg Gadamer, *Truth and Method* (New York: Crossroad, 1982), pp.162f.

41. Schleiermacher, *Hermeneutics: The Handwritten Manuscripts,* ed. H. Kimmerle, trans. J. Duke and J. Forstman (Missoula, MT: Scholars Press, 1977), p.100. My emphasis.

42. Friedrich Schleiermacher, *Werke* III (Berlin: Riemer, 1838). pp.354–65.

43. *The Handwritten Manuscripts,* p.63. For a contemporary version of romantic hermeneutics see E.D. Hirsch, *Validity in Interpretation* (New Haven: Yale University Press, 1967). Hirsch attempts to use phenomenological notions of intentionality in speaking of the author's intent to move beyond Schleiermacher's "psychologism" and beyond the vagueness and mystery of the method of "divination."

44. Wilhelm Dilthey, *G.S.,* Vol. 7: *Der Aufbau der geschichtlichen Welt in den Geisteswissenschaften,* ed. B. Groethuysen (Stuttgart: Teubner, 1958), p.171. As translated by Schaeder, *Hebrew Humanism,* p.43.

45. Wilhelm Dilthey, *W. Dilthey: Selected Writings,* trans. and ed. H. P. Rickman (London: Cambridge, 1976), p.178. See Dilthey's discussion of lived experience in "Fragments of a Poetics," in his *Selected Works,* Vol. V: *Poetry and Experience,* ed. R. Makkreel and F. Rodi (Princeton: Princeton University Press, 1985). In lived experience, "we move not in the sphere of sensations, but that of objects; not in the sphere of feelings, but that of value, meaning, etc." (p.228). For a discussion of the movement in Dilthey's thought about *Erlebnis* toward a notion of experience which is more seriously contextualized by society see Michael Ermarth, *Wilhelm Dilthey: The Critique of Historical Reason* (Chicago: University of Chicago Press, 1978), pp.225ff.

46. Hans-Georg Gadamer, *Truth and Method,* p.55. See also pp.58–63.

47. Wilhelm Dilthey, *G.S.,* Vol. 1: *Einleitung in die Geisteswissenschaften,* ed. B. Groethuysen (Stuttgart: Teubner, 1959), pp.xv–xix, and *G.S.,* Vol. 7, pp.79–88.

48. For a more detailed discussion of these two methods and their significance for religious studies see my "Bridging the Gap Between Understanding and Explanation Approaches to the Study of Religion," *Journal for the Scientific Study of Religion,* 25:4

(December 1986), 504–13. And my "In Pursuit of Dialogue," *JSSR*, 27 (December 1988), 645–50. The significance of these methods for Buber's hermeneutics will be discussed in the following three chapters.

49. "It is crucial to see that for Dilthey it is not only through expression that others receive and understand my experience but it is also through expression that I understand my own lived-experience." Ermarth, *Dilthey: The Critique*, p.280.

50. From "Das Verstehen anderer Personen und ihrer Lebensäusserungen," *G.S.*, Vol. 7, p.208. I use the new translation from Kurt Mueller-Vollmer, "The Hermeneutics of the Human Sciences," in Mueller-Vollmer, ed. and trans., *The Hermeneutics Reader* (New York: Continuum, 1985), p.155.

51. Dilthey, "Fragments of a Poetics," *Selected Works*, Vol. 5: *Poetry and Experience*, eds. R. Makkreel and F. Rodi (Princeton: Princeton University Press, 1985), p.228.

52. Borrowing from Hegel, Dilthey refers to the highest, more permanent forms of expression: custom, law, religion, art, science, and philosophy as "Objective Mind." See Mueller-Vollmer, *The Hermeneutics Reader*, p.155. Objective Mind, or what we may call concretized and time-tested expressions, then becomes the medium and context within which new expressions are understood. "It is the medium in which the understanding of other persons and their life-expressions takes place." *Ibid.* Ermarth believes that Dilthey's notion of expression moved him away from the Romantics who mistrusted the capacity of language or form to express human experience. See *Dilthey: The Critique*, p.280.

53. Dilthey, *Selected Writings*, pp.6–11.

54. "The Development of Hermeneutics," in Dilthey, *Selected Writings*, p.247. (This essay appears in Dilthey, *G.S.*, Vol. 5, pp.317–37 and is also translated in Mueller-Vollmer, *The Hermeneutics Reader*.)

55. *Ibid.*, p.248.

56. Dilthey, "Der Aufbau der geschichtlichen Welt," *G.S.*, Vol, 7, p.191; *Selected Writings*, trans. Rickman, p.208. "Understanding is the rediscovery of the I in the Thou. . . . This identity of the mind in the I and the Thou . . . makes successful co-operation between different processes in the human studies possible." Buber, of course, developed a different notion of the relationships between the I and Thou which assumed not an "identity of mind" but, rather, an essential difference.

57. Dilthey, *Selected Writings*, p.159. Because self-reflection is so important to the empathic method, autobiography, one's own attempt to bring to expression one's important life-experiences, is a primary preparatory tool for the task of hermeneutics. See *Selected Writings* pp.214ff.

58. Understanding, proper, is based upon what Dilthey called "elementary understanding"—an assumed understanding of basic cultural codes, e.g., language, gestures, facial expressions. Dilthey, "The Hermeneutics of the Human Sciences," in Mueller-Vollmer, *Hermeneutics Reader*, p.154.

59. *Ibid.*, p.159 [my italics].

60. *Ibid.*

61. Dilthey, *G.S.*, Vol. 7, p.215.

62. Dilthey asserts that the relation between creation and creator is not the only one which the interpreter is concerned with. He/she must also be concerned with "the relation of the expression to the expressed" ("The Hermeneutics of the Human Sciences," in Mueller-Vollmer, *Hermeneutics Reader*, p.157), understood not as the author's *Erlebnis* but as the "objective meaning" of the work outside of the author's mental state. Paul Ricoeur has tried to argue that Dilthey's recognition of an "objective referent" in a work constitutes a major shift away from his earlier subjectivist hermeneutics. Ricoeur, *Interpretation Theory* (Fort Worth: Texas Christian University Press, 1976), pp.90–91. Michael Ermarth summarizes the move as follows.

> Particularly after his reading of Husserl, he extended his notion of meaning to include the relation between the sign and the thing signified and stipulated that

what is signified cannot be resolved into experiential components and con-figurations. *Verstehen* is just not simply the "resubjectifying" of objectivations in a "backward" movement from the objective expression to the immanent subjective experiences of the expresser, but also a "forward movement," from the sign to its intentional object. (*Dilthey: The Critique,* p.274)

63. The English word "genius" does not adequately capture the German romantic use of the term *ingenium,* which means something less exclusive than our "genius." The meaning is closer to our word "inspiration" or "invention." Gadamer explains it this way:

> Wherever one must 'come upon something' that cannot be found through learning and methodical work alone, i.e., wherever there is *invention,* where something is due to inspiration and not to methodical calculation, the important thing is *in-genium,* genius. (Gadamer, *Truth and Method,* p.50)

64. Understanding and interpretation are intricately related for Dilthey, as with many in the *verstehen* tradition. See Gadamer: "Alles Verstehen ist Auslegen," in his *Wahrheit und Methode,* 2nd edition (Tübingen: Mohr, 1965), p.366.

65. Dilthey, in Mueller-Vollmer, *Hermeneutics Reader,* p.161.

66. Martin Buber, *The Legend of the Baal-Shem* (New York: Schocken Books, 1969), p.10. Buber's correspondence shows that Buber's wife, Paula Winkler, who herself was a New Romantic poet and novelist, helped him write many of the Baal-Shem legends. See Buber, *Briefwechsel* I, letters nos. 109–11, pp.249–51. Mendes-Flohr reports that the original drafts of these stories, available in the Buber Archive, also show Winkler's hand in the writing of the tales. Mendes-Flohr, "Orientalism," p.112.

67. Martin Buber, "My Way to Hasidism," in Buber, *Hasidism and Modern Man,* trans. M. Friedman (New York: Harper, 1966), pp.61–62.

68. Buber, *Briefwechsel* I, letter no.12, p.156.

69. Martin Buber, "My Way to Hasidism," p.62. Hans Kohn states that Buber was very much influenced by Gustav Landauer, who, in turn it seems, was influenced by Dilthey in his modern German translation of Meister Eckhart's work. Hans Kohn, *Martin Buber: Sein Werk und Sein Zeit* (Cologne: Joseph Melzer, 1961), p.30. Kohn quotes from the publication prospectus for Landauer's Eckhart translation which includes observations that could very easily be said by Buber's publisher about his translations of the tales of Nahman and the Baal Shem.

> Landauer believes himself to have found the key to Eckhart's secrets from a certain kinship with his being. He joyfully went about his work with sincere belief in his intellectual and spiritual affinity, and since he was successful in understanding Eckhart and in linguistically and conceptually forming the material anew, he was able to separate out from the extant writings of the Meister that which was uniquely Eckhart's. . . . Only he could presume to sift through this material who felt and revered Eckhart completely, as full of life and vitalizing. Therefore, designations for this book as a selection or modernization would be totally false. . . . It is the return of a forgotten one who should not be evaluated historically but rather should be filled [*erfüllt*] anew with life, (p.293 n.2, my translation)

See, also, Dilthey's use of the term *Erfüllung* in *G.S.,* Vol. 6, p.315. I must thank Paul Mendes-Flohr for pointing me to the parallel between Buber and Landauer which is suggested in Kohn's book.

70. Buber, "Hasidism and Modern Man" [1956], in *Hasidism and Modern Man,* p.26.

71. Buber, "My Way to Hasidism," p.62.

72. This suggestion of Buber's (that he was more faithful to the Hasidic master than were the immediate disciples) may seem somewhat presumptuous but it parallels the romantic hermeneutic assertion that an interpreter can understand the author better than the author can understand himself. Knowing Buber's hermeneutic assumptions, Buber's statement may appear less radical.

73. Buber, "Replies to My Critics," in P. Schilpp and M. Friedman, eds., *The Philosophy of Martin Buber* (La Salle, IL: Open Court, 1967), p.731.

74. Martin Buber, *The Tales of Rabbi Nachman,* trans. M. Friedman (New York: Horizon, 1956) p.i.

75. *Ibid.*

76. Gadamer, *Truth and Method,* pp.277, 361.

77. Buber, *Briefwechsel* I, letter no.104, p.244.

78. *Ibid.* Arthur Green seems to agree with Buber as he states that Nahman's stories were recorded in a "poverty of language and style." Green, *Tormented Master: A Life of Rabbi Nahman of Bratslav* (University, AL: University of Alabama, 1979), p.344.

79. Arnold Band, *Nahman of Bratslav: The Tales* (New York: Paulist Press, 1978), pp.44–46.

80. Buber, "Replies," p.731.

81. Buber included only six of the thirteen tales of Nahman and tells us that the other seven tales, which he did not include in his 1906 publication, were the most "garbled and fragmentary." *The Tales of Rabbi Nachman,* p.45. However, Michael Brocke has recently uncovered, in a rare collection of stories for youths published in 1905, a seventh tale: "The Story of the Traveling Princess," which Buber translated. Brocke published this tale side by side with a literal German translation of the original Nahman story and used the work of Harold Bloom to argue that Buber, like creative writers and interpreters of any literary tradition, produced a "strong misreading" of the original Nahman tale to negate the past tradition and remake it anew. See Michael Brocke, "Martin Bubers *Misreading* des R. Nachman von Bratzlaw: *Die unbekannte 'Geschichte von der fahrenden Prinzessin,'*" *Spiel—Räume,* ed. H. G. Heimbrock (Neukirchener Verlag, 1983). This application of Bloom to Buber's retelling of the Nahman tales certainly illuminates what may be called the "Oedipal aspect" of Buber's project, yet I believe still deeper insight can be found by locating Buber's work in the context of the German romantic hermeneutic tradition out of which Buber toiled and which Brocke fails to mention. Laurence Silberstein uses Bloom along with Rorty, Hayden White, and others to recontextualize Buber's interpretation of Hasidism with postmodern deconstruction theories (*Buber's Social and Religious Thought,* ch.2). Although I have great sympathy with Silberstein's overall approach, I do think that Buber is better placed in the context of German hermeneutics than in that of contemporary French and French-influenced American deconstructive hermeneutics.

82. *Die Geschichten des Rabbi Nachman* (Frankfurt am Main: Rütten und Loening, 1918), pp.45, 85, 133. Buber, in fact, employs some of the German linguistic conventions of Grimm. For example: "Es war einmal ein Rabbi, der hatte sein Leben der Thora dargebracht." The use of the demonstrative "der" in the second clause instead of a relative makes the meaning: "Once there was a rabbi, he had devoted his life to Torah" instead of "There once was a rabbi, who had devoted. . . ."

83. My translations are from Buber, *Die Geschichten des Rabbi Nachman* (1918), and from Rabbi Nahman, *Sippurey Ma'asiyot* (Berlin: Hebräischer Verlag, 1922) and *Sippurey Ma'asiyot,* (14th ed.; Jerusalem: Association of Bratslav Hasidim, 1969). I call these editions "traditional" because they have been held to be so by contemporary scholarship and by Bratslav Hasidim. I have not been able to establish, through the Buber Archives, if these were indeed the editions that Buber used. But I think we can assume that Buber's editions were close enough to these for me to make the hermeneutical points in my comparisons. Following Mendel Piekarz, *Hasidut Braslav* (Jerusalem, 1972), who argues that the language which the tales were first written down in was Hebrew, my translation, generally, follows the Hebrew text though I do also consult the Yiddish (cf. Green, *Tormented Master,* p.367 n.1). For another comparison of the Buber and Nahman texts see Hans Hermann Blettgen, "Der Rabbi und Sein Sohn: Martin Bubers Verarbeitung einer Geschichte des Rabbi Nachman von Bratzlaw," in M. Brocke, ed. *Beter und Rebellen Aus 1000 Jahren Judentum in Polen* (Berlin: Institut Kirche und Judentum, 1983).

84. An unfortunate aspect of this contrast, which is characteristic of Buber's in-

terpretation of all of Hasidism, is that it establishes a radical gulf between the strict rabbinic *halakhist* and the "spiritual" Hasid. This contrast suggests, quite wrongly, that the Hasidim were not diligent in following *halakhah,* and that the *halakhic* observance of the *mitnagdim* made them less spiritual.

85. Here are the two German sentences in their entirety:

Aber seine Seele konnte über den Büchern nicht verharren, und sein Blick hielt sich nicht auf der unendlichen Fläche der kleinen starren Lettern, sondern glitt immer wieder hinaus über die gelbe Flut der ähren hin and bis zu dem dunklen Strich der fernen Tannenwälder. Und mit seinem Blick glitt seine Seele hinaus und wiegte sich in der stillen Luft, scheu wie ein junger Vogel. (Buber, *Die Geschichten des Rabbi Nachman,* p.55)

86. The son achieved, according to the Jewish mystical kabbalistic system, the first level of spiritual growth—the "small light" or the *sefirah* of *malkut.* The zaddik has achieved the "great light," the *tiferet* or *yesod,* the seventh or ninth level. See the commentary on Nahman's tales by Arnold Band in Band, *Nahman of Bratslav: The Tales,* p.307.

87. The Yiddish explains: he is *"kein ehrlicher Yehudi,"* no honorable Jew.

88. I have been aided here by an unpublished paper of my former student Pamela Nelson, "The Scholar and the Philosopher: A Tale of Rabbi Nahman's Translators."

89. See the commentaries of Band, *Nahman of Bratslav,* pp.309–10, and Adin Steinsaltz, *Beggars and Prayers* (New York: Basic Books, 1985), pp.133–47.

90. Buber, *The Tales of Rabbi Nachman,* pp.80–82.

91. *Ibid.,* p.85.

92. Martin Buber, *Good and Evil* (New York: Scribner's, 1953), pp.139–43.

93. Steinsaltz, *Beggars,* pp.146–47.

94. The Buber-Scholem controversy over the interpretation of Hasidic texts will be addressed in the next chapter.

95. I will argue, in the next chapter, that if the interpreter is limited to the task of discerning the meaning of a text in its initial context she or he will fail in the hermeneutical task of making the text relevant to contemporary audiences. Yet, I will also argue, that knowledge of the original form and context of a text will assist and not hinder the interpreter in the attempt to discern the text's contemporary relevance.

96. I am indebted to Maurice Friedman for pointing me to the difference between Buber's early and later methods of interpreting Hasidic texts when I gave a very early draft of this chapter at the American Academy of Religion meetings in Chicago, December, 1984.

2. *I and Thou* and the Dialogical Hermeneutic Method

1. As we will see, Buber's later hermeneutic method cannot be considered a total break with romanticism. Buber appears to have retrieved aspects of the first, "grammatical" stage of romantic hermeneutics with its attention to the details of the language of a particular text and rejected the more famous, second, "psychological" stage. See chapter 3. Because of this tie to the romantics and for other reasons (see below) I oppose Gadamer and refer to Buber's dialogical hermeneutics as a "method."

2. An additional influence on Buber's revised hermeneutic approach stemmed from his involvement with Franz Rosenzweig in their joint project of translating the Hebrew Bible into German, which was started in May 1925.

3. Martin Buber, *Der Grosse Maggid und seine Nachfolge* (Frankfurt: Rütten und Loening, 1922), p.14 (my translation).

4. Martin Buber, *Tales of the Hasidim: Early Masters,* trans. Olga Marx (New York: Schocken Books, 1947), p.xi.

5. *Ibid.,* p.viii.

6. *Ibid.,* p.x.

7. The Friedman translation of *The Legend of the Baal-Shem* leaves out this sen-

tence *(Er ist die Schale, die du zerschlagen sollst)* with its obvious reference to the kabbalistic *kelipot,* the evil husks or shells that encase the divine sparks within all creatures and things. See Gershom Scholem, *On the Kabbalah and Its Symbolism* (New York: Schocken, 1969), pp.114f.

8. My English translation of the "Werewolf" is from Martin Buber, *Die Legende des Baal-Shem* (Frankfurt: Rütten und Loening, 1920). Although, as was noted in chapter 1, Buber's wife, Paula, wrote some of the Baal-Shem legends, from the evidence of their correspondence it appears that the first legend, the "Werewolf," was written by Buber himself.

9. Dan Ben-Amos and Jerome Mintz, in their English translation of the legends of the Baal-Shem Tov, translate this line as: "I see that you will light my candle." And they regard this as a reference to the *jahrzeit* or "memorial" candle which children light after the death of a parent. *In Praise of the Baal-Shem Tov* (Bloomington: Indiana University Press, 1970), p.11. But Buber's rendering cannot be considered a creative retelling, for the Hebrew is ambiguous *(roeh ani sh'atah ta'er nari)* and can be translated either way.

10. My translation is from Martin Buber, *Die Erzählungen der Chassidim* (Zurich: Manesse Verlag, 1949), and the Hebrew rendition in Buber, *Or ha-Ganuz* (Jerusalem: Schocken, 1946). In these renditions the "Werewolf" story is presented in three, separate short tales: "His Father's Word" (which we present above), "The Vain Labor," and "The First Fight."

11. Buber, "Hasidism and Modern Man," p.24.

12. Martin Buber, *Ecstatic Confessions,* ed. P. Mendes-Flohr, trans. E. Cameron (San Francisco, CA.: Harper and Row, 1985), pp.5–7. Mendes-Flohr shows, in his preface to *Ecstatic Confessions* (pp.xiv–xv, xix–xx), how Buber was echoing the views of other neo-romantics. Mendes-Flohr remarks that Fritz Mauthner, in his *Beiträge zu einer Kritik der Sprache,* "questioned whether language . . . is suitable for gaining and expressing genuine knowledge." In his, *Skepsis und Mystik,* Buber's close friend and mentor, Gustav Landauer, summarized the views of Mauthner and stated that "Language . . . cannot serve to bring the world closer to us." Mendes-Flohr notes that Robert Musil saw language as "faulty and fraudulent" and Hofmannsthal expressed similar skepticism.

13. Translation of *Das neue Denken* in Nahum Glatzer, *Franz Rosenzweig: His Life and Thought* (New York: Schocken, 1961), p.198. In his great theological work, *Der Stern der Erlösung* [1921], Rosenzweig refers to language as "the centerpiece, as it were, of this entire book." *The Star of Redemption,* trans. William Hallo (Boston: Beacon, 1972), p.172. Rosenzweig retrieved the high valuation of language characteristic of Judaism. For a discussion of language in Judaism see Josef Stern, "Language," in *Contemporary Jewish Religious Thought,* ed. A Cohen and P. Mendes-Flohr (New York: Scribner's, 1987); see also Mendes-Flohr, "Introduction," to Buber, *Ecstatic Confessions,* p.xxiii.

14. Rivka Horwitz, *Buber's Way to I and Thou* (Heidelberg: Lambert Schneider, 1978), p.222; see chs. 5, 6.

15. Martin Buber, *I and Thou,* trans. R. G. Smith (New York: Scribner's, 1958), p.3. All references to *I and Thou* will be taken from this translation unless otherwise noted. Kaufmann's more recent translation distinguishes itself by translating "Ich und Du" as "I and You" rather than "I and Thou." This is more in line with the personal German meaning of "du" that Buber wants to convey. Yet, by now "I and Thou" has become a term which so many know and associate with Buber's thought that "I and You" seems to add to confusion. The Smith translation also captures the poetic quality of the original better than does Kaufmann's translation. See Maurice Friedman, *Martin Buber: Early Years* (1981), pp.428–29, for a more in-depth comparison of the two translations. Friedman also prefers the Smith translation. That this view is shared by the Buber estate is evidenced by the fact that the latest Scribner edition of *I and Thou* uses the Smith translation.

16. Martin Buber, *I and Thou,* trans. W. Kaufmann (New York: Scribner's, 1970), p.53.

17. *I and Thou*, trans. Smith, p.4.

18. Recall a statement of Dilthey's quoted in the preceding chapter: "Understanding is the rediscovery of the I in the Thou. . . . This identity of the mind in the I and the Thou . . . makes successful co-operation between different processes in the human studies possible." *Dilthey: Selected Writings* (1976), trans. Rickman, p.208.

19. *I and Thou*, p.6.

20. From a letter of Buber to Ronald Smith, which Smith reported in his *Martin Buber* (Richmond, VA: John Knox, 1967), p.16, n.19. For another good discussion of how to translate the term *geistige Wesenheiten*, see Robert Wood, *Martin Buber's Ontology* (Evanston IL: Northwestern University Press, 1969), p.43 and n.38.

21. The expression "prime analogate" is Wood's; *Ontology*, p.50. Buber's first mention of *geistige Wesenheiten* in *I and Thou* refers to "forming, thinking, acting" (p.6). His next reference is to "language, art, and action" (p.39), which is followed by paragraphs on knowledge, art, and action (pp.40–42). The discussions of art seem primary because it is out of them that Buber develops most fully his notion of a form of spirit that has become concrete.

22. Buber, *I and Thou*, p.9.

23. See Dilthey, *G.S.*, Vol.6, *Die geistige Welt* II, pp.313–20.

24. *I and Thou*, pp.9–10.

25. Because works of art have an element of "Geist," of spirit, they are more than just human products and can, when approached with the attitude of I-Thou, allow a "glimpse" of the eternal Thou.

26. Buber, *I and Thou*, p.39.

27. Buber's references to *Geist* in *I and Thou* range from transcendent notions of spirit as "in its own realm" (p.51), the "starry heaven," and the "deep mystery" (p.42), to the religious designation, the "word" (p.39), to more immanent notions of spirit as encompassing nature (p.24), to human and cultural notions: "language . . . art . . . and action" (p.39). Wood has tried to establish some order in Buber's use of the term by suggesting that the purest form of spirit is transcendent and labeled "the word" and its manifestations are found in the forms of spirit: art, knowledge, action. *Ontology*, p.74.

28. Buber moves away from this Idealist notion of the origin of art in a later essay on aesthetics, *"Der Mensch und sein Gebild"* [1955]. Here, he suggests that the "forms" to which the artist relates exist in perceived and sensed reality. Art is stimulated by the perceptions and sensations, the shapes, sounds, and smells which come from the world. Art makes the world into expression—it thrusts the world into relief. It is fashioned through an encounter with the sensual in the world. "The artist . . . may establish his work only by means of what happens to him in the sphere of the bound life of his senses—in the fundamental events of perception." "Der Mensch und sein Gebild," *Werke* I (Heidelberg: Lambert Schneider, 1962), pp.424–41; published in English as "Man and His Image-Work," in *The Knowledge of Man*, ed. M. Friedman (New York: Harper, 1965) (p.151). Cf. Gadamer: In art, "what is given to the senses . . . is itself made present." *Truth and Method*, p.446. See Buber's "Spirits and Men," *A Believing Humanism* (pp.52–54), for an interesting discussion of the work of Buber's wife, Paula, as an example of an artistic form of spirit.

29. Buber, *I and Thou*, p.10.

30. *Ibid.*

31. *Ibid.*, pp.10, 40.

32. Buber, "Ich und Du," *Werke* I, p.84.

33. Louis Hammer, "The Relevance of Buber to Aesthetics," in Schilpp and Friedman, eds., *The Philosophy of Martin Buber*, p.627.

34. Buber, *I and Thou*, pp.128–129.

35. Martin Buber, "Dialogue," *Between Man and Man*, trans. R. G. Smith (New York: Macmillan Co., 1965), p.9.

36. Buber, "Man and His Image-Work," *The Knowledge of Man*, p.150.

37. Buber's notion of the "reality" and "truth" which art discloses has some affinities with Heideggerian aesthetics and its "disclosure model" for truth. See Heidegger, "The Origin of the Work of Art," *Poetry, Language, Thought,* trans. A. Hofstadter (San Francisco: Harper and Row, 1971). Also W. Spanos, ed., *Martin Heidegger and the Question of Literature* (Bloomington: Indiana University Press, 1979).

38. Hammer, "Relevance," p.614.

39. "Der Mensch und sein Gebild," *Werke* I, p.424.

40. Buber, *I and Thou,* trans. W. Kaufmann, p.62.

41. Maurice Friedman, "Introductory Essay," in Martin Buber, *The Knowledge of Man,* p.53.

42. We can use Donald Berry's analysis of how it is we can have a "mutual" I-Thou relation with nature to explain the mutual relationship with a work of art. Berry suggests that we establish a notion of varying "degrees" or levels of mutuality. See Donald Berry, *Mutuality: The Vision of Martin Buber* (Albany: SUNY Press, 1985), ch.1. The I-Thou relation I have with a tree is not the fully mutual relationship I have with my friend, but there are aspects of give and take in the relationship that make it more than a relationship of objectification or I-It. Similarly we could say that we do not have a fully mutual relationship with a work of art, but there can be a give and take, a "dialogue" with the work when I approach it with the attitude of Thou.

43. Buber, "Dialogue," p.25.

44. See *Truth and Method,* pp.153–214. I am grateful for the very clear summary of Gadamer's critique of romantic hermeneutics in Georgia Warnke, *Gadamer: Hermeneutics, Tradition and Reason* (Cambridge, UK: Polity, 1987), ch.1.

45. Gadamer, *Truth and Method,* p.165.

46. *Ibid.,* p.445.

47. *Ibid.,* pp.91ff.

48. *Ibid.,* p.94.

49. *Ibid.,* p.95.

50. *Ibid.,* p.278.

51. *Ibid.,* p.321.

52. Others, such as F. Rosenzweig, E. Rosenstock-Huessy, and F. Ebner, employed the term, but its most sustained development is found in Buber's work and its worldwide recognition is also due to Buber. For a historical discussion of the term see Buber, "The History of the Dialogical Principle" [1954], in *Between Man and Man* (1965), and Michael Theunissen, *The Other,* trans. C. Macann (Cambridge: MIT Press, 1984), pp.256–71.

53. Gadamer, *Truth and Method,* p.321.

54. *Ibid.,* p.323.

55. Cf. Buber, *I and Thou,* p.4, and "Dialogue," p.8, where Buber speaks of the objective way of perceiving, which he calls "observing."

56. Gadamer, *Truth and Method,* p.262.

57. *Ibid.,* p.322.

58. *Ibid.,* pp.262–63.

59. Martin Buber, "Distance and Relation," *The Knowledge of Man,* p.60.

60. *Ibid.,* p.69.

61. Gadamer, *Truth and Method,* p.324.

62. *Ibid.,* p.325.

63. *Ibid.,* p.443.

64. *Ibid.,* p.326.

65. *Ibid.,* p.331.

66. For an elaborate theory of the importance of the way in which texts are successively interpreted through history see Hans Robert Jauss, *Toward an Aesthetic of Reception* (Minneapolis: University of Minesota Press, 1982). Part of the radicality of Buber's interpretation of Hasidism can be seen in his failure to pay attention to

traditional Jewish scholars of Hasidism who preceded him. If these scholars had an effect on him it was a negative effect, that is, Buber denied much of the traditional Jewish context and attempted to graft Hasidism onto modern existentialist and humanist thought. Given Buber's denial of the traditional Jewish interpretations that preceded him, Michael Brocke's oedipal reading of Buber (adapted from Harold Bloom's work) makes some good sense. Brocke, "Martin Bubers *Misreading* des R. Nachman von Bratzlaw."

67. Gadamer, *Truth and Method,* pp.267ff.

68. Buber, "Über das Erzieherische," *Werke,* I, pp.801ff.

69. Buber, "Education," *Between Man and Man,* p.97.

70. Gadamer, *Truth and Method,* p.273.

71. *Ibid.,* p.341. Buber gives moving examples of transforming dialogues in his essay "Dialogue," pp.3–6.

72. Gadamer, *Truth and Method,* p.274.

73. *Ibid.,* p.278.

74. *Ibid.,* p.297.

75. *Ibid.,* pp.263–64.

76. Buber, "Hasidism and Modern Man," p.38.

77. Buber, "Replies to My Critics," in *The Philosophy of Martin Buber,* p.737.

78. Gadamer, *Truth and Method,* p.275. This is not to say that every new interpretation is a correct interpretation. Interpretation, as Gadamer suggests in the final sentence of *Truth and Method,* must "be achieved by a discipline of questioning and research" (p.447). Georgia Warnke explains that this means that for Gadamer "understanding" *(verstehen)* is a matter of coming to an understanding *(Verständigung)* with others" *(Gadamer,* p.4). David Tracy has interpreted this to mean that each person's interpretation of a text must be subjected to the questioning and research of other serious readers. A dialogue must also be engendered between interpreters. "The larger dialogue with the entire community of capable readers is a major need for any claim to relative adequacy in interpretation." Tracy, *The Analogical Imagination* (New York: Crossroad, 1981), p.121. Richard Bernstein summarizes Gadamer's position on a "true" interpretation in this way: it is "what can be argumentatively validated by the community of interpreters who open themselves to what [the text of a] tradition says to us." *Beyond Objectivism and Relativism: Science, Hermeneutics and Praxis* (Philadelphia: University of Pennsylvania Press, 1983), p. 154. Although Buber also requires that the interpreters bring their interpretations to a public forum, the logic of dialogue which aims to preserve difference means that Buber would be more open to variety in interpretation. See chapter 4.

79. Gadamer, *Truth and Method,* p.350.

80. Buber, *I and Thou,* trans. Kaufmann, p.57. For a discussion of Buber's notion of language in *I and Thou* see my University of Chicago dissertation, "Martin Buber's Stories and Contemporary Narrative Theory," (1983) ch. 1.

81. *I and Thou,* pp.102–03.

82. *Ibid.,* p.11.

83. *Ibid.*

84. *Ibid,* pp.4, 17.

85. Grete Schaeder, *Hebrew Humanism,* p.150. Robert Wood, *Ontology,* pp.36–37. Paul Mendes-Flohr, in a seminar at the University of Virginia on Buber (Fall 1986) also interpreted Buber's use of the terms "primary words," "speech," and "language," metaphorically.

86. See chapter 4.

87. The list of those who have severely criticized Buber to the point of dismissing his writings on Hasidism is long and it is somewhat surprising that it includes not only historians of Hasidism but also such philosophers and theologians as Louis Jacobs, Arthur Cohen, and Steven Katz, who one might think would have more sympathies with philosophical approaches. Indeed, I have been trying to show that it was Buber's

philosophical training that led him to his particular interpretation of Hasidism and that the interpretation remains philosophically defensible.

88. Buber, "Replies," p.731.

89. See Gadamer, *Truth and Method,* pp.324–25.

90. Gershom Scholem, "Martin Buber's Interpretation of Hasidism," *The Messianic Idea in Judaism,* trans. M. Meyer (New York: Schocken, 1971), p.230.

91. Rudolf Bultmann, "The Problem of Hermeneutics," *New Testament and Mythology,* trans. and ed. S. Ogden (Philadelphia: Fortress Press, 1984), p.72.

92. Martin Buber, "Interpreting Hasidism," *Commentary,* 36:3 (Sept. 1963), 218.

93. The Science of Judaism shares some intellectual roots with the tradition of romantic hermeneutics. Both movements grew out of a great appreciation for history and an attempt to develop more adequate methods for interpreting important cultural expressions and historical movements of the past. For both movements, figures such as Friedrich Ast, Friedrich August Wolf, and Hegel were very important. Yet where the romantics complemented philology with divinatory and empathic methods, the Science of Judaism relied exclusively on philological and historical critical methodologies.

94. This quotation from August Wilhelm Schlegel appears in Paul Mendes-Flohr and Jehuda Reinharz's discussion of the presuppositions of the Science of Judaism, *The Jew in the Modern World: A Documentary History,* ed. P. Mendes-Flohr and J. Reinharz (Oxford: Oxford University Press, 1980), p.183.

95. *Ibid.*

96. *Ibid.*

97. Leopold Zunz, "On Rabbinic Literature," from *Gesammelte Schriften* Vol. 1 (1875), trans. A. Schwartz in P. Mendes-Flohr and J. Reinharz, *The Jew in the Modern World,* p.202.

98. *Ibid.*

99. *Ibid.,* p.200.

100. *Ibid.,* p.197.

101. Scholem, "The Science of Judaism: Then and Now" [1959], in *The Messianic Idea,* p.305.

102. Steinschneider, as quoted by Scholem, *ibid.,* p.307.

103. Scholem, *ibid.,* p.312.

104. Scholem was not, of course, primarily a historian of Hasidism but of the Jewish mysticism that preceded it.

105. Gershom Scholem, *Major Trends in Jewish Mysticism* (New York: Schocken, 1946). Lecture 9.

106. Scholem, "Buber's Interpretation of Hasidism," in *The Messianic Idea,* pp.230–31.

107. *Ibid.,* p.231.

108. Rivka Schatz-Uffenheimer also criticizes Buber's interpretation of the Hasidic relationship to the profane sphere. See her "Man's Relation to God and World in Buber's Rendering of the Hasidic Teaching," in P. Schilpp and M. Friedman, *The Philosophy of Martin Buber,* (La Salle, IL: Open Court, 1967). And Steven Katz has also tried to support Scholem's contention that Buber mistakenly elevated the narrative literature over the theoretical. See Katz, "Martin Buber's Misuse of Hasidic Sources," *Post-Holocaust Dialogues* (New York: New York University Press, 1984). Arthur Green, however, has supported Buber on this latter issue and I have tried to provide some theoretical justification for the primacy of narrative to Hasidism on the basis of recent work in narrative theology. Arthur Green, *Tormented Master,* p.368 n.4. Steven D. Kepnes, "Martin Buber's Stories and Contemporary Narrative Theory," University of Chicago dissertation (1983), chs. 2 and 3.

109. Scholem, "Buber's Interpretation of Hasidism," p.247.

110. Given the contemporary debates in the philosophy of history, one cannot label Scholem's work as a form of explanation without addressing the issue of whether or not history itself is a form of explanation or understanding. In his recent book *Time and*

Narrative, Paul Ricoeur argues that history is a hybrid science, including elements of narrative and *verstehen* as well as elements of argument and explanation. *Time and Narrative,* Vol. I, trans. K. McLaughlin and D. Pellauer (Chicago: University of Chicago Press, 1984), chap. 6. However, I believe that we can isolate the explanatory element in history in its historical critical methodologies, and it is this aspect of Scholem's presentation of Hasidism that I am interested in here.

111. Gadamer, *Truth and Method,* p.299.

112. Baruch Kurzweil, who came from a religious orientation opposite that of Buber, also levied a critique of Scholem's belief in the value and ideology-free character of the Science of Judaism. He did so, however, not to argue for a new application of Jewish texts to modern life, but to discredit the academic study of Judaism and the secular movement of Zionism (with which Scholem was associated) so as to encourage a renewed dedication to the traditional Judaism of the past. See the fine article of David Myers, "The Scholem-Kurzweil Debate and Modern Jewish Historiography," *Modern Judaism* 6:3 (October 1986), pp.261–86.

113. Current representatives are Hayden White, Louis Mink, W. B. Gallie, and Arthur Danto. For a thorough review of the positions of these figures see Paul Ricoeur, *Time and Narrative,* Vol. I, Part II.

114. For a Wittgensteinian argument against the possibility of pure "objectivity" in social science and for the language and situation-dependent character of all social science and the determinative role that the subjectivity of the investigator must play in the social sciences, see Peter Winch, *The Idea of a Social Science and Its Relation to Philosophy* (London: Routledge and Kegan Paul, 1964), and Charles Taylor, "Interpretation and the Sciences of Man," *Review of Metaphysics* 25 (1971), pp.3–51. For a more radical presentation of the view that "objectivity" is impossible to establish and that there are no qualitative differences between the human, the social, and the hard sciences, see Richard Rorty, *Philosophy and the Mirror of Nature* (Princeton: Princeton University Press, 1979). For a presentation of the mutual uses of metaphor, models, and imagination in science and religion, see Mary Gerhart and Alan Russell, *Metaphoric Process: The Creation of Scientific and Religious Understanding* (Fort Worth: Texas Christian University Press, 1984).

115. Paul Ricoeur, "Explanation and Understanding," *The Philosophy of Paul Ricoeur* (New York: Beacon, 1978), pp.149–67. See also Ricoeur, *Interpretation Theory* (Fort Worth: Texas Christian University Press, 1976), chap. 4.

116. Ricoeur, "Explanation and Understanding," p.165.

117. *Ibid.,* p.153, Ricoeur's emphasis.

118. See Bultmann, "The Problem of Hermeneutics," p.86.

119. Yosef Yerushalmi, *Zakhor* (Seattle: University of Washington Press, 1982), p.110.

120. Under this distinction, as Robert Wood and Steven Katz have pointed out, lies the Kantian dichotomy between the noumenal and phenomenal realms. Wood, *Ontology,* p.35. Katz, "Martin Buber's Epistemology: A Critical Appraisal," *Post-Holocaust Dialogues.*

121. Gadamer, *Truth and Method,* pp.302–03. For Ricoeur's critical comments on Gadamer's attempts to exclude explanatory methods from the interpretation of texts see Ricoeur, "The Hermeneutical Function of Distanciation," *Philosophy Today* 17 (Summer 1973), 129–30. In chapter 4 we will review the important criticism of Jürgen Habermas, who maintains that certain texts are "systematically distorted" by ideologies and that they require critical explanatory theories, like those provided by Marx and Freud, if they are to be properly understood. Habermas, *Hermeneutik and Ideologiekritic* (Frankfurt: Suhrkamp, 1971). See also the debates between Habermas and Gadamer in *Continuum* 8 (1970), 77–96, 123–28.

122. I know of only one study that uses a methodological approach like the one Ricoeur suggests and that is the method Arthur Green employs in his *Tormented Master.* Green uses historical critical tools to establish social and historical context and he also

employs psychological theory to establish the psychobiographic context of Nahman's life and work. These explanatory methods are complemented by an attempt to understand the theological meaning of Nahman's life and work, not only for Nahman's contemporaries but for Jewish life today. We see Green's complex method employed on a Hasidic text in his interpretations of Nahman's famous tales. See Excursus II.

3. Buber's Biblical Hermeneutics

1. I am grateful to Gary Anderson of the University of Virginia for his helpful comments on an early draft of this chapter.

2. Gershom Scholem, "Martin Buber's Conception of Judaism," *On Jews and Judaism in Crisis* (New York: Schocken, 1976), p.165.

3. Nahum Glatzer, "Buber as an Interpreter of the Bible," *The Philosophy of Martin Buber*, p.366.

4. Benyamin Uffenheimer, "Buber and Modern Biblical Scholarship," H. Gordon and J. Bloch, eds., *Martin Buber: A Centenary Volume* (New York: KTAV, 1984), p. 163.

5. Michael Fishbane, "Introduction," in Martin Buber, *Moses* (Atlantic Highlands: Humanities Press, 1987), p.xv.

6. Martin Buber, "*Ich und Du*," *Werke* I, p.84.

7. Martin Buber, "Zu einer neuen Verdeutschung der Schrift," *Beilage*, to *Die fünf Bücher der Weisung* (Köln: Jakob Hegner, 1968 [1954]), p.2. This appendix to the 1954 and 1968 revised publication of the translation of the Pentateuch summarizes many of Buber's earlier essays on the translation from Martin Buber and Franz Rosenzweig, *Die Schrift und Ihre Verdeutschung* (Berlin: Schocken, 1936). Most of these essays are also found in Martin Buber, *Werke* II, (Heidelberg: Lambert Schneider, 1964), pp.847–71 and pp.1093–1187, and some in Buber, *Darkho shel Mikra* (Jerusalem: Mosad Bialik, 1964), pp.272–307, 344–59. All translations from this appendix are my own.

8. Harold Stahmer reports that, in a letter written to him by Buber, Buber specifically pointed to his biblical studies as a major source of his views on language. Harold Stahmer, "*Speak that I May See Thee*": *The Religious Significance of Language* (New York: Macmillan, 1968), p.192. This book is helpful for placing Buber's views on language in the context of the views of other German religious thinkers such as Hamann, Rosenstock-Huessy, Rosenzweig, and Ebner.

9. Everett Fox, "Technical Aspects of the Translation of Genesis of Martin Buber and Franz Rosenzweig." Dissertation, Brandeis University, 1975, p.6.

10. For a history of the translation and the procedures used to execute it see "Aus dem Anfängen unserer Schriftübertragung," in Martin Buber and Franz Rosenzweig, *Die Schrift*. Also Martin Buber, *Darkho shel Mikra*, pp.344ff.

11. Nahum Glatzer, *Franz Rosenzweig: His Life and Thought* (New York: Schocken, 1961), pp.359–60.

12. *Ibid.*, p.252.

13. *Ibid.*, p.253.

14. Buber, "Neue Verdeutschung," p.4.

15. *Ibid.*, p.6.

16. *Ibid.*

17. *Ibid.*, p.5.

18. *Ibid.*, p.9.

19. *Ibid.*

20. *Ibid.*, p.6.

21. Martin Buber, *Moses: The Revelation and the Covenant* [1945] (New York: Harper and Row, 1958), p.9.

22. Buber, "Neue Verdeutschung," p.13.

23. *Ibid.*

24. Benno Jacob and M. D. Cassutto used Buber's principle of *Leitworte* extensively in their commentaries on the Hebrew Bible and attempted to discredit the documentary hypothesis and trace out a unity throughout the text by using *Leitworte*.

25. Buber, "Neue Verdeutschung," p.8.
26. *Ibid.*
27. See Fox, "Technical Aspects," p.32, for traditional Jewish and modern scholarship that supports this view.
28. In an early publication on Jewish art Buber already was convinced that the voice and hearing were primary to biblical sensibility. "The Jew of antiquity is more of a 'hearing-man,' than a 'seeing-man.'" Martin Buber, *"Einleitung," Jüdische Künstler* (Berlin: Jüdischer Verlag, 1903), p.7.
29. Buber, *Werke* II, p.869.
30. Buber, "Neue Verdeutschung," p.8.
31. *Ibid.*, p.18; cf. Buber and Rosenzweig, *Die Schrift*, pp. 76–85. For a fine discussion of the colometric representation of lines and all the other translation techniques see Uffenheimer, "Buber and Biblical Scholarship," pp.168ff.
32. Buber, "Neue Verdeutschung," p.41.
33. *Ibid.*
34. Buber, *Werke* II, p.869.
35. Everett Fox, *In the Beginning* (New York: Schocken, 1983). Fox shows how the Buber-Rosenzweig translation of Genesis 1:1 is "akin to poetry" (p.xiv).
36. Buber, "Neue Verdeutschung," p.9.
37. *Ibid.*, p.19.
38. *Ibid.*, p.20.
39. Buber and Rosenzweig, *Die Schrift*, p.285.
40. Buber, "Neue Verdeutschung," p.20.
41. *Ibid.*, p.18.
42. *Ibid.*, p.20.
43. This translation was suggested to me by Maurice Friedman.
44. *Ibid.*, p.27. Cf. Buber and Rosenzweig, *Die Schrift*, pp.279–81.
45. Additional examples of the semantic importance of the direct translation method are found in the rendering of names and places. Cf. Everett Fox, *In the Beginning*, pp.xvff.
46. Buber, "Neue Verdeutschung," p.15, and *Werke* II, p.1131.
47. "Neue Verdeutschung," p.13. Buber refers to the final redactor of the Hebrew Bible as "the consciousness of unity which constructed the great halls of the Bible out of handed down structures and fragments." Rosenzweig refers to this redactor with the reverential term *Rabbenu, unser Lehrer*—our rabbi, our teacher, *op. cit.*, p.7.
48. *Ibid.*, p.18.
49. The translation is from Fox, *In The Beginning*. I have benefited from his analysis of the *Leitwort panim*, p.xiii. For other discussions of *Leitworte* see Uffenheimer, "Buber and Biblical Scholarship," pp.172–78, and Michael Fishbane, "Martin Buber as an Interpreter of the Bible," *Judaism*, 27:2 (Spring 1978), 184–95. Buber's German of Gen. 32:21–22 is:

> Denn er sprach zu sich:
> Bedecken will ich sein Antlitz
> mit der Spende, die vor meinem Antlitz geht,
> danach will ich sein Antlitz sehn,
> vielleicht hebt er mein Antlitz empor.
> Die Spende schritt seinem Antlitz voraus.

50. My italics. Here is the German of Genesis 33:10:

> Nimmer doch!
> möchte ich doch Gunst in deinen Augen gefunden haben,
> daß du meine Spende aus meiner Hand nehmest.
> Denn ich habe nun doch einmal dein Antlitz angesehn, wie man Gottheitsantlitz
> ansieht.
> und du warst mir gnädig.

51. The leading-word philology, however, is more like that rabbinic form of linguistic

analysis which Yitzchak Heinemann called "creative philology," than the formal philology of Schleiermacher. *Darkhei ha-Aggadah* (Jerusalem: Magnes, 1970), pp.4ff. By saying that Buber retrieves aspects of romantic hermeneutics I am suggesting that he recovers the first, grammatical, stage and not the second, psychological, stage, which his dialogical hermeneutics was meant to supersede.

52. Chapters of *Der Gesalbte* were published separately in 1938, 1950, and 1951. The work first appeared as a whole in *Werke* II (1964), pp.725–846, and in *Darkho shel Mikra* (1964), pp.164–272. For the full publication history see *Werke* II, p.1233.

53. Martin Buber, *Kingship of God* [1932], trans. R. Scheimann (New York: Harper and Row, 1967), p.67.

54. *Moses*, pp.15–16. Here, again, we are reminded of themes of Romanticism—returning to the "original nucleus of the saga," attempting to get back to the "original event of dialogue." To the extent that the I-Thou event of original disclosure and revelation remains determinative of Buber's biblical hermeneutics and theology Buber does remain "romantic." Yet this can also be said of Heidegger, Gadamer, and Ricoeur and their quest for the event of disclosure or manifestation of "Being" and "truth" in art and text. As David Tracy has said, "We are all heirs to this [romantic] movement insofar as we accord some primacy to truth as manifestation." David Tracy, *Plurality and Ambiguity* (San Francisco: Harper and Row, 1987), p.31.

55. Martin Buber, *The Prophetic Faith* [1942], trans. C. Witten-Davies (New York: Harper and Row, 1960), p.88.

56. Buber, *Kingship of God,* p.15.

57. *Ibid.,* p.17.

58. *Ibid.* Although Buber was often critical of the documentary hypothesis, he regarded it as a given of modern biblical interpretation. However, he believed that the interpreter had to go beyond the fragmentation of the Bible which the documentary hypothesis caused and seek the hints of unity throughout a section or book of the Bible. See Martin Buber, "Herut" [1919], *On Judaism,* ed. N. Glatzer (New York: Schocken, 1972), p.172, and Buber, "Abraham the Seer" [1939], *On the Bible,* ed. N. Glatzer (New York: Schocken, 1982), p.25.

59. Buber, *The Prophetic Faith,* p.6.

60. *Ibid.,* pp.6–7.

61. Buber, *Moses,* p.8.

62. *Ibid.*

63. Nicht ich will über euch walten,
    nicht mein Sohn soll über euch walten

64. Was taugt euch besser,
    daß über euch siebzig Männer walten, alle Söhne Jerubbaals,
    oder daß ein *einziger* Mann über euch walte?

65. Buber, *Kingship of God,* ch.3.

66. Edward Greenstein, "Biblical Narratology," *Prooftexts* 1:2 (May 1981), p.202.

67. Fishbane, "Martin Buber as an Interpreter of the Bible," pp.184–95, and "Introduction" to *Moses.* See also *Garments of Torah* (Bloomington: Indiana University Press, 1989).

68. Harold Bloom, "Introduction" to Buber, *On the Bible.*

69. Meir Sternberg, *The Poetics of Biblical Narrative* (Bloomington: Indiana University Press, 1987), p.13.

70. Robert Grant and David Tracy, *A Short History of the Interpretation of the Bible* (Philadelphia: Fortress Press, 1984), p.154.

71. Buber, "Neue Verdeutschung," p.20.

72. *Ibid.,* p.2.

73. Gadamer, *Truth and Method,* p.274.

74. Buber, *The Prophetic Faith,* p.205.

75. *Ibid.,* p.103.

76. Buber, "Neue Verdeutschung," p.7.
77. *Ibid.,* p.8.
78. *Ibid.,* p.7.
79. *Ibid.,* p.15.
80. *Ibid.,* p.7.
81. "Biblical Humanism" [1933], in Buber, *On the Bible.*
82. *Ibid.,* p.215.
83. Martin Buber, "Dialogue Between Heaven and Earth" [1951], *On Judaism,* p.221. Buber refers to this direct dialogue only very briefly in the third part of *I and Thou.* Most of *I and Thou* is concerned with more mediated forms of dialogue through which the direct dialogue is only glimpsed.
84. Buber, *The Prophetic Faith,* p.2.
85. *Ibid.,* p.164.
86. For another presentation of the power and meaning of the spoken word of God and of persons which is quite Buberian in spirit see Walter Ong, *The Presence of the Word* (New Haven: Yale University Press, 1967).
87. Buber, *The Prophetic Faith,* p.164.
88. Jer. 23:29 as quoted in Buber, *ibid.,* p.170.
89. *Ibid.,* p.177.
90. Buber, "Dialogue Between Heaven and Earth," p.221.
91. Buber, *The Prophetic Faith,* p.164.
92. *Ibid.,* p.58.
93. An anonymous referee of this book has asked whether Buber really could think that God and humanity "speak" to each other in human language. Assuming that they could not, the referee refers me to Julian Jaynes, *The Origin of Consciousness in the Breakdown of the Bicameral Mind* (Boston: Houghton Mifflin, 1976). Here Jaynes suggests that humans who hear the voice of God are hallucinating. They "lack an internal mind-space to reflect upon" and "obeyed these hallucinated voices because [they] could not 'see' what to do by [themselves]" (p.75). This psychological explanation for the dialogue between God and human persons, however, would be totally unacceptable to Buber. The God of the Bible is not part of human consciousness but absolutely other. The dialogue between humans and this God must take the shape of human language, at some points, if humans are to grasp the message that God is relating to them. Also, if humans could not speak to God in their language then the act of prayer would be meaningless. See chapter 6 note 79 for my discussion of Buber's response to C. G. Jung's psychological treatment of God.
94. *Ibid.,* p.170.
95. *Ibid.,* pp.164–65.
96. Buber's favorite example of this is the Decalogue. He states that the "soul of the Decalogue, is to be found in the word 'Thou.' " Buber avers that to properly receive the message of the Decalogue one must feel as if he or she is actually addressed. "Only those persons really grasp the Decalogue who literally feel it as having been addressed to them" (Buber, *Moses,* p.130). The Ten Commandments "were uttered by an *I* and addressed to a *Thou.*" Buber, "What Are We to Do about the Ten Commandments?" [1929], *On the Bible,* p.118.
97. Buber, *The Prophetic Faith,* p.165.
98. Buber, "Dialogue Between Heaven and Earth," p.215.
99. Buber, "Biblical Humanism," p.213.
100. *Ibid.,* pp.214–15.
101. For Buber God certainly does not speak only in Hebrew (see "Biblical Humanism," p.213). Buber's general humanism would prohibit him from making that exclusive a statement. However, I would note that Buber's article "Biblical Humanism" was altered and published in Hebrew with the title "Hebrew Humanism" [1941], not only to address issues of language in the Bible but also to arouse interest in the Hebrew

language and build support for Zionist attempts to revive Hebrew as a spoken language and bring about a Jewish cultural and spiritual "Renaissance" in Palestine.

102. Buber, *Moses*, p.139.
103. *Ibid.,* p.140.
104. Buber, "The Man of Today," p.4.
105. Buber, "Biblical Humanism," p.213.
106. *Ibid.*
107. Buber, *The Prophetic Faith,* p.169.
108. Buber, "Biblical Humanism," p.213.
109. Buber, "Dialogue Between Heaven and Earth," p.216.
110. Buber, "Biblical Humanism," p.215.
111. *Ibid.*
112. *Ibid.,* p.214.
113. *Ibid.*
114. *Ibid.,* p.215.
115. *Ibid.*
116. Gadamer seems to disagree with Buber's assessment of the Platonic dialogues. Gadamer sees not a formal and worked-over series of dialogues, but a "discussion" which contains the "live play of risking assertions, of taking back what we have said, of assuming and rejecting, all the while proceeding on the way to reaching an understanding." Gadamer, *Dialogue and Dialectic: Eight Hermeneutical Studies of Plato* (New Haven: Yale University Press, 1980), p.5. Still, one could question whether there really is the risk of genuine dialogue when Socrates always seems to be in control of the dialogues and able to lead his partners to his (brilliant) conclusions.
117. Buber, "Biblical Humanism," p.214.
118. *Ibid.,* p.215.
119. *Ibid.*
120. In *Truth and Method* (pp.10–19) Gadamer endeavors to show that the concept of *Bildung* was of crucial importance to humanism and the "human sciences" from Goethe to Hegel. Gadamer tells us that with Hegel, *Bildung* "requires the sacrifice of particularity for the sake of the universal" (p.13). Here, we see how far we have gone from biblical sensibility where the particular is never sacrificed for the universal but is exalted as the route to the universal.
121. Buber, "Biblical Humanism," p.216.
122. *Ibid.,* p.216.

4. Constructing a Buberian Hermeneutic Theory

1. Although Buber studied linguistics in his university days he does not appear to have made the study of linguistics a regular part of his continuing intellectual diet. "The Word That Is Spoken" makes references to Wilhelm von Humboldt, J. G. Hamann, and Edward Sapir but not to Saussure and other linguists. Von Humboldt did have a notion of linguistic diversity but he finally developed an individualistic basis for language and therefore could not have been much help to Buber in his attempt to develop a notion of language based on human dialogue. Hamann and Sapir, with their more socially oriented views of language, were obviously more help. Unfortunately, at the time of the writing of "The Word That Is Spoken," Buber appears to have been unaware of the work of the one modern figure in linguistics with whom he has most in common, Mikhail Bakhtin.

2. Martin Buber, "Replies to My Critics," *The Philosophy of Martin Buber,* p.696.

3. Martin Buber, *"Das Wort, das gesprochen wird," Werke* I, "The Word That Is Spoken," trans. M. Friedman, *The Knowledge of Man,* p.115. I use the Friedman translation often in this chapter and am very grateful to him for this translation.

4. *Ibid.,* p.117.

5. Martin Heidegger, *Poetry, Language, Thought,* trans. A. Hofstadter (San Francisco: Harper and Row, 1971), p.190. Could it be that it was Heidegger's failure to

connect language to the concrete human and historical situation and to the word that is spoken from person to person that allowed him to be taken over by Nazism and the perverse use of language that was common to it?

6. Buber, "The Word," p.117.

7. Buber, "Biblical Humanism," p.215.

8. Jacques Derrida, *L'Écriture et la différence* (Paris: Seuil, 1967).

9. I am grateful to Nathan Scott, Jr., for his discussion of Bakhtin in "The House of Intellect in an Age of Carnival: Some Hermeneutical Reflections," *Journal of The American Academy of Religion,* 55,1. I also benefited from the fine reviews of Bakhtin's work by Giles Gunn in *The Culture of Criticism and the Criticism of Culture* (New York: Oxford, 1987), ch. 6.; Allon White, "Bakhtin, Sociolinguistics and Deconstruction," in F. Gloversmith, ed., *The Theory of Reading* (Totowa, NJ: Barnes and Noble, 1984); Katerina Clark and Michael Holquist, *Mikhail Bakhtin* (Cambridge: Harvard University Press, 1984); and Tzvetan Todorov, *Mikhail Bakhtin: The Dialogical Principle,* trans. W. Godzich (Minneapolis: University of Minnesota Press, 1984). This latter book includes English translations of a number of Russian texts not otherwise available and I quote from some of these translations.

10. As quoted in Joseph Frank, "The Voices of Mikhail Bakhtin," *New York Review of Books,* XXXIII, No. 16 (Oct. 23, 1986), p.56,n.2. Frank quotes these remarks of Bakhtin from Mariya Kaganskaya, "Shutovskoi Khorovod," *Sintaksis,* 12 (1984), p.141. Bakhtin does not refer to Buber very much in his writings, but he cites the antisemitism of some of his friends as one reason he was reluctant to speak more about Buber.

11. Mikhail Bakhtin, *The Dialogic Imagination,* ed. M. Holquist, trans. C. Emerson and M. Holquist (Austin: University of Texas Press, 1981), p.412.

12. *Ibid.,* p.293. For a theory of language and interpretation that, like Bakhtin's and Buber's, locates the source of writing in speech and stresses the referential capacities of language see Paul Ricoeur, *Interpretation Theory,* chs. 1,2,4.

13. Maurice Friedman has informed me that Buber would have to have been aware of the work of Bakhtin when he read and commented on the 1963 edition of Friedman's *Problematic Rebel.* In this book Friedman uses Bakhtin in his discussion of Dostoevsky.

14. In her recent article on Buber and Bakhtin, Nina Perlina cites a number of recent publications by and on Bakhtin to argue that "Bakhtin was familiar with the early writings of Buber including *Reden über das Judentum,* 1911–23; *Daniel* 1913; and *Ich und Du,* 1923." Perlina, "Mikhail Bakhtin and Martin Buber: Problems of Dialogic Imagination," *Studies in Twentieth Century Literature,* 9:1 (Fall 1984), p.26n.4. Perlina's article came to my attention after I wrote this chapter. Our two different analyses support each other. Each uses different textual warrants to illustrate the striking similarities between Buber and Bakhtin.

15. On the Bakhtin circle of intellectuals and their "Kantian Seminars" held in the cities of Nevel and Vitebsk see Katerina Clark and Michael Holquist, *Mikhail Bakhtin* (Cambridge: Harvard University Press, 1984), ch.2. Clark and Holquist tell us that Bakhtin's early notebooks of the 1920s were "highly colored by the characteristic topics and terms of the Marburg School of neo-Kantianism" (p.54) and that one of Bakhtin's most important intellectual conversation partners in his early years was the Jewish disciple of Hermann Cohen, Matvei Kagan (pp.41ff.).

16. *Ibid.,* p.128. Clark and Holquist mention three different religious groups in the 1920s that Bakhtin was associated with: "The scholarly Brotherhood of Saint Sophia, the public and eclectic Volfila and the more private Voskresenie" (p.130). Bakhtin adhered to a liberal and ecumenical philosophy of religion but was also attracted to the deep spirituality of the devout Russian Orthodox Brotherhood of Saint Seraphim. In fact, one of the charges that brought his arrest in January 1929 was that he was a member of this order. Clark and Holquist tell us that in the 1930s Bakhtin moved away from religion toward "secular and sociological" concerns (p.131). They claim that this movement was not motivated by Soviet repression of religion but by Bakhtin's own developing "anti-

metaphysical and anti-idealist standpoint" *(ibid.)*. We can see Bakhtin's concern for a spontaneous, nonrational, quasi-religious principle in his later notion of the "carnival" in literature and culture. See Bakhtin, *Rabelais and His World* (Cambridge: MIT Press, 1968).

17. Buber, *"Gemeinschaft," Worte an die Zeit*, II (München: Drieländerverlag, 1919). See Mendes-Flohr, *From Mysticism to Dialogue*, chs.2 and 5, for an extended discussion of Buber's understanding of *gemeinschaft* and its connections to sociology and to religion.

18. Clark and Holquist, *Mikhail Bakhtin*, p.9.

19. Bakhtin's dialogical notion of self, his view of self as "defined by the pattern of its responses to the world" *(ibid.,* p.54), is shown over and over again in the recently published and translated collection of his first works: *Art and Answerability*, ed. M. Holquist and trans. V. Liapunov (Austin: University of Texas Press, 1990). For Buber's notion of the "dialogical self" see my discussion in chapter 6.

20. Since Buber did not live in the USSR, the issue of socialist cultural unanimity and repression of dissent was not as crucial an issue for him as it was for Bakhtin. Yet Buber did speak out against centralized state socialism and for the small decentralized socialist communities represented by the early kibbutz communities of Israel. See Buber, *Paths in Utopia*.

21. Mikhail Bakhtin, *Problems of Dostoevsky's Poetics*, trans. C. Emerson (Minneapolis: University of Minnesota Press, 1984), p.64.

22. *Ibid.,* p.59.

23. Perlina seems to believe that Buber and Bakhtin are, ultimately, not far off "in the area of ontology" and on the issue of "the dialogue between man and God" (p.25). Perlina argues that the two complement each other quite nicely in these areas: "Bakhtin's discourse-utterance theory provides the linguistic apparatus for the existentialist . . . philosophy of Martin Buber. Reading Bakhtin for Buber results in bringing more structure and regulation into the latter's emotional and descriptive writings" *(ibid.)*.

24. Buber, "The Word," p.110.

25. *Ibid.*

26. *Ibid.*

27. Bakhtin, *The Dialogic Imagination*, pp.262–63. In his sensitivities to the social and political dimensions and the relations of power and class inherent in the different languages used by societies Bakhtin goes well beyond Buber and beyond many modern linguists. See Allon White, "Bakhtin, Sociolinguistics and Deconstruction." White believes that Bakhtin's sociolinguistics can be used to critique the asocial and atemporal aspect of deconstructive linguistics.

28. Buber, "The Word," p.111.

29. *Ibid.* For another discussion of Buber's notion of the power of the spoken word see Maurice Friedman, *Buber: Life and Work: Early Years*, pp.315f.

30. Buber, "The Word," p.111.

31. *Ibid.,* p.112.

32. Bakhtin, *The Dialogic Imagination*, p.280.

33. Buber, "The Word," p.113.

34. *Ibid.,* p.115.

35. Bakhtin, *The Dialogic Imagination*, p.279.

36. *Ibid.,* p.279.

37. *Ibid.,* p.410.

38. *Ibid.,* p.277.

39. *Ibid.,* p.270.

40. Buber, "The Word," p.115.

41. *Ibid.,* p.115. In Buber's, "Autobiographical Fragments," he includes a "Report on a Talk" which he had with the Neo-Kantian philosopher Paul Natorp about the old and worn word "God." Natorp asks Buber:

"How can you bring yourself to say 'God' time after time?. . . . What word of human speech is so misued, so defiled, so desecrated as this?"

And Buber answers:

"Yes, . . . it is the most heavy-laden of human words. None has become so soiled, so mutilated. Just for this reason I may not abandon it. Generations of men have laid the burden of their anxious lives upon this word and weighed it to the ground; it lies in the dust and bears their whole burden. . . . Where might I find a word like it to describe the highest! . . . We cannot cleanse the word 'God' and we cannot make it whole; but, defiled and mutilated as it is, we can raise it from the ground and set it over an hour of great care," (pp.30–31)

42. Bakhtin, "From the Prehistory of the Novelistic Discourse," in *The Dialogic Imagination.*

43. Buber, "The Word," p.117.

44. *Ibid.,* p.116.

45. Bakhtin, "Discourse in Life and Discourse in Poetry," quoted in Todorov, *The Dialogical Principle,* p.41. Italics in original quotation.

46. Buber, *"Der Mensch und sein Gebild"* (Heidelberg: Lambert Schneider, 1955); also in *Werke* I, 1962. Translated as "Man and His Image-Work," *The Knowledge of Man.*

47. Buber, "Man and His Image-Work," pp.160–61.

48. Buber, "The Word," p.111.

49. Buber, *The Prophetic Faith,* pp.88ff.

50. Buber, "The Word," p.120.

51. *Ibid.,* p.118. In "Man and His Image-Work," Buber asserts that because poetry "is not obedient to anything other than language" (p.162), it ranks among the highest forms of art. Here we can document Buber's movement from his emphasis on the plastic arts in *I and Thou* to the written arts and to a deepened appreciation for language as positive language in his late writings.

52. We must be clear that, unlike Buber, Bakhtin did not find the Bible to be a rich repository of human dialogue. Bakhtin included biblical literature under his category of the epic, which is far too formalized, cut off from the present, and "monochronic" to relate the living speech of the present moment of dialogue. Bakhtin, *The Dialogic Imagination,* pp.14–16.

53. *Ibid.,* pp.278–79.

54. *Ibid.,* p.410. Bakhtin also believes that the text produced is itself in dialogical, or, to use the word that Julia Kristeva has made famous, "intertextual," relation with the author's previous texts and other texts of its genre. See Todorov, *The Dialogical Principle,* ch. 5. For more on Bakhtin's views on artistic creativity see Todorov pp.99f.

55. Buber, "The Word," p.118.

56. *Ibid.,* p.111.

57. *Ibid.,* p.118.

58. As translated by Todorov, *The Dialogical Principle,* p.99.

59. Buber, "Autobiographical Fragments," p.35.

60. Quoted in Todorov, *The Dialogical Principle,* p.109.

61. *Ibid.,* p.97.

62. *Ibid.,* p.104.

63. *Ibid.,* p.110.

64. Buber, *Dem Gemeinschaftlichen folgen, Die Neue Rundschau* LXVII/4 (Oct. 1956), 582–600. Also in *Werke* I. Translated as "What Is Common to All," *The Knowledge of Man,* p.104.

65. *Ibid.,* p.106.

66. *Ibid.,* p.104.

67. In the process of dialogue on the meaning of an interpretation Buber suggests that the human community, the human "world-shape," or the human "cosmos," is formed and reformed. *Ibid.,* pp.98ff.

68. Bamidbar [Numbers] Rabbah, 13:15. Cf. "Is not My word like . . . a hammer that

breaks the rock into pieces? [Jer. 23:29] As the hammer splits the rock into many splinters, so will a scriptural verse yield many meanings." Sanhedrin 34A.

David Stern cautions that recent attempts to incorporate Rabbinic midrash into contemporary literary theory are fraught with the danger of misrepresenting the historical context and religious aims of Rabbinic midrash. In his "Midrash and Indeterminacy," *Critical Inquiry,* 15:1 (Autumn 1988), Stern takes on the attempt to correlate the Rabbinic technique of multiple interpretation with the deconstructive notion of the "indeterminacy" of meaning in a text (cf. Gerald Graff, "Determinacy/Indeterminacy," in *Critical Terms,* ed. Lentricchia). Stern states in the beginning of his essay, "I hope to show [that] multiple interpretation in midrash bears little connection to the [contemporary literary] notion of indeterminacy" (p.135). Although I am not convinced that there are not a lot of fruitful points of intersection between Rabbinic midrash and contemporary deconstructive theories of text and interpretation I am definitely convinced that there are very fruitful points of intersection between the dialogic hermeneutics of Bakhtin and Buber and Rabbinic midrash. The advantage of dialogic hermeneutics over deconstruction is found in the ability of the former to deal with issues of referentiality and meaning. Certainly Buber, like the Rabbis, wants to find ways of talking about the extent to which texts point to and give meaning to our human temporal condition, and Buber is also concerned with developing an interpretative approach that would "recapture the fullness of divine presence" (Stern, p.161) in a text. For an attempt to make the strongest connections between Rabbinic midrash and deconstructive theories see Susan Handelman, *The Slayers of Moses* (New York: SUNY Press, 1982). For a view somewhere between that of Handelman and Stern see Betty Roitman, "Sacred Language and Open Text," *Midrash and Literature,* ed. G. Hartman and S. Budick (New Haven: Yale University Press, 1986).

69. Bakhtin, "Concerning Methodology in the Human Sciences," as quoted in Todorov, *The Dialogical Principle,* p.110.

70. Buber, "The Demonic Book," *A Believing Humanism,* p.46.

71. Buber, "Advice to Frequenters of Libraries," *Books for Your Vacation,* Branch Library Book News, The New York Public Library, XXI/5, v.1944, pp.81–82.

72. *Ibid.,* p.81.

73. *Ibid.*

74. David Tracy, *The Analogical Imagination,* ch.3.

75. Buber, "Advice," p.81.

76. Buber, *I and Thou,* trans. Kaufmann, p.54.

77. Buber, "Distance and Relation," *The Knowledge of Man,* p.71.

78. Buber, "Elements of the Interhuman," *The Knowledge of Man,* p.76.

79. Hans-Georg Gadamer, "On the Scope and Function of Hermeneutical Reflection," *Continuum,* 8:1 (Spring 1970), p.85.

80. Jürgen Habermas, "On Systematically Distorted Communication," *Inquiry,* 13:3 (Autumn 1970), 205–19; "Summation and Response," *Continuum* 8:1 (Spring 1970), p.118. See also Habermas, "A Review of Gadamer's *Truth and Method,*" *Understanding and Social Inquiry,* ed. F. Dallmayr and T. McCarthy (Notre Dame: University of Notre Dame Press, 1977); Habermas, *Knowledge and Human Interests,* trans. J. Shapiro (Boston: Beacon, 1970), pp.283ff. and Habermas, *Theory and Practice,* trans. J. Viertel (Boston: Beacon, 1975), pp.30–31.

81. Habermas, "Summation and Response," p.121. See also "Introductory Remarks for a Theory of Communicative Competence," *Inquiry,* 13:4 (Winter 1970), 360–76 and *Communication and the Evolution of Society,* trans. T. McCarthy (Boston: Beacon, 1979). For a good secondary source see Thomas McCarthy, "Rationality and Relativism: Habermas's 'Over-coming' of Hermeneutics," in *Habermas: Critical Debates,* ed. D. Held and J. Thompson (Cambridge: MIT Press, 1982). Gadamer believes that bringing prejudgments to consciousness does not do away with them, for they are part of what it means to live in a temporally conditioned world. Bringing prejudgments to conscious-

ness merely helps us to do away with some of the more gross and biased prejudgments. Here, Gadamer is very different from Habermas, who believes that critical theories and systematic attention to the conditions of ideal communication can open a sphere of objectivity in which cultural, historical, and linguistic conditioning factors are all but eradicated.

82. Many have argued that Buber interpreted all Jewish texts with an anti-*halakhic* ideology, a pregiven, systematic aversion to the religious power and spiritual efficacy of Jewish law. More than any other critique it is this criticism of a fundamental conviction of Buber's—that Judaism, which for centuries had lived and survived on *halakhah*, no longer needed to regard *halakhah* as the central path of modern Jewish religious expression—that haunts Buber's interpretations of Jewish texts. Buber certainly did not hide his prejudgments or prejudices regarding Jewish law, but it remains a question whether or not he was aware of the distorting character of these prejudgments and whether they functioned, ideologically, to systematically distort his interpretations of Jewish texts.

83. Buber, "Pfade in Utopia," *Werke* I, trans. R. F. C. Hull, *Paths in Utopia* (Boston: Beacon, 1958).

84. Buber, *I and Thou,* part II.

85. Buber, "Advice," p.81.

86. For examples of deconstruction as literary criticism see Harold Bloom, et al., *Deconstruction and Criticism* (New York: Seabury, 1979). For application of deconstruction to theology see Thomas Altizer, et al., *Deconstruction and Theology* (New York: Crossroad, 1982).

87. David Tracy speaks of the capacity of explanation to "challenge, correct, refine, complicate and confront" a reader's original understanding of a text. Tracy includes, in the repertoire of explanatory methods available to the interpreter, not only historical criticism but semiotic and deconstructionist methods. Tracy, *The Analogical Imagination,* p. 115. By allotting deconstruction a role in the middle, "explanatory," stage of interpretation, Tracy believes that the interpreter can take advantage of the deep sensitivity to language and rhetoric and the playful ability of deconstruction to unravel a text, to open new possibilities of reading a text, at the same time that the deconstructive ideology against meaning and reference can be bypassed. This is done by moving to a final "post-explanatory," "post-deconstructive," stage of interpretation, when the interpreter turns from semiotic and deconstructive analyses to wager an interpretation of the meaning of the text and of its applicability to life. A similar move is suggested by Ricoeur's tripartite "understanding, explanation, understanding" model for interpretation (Ricoeur, "Explanation and Understanding," p.165) and by Wayne Booth's theory of "critical understanding." Booth avers that the "violations" which deconstruction exercises on texts can be "vitalizing," especially when deconstruction is combined with other, more traditional reference-oriented methods of interpretation. *Critical Understanding: The Powers and Limits of Pluralism* (Chicago: University of Chicago Press, 1979), pp.220–23, 244–59.

88. Buber, "Distance and Relation," p.62.

89. Tracy, in Robert Grant and David Tracy, *A Short History of the Interpretation of the Bible,* p.154.

90. Paul Ricoeur, "Ethics and Culture," *Philosophy Today* 17:2/4 (Summer 1973), p.157.

91. Paul Ricoeur, "The Hermeneutical Function of Distanciation," *Philosophy Today,* 17:2/4 (Summer 1973), p.130.

92. *Ibid.,* p.134.

93. Buber, "Advice," p.81.

94. Buber, "Image-Work," p.149.

95. Buber, "The Word," p.118. Buber does also make statements about the importance of the author's intention (e.g., "Advice," p.82) that contradict the statements

quoted here. But in this constructive attempt to map out a general dialogical hermeneutic method I am stressing the post-romantic side of Buber's writings.

96. Mikhail Bakhtin, *Problems of Dostoevsky's Poetics*, p.58.

97. Emmanuel Levinas, *Collected Philosophical Papers*, trans. A. Lingis (Dordrecht: Martinus Nijhoff, 1987), p.55. See also Levinas, *Totality and Infinity*, trans. A. Lingis (Pittsburgh: Duquesne University Press, 1979), pp.81f.

98. Levinas, "La trace de l'autre," *En découvrant l'existence avec Husserl et Heidegger* (Paris, Vrin, 1967).

99. Gadamer, *Truth and Method*, pp.274ff.

100. Ricoeur, "The Hermeneutical Function of Distanciation," p.141.

101. Buber, "Biblical Humanism," p.213.

102. Buber, "Advice," p.82.

103. *Ibid.*

104. Nathan Scott, Jr., "The House of Intellect," p.13.

105. One could also argue that Richard Rorty, who made Michael Oakeshott's phrase "the conversation of mankind" the leitmotif of contemporary hermeneutics, could also be included in the "dialogical group" (Rorty, *The Mirror of Nature*, ch.8:5). Rorty's most recent work probably places him too close to the deconstructionists for Nathan Scott, however.

106. Habermas, "Summation and Response," p.121.

107. Although dialogical hermeneutics requires that the wide variety of methods and tools that are available to contemporary critics be employed, a haphazard eclecticism is plainly discouraged. At the same time that Ricoeur has argued for the need for both methods of understanding and explanation he always demands that the different methods be kept distinct. In Ricoeur's hermeneutic model, explanation represents a second "moment" in the interpretative process which is preceded by an initial precritical attempt at understanding and which is followed by a "post-critical moment" ("Ethics and Culture," p.157) of understanding sometimes called the moment of second naïveté. Wayne Booth, a proponent of what he calls a hermeneutics of "critical dialogue" or "critical understanding," has argued for "the possibility of a full embrace of more than one critical method without reducing pluralities to one (a supreme monism), . . . or cancelling them out into zero [eclecticism]" (*Critical Understanding*, p.25).

108. Scott, "The House of Intellect," p.14.

109. *Ibid.*, p.15.

110. Scott finds the deconstructionist method to be antithetical to dialogue. "The very nature of the deconstructionist project militates against its according equality to any other cultural project: it is simply a matter of fundamental method." Ibid., p.8. Scott argues that the deconstructionist "procedure would cut the vital nerve of dialogical possibility itself at the very outset." *Ibid.*, p.9. For an extended critique of deconstructionism see, also, Nathan Scott, Jr., "The New Trahison des Clercs: Reflections on the Present Crisis in Humanistic Studies," *The Virginia Quarterly Review*, 62:3 (Summer 1986), pp.402–22.

111. Scott, "The House of Intellect," p.16.

112. *Ibid.*

113. David Tracy, *Plurality and Ambiguity: Hermeneutics, Hope, Religion*, (San Francisco: Harper and Row, 1987), pp. 22–23. For the particular relevance of Tracy's notion of truth for modern theology see *The Analogical Imagination*, p.58 and p.86n.34.

114. Gadamer, "Truth and Method," p.447.

115. Gadamer, "On the Scope and Function of Hermeneutics," p.81.

116. Tracy, *Plurality and Ambiguity*, p.25.

117. *Ibid.*, p.23.

118. *Ibid.*, p.25.

119. Wayne Booth, *Critical Understanding*, pp.219ff.

120. *Ibid.*, p.226.

121. *Ibid.*, p.237.

122. I have learned a great deal from and am indebted to David Tracy for his four hermeneutical steps as he outlines them in *The Analogical Imagination*, pp.118ff. and p.152. My Buberian hermeneutic differs from Tracy's in that it is somewhat less involved than Tracy's is in establishing the "truth" of a particular interpretation and more focused on allowing for a plurality of interpretations.

5. Narrative and the Philosophy of I and Thou

1. For example, the first chapter of *Werke* I, "Daniel," is a narrative told in dialogue form. The second chapter, *Ich und Du,* employs narrative expression at a number of crucial points. Part 3 contains an important anecdote about Buber's relation to his house cat to illustrate his point that "an animal's eyes have the power to speak a great language" (p. 96 Smith trans.). And the postscript to *I and Thou* includes a tale about Buber's encounter with a Doric pillar to illustrate the I-Thou encounter with art (pp. 128–29 Smith trans.). I will show below how important narratives are to *"Zwiesprache,"* the third article in *Werke* I. And one can find narratives throughout the rest of the collection of philosophical essays in *Werke* I.

2. Martin Buber, "Dialogue," *Between Man and Man*, trans. R.G. Smith (New York: Macmillan, 1965), p.xi.

3. *Ibid.*, p.5.

4. *Ibid.*, p.3.

5. *Ibid.*

6. *Ibid.*, pp.3–4.

7. *Ibid.*, p.4.

8. *Ibid.*

9. *Ibid.*

10. *Ibid.*

11. *Ibid.*, p.5.

12. *Ibid.*

13. *Ibid.*, p.6.

14. *Ibid.*

15. *Ibid.*, p.23.

16. *Ibid.*

17. Here is the German:

Wenn ich über die mächtige, zuweilen verwunderlich glattgekämmte, zu andern Malen ebenso erstaunlich wilde Mähne strich und das Lebendige unter meiner Hand leben spürte, was es, als grenzte mir an die Haut das Element der Vitalität selber, etwas, das nicht ich, gar nicht ich war, gar nicht ichvertraut, eben handgreiflich das Andere, nicht ein anderes bloβ, wirklich das Andere selber, und mich doch heranlieβ, sich mir anvertraute, sich elementar mit mir auf Du und Du stellte. Der Schimmel hob, auch wenn ich nicht damit begonnen hatte ihm Hafer in die Krippe zu schütten, sehr gelind den maβigen Kopf, an dem sich die Ohren noch besonders regten, dann schnob er leise, wie ein Verschworner seinem Mitverschwornen ein nur diesem vernehmbar werden sollendes Signal gibt, und ich war bestätigt. (*Werke* I, p.196)

18. "Dialogue," p. 23.

19. *Ibid.*, p.xiii.

20. Roland Barthes has given clear expression to the ubiquity of narrative in human culture.

Narrative is present in myth, legend, fable, tale, novella, epic, history, tragedy, drama, comedy, mime, painting (think of Carpaccio's *Saint Ursula*), stained glass windows, cinema, comics, news item, conversation. Moreover, under this almost infinite variety of forms, narrative is present in every age, in every place, in every society; it begins with the very history of mankind and there nowhere is nor has been a people without narrative. . . . Narrative is international, transhistorical, transcultural: it is simply there, like life itself.

"Introduction to the Structural Analysis of Narratives," *Image, Music, Text,* trans. Stephen Heath (New York: Hill and Wang, 1977), p.79.

21. Frank Kermode, *The Sense of an Ending* (Oxford: Oxford University Press, 1966), p.46.

22. *Ibid.,* p.45.

23. Kermode is particularly interested in the Christian Apocalyptic, which transforms the endings of all Hebrew narratives into middles and refashions their meaning by attaching the Christian ending.

The Bible . . . begins at the beginning ('In the beginning . . .') and ends with a vision of the end ('Even so, come, Lord Jesus'); the first book is Genesis, the last Apocalypse. Ideally, it is a wholly concordant structure, the end is in harmony with the beginning, the middle with beginning and end. The end, Apocalypse, is traditionally held to resume the whole structure. *(Ibid.,* p.6)

Unfortunately, Kermode does not comment on the negative repercussions for Judaism that went along with the hermeneutic move to transform the endings of Hebrew narratives into "middles" that are brought to their fulfillment in Christian Apocalypse. In this hermeneutic move lies the source of Christian doctrines of supersession beyond a Judaism that is incomplete or moribund.

24. *Ibid.,* p.39.

25. *Ibid.,* p.155.

26. Frank Kermode, *The Genesis of Secrecy* (Cambridge: Harvard University Press, 1979), p.24.

27. *Ibid.,* p.53.

28. *Ibid.,* p.3.

29. Michel Foucault, *Madness and Civilization,* trans. R. Howard (New York: Random, 1965), and *Power/Knowledge,* ed. C. Gordon (Brighton: Harvester Press, 1980). Hayden White, *The Tropics of Discourse* (Baltimore: Johns Hopkins University Press, 1978), and "The Value of Narrativity in the Representation of Reality," *Critical Inquiry* 7:1 (Autumn 1980), 5–27.

30. Here is the verse from Mark:

[When Jesus was arrested the disciples] all forsook him and fled. And a young man followed him, with nothing but a linen cloth about his body; and they seized him, but he left the linen cloth and ran away naked.

31. Kermode, *Genesis,* p.57.

32. To provide more support for his thesis on the opaque nature of narrative, Kermode makes use of an ancient interpretation of why it was that Jesus spoke in parables. This interpretation suggests that Jesus used the narrative parable form deliberately to lead his "enemies" [too often presented as the pharisees] astray. Jesus spoke in narrative form "to ensure that they would miss the point" (p.30). Jesus tells narratives not to "utter" the clear message of the end but to, as he himself says, "utter what has been hidden" (Matthew 13:34).

33. As quoted in *Genesis,* p.64.

34. *Ibid.,* p.40.

35. *Ibid.,* p.47.

36. *Ibid.,* p.47.

37. *Ibid.,* p.145.

38. *Time and Narrative,* Vols. 1 and 2, trans. Kathleen McLaughlin and David Pellauer (Chicago: University of Chicago Press, 1984–85); Vol. 3, trans. Kathleen Blamey and David Pellauer (Chicago: University of Chicago Press, 1988). French original, *Temps et Récit,* Vols. 1–3 (Paris: Editions de Seuil, 1983–85).

39. Because of the work of the nonnarrative historians, the assertion that history is a form of narrative cannot be taken as a given. To make this claim Ricoeur must evaluate the arguments of those historians who have attempted to undermine the import of narrative to history. Ricoeur undertakes this analysis in Part 2 of Volume 1 of *Time and Narrative*. His analysis begins with two radical challenges to the notion of the narrative quality of history. The first challenge is from the Annales School of economic and social history (founded in 1939 by Lucien Febvre and Marc Bloch) and the second challenge is from the Logical Positivist philosopher Carl Hempel.

Members of Annales challenge the importance of narrative to history by challenging the importance of single events and human agents. The Annales School is interested in social and economic conditions and structures that are detected over long time spans. The single temporal event whose story narrative relates is swallowed up in the "total social fact" (p.102). The other major attack on the role of narrative in history comes from Carl Hempel and the Logical Positivists, who have attempted to delineate the "scientific" character of history. In "The Function of General Laws in History" Hempel argues that laws function in history as they do in physics or any hard science. Historical events are "explained" by subsuming them under the laws of history as physical events are explained by subsuming them under the laws of physics.

With regard to Annales, Ricoeur argues that even the social history which the Annales School describes uses narrative elements such as plot, character, and event. Where Ricoeur finds a structure analogous to plot in Annales history is in its notion of a trend or cycle. A cycle includes a rise and fall with a crisis in between (p.264n.47). And in the notion of crisis and change, Ricoeur locates an analogy to event in plot. What takes the place of characters in social history are the major entities whose fate history follows: empire, civilization, society (p.200).

With regard to Hempel, Ricoeur argues that the historian is not primarily interested in establishing laws and subsuming events under regularities. Rather, the historian is interested in the uniqueness of an event. And it is primarily the narrative element in history, its ability to reveal the details of an historical event, that discloses historical uniqueness (p.124). Thus, through its variety of connections to the basic elements of narrative, Ricoeur argues that history cannot be severed from narrative.

40. Ricoeur, *Time and Narrative*, Vol.1, p.3.

41. Kermode is equivocal on the issue of reference in his later book, *The Genesis of Secrecy*. For though he allows that narratives may "mime the fortuities of real life" (p. 54), he also argues that modern interpreters are compelled to accept that sense and reference are divorced and that the text is "not referring to what is outside or beyond it" (p.122).

42. See Tzvetan Todorov, *Les Genres du Discourse* (Paris: Seuil, 1978). Gérard Genette, *Nouveau Discours du récit* (Paris: Seuil, 1983). Algirdas-Juilien Griemas, *On Meaning: Selected Writings in Semiotic Theory*, trans. Paul Perron and Frank Collins (Minneapolis: University of Minnesota Press, 1987).

43. Ricoeur, *Time and Narrative*, Vol.1, pp.77–78.

44. *Ibid.*, p.78. To avoid the naïve assumption that narrative can fully capture the reality to which it refers, Ricoeur comes to use the term "refiguration" rather than "reference" when speaking of the relation of narrative to the reality to which narrative points. See Ricoeur, *Time and Narrative*, Vol.3, p.100.

45. Ricoeur, *Time and Narrative*, Vol.1, p.34.

46. See the work of the Aristotelian School of literary criticism: Northrop Frye, Richard McKeon, Erich Auerback, Ronald Salmon Crane.

47. Ricoeur, *Time and Narrative*, Vol.1, p.54.

48. Ricoeur, "The Narrative Function," *Semeia*, 13 (1978), p.189.

49. *Ibid.*, p.194.

50. In *Time and Narrative*, Ricoeur follows Karl Heussi in arguing that the past is the

Gegenüber "to which historical knowledge tries to correspond in an appropriate manner" (Vol.3, p.143). Ricoeur argues that if history cannot truly represent the "reality of the past," history remains subject to that past.

Through documents and their critical examination of documents, historians are subject to what once was. They owe a debt to the past, a debt of recognition to the dead, that makes them insolvent debtors. (Vol.3, pp.142–43)

51. Ricoeur, "Narrative Function," p.198.

52. Ricoeur, *Time and Narrative,* Vol.2, p.101.

53. Ricoeur explains:

It is clear that discontinuous structure suits a time of dangers and adventures, that a more continuous, linear structure suits a *Bildungsroman* where themes of growth and metamorphosis predominate, whereas a jagged chronology, interrupted by jumps, anticipations, and flashbacks, in short, a deliberately multidimensional configuration, is better suited to view a time that has no possible overview, no overall internal cohesiveness. (*Time and Narrative,* Vol.2, p.81)

54. Ricoeur, *Time and Narrative,* Vol.3, p.188.

55. See the work of Elie Wiesel. Wiesel, through one of his characters in *The Testament,* has pointed to the ultimate similarity between history and fiction.

The work of the poet and the historian are identical. . . . Both illuminate the summit and proceed by the process of elimination, retaining only one word in ten, one event in a hundred. The difference between poetry and history? Let's say poetry is history's invisible dimension.

The Testament, trans. M. Wiesel (New York: Summit Books, 1981), p.59.

56. Augustine, *Confessions,* trans. R.S. Pine-Coffin (New York: Penguin, 1961), 14:17.

57. Ricoeur, *Time and Narrative,* Vol.3, p.12

58. This analysis is taken from Ricoeur's brief and succinct analysis of "within-time-ness" in "Narrative Time," *Critical Inquiry,* 7:1 (Autumn 1980), 169–91. For a more extended discussion see *Time and Narrative,* Vol.3, pp.82ff.

59. Ricoeur, "Narrative Time," p.173. Cf. *Time and Narrative,* Vol.1, p.63.

60. Ricoeur, "Narrative Time," p.175.

61. *Ibid.,* p.180.

62. *Ibid.,* p.180.

63. *Ibid.,* p.182. Ricoeur locates the process of repetition in the configurational aspect of plot. The configurational aspect of plot groups together and organizes events around a theme which is usually made explicit at the end of the plot.

64. Ricoeur, *Time and Narrative,* Vol.1, p.67.

65. *Ibid.,* pp.66–67.

66. Ricoeur, "Narrative Time," p.180. We can see the process of repetition working quite clearly in self-authored narratives, in autobiographies (*ibid.,* pp.186ff.) In autobiography, an individual constructs and repeats the events of the past to find out who he or she is and to retrieve the potentialities of his/her birth. Individuals seek the roots of their present moment in their past. An individual finds her present, her story's "end," in her beginning. The configuration of the autobiographical plot, the personal "theme" which is apprehended by the individual in constructing an autobiography, may be considered as the equivalent of Heidegger's notion of individual fate. Ricoeur suggests that we consider retellings of great societal stories—myths and histories—as "communal acts of repetition" (p.189) in which a sense of communal "destiny" (p.188), a sense of heritage and "tradition," is retrieved.

67. Ricoeur, *Time and Narrative,* Vol.3, p.76. Ricoeur is careful to point out that, for Heidegger, the deeper dimensions of historicality and repetition are only actualized by the heroic and truly "authentic" individual. In this sense these temporal dimensions are "existential" and not "existentiell." *Time and Narrative,* Vol.3, pp.65–66.

68. *Ibid.,* p.76.

69. *Ibid.*

70. Kermode, *Sense of an Ending,* p.7.
71. Ricoeur, *Time and Narrative,* Vol.3, p.83.
72. *Ibid.,* p.254.
73. *Ibid.,* p.241 (my emphasis).
74. In a discussion of what temporal dimension and what part of a narrative should take priority, the end or the middle, we cannot fail to note that the beginning also has its champions, most notably Edward Said, *Beginnings* (New York: Basic, 1975).
75. Ricoeur mentioned to me, in a conversation we had, that he thought that the notion of *peripeteia* could account for Buber's middle. However, as I try to show below, Buber's middles encompass more than what is included in the concept of *peripeteia.*
76. Ricoeur, *Time and Narrative,* Vol.1, p.43.
77. Kermode, *Sense of an Ending,* p.18.
78. *Ibid.,* p.53.
79. *I and Thou,* Smith trans., p.80.
80. Sokell did this in a series of lectures on Heidegger given at the University of Virginia in the Fall of 1986.
81. Kermode, *Sense of an Ending,* p.27.
82. In light of these discussions of favored temporal moments, it is interesting that Eliade has argued that the temporal orientation of "archaic" religious myth is toward the past and beginnings, toward the time of *illo tempore. The Myth of the Eternal Return,* trans. W. Trask (Princeton: Princeton University Press, 1971), ch.2. These perhaps all too simple schema that we are developing here suggest that "archaic" or primal religious narratives look to the past, Christianity toward the future, and Judaism toward the present.
83. Jacob Neusner, *Between Time and Eternity* (Encino CA: Dickenson, 1975), p.2. See Neusner's, more recent, *Scriptures of the Oral Torah* (New York: Harper, 1987). Here, he argues that if the Rabbis were first concerned with "sanctification in this world," that was not their sole concern; Rabbinic Judaism also came to concerns of the nature of "salvation in time to come" (p.10).
84. David Roskies points out that at the time of the establishment of the canon in 70 C.E. at Yavneh, the Rabbis "triumphed" and "most of the apocalyptic writings were excluded from the biblical canon." "Memory," *Contemporary Jewish Religious Thought,* p.582.
85. Buber and Scholem do have different ideas about the aims and goals of this neutralization. Both Buber and Scholem seem to agree that the neutralization occurred, at least partially, because of the failed messianism of Shabbati Zvi. But for Buber the goal of the neutralization was the sacralization of the human community, human acts, and everyday behaviors, i.e., the "hallowing of the everyday." Against this Scholem argues that the neutralization of messianism in early Hasidism resulted in a move of the Hasidim within themselves and beyond the everyday toward mystical contact with the divine. "The immediate goal of Hasidism . . . was no longer the redemption of the nation from exile and the redemption of all being. *That* would be messianism. . . . the goal, as formulated in the works of Rabbi Polnoye, is the mystical redemption of the individual here and now." Scholem, "The Neutralization of Messianism," *The Messianic Idea in Judaism* (New York: Schocken, 1971), p.195.
86. Kermode, *Sense of an Ending,* pp.82–89.
87. Ted Estess, "The Inenarrable Contraption," *Journal of the American Academy of Religion,* 42 (Sept. 1974), 419.
88. *Ibid.,* p.424.
89. *Ibid.,* p.421.
90. In his essay "New Novel New Man," Robbe-Grillet tells us that "Before the work of art, there is nothing, no certainty, no thesis, no message." *For a New Novel,* trans. R. Howard (New York: Grove, 1965), p.141.
91. Kermode, *Sense of an Ending,* p.20.

92. *Ibid.,* p.140.

93. Kermode, *Genesis,* p.16.

94. I have adapted this phrase from Wayne Booth, *The Rhetorics of Fiction* (Chicago: University of Chicago Press, 1961), pp.158–59.

95. There is at least one clear case where Buber's reliability as an author has been called into question. Rivka Horwitz has pointed out that an early version of story number 14, "Question and Answer," in Buber's "Autobiographical Fragments" contradicts a version given in Buber's *"Religion als Gegenwart"* lectures. In this story Reverend Hechler, a friend of Herzl and an ardent Zionist, asks Buber if he believes in God. Buber tells us in the lectures that he couldn't really answer the man at the time, but at a later time, while he was riding in a train, the answer came to him. I do not believe in God "if to believe in God means to speak to him in the third person . . . , God must always be addressed in the second person" (as quoted in Horwitz, p.176). In the version of the story told in the "Autobiographical Fragments," Buber tells us that the answer came to him after parting with Hechler at "that corner where the black path issued into our street" (p.24). This change makes the narrative more dramatic and more exciting as a story, yet Horwitz makes a convincing case that the earlier version is closer to the facts. Rivka Horwitz, *Buber's Way to I and Thou* (Heidelberg: Lambert Schneider, 1978).

96. Even though I am not sure it is correct to answer my own rhetorical question, I feel I must make some response to the very radical question that I have just posed. The most direct response I could offer is that there is no way to "authenticate" or "verify" the I-Thou dialogue. Offering this verification, however, was never Buber's goal. Laurence Silberstein has aptly adopted Richard Rorty's (1979) notion of the "edifying" philosopher to describe Buber's aim in addressing the I-Thou relationship. Buber's task was not to verify I-Thou through "objectification and rational analysis" but to "point a way" to I-Thou, to "carry on a conversation" about I-Thou and the non-alienating "way of living" relating to the world and others that the I-Thou relationship suggests. Silberstein, *Martin Buber's Social and Religious Thought,* pp.106–07. My argument here has been that Buber's narratives provide a privileged form of discourse for pointing to and beginning conversation about the I-Thou relationship.

97. See, for example, the end of the story about the two silent seated partners which we reviewed earlier. "Where unreserve has ruled, even wordlessly, between men, the word of dialogue has happened sacramentally" ("Dialogue," p.4).

98. Ricoeur, *Time and Narrative,* Vol.3, p.159.

99. Ricoeur, *Time and Narrative,* Vol.1, p.80.

6. "Autobiographical Fragments": Becoming Self through the Other

1. Ricoeur quotes Aristotle in *The Poetics:* "For tragedy is not an imitation of men but of actions and of life. . . . What is more, without action there could not be a tragedy, but there could be without characterization." *Time and Narrative,* Vol.1, p.37.

2. In his fine summary of narrative theory, Seymour Chatman notes that "It is remarkable how little has been said about the theory of character in literary history and criticism." *Story and Discourse* (Ithaca: Cornell University Press, 1978), p.107. Since Aristotle stressed the centrality of action and incident to tragedy, literary criticism has tended to stress the import of plot over character. This is true even for modern Formalist and Structuralist theories where characters are portrayed as a "function of plots" (p.113). Chatman, however, argues that in modern literature and film, where the psychological investigation of character has become a central concern, characterization deserves more attention and should be regarded as "equally important" as plot in narrative theory (p. 110).

3. For a more in-depth analysis of the import of character to the novel see Henry James, "Preface to The Portrait of a Lady," in R. Blackmur, ed., *The Art of the Novel* (New York: Scribner's, 1934), ch.3.

4. Kermode, *Genesis of Secrecy,* p.77.

5. Ian Watt, *The Rise of the Novel* (Berkeley: University of California Press, 1967), p.13.

6. James Olney, "The Style of Autobiography," in J. Olney, ed., *Autobiography: Essays Theoretical and Critical* (Princeton: Princeton University Press, 1980), p.19.

7. William Howarth, "Some Principles of Autobiography," in Olney, *Autobiography,* p.85.

8. Jean Starobinski, "The Style of Autobiography," in Olney, *Autobiography,* p.74.

9. Georges Gusdorf, "Conditions and Limits of Autobiography," in Olney, *Autobiography,* p.19.

10. Henri Beyle Stendhal, *The Life of Henri Brulard,* trans. J. Stewart and B. Knight (New York: Minerva, 1968), p.2.

11. Gusdorf, "Conditions and Limits," p.29.

12. Maurice Friedman tells us that he even had a role in helping Buber select anecdotes from existing publications. "Introduction" to Martin Buber, *Meetings* (La Salle, IL: Open Court, 1973), p.4.

13. Buber, "Autobiographical Fragments," in Schilpp and Friedman, eds., *The Philosophy of Martin Buber,* p.3.

14. *Ibid.,* p.4. Although there is a tendency to stress the importance of meetings over mismeetings in discussions of I-Thou relationships and the self, Buber's autobiography reveals that mismeetings can be at least as important. Buber tells us that two mismeetings, one with his mother and the other with a forlorn student, were "decisive" for his thinking about I-Thou relatiolnships; *ibid.,* pp.4 and 25.

15. Roy Pascal, *Design and Truth in Autobiography* (Cambridge: Harvard University Press, 1960), p.9.

16. Martin Buber, *Briefwechsel aus sieben Jahrzehnten,* Vol.III, ed. G. Schaeder (Heidelberg: Lambert Schneider, 1975), p.293. [My translation.]

17. James Olney, *Metaphors of Self* (Princeton: Princeton University Press, 1972), p.35.

18. Karl Weintraub, "Autobiography and Historical Consciousness," *Critical Inquiry,* 1:4 (June 1975), 834.

19. Gusdorf, "Conditions," p.29.

20. Cf. Mircea Eliade, *The Myth of the Eternal Return* (Princeton: Princeton University Press, 1971), chs.2–3.

21. Gusdorf, "Conditions," p.31.

22. *Ibid.*

23. *Ibid.,* p.34.

24. Weintraub, "Autobiography," p.846.

25. *Ibid.,* p.847. Each different commentator on autobiography seems to have his or her candidate for the "first" or "primary" case. Huck Gutman has made a strong case for Rousseau's *Confessions.* "Rousseau reveals and celebrates the automistic, autonomous self: He is perhaps the first human being to insist upon his own singularity." Gutman quotes Rousseau: "My mind needs to go forward in its own time, it cannot submit itself to anyone else's. For I knew that my experience did not apply to others." Gutman, "Rousseau's Confessions: A Technology of the Self," in L. Martin, H. Gutman, P. Hutton, eds., in *Technologies of the Self* (Amherst: University of Massachusetts Press, 1988), p.100.

26. Although Avrom Fleishman, in his *Figures of Autobiography* (Berkeley: University of California Press, 1983), has argued that autobiography and the notion of individuality is not unique to the West, I tend to side with Gusdorf and Weintraub. Certainly we have autobiographic-like writings before the sixteenth century and in other cultures. But the sustained use of the genre and the celebration of the individual as unique and separate from the larger community is first seen as a widespread phenomenon in the West.

27. Howarth, "Some Principles," p.88.

28. Karl Weintraub, *The Value of the Individual* (Chicago: University of Chicago Press, 1978), p.45.

29. Howarth, "Some Principles," p.104.

30. In Freud's depth psychology the self has a "static" quality. Freud likened the psychoanalyst to the archeologist. Classical psychoanalysis is an attempt to excavate a buried self, the self determined by the conflicts of infancy. Once excavated, the self stands set in the confines of the narrative of the case history, See Steven Kepnes, "Telling and Retelling: The Use of Narrative in Psychoanalysis and Religion," in S. Kepnes and D. Tracy, eds., *The Challenge of Psychology to Faith* (New York: Seabury, 1982) and Sigmund Freud, *Dora: An Analysis of a Case of Hysteria* (New York: Macmillan, 1963), pp.31–32.

31. Weintraub, "Autobiography," p.847.

32. Lawrence Kaplan, *Bibliography of American Autobiography* (Madison: University of Wisconsin Press, 1961).

33. Cf. Robert Bellah *et al., Habits of the Hearts* (Berkeley: University of California Press, 1985). Christopher Lasch, *The Culture of Narcissism* (New York: W.W. Norton, 1978). Philip Rieff, *The Triumph of the Therapeutic* (New York: Harper and Row, 1966).

34. Buber was inspired by what Ferdinand Tönnies described as the *Gemeinschaft* nature of society in premodern Europe. Tönnies, *Community and Society,* trans. C.P. Loomis (New York: Harper, 1963). Buber saw the communitarian life of Hasidic societies as an example of genuine *Gemeinschaft.* But he ultimately wanted to bring the communal spirit and sense of human bonding of these communities into the modern world. For a discussion of Buber's notion of *Gemeinschaft* see Mendes-Flohr, *From Mysticism to Dialogue,* chs.2, and 5.

35. Buber, *I and Thou,* trans. W. Kaufmann, p.54. Buber does draw a distinction between the self of the I-Thou relationship, the "Thou-I," and the self of the "I-It" relationship, the "It-I." The former gives rise to the development of "persons" and the latter produces "individuals," Buber, *I and Thou,* trans. R. G. Smith, p. 62.

> Individuality makes its appearance by being differentiated from other individualities. A person makes his appearance by entering into relation with other persons. *(Ibid.)*

Since the "Thou-I," the person, represents the fullness of selfhood we will focus on it, following Buber's emphasis.

36. Buber, *I and Thou,* trans. Kaufmann, p.80. Roy Steinhoff Smith has attempted a creative developmental presentation of Buber's relational view of self. Smith argues that, for Buber, "only in relational events does the unified I come into being as a fully differentiated form." Roy Steinhoff Smith, "The Becoming of the Person in Martin Buber's Philosophical Anthropology and Heinz Kohut's Psychology of Self," diss., University of Chicago, 1985, p.41.

37. Martin Buber, "Distance and Relation," in *The Knowledge of Man,* p.71. For another discussion of the relational self in Buber's writings, see my "Buber's Ark: The Dialogic Self," in Donald Capps and Richard Fenn, eds., *The Endangered Self* (Philadelphia: Augsburg Fortress Press, 1992).

38. Buber, "Distance and Relation," p.71.

39. *Ibid.* For an application of Buber's views on the confirmation of otherness to the areas of family and social life see Maurice Friedman, *The Confirmation of Otherness* (New York: Pilgrim Press, 1983).

40. Michael Theunissen, *The Other: Studies in the Social Ontology of Husserl, Heidegger, Sartre, and Buber,* trans. C. Macann (Cambridge: MIT Press, 1984), p. 284.

41. Martin Buber, "The Question to the Single One," *Between Man and Man,* p. 57. Robert Perkins has shown us that Buber was rather sloppy and very choosy in which texts of Kierkegaard he used to paint his picture of Kierkegaard as antisocial and overly individualistic. Perkins, "Buber and Kierkegaard: A Philosophic Encounter," in Gordon

and Bloch, eds., *Martin Buber: A Centenary Volume.* Certainly Kierkegaard was concerned with society, with social critique, and with bringing about more authentic public discourse on matters of true import. Yet his solutions to social problems revolved around arriving at authentic subjectivity and a genuine relation of the self to God. Buber would argue that these first moves isolate the self instead of involving it, from the beginning, with other human selves and the community.

42. Kermode, *Genesis,* p.78.

43. Buber, "Dialogue," p.13.

44. Weintraub, "Autobiography," p.828.

45. *Ibid.,* p. 824.

46. Buber, "Dialogue," pp.10–11.

47. Martin Buber, "The Unconscious," ed. and trans. M. Friedman, *A Believing Humanism* (New York: Simon and Schuster, 1967), p. 168.

48. Erik Erikson, *Childhood and Society* (New York: Norton, 1963).

49. Bertram Cohler, "Personal Narrative and Life Course," in P. Baltes and O. Brim, eds., *Life-Span Development and Behavior,* Vol.4 (New York: Academic Press, 1982), p.210.

50. To argue for the novelty of Buber's ideas in Continental thought Theunissen shows that Buber posits "the between" as his point of departure for discussion of self and reality whereas Husserl, Heidegger, and Sartre begin from the "sphere of subjectivity." Theunissen, *The Other,* p.276. He distinguishes Buber's notion of self from that of Husserl by showing that for Husserl the I of phenomenological subjectivity "stands in no relation to a Thou and is not a member of a We." *Ibid.,* p.20. He distinguishes Buber from Heidegger stating that: "According to Heidegger the self can only come to itself to a voluntary separation of itself from the other self, according to Buber, it has its being solely in the relation." *Ibid.,* p.284.

51. Charles Brice has labored to distinguish Buber from seemingly obvious allies in the area of psychological theory, the "Object-Relation" psychologists (W.R.D. Fairbairn, Harry Guntrip, Donald W. Winnicott, Otto Kernberg, Margaret Mahler). Although these psychologists assert the primal importance of other persons for the development of the self, the other person is important only as "psychical representation," as "object" not as real person.

> In its precise theoretical usage, the term "object relation" does not describe the meeting between person and other and certainly not the meeting between I and Thou. The term is restricted to an internal relationship between self, image of self, and internal image of other, i.e., between self and self.

Charles Brice, "Pathological Modes of Human Relating and Therapeutic Mutuality: A Dialogue Between Buber's Existential Theory and Object-Relations Theory," *Psychiatry,* 47:2 (1984), p.119.

52. Although Paul Pfuetze, *Self, Society, Existence* (New York: Harper and Row, 1961), has tried to show the affinities between Buber's relational notion of self and the social self of Mead, there are important differences. Here is a characteristic statement of Mead on the social self. "It is only as the individual finds himself acting with reference to himself as he acts towards others, that he becomes a subject to himself." George Herbert Mead, *Selected Writings* (New York: Bobbs Merrill, 1964), p.143. Here the self becomes a subject, not through genuine meetings with others, but by acting toward himself as he acts toward others.

53. Fleishman, *Figures,* p.13; Barrett Mandel, "Full of Life Now," in Olney, *Autobiography,* p.64; Starobinski, "The Style of Autobiography," p.75; Weintraub, "Autobiography," p.824.

54. Olney, "Autobiography," p.24.

55. *Ibid.,* p.25.

56. Louis Renza, "The Veto of the Imagination: A Theory of Autobiography," in Olney, *Autobiography,* p. 295.

57. Michel Foucault, "What Is an Author?" in D. Bouchard, ed., *Language, Counter-Memory, Practice* (Ithaca: Cornell University Press, 1977), p.116.

58. *Ibid.*, p.117. The views of Foucault and Barthes (whom I quote below) on the death of the author cannot be equated. Where Barthes celebrates the "Death" of the author, Foucault is sensitive to some of the problems caused by the author's demise and he does try to constructively address these problems with his notion of the "foundational author" (*Ibid.*, p.132f.).

59. Roland Barthes, "The Death of the Author," *Image, Music, Text,* trans. S. Heath (New York: Hill and Wang, 1977), p.142.

60. Calvin Schrag, *Communicative Praxis and the Space of Subjectivity* (Bloomington: Indiana University Press, 1986), p.viii.

61. Foucault, "What Is an Author?" p.137.

62. Jacques Derrida, "Structure, Sign and Play in the Discourse of the Human Sciences," in R. Macksey and E. Donato, eds., *The Languages of Criticism and the Sciences of Man* (Baltimore: Johns Hopkins University Press, 1970), p.271, as quoted in Schrag, p.129.

63. Schrag, *Communicative Praxis,* p.viii.

64. *Ibid.*, p.4. Richard Rorty, in describing the "contingency of selfhood," has also employed the notion of a "web of relations" to refer to what he calls the "incomplete" postmodern self. The self "cannot get completed because there is nothing to complete; there is only a web of relations to be rewoven, a web which time lengthens every day. . . . [W]e shall be content to think of any human life as the always incomplete, yet sometimes heroic reweaving of such a web." Rorty, *Contingency, Irony, and Solidarity* (Cambridge: Cambridge University Press, 1989), p.43.

65. Schrag, *Communicative Praxis,* pp.4–6.

66. *Ibid.*, p.125.

67. The one who thinks is bound, in different degrees of substantiality but never purely functionally, to a spatial realm, to a historical hour, to the genus man, to a people, to a family, to a society, to a vocational group, to a companionship in convictions. This entanglement in a manifold We . . . wards off the temptation of the thought of [individual] sovereignty.
Buber, "The Question to the Single One," *Between Man and Man,* p.80.

68. Buber, "What Is Common to All," *The Knowledge of Man,* p.91.

69. Schrag, *Communicative Praxis,* p.200.

70. *Ibid.*, p.202.

71. *Ibid.*

72. Buber, "Dialogue," pp.16–17.

73. The question may be asked, why need we turn to a discussion of God? Why does the relational self require relationship to God? Some scholars, most notably Michael Theunissen, have argued that Buber developed a "social ontology" that does not require reference to God. Theunissen, *Der Andere: Studien zur Sozialontologie* (Berlin: W.de Gruyter, 1965), pp.333ff. Yet I side with Yehoshua Amir, who has argued that the relationship to God cannot be severed without radically altering Buber's program. Amir, "The Finite Thou and the Eternal Thou in the Work of Buber," in H. Gordon and J. Bloch, eds., *Martin Buber: A Centenary Volume* (New York: KTAV, 1984). Indeed, as I will show below, Buber argued that it is God, as eternal other, who insists on relationship to otherness and demands relationship of self to other humans and the world.

74. Buber, "Dialogue," p.35.

75. Buber, "Replies to My Critics," in *The Philosophy of Martin Buber,* p.689.

76. Buber, *I and Thou,* trans. Smith, p.75.

77. Paul Mendes-Flohr, "Martin Buber's Conception of God," in A. Babolin, ed., *Teologia Filosofica E Filosofia Della Religione* (Perugia: Editrice Benucci, 1986), p.176. Cf. Buber, *I and Thou,* pp.114–15.

78. Buber, "Man and His Image-Work," *The Knowledge of Man,* p.150.

79. Buber, "Dialogue," p.178. Buber's concern for otherness in religious life often pitted him against modern psychological interpreters of religion, like C.G. Jung, who would find God in the depths of the self. Buber argues that in collapsing the transcendent God into a psychological category, the "self," the genuine relationship to God as transcendent other, as eternal Thou, is lost.

> For if religion is a relation to psychic events, which cannot mean anything other than to events of one's soul, then it is implied by this that it is not a relation to a Being or Reality which, no matter how fully it may from time to time descend to the human soul, always remains transcendent to it. More precisely, it is not the relation of an I to a Thou.

Martin Buber, *The Eclipse of God*, trans. M. Friedman (New York: Harper and Row, 1952), p. 79.

In Buber's view, the dangerous consequence of presenting God as part of the psyche and doing away with God's transcendence, God's radical "otherness," is the concomitant loss of respect for the otherness of persons and world and hence the loss of relationship. Cf. Carl G. Jung, *Memories, Dreams, Reflections*, trans. R. and C. Winston (New York: Vintage, 1963), pp.4–5. In interpreting the central religious vocation as a relationship between the I and the self, as Jung does, the life of the created world dims in value. This leads to a phenomenon which Buber calls "the psychologizing of the world": people, places, world itself, lose their reality. Martin Buber, "On the Psychologizing of the World," trans. M. Friedman, *A Believing Humanism.*

80. See my discussion of autobiography and Judaism below.

81. Despite Christianity's concern for the separate individual, it is precisely the uniform and set patterning of the self, the attempt to discourage idiosyncracy and form the self to a Christian paradigm, that makes traditional Christian notions of the self and Christian autobiography "premodern."

82. Buber is particularly critical of the autobiographies of Christian mystics who lose their self in God. In the search for union with God the I is "absorbed" and "merged" (*I and Thou*, trans. Smith, p.84.) in the eternal Thou and human relationships are bypassed. As an example I quote from Saint Teresa of Avila.

> In the orison of union the soul is completely awake as regards God, but wholly asleep as regards things of this world and respect of herself. During the short time the union lasts she is deprived of every feeling and even if she would, she could not think of any single thing. Thus she needs to employ no artifice in order to arrest her understanding: it remains so stricken with inactivity that she neither knows what she loves nor in what manner she loves, nor what she wills.

As quoted in William James, *The Varieties of Religious Experience* (New York: Penguin, 1982), p.408.

As we see in the case of Saint Teresa, the I is deprived of its feeling and will; the I is obliterated, "swallowed up by the Thou" (*I and Thou*, p.84). Therefore, in Buber's view, true relationship between the I and the eternal Thou does not occur.

83. Janet Varner Gunn, "The Religious Hermeneutic of Autobiography," in R. Detweiler, ed., *Art/Literature/Religion*, JAAR Thematic Studies, 49:2 (Chico, CA: Scholars Press, 1983). See also Gunn, *Autobiography: Toward a Poetics of Experience* (Philadelphia: University of Pennsylvania Press, 1982), chs. 1,5.

84. Sallie McFague, *Speaking in Parables* (Philadelphia: Fortress Press, 1975), p.154, as quoted in Donald Capps, "Parabolic Events in Augustine's Autobiography," *Theology Today*, 40:3 (Oct. 1983), 270. Kenneth Kramer has argued for the value of autobiography on slightly different grounds. When autobiography is used for theology the pitfalls of scholasticism can be avoided. "Today's theological task must be autobiographical . . . for without personal history theology reverts to scholasticism." Kramer, "Autobiographical World Theology," *Horizons*, 13:1 (Spring 1986), 105.

85. It is curious to me that Gunn's argument for the time-boundedness or "worldliness" of autobiography in her book is made in reference to Augustine when other figures

188   *Notes for Pages 117–118*

that Gunn investigates—Thoreau, Wordsworth, Proust, more modern figures—may have been better resources to make this claim. Cf. *Autobiography,* ch.5.

86. Buber, "The Silent Question" [1952], *On Judaism,* p. 209.

87. Buber, "Dialogue," p.4.

88. Buber, "The Dialogue Between Heaven and Earth" [1951], *On Judaism,* p.221.

89. The earliest example of Jewish autobiography is arguably found in the memoirs of Glueckel of Hameln, 1646–1724, and this was written for "her children," so that they might know of their father who died. It was certainly not a record of a religious or self-quest and it was private and unknown until the twentieth century. Glueckel Hameln, *The Memoirs of Glueckel of Hameln,* trans. M. Lowenthal (New York: Schocken, 1977).

90. David Roskies, "Memory," in Cohen and Mendes-Flohr, eds., *Contemporary Jewish Religious Thought,* p.582.

91. *Ibid.*

92. Richard L. Rubenstein, "The Promise and Pitfalls of Autobiographical Theology," in R. Detweiler, ed., *Art/Literature/Religion,* JAAR Thematic Studies, 49:2 (Chico, CA: Scholars Press, 1983), pp.125–26. One does begin to find spiritual autobiography in Judaism only in the modern period. In Eastern Europe, Hasidism, which often stressed the import of the individual's spiritual quest, did give rise to biographies, personal confessions, and spiritual autobiographies. And in the West, where the grip of tradition loosened, and were the question of identity for Jews has become a central issue, there have been an abundance of autobiographies written by Jews. We could simply place Buber's autobiography in the category of the quest of the modern Jew for identity but the style of the work does not quite fit with the many Jewish autobiographers who have adopted the reigning Western paradigm of the singular self and the style of what we have called the "monumental autobiography."

93. Buber, "Judaism and The Jews" [1911], *On Judaism,* p.16.

94. *Ibid.,* p.18.

95. Buber, "Love of God and Love of Neighbor" [1943], *Hasidism and Modern Man,* M. Friedman ed. and trans. (New York: Harper, 1958/1966), p.237.

96. *Ibid.,* p.233. The fundamental way in which Daniel Breslauer, in his "Guide to the Jewishness of Buber's I and Thou," ties Buber's philosophy to Judaism is through an investigation of Buber's twofold affirmation of the "need of organic social life as well as the need of God," Daniel Breslauer, *The Chrysalis of Religion: A Guide to the Jewishness of Buber's I and Thou* (Nashville: Abingdon, 1980), p.16. Among the many tales and texts that Breslauer quotes is the story of the Rebbe of Zans. "Buber tells of the Rebbe of Zans who complained that he had reached old age without fully turning to God. He was rebuked and told 'You are thinking only of ourself. How about forgetting yourself and thinking of the world' " (p.15). For a discussion of the Jewish religious importance of good relations between individuals in society that draws on talmudic sources see Chaim Reines, "The Self and the Other in Rabbinic Ethics," in Menachem Kellner, ed., *Contemporary Jewish Ethics* (New York: Sanhedrin, 1978).

97. In *Totality and Infinity* (Hague: Martinus Nijhoff, 1979) Levinas states: "My being is produced in producing itself before the others in discourse; it is what it reveals of itself to the others" p.253. He has also said: "My ethical relation of love for the other stems from the fact that the self cannot survive by itself alone, cannot find meaning within its own being-in the-world." E. Levinas and R. Kearney, "Dialogue with Emmanuel Levinas," in R. Cohen, ed., *Face to Face* (New York: SUNY, 1986), p.24. For Rosenzweig's notion of the social self see *The Star of Redemption,* pp.206–15. I am grateful to Yudit Greenberg for her comments to me on the social self in Levinas and Rosenzweig.

98. Although Husserl was Jewish he did not attempt to connect his Jewishness and Judaism to his philosophical positions as did Buber, Rosenzweig, and Levinas.

99. See my forthcoming book *The Social Self in Modern Jewish Philosophy.*

100. In speaking to the B'nai Brith organization Freud once attributed his courage in developing his new theories to his Jewish sense of being "other." "Because I was a Jew I

found myself free of many prejudices which restrict others in the use of the intellect; as a Jew I was prepared to be in the Opposition and to renounce agreement with the 'compact majority.' " Sigmund Freud, "Lecture to Society of B'nai Brith" [1926], *Standard Edition of the Complete Psychological Works,* Vol.20, trans J. Strachey (London: Hogarth Press, 1959), p.274.

7. Narrative Biblical Theology: Responding to the Eclipse of God

1. Buber, "The Man of Today and The Jewish Bible," *On the Bible,* p.10 (From *Die Schrift und ihre Verdeutschung,* 1936).

2. Buber, "Elements of the Interhuman," *The Knowledge of Man,* p.71, cf. p.83.

3. One could argue that Buber's work on Hasidic texts also enlarged his immediate temporal framework by bringing him to study Jewish Hasidic culture of the eighteenth and nineteenth centuries and the Kabbalah of medieval Judaism. But I would suggest that the biblical texts were more important in enlarging Buber's temporal frame because of the centrality of biblical notions of creation (the beginning of time) and redemption (the future end of time). What Buber seems to focus on in Hasidism is its sense of hallowing the present moment of now.

4. Buber, *The Legend of the Baal-Shem,* pp.10ff.

5. Buber, "Replies to My Critics," in *The Philosophy of Martin Buber,* p.690.

6. Barry Mesch has begun to investigate the role of narrative in medieval Jewish philosophy. Although Saadya Gaon seemed to see only biblical narrative as a route to *mitzvot* and Maimonides saw the narratives as symbolic of eternal truths, Judah Halevi appreciated the narratives as disclosive of God's revelatory presence in public events and his work could be seen as an early attempt at a narrative Jewish theology. See Barry Mesch, "Ta'amey Ha-Mitzvot and Ta'amey Hasippurim: The Biblical Narrative in Saadya, Halevi and Maimonides," unpublished paper delivered at the Association of Jewish Studies Meetings, Dec. 1989.

7. Buber, "Abraham the Seer," *On the Bible,* p.26. From *Shelihut Avraham, Haaretz* (Tel Aviv: 1939).

8. In the preface to *Königtum Gottes,* "The Kingship of God," Buber explains that he originally wanted to write a theological commentary to the entire Hebrew Bible but was forced by the sheer magnitude of the project to concentrate on the subjects which interested him most. What Buber chooses represents a fundamental hermeneutic move. It represents the construction of Buber's own "canon within the canon" of biblical books, the books which establish his series of hermeneutical questions and structure his responses.

9. Emil Fackenheim, *God's Presence in History,* p.9.

10. Paul Mendes-Flohr argues that "Buber interpreted the central concepts of biblical religion—Creation, Revelation, and Redemption—not theologically, but, . . . phenomenologically, as concepts which point to the experienced reality of dialogue." Mendes-Flohr, "M. Buber's Conception of God," pp.197ff. For Rosenzweig these three concepts led him to the assertion of certain theological attributes, e.g., the biblical account of creation suggests that God has a "will" and is separate from nature and revelation gives evidence to God's "reason." Mendes-Flohr shows that Buber could not accept Rosenzweig's "metaphysical" assertions about God's attributes and, instead, was concerned with the implications of creation, revelation, and redemption for humanity. Although I would not contest Mendes-Flohr's position here, I am confident that he would agree that Rosenzweig was concerned not only with purely theological issues but that he, too, was concerned with the implications of creation, revelation, and redemption for human experience. And I believe that Mendes-Flohr would also agree that Buber and Rosenzweig found some agreement on these human implications.

Very briefly I would summarize Buber's view of the three concepts we are discussing as follows: Creation establishes the precondition through which humans can be addressed in their existence by God. Revelation is the moment of address by God. And redemption is the fulfillment of address in the world. See Buber, "The Man of Today," pp.7ff.

11. Buber, "Why We Should Study Jewish Sources" [1933], *Israel and the World* (New York: Schocken, 1963), p.146. With all due respect to Yosef Yerushalmi and his most helpful book, *Zakhor,* on the relation between the Jewish common memory and modern historiography, I believe that it is not true that "the Jewish collective memory . . . is yet to be explored." *Zakhor: Jewish History and Jewish Memory* (Seattle: University of Washington Press, 1982), p.xvi. Indeed, Buber's discussion of the Jewish common memory and his notion of "saga" (see below) provides us with some very valuable insights into the nature of the "common memory" of the Jews.

12. Buber, "The Man of Today", p.9. Stephen Crites argues that both our sense of the past and our sense of the future, our memory and our anticipation of the future, are structured by narrative. He refers to memory as an "incipient narrative" and "primitive chronicle." Memory holds events in the "simple temporality of sequence, before and after." We anticipate the future by imagining a "scenario," by "framing little stories about how things may fall out." Crites, "The Narrative Quality of Experience," pp.298, 302.

13. Buber, *Kingship of God,* p.63.

14. I have been aided in my understanding of Buber's notion of "common memory" by Laurence Thomas's notion of an "affirming past." See Thomas, *Vessels of Evil* (forthcoming).

15. Buber, *The Prophetic Faith,* p.51.

16. Here we can see the relevance of Ricoeur's presentation of the Heideggerian notion of "repetition." Through repeating the primal Passover story a sense of common Jewish identity and destiny is forged.

17. Buber refers to the Torah as "a book of teachings and laws edited at that time [the rule of Hezekiah] and ascribed to Moses." *Good and Evil* (New York: Schribner's, 1953), p.51.

18. Buber, *The Prophetic Faith,* ch.4.

19. Buber's writings on the Bible were calculated to elevate the view of the "Old Testament," whose importance had been denigrated by such figures as Adolph Harnack and Rudolf Bultmann. For an interesting discussion by a number of Christian theologians and Bible scholars of Bultmann's rather reserved opinion of the importance of the Old Testament presented in his "The Significance of the Old Testament for the Christian Faith," see B. Anderson, ed., *The Old Testament and Christian Faith* (New York: Harper and Row, 1963).

20. Buber, "Why We Should Study Jewish Sources," p.148.

21. Buber, "The Man of Today," p.7.

22. Benyamin Uffenheimer, "Buber and Modern Biblical Scholarship," *Martin Buber: A Centenary Volume,* p.163.

23. Buber, "The Man of Today," p.1.

24. Buber, "Distance and Relation," in *The Knowledge of Man,* p.60.

25. Buber, "The Man of Today," p.7.

26. *Ibid.,* pp.5–6. Despite Buber's interesting remarks on the cultic context of the Jewish common memory in his discussion of the Passover Festival, our present quotation from "The Man of Today" suggests that, for Buber, access to the Jewish common memory is a hermeneutical event that can occur "any time" one opens the biblical text and approaches it with the attitude of I-Thou. Other commentators, however, have stressed the necessity of halakhic and ritual contexts for access to the Jewish common memory. Thus, Moshe Spero argues that Jewish common memory is "enhanced and safeguarded" by "the basic halakhic parameters governing ritual observance." "Remembering and Historical Awareness Part II" *Tradition,* 19:1 (Spring 1981), 71. David Roskies traces the path of the common memory from the Bible to rabbinic texts to its home in the medieval "liturgy" and in post-Holocaust "communal rituals." "Memory," *Contemporary Jewish Religious Thought,* pp.583, 585. And Fackenheim argues that the

efficacy of the common memory is dependent on the integrity of the "midrashic framework." *God's Presence,* p.49.

27. Buber, "Judaism and the Jews," *On Judaism,* p.16.

28. *Ibid.*

29. Buber, "The Man of Today," p.7.

30. *Ibid.,* p.6.

31. *Ibid.,* p.8.

32. *Ibid.,* p.1.

33. *Ibid.,* p.2.

34. Erich Auerbach, *Mimesis,* trans. W. Trask (Princeton: Princeton University Press, 1953), p.15.

35. Even though Hans Frei, in his *Eclipse of Biblical Narrative* (New Haven: Yale University Press, 1974), follows Auerbach in his assertion of the univocal and autocratic nature of biblical narrative, it becomes clear that it is the dogmatic strand in Christian hermeneutics up until the eighteenth century that is at the root of the supposed univocal and authoritarian nature of the "Old Testament" narratives and not the text itself. Although rabbinic hermeneutics is not without its authoritarian qualities the strictness was focused on halakhic hermeneutics *(midrash halakhah),* leaving theological hermeneutics *(midrash aggadah)* much more freedom.

36. One will note aspects of Tillich's notion of theology as a correlation of the "message" of the religious tradition with the "question implied in the [contemporary] situation" through which the questions are "answered." *Systematic Theology* (Chicago: University of Chicago Press, 1966), pp.3–6. Cf. Abraham J. Heschel, *God in Search of Man* (New York: Harper, 1966), p.3. Yet my definition includes a number of important differences from Tillich's and is much closer to Tracy's hermeneutical notion of theology as "a reinterpretation of the tradition for the present situation." *Analogical Imagination,* p.64. I would argue that in "retelling" biblical narratives we interpret them, and when we retell them for the contemporary situation we do not provide "answers" to the questions of that situation but "expression for" and "responses" to the contradictions and joy in that situation.

I have been aided in my formulation here by Larry Bouchard's discussion of tragedy as an expression of and not an answer to the theological problematics of evil; see his *Tragic Method and Tragic Theology* (University Park: Pennsylvania State University Press, 1989).

37. Buber, "The Man of Today and the Jewish Bible," p.7. (slightly altered).

38. Martin Buber, *Moses: The Revelation and the Covenant,* p.14.

39. Yerushalmi is just one among many who have argued that "It was ancient Israel that first assigned a decisive significance to history." *Zakhor,* p.8.

40. Harold Bloom, "Introduction," in Buber, *On The Bible,* p.xxiii.

41. Buber's "saga" has some affinities with H. Richard Niebuhr's notion of "inner history," which he distinguishes from "external history." "From the realistic point of view we are concerned in external history to abstract from all that is merely secondary, from subjective and partisan accounts of what happened. . . . In internal history . . . we are concerned . . . with 'values,' . . . verifiable in a community of selves." Niebuhr, *The Meaning of Revelation* (New York: Macmillan, 1941), pp.48–49.

42. Yerushalmi discusses this point at length beginning with this piece of biblical witticism. "The biblical appeal to remember thus has little to do with curiosity about the past. Israel is told only that it must be a kingdom of priests and a holy nation; nowhere is it suggested that it become a kingdom of historians." *Zakhor,* p.10ff.

43. Buber, *Moses,* p.16.

44. *Ibid.,* p.13.

45. *Ibid.,* p.14.

46. *Ibid.* Buber quotes the Iranologist Ernst Herzfeld's *Mythos und Geschichte* (1933) here. His distinction between "Saga" and "history" is also influenced by the work of

philologist Hermann Usener. Buber's views on the significance of event and narrative in the Bible are echoed in G. Ernest Wright, *God Who Acts* (London: SCM Press, 1952). David Kelsey has a fine discussion of these issues in Protestant Neo-Orthodox thought in his *The Uses of Scripture in Recent Theology* (Philadelphia: Fortress Press, 1975). In brief, Barth, Bultmann, and Tillich have a great appreciation for the revelatory "event" in scripture but a weak conception of the importance of the narrative vehicles for expression of these events.

47. Buber, *Moses*, p.14.

48. *Ibid.*

49. *Ibid.*

50. Buber, *Kingship of God*, p.63.

51. Buber, *Moses*, p.15.

52. *Ibid.*

53. Yerushalmi also describes how different genres of relating the past are "held together in a web of delicate and reciprocal relationships" (*Zakhor*, p.14) in the Bible and he goes on to show how this web is "pulled asunder" *(ibid.)* in rabbinic literature in favor of more purely mythological and legendary narrative forms.

> Unlike the biblical writers the rabbis seem to play with Time as though with an accordion, expanding and collapsing it at will. Where historical specificity is [the] hallmark of the biblical narratives, that acute biblical sense of time and place often gives way to rampant and seemingly unselfconscious anachronism. *(Ibid.* p.17)

54. The "mixed discourse," the use of history, literature, music, poetry, ritual, philosophy, and theology to express and address the issues surrounding the Holocaust is a good example of the way in which contemporary Jewry is utilizing what I would call "biblical mimetic methodologies" in its attempt to respond to the Holocaust.

55. Martin Buber, *Werke* II (Heidelberg: Lambert Schneider, 1964), p.19.

56. Buber, *Moses*, p.14.

57. Buber, *Kingship of God*, p.126.

58. Fishbane, *Biblical Interpretation in Ancient Israel* (Oxford: Clarendon Press, 1984).

59. Buber, "The Man of Today," p.1.

60. If Buber's writings are finally ruled by the attempt to discern a message for the contemporary situation we can understand Buber's biblical writings not only as a response to the Holocaust but also as a response to the struggle for Jewish cultural renewal and Jewish national renewal. As Benyamin Uffenheimer has pointed out, Buber's attention to the style, the rhythm, the narrative form, and the "spokenness" of biblical Hebrew must be viewed in relation to the revival of Hebrew as a spoken language ("Buber and Biblical Scholarship," p.164). Buber's very attention to the Bible developed out of hope for a Jewish cultural renewal in which the Hebrew Bible would play a central role.

61. Buber, "The Man of Today," p.1.

62. Buber, *The Prophetic Faith*, p.31.

63. Buber, *Kingship of God*, p.100.

64. It is interesting to see how the intimacy between God and Moses is constantly punctuated, one may even say preserved, by strategies of distance. For example: "Do not come near to here,/ put off your sandal from your foot" (Ex. 3:5). "You cannot see My face,/ for no human can see Me and live" (Ex 33:20). "I will place you in the cleft of the rock,/ and screen you with My hand/until I have passed by./Then I will remove My hand;/ you shall see My back,/ but My face shall not be seen" (Ex. 33:22–23). For a discussion of two types of distancing, one that induces and the other that hinders dialogue, see the section on "Distance and Repair" below.

65. The Exodus translations are taken from Everett Fox, *Now These Are the Names* (New York: Schocken, 1986), which, like Fox's Genesis translation, *In the Beginning*, is an attempt to use Buber and Rosenzweig's translation techniques to create a "Hebrew-like" English translation of the Bible.

66. Buber, *Moses,* p.52. Mendes-Flohr points out that it was Rosenzweig who first showed Buber the problematic nature of the translation of YHVH as "I am that I am" and suggested that alternative: "I am there such as I am there" [*Ich bin da als der ich da bin*]. Mendes-Flohr, "Buber's Conception of God," p.197.

67. Buber, *Moses,* p.52.

68. *Ibid.,* p.76.

69. Cf. *ibid.,* pp.101ff.

70. *Ibid.,* p.54.

71. Buber, *Kingship of God,* p.86.

72. *Ibid.,* p.95.

73. *Ibid.,* p.102.

74. Cf. the officers of I Kings 4:7.

75. Cf. 2 Sam. 20:26.

76. Buber, *Moses,* p.106.

77. *Ibid.,* p.107.

78. *Ibid.,* p.106.

79. Buber, *Kingship of God,* p.92.

80. *Ibid.,* p.93.

81. Buber, borrowing from the work of Max Weber, describes the basis of the human authority of this period as "charismatic authority." It is won only through the "charisma" of the individual leader-warrior or prophet, endowed with the spirit, the *ruah,* and given a mission by God. The deity of this period is unencumbered by a priesthood and set dwelling place, be it mountain or temple. YHVH wanders with His people and His presence is symbolized, after Sinai, by the portable tent and Ark of the Covenant, which moves with the people and provides a place "for God to manifest himself in or on" (*Moses,* p.159).

82. Buber, *Two Types of Faith,* trans. N. Goldhawk (New York: Macmillan, 1951), p.10.

83. *Ibid.,* p.8.

84. *Ibid.,* p.10.

85. *Ibid.,* p.29.

86. Paul Mendes-Flohr describes Buber's notion of trust as "a *secondary* phenomenon—it is a consequence of an original experience of dialogue." "Buber's Conception of God," p.187.

87. Buber, *Two Types of Faith,* p.49.

88. Mendes-Flohr, "Buber's Conception of God," p.185.

89. Buber, *Two Types of Faith,* p.9.

90. *Ibid.,* p.8. It is interesting that Buber's conception of faith as trust fits nicely with Erik Erikson's notion of religion. In *Childhood and Society* (New York: Norton, 1963), Erikson correlates the first and most important psychological stage of development, which he calls "basic trust," with religion. "Trust born of care is, in fact, the touchstone of *actuality* of a given religion. All religions have in common the periodic childlike surrender to a Provider or providers who dispense earthly fortune as well as spiritual health" (p.250). Erikson sees in the notion of religion as trust a fundamental maternal dimension. The issue of the break in trust is an issue that recalls separation of the infant from the mother and atonement is, then, an attempt to restore the trusting relationship with God as mother. ". . . [T]he most primitive layer in all religions and the religious layer in each individual abound with efforts of atonement which try to make up for vague deeds against a maternal matrix and try to restore faith in the goodness of one's strivings and in the kindness of the powers of the universe" (pp.250–51). Although Buber would regard Erikson's analysis as a dangerous reduction of religion to psychology one could develop a fascinating psychological study of Buber's view of God and faith using contemporary object-relations psychology (Winnicott, Fairbairn, Guntrip, M. Mahler), which highlights the earliest mother-child relation and issues of trust instead of the later father-child relation and issues of guilt.

91. Buber, *Prophetic Faith,* p.89.

92. Cf. Deut. 31:18.

93. The following analysis is taken from Buber, "The Leading Word and the Paradigmatic Form of Divine Speech," (Hebrew) *Darkho shel Mikra,* pp.300–307. (The translations are my own).

94. Fox's commentary in *Now These Are the Names,* p.181.

95. Buber, "The Leading Word . . . ," p.302.

96. *Ibid.,* p.300.

97. *Ibid.,* p.303.

98. Buber, *Moses,* p.109.

99. The prophetic faith, for Buber, never was an establishment faith, a faith of celebration of the status quo, but a faith of wandering and hope for the future, a faith dependent only on direct contact with God, a faith which included in it a demand for criticism of the given order. The writing prophets stood outside the monarchy and the people and criticized them from the perspective of their faith in God as king and leader. Buber seemed to see himself as part of this prophetic tradition, standing outside the mainstream of Zionism led by Ben-Gurion and criticizing it from the values presented in prophetic Judaism.

100. Buber, *The Prophetic Faith,* p.129.

101. Buber, "The Dialogue Between Heaven and Earth," p.219.

102. Buber, *The Prophetic Faith,* p.124.

103. *Ibid.,* p.140.

104. *Ibid.,* p.142.

105. *Ibid.*

106. *Ibid.,* p.153.

107. *Ibid.*

108. *Ibid.,* p.144.

109. *Ibid.*

110. Richard Rubenstein, "The Dean and the Chosen People," *After Auschwitz* (Indianapolis: Bobbs Merrill, 1968). Irving Greenberg, "Cloud of Smoke, Pillar of Fire: Judaism, Christianity, and Modernity After the Holocaust," p.23f. Fackenheim, *God's Presence,* pp.5–6.

111. Buber, *The Prophetic Faith,* p.1.

112. I must thank Lou Silberman for first pointing me to this section of *The Prophetic Faith* as a resource to address the Holocaust in a seminar I took with him at the University of Chicago in 1978.

113. *Ibid.,* p.184.

114. *Ibid.,* p.234.

115. *Ibid.*

116. Irving Greenberg has also used the "Suffering Servant" motif to respond to the Holocaust. Greenberg connects the motif to symbols of "vicarious suffering" throughout Jewish tradition.

> The Suffering Servant in Isaiah 53 sounds like a passage out of Holocaust literature. He is led as a sheep to slaughter. . . . He is despised and forsaken of men. . . . Of course the concept of vicarious suffering is not new to Jewish tradition. It is one of the great themes of the High Holiday liturgy. Isaac's binding, in particular, is held up as a paradigm of suffering. ("Cloud of Smoke," p.36)

One of the most elegant uses of the Suffering Servant motif in all of Holocaust literature is found in André Schwarz-Bart's use of the legend of the "Lamed-vov," the 36 righteous who uphold the world through their suffering. *The Last of the Just,* trans. S. Baker (New York: Atheneum, 1960).

117. Buber, *The Prophetic Faith,* p.1.

118. Fackenheim, *God's Presence in History,* p.49.

119. Richard Rubenstein states in *After Auschwitz:*

> If I believed in God as the omnipotent author of the historical drama and Israel as His Chosen People, I had to accept . . . [the] conclusion that it was God's will that Hitler committed six million Jews to slaughter. I could not possibly believe in such a God nor could I believe in Israel as the chosen people of God after Auschwitz. (p.46)

Greenberg describes "dialectical faith," in "Cloud of Smoke":

> The Holocaust challenges the claims of all the standards that compete for modern man's loyalties. Nor does it give simple clear answers and definitive solutions. . . . The Holocaust offers only dialectical moves and understandings. The classic normative experiences [of faith are] . . . tested and reformulated—dialectically attacked and affirmed—as they pass through the fires of the new revelatory event. (p.23–24)

Fackenheim articulates the 614th commandment in *God's Presence in History* with this declaration:

> Jews are forbidden to hand Hitler posthumous victories. They are commanded to survive as Jews, lest the Jewish people perish. . . . A Jew may not respond to Hitler's attempt to destroy Judaism by himself cooperating in its destruction. (p.84)

120. Greenberg speaks of this issue in the context of the Holocaust.

> [The Holocaust] ends the easy dichotomy of atheist/theist. . . . It makes clear that faith is a life response of the whole person to the Presence of life and history. Like life this response ebbs and flows. The difference between the skeptic and the believer is the frequency of faith. ("Cloud of Smoke," p.27)

121. For example, Steven Katz fails to include Buber in his survey: "Jewish Faith After the Holocaust: Four Approaches," *Post-Holocaust Dialogues.*

122. Buber, *The Prophetic Faith*, p.182.

123. *Ibid.,* p.147

124. *Ibid.,* p.183.

125. *Ibid.,* p.189.

126. *Ibid.*

127. *Ibid.*

128. Buber, "Dialogue Between Heaven and Earth," p.224.

129. *Ibid.*

130. Buber, *Two Types of Faith*, p.28.

131. Buber, *The Prophetic Faith*, p.193.

132. *Ibid.*

133. *Ibid.*

134. *Ibid.,* p.194.

135. *Ibid.*

136. In *Good and Evil* Buber argues that the Hebrew for "to know," *leda'at,* indicates "contact" and not "reflection." "The decisive event for 'knowing' in biblical Hebrew is not that one looks at an object, but that one comes into touch with it. . . . At the center is not a perceiving of one another, but the contact of being, intercourse" (p.56).

137. Buber, "Dialogue Between Heaven and Earth," p.224.

138. Buber, *The Prophetic Faith*, p.192.

139. *Ibid.,* p.193.

140. In *The Eclipse of God* Buber has a helpful interpretation of what it means to have the "fear of God."

> All religious reality begins with what Biblical religion calls the "fear of God." It comes when our existence between birth and death becomes incomprehensible and uncanny, when all security is shattered through the mystery. . . . Through this dark gate the believing man steps forth into the everyday which is henceforth hallowed as the place in which he has to live with the mystery. (p.36)

141. Buber, *The Prophetic Faith*, p.195.

142. Buber, "Man of Today," p.8. I would offer that Abraham Joshua Heschel's initial

turn to nature as a "way to His presence," and his stress on the sense of "Wonder," "Mystery," "Awe," and "Glory" that nature inspires are also motivated by an attempt to bring contemporary Jews back to the God of Judaism through the God of creation. See Heschel, *God in Search of Man* (New York: Harper, 1955), chs.2–8.

143. I use the translation of the Hebrew Bible, *Tanakh* (New York: Jewish Publication Society, 1985).

144. Buber, *The Prophetic Faith*, p.195.

145. Frankl tells us that the camp inmate experienced nature's beauty "as never before."

> If someone had seen our faces on the journey from Auschwitz to a Bavarian camp as we beheld the mountains of Salzburg with their summits glowing in the sunset, through the little barbed windows of the prison carriage, he would never have believed that those were the faces of men who had given up all hope of life and liberty. Despite that factor—or maybe because of it—we were carried away by nature's beauty, which we had missed for so long.

Man's Search for Meaning (New York: Simon and Schuster, 1962) pp.38–39.

146. Buber, "Dialogue Between Heaven and Earth," p.225.

147. The insight into the hope that the God of Creation represents came to me, personally, after seeing *Shoah*, the documentary film on the Holocaust, for the second time. I became fascinated with the green grass that had grown up at Auschwitz. What was that beautiful, lush, green grass doing there? How could grass grow in that evil place, that endless, sunless night, that living hell? Should it not be barren forever? These questions baffled me. In thinking about them, however, I suddenly saw that green grass as a sign of hope. Life goes on, surges forth, life grows even in and after Auschwitz. I came to see that there was a similarity between my expectation that God would intervene in Auschwitz and my expectation that God would prevent grass from ever growing there. Because those people were so innocent and in need of help, God should have come to help them, I had thought. Because that place, Auschwitz, was so evil, God should prevent grass from growing there, I had thought. But inexorably life goes on. Life is rejuvenated. Inmates who at the end of the war weighed 65 pounds, only skin and bones, did find that their bodies healed. Survivors lived on and had children and those children, like all kids, laughed and played and celebrated and celebrate life.

So the life that continues and surges forth after the Holocaust means that there is still hope and goodness and reason to praise God for the life that he gives and sustains and heals. The tradition teaches in its doctrine of creation that the created world is good. "And God saw all that He created and Behold it was very good," we read in Genesis. This basic goodness of life, this goodness which we can perceive in the extent to which so many of us seek not only to continue to survive but to work and build and find pleasure in living, is the gift from God that all of us can acknowledge. Continually, daily, life is created, healing happens, new life is born, and this must be a signal of hope.

148. Buber, "Dialogue Between Heaven and Earth," p.224.

149. *Ibid.*, p.222.

150. *Ibid.*, p.225.

151. *Ibid.*, p.224.

152. I wish to thank Brian Mahan for his comments on the relevance of Buber's *Good and Evil* to issues of suffering and faith.

153. Martin Buber, *Briefwechsel aus sieben Jahrzehnten*, Vol. II, ed. G. Schraeder, p.111.

154. For the definitive collection of all of Buber's writings on the bi-national State and the Arab-Israeli conflicts of his day see Buber, *A Land of Two Peoples*, ed. P. Mendes-Flohr (Oxford: Oxford University Press, 1983). Buber's biblical writings must also be seen as a response to the attempt to build a Jewish State in Palestine. In this regard, it is significant that it was the Israelite nomadic wandering faith that Buber pointed to as ideal and not the faith of establishment in the land, the faith centered in Jerusalem and

in the Davidic monarchy. In fact, Buber seems to purposely desist from stressing the biblical passages which speak of the holiness of the land of Israel and the divine sanction of Jewish possession of this land.

Henry Abramovitch has pointed out that when Buber wrote "Abraham the Seer" (1939), he omitted mention of YHVH's promise to give Israel to Abraham's seed and also underemphasized the expulsion of Ishmael from the land. Buber argued that, ultimately, the land belonged neither to the Jews nor to the Arabs but to God. "The desire for ownership of land is not prohibited, renunciation [of it] is not invited, but the owner of the land is God—man only 'dwells temporarily,' *'Beisass,'* and the owner establishes the rhythms of the temporary settlement so that an overpowering disparity will not cause the relationship between the partners to break" (*"Zu einer neuen Verdeutschung,"* p.1). Abramovitch believes this is so because "to call attention to Abraham's rejection of Ishmael would not have helped the cause of reconciliation" between Arab and Jew which was so important to Buber's work in the League for Jewish-Arab Rapproachement and Cooperation. Henry Abramovitch, "The Psychobiography of a Dialogue: Martin Buber and the Biblical Abraham," *Judaism,* 34:4 (1985), 411. Buber's biblical narrative is designed to give hope to the new settlers, to give them a sense that God is with them, at the same time that it allows for the legitimate claims of another people, the Arab residents of Palestine.

155. In 1950 Buber spoke of the war for Israeli independence, which dashed his hopes for a bi-national state, as "the most grievous" of the three wars he experienced. *Two Types of Faith,* p.15. In volume three of *Buber's Life and Work* (New York: Dutton, 1983), Maurice Friedman shows how Buber responded to each of the tragedies of the later period of his life.

156. Buber, *Good and Evil,* p.3.
157. *Ibid.,* p.7.
158. *Ibid.,* p.9.
159. *Ibid.*
160. *Ibid.,* p.13.
161. *Ibid.,* p.47.
162. *Ibid.,* p.34.
163. *Ibid.,* p.51.
164. *Ibid.,* p.34.
165. *Ibid.,* p.53.
166. *Ibid.*
167. *Ibid.,* p.55.
168. *Ibid.,* p.54.
169. *Ibid.,* p.55.
170. *Ibid.,* p.60.
171. *Ibid.,* p.31.
172. *Ibid.,* p.6.
173. *Ibid.,* p.20.

174. I am re-appropriating this expression from its use by Peter Ochs in his very fine attempt to correlate the post-liberal Christian theology of Lindbeck with what Ochs calls the theology of Jewish "Aftermoderns." Peter Ochs, "A Rabbinic Pragmatism," in B. Marshall, ed., *Theology and Dialogue* (Notre Dame: Notre Dame University Press, 1990).

8. Conclusion: Buber and the Narrative Theologians

1. Gary Comstock, "Two Types of Narrative Theology," *JAAR,* 55:4 (Winter 1987), 687–717. Comstock puts "the anti-foundational, cultural-linguistic, Wittgensteinians" Hans Frei, George Lindbeck, Stanley Hauerwas and David Kelsey in the "pure" group. And the "revisionist, hermeneutical, Gadamerians" Paul Ricoeur, David Tracy, Julian Hartt, and Sallie McFague in the second, "impure" group.
2. George Lindbeck, *The Nature of Doctrine* (Philadelphia: Westminster, 1984).

3. See Michael Goldberg, *Theology and Narrative,* ch.6.

4. Buber, "Dialogue," pp.1–2.

5. *Ibid.,* pp.2–3.

6. *Ibid.,* p.2.

7. Buber's general hermeneutics (ch.4.) and the argument below will suggest that Buber's narrative biblical theology and his response to the Holocaust need to be brought to and tested in public discourse where philosophic as well as narrative language is employed.

8. See *I and Thou,* Smith trans., pp.18ff.

9. *Ibid.,* p.17.

10. Buber, "Distance and Relation," p.71. There is also a statement in *I and Thou* which suggests that the I is aided in relationships with other Thous by a "knowledge" of its separateness from others.

> Through the Thou a man becomes I. That which confronts him comes and disappears, relational events condense, then are scattered, and in the change consciousness of the . . . I grows clear . . . till a time comes when it bursts its bonds, and the I confronts itself for a moment, separated as though it were a Thou; as quickly to take possession of itself and from then on to enter into relations in consciousness of itself. (p.29)

11. Buber, *Good and Evil,* p.66.

12. Paul Ricoeur makes a similar point in *Symbolism of Evil,* trans. E. Buchanan (Boston: Beacon, 1967).

13. "Interrogation of Martin Buber by M. Friedman," in S. Rome and B. Rome, eds., *Philosophical Interrogations* (New York: Holt, Rinehart, Winston, 1964), p.53; cf. pp.46,48,56.

14. Buber, "What Is Common to All."

15. *Ibid.,* p.104.

16. *Ibid.,* p.105.

17. *Ibid.,* p.104.

18. *Ibid.,* p.107.

19. Buber, "Hasidism and Modern Man," p.42.

20. Buber, "What Is Common," p.107.

21. In the end of my "A Narrative Jewish Theology," I discuss some of the limits of narrative and reasons why Jewish theology cannot rest on narrative *aggadah* alone. First, and foremost, there is the issue of the central place of law, *halakhah.* Chaim Bialik, in his classic *Halakhah and Aggadah* (London: Zionist Federation, 1944) has argued that Judaism cannot rest with narratives but that *halakhah* is the "inevitable continuation and sequel of *aggadah*" (p.26). For a helpful discussion of the "limits" of narrative discourse for philosophy and Christian theology see George Aichele, Jr., *The Limits of Story* (Chico, CA: Scholars Press, 1985).

22. Buber, "What Is Common," p.104.

23. Here I aim to expand Todorov's Bakhtinian phrase "dialogics of culture" (*The Dialogical Principle,* p.104) beyond one culture to refer to the dialogue between many cultures.

24. Buber, "Genuine Dialogue and the Possibilities of Peace," [1953] *Pointing the Way,* p.235.

BIBLIOGRAPHY

A. Buber's Works Cited

Buber, Martin. "On Viennese Literature." [Polish] *Weekly Review of Social Life, Literature, and Fine Arts,* 32:25,27 (June and July 1897), 297–98, 321–22, Warsaw. [English translation: In W. Johnston, "Martin Buber's Literary Debut," 1974.]

———. "Ein Wort über Nietzsche und die Lebenswerte." *Die Kunst im Leben,* I/2, xii (1900), 13.

———. "Von Jüdischer Kunst." *Die Welt,* 46 (Nov. 11, 1901), 10.

———. "Die Schaffenden, das Volk und die Bewegung." *Jüdischer Almanach.* Berlin: Jüdischer Verlag, 1902.

———. ed. *Jüdische Künstler.* Berlin: Jüdischer Verlag, 1903.

———. "Gustav Landauer." *Die Zeit,* 39:506 (June 1904), 127–28.

———. *Die Geschichten des Rabbi Nachman: Ihm nacherzählt von Martin Buber.* Frankfurt a.M: Rütten und Loening, 1906 and 1918. [English translation: *The Tales of Rabbi Nachman.* 1956.]

———. *Die Legende des Baal-Shem.* Frankfurt o. M.: Rütten und Loening, 1908. Revised edition, 1920. [English Translation: *The Legend of the Baal-Shem.* 1969.]

———. "Das Judentum und die Juden." In *Drie Reden über das Judentum.* Frankfurt o.M.: Rütten und Loening, 1911. [English translation: "Judaism and the Jews." In *On Judaism.* 1972.]

———. "*Mein Weg zum Chassidismus.*" Frankfurt o.M.: Rütten und Loening, 1918. [English translation: "My Way to Hasidism." In *Hasidism and Modern Man.* 1966.]

———. *Cherut: Eine Rede über Jugend und Religion.* Vienna: Löwit, 1919. [English Translation: "Herut," In *On Judaism.* 1972.]

———. "Gemeinschaft." *Worte an die Zeit: Eine Schriftenreihe* II. Munich: Drieländerverlag, 1919.

———. *Die Jüdische Bewegung: Gesammelte Aufsätze und Ansprachen* I. Berlin: Jüdischer Verlag, 1920.

———. *Ekstatische Konfessionen.* Leipzig: Insel Verlag, 1921. [English translation: *Ecstatic Confessions. 1985.]*

———. *Der Grosse Maggid und seine Nachfolge.* Frankfurt o. M.: Rütten und Loening, 1922.

———. *Ich und Du.* Leipzig: Insel Verlag, 1923. [1962, *Werke* I]. [English translation: *I and Thou.* trans. R. G. Smith, 1958. trans. W. Kaufmann, 1970.]

———. "Über Stefan George." *Die Literarisch Welt* (July 13, 1928).

———. "Zweisprache." *Die Kreatur,* III/3 (1929), 201–222. [English translation: "Dialogue." In *Between Man and Man.* 1965.]

———. "Was soll mit den zehn Geboten geschehen?" *Die Literarisch Welt* (July 7, 1929), 3. [English translation: "What Should We Do About the Ten Commandments?" In *Israel and the World.* 1963.]

———. *Königtum Gottes.* Berlin: Schocken, 1932. [English translation: *Kingship of God.* 1967.]

———. "Why We Should Study Jewish Sources." [German] In *Kampf um Israel.* Berlin: Schocken, 1933. [In *Israel and the World.* 1963.]

———. "Biblischer Humanismus." *Der Morgen,* 9:4 (Oct. 1933), 241–45. [English translation: "Biblical Humanism." In *On the Bible.* 1982.]

————. *Die Frage an den Einzelnen.* Berlin: Schocken: 1936 [English translation: "The Question to the Single One." In *Between Man and Man.* 1965.]

————. "Der Mensch von heute und die jüdische Bibel." In Buber and F. Rosenzweig. *Die Schrift und ihre Verdeutschung.* Berlin: Schocken, 1936 [English translation: "The Man of Today and the Jewish Bible." In *On the Bible.* 1982]

————. "Shelihut Avraham." *HaAretz* (Feb. and March 1939). "English translation: "Abraham the Seer." In *On the Bible.*1982.]

————. *Humaniut Ivrit. Hapoel Hatzair,* 34:18 (May 1941). [English translation: "Hebrew Humanism." In *Israel and the World.* 1963.]

————. *Torat HaNeviim.* Tel Aviv: Bialik, 1942. [English translation: *The Prophetic Faith.* 1960.]

————. "Advice to Frequenters of Libraries." *Books for Your Vacation.* Branch Library Book News. The New York Public Library, XXI/5 (1944), 81–82.

————. "Love of God and Love of Neighbor." [Hebrew] In *B'Pardas Ha'Hasidut.* Tel-Aviv: Bialik, 1945. [English translation from the German (1952): In *Hasidism and Modern Man.* 1958.

————. *Moshe.* Jerusalem: Schocken, 1945. [English translation: *Moses.* 1958.]

————. *Or Ha'Ganuz.* Jerusalem: Schocken, 1946. [English translation: *Tales of the Hasidism: Early Masters.* 1947.

————. *Ntivut b'Utopia.* Tel Aviv: Am Ovad, 1947. [English translation: *Paths in Utopia* 1958.]

————. "Das Problem des Menschen." In *Dialogisches Leben.* Zurich: G. Müller, 1947. [English translation: "What Is Man?" In *Between Man and Man.* 1965.]

————.*Tales of the Hasidim: Early Masters.* [Hebrew, 1946] Translated by Olga Marx. New York: Schocken Books, 1947.

————. *Tales of the Hasidim: Later Masters.* [Hebrew, 1946]Translated by Olga Marx. New York: Schocken Books, 1948.

————. *Die Erzählungen der Chassidim.* [Hebrew, 1946] Zurich: Manesse Verlag, 1949.

————. "Urdistanz und Beziehung," *Studia Philosophica Jahrbuch des Schweizerischen Philosophischen Gesellschaft, Separatum* X. Basel: Verlag für Recht und Gesellschaft, 1950, 7–19. [English translation: "Distance and Relation." In *The Knowlege of Man.* 1965.]

————. *Pfade in Utopia.* [1962, *Werke I*] Heidelberg: L. Schneider, 1950. [English translation: *Paths in Utopia.* 1958.]

————. *Zwei Glaubensweisen.* Zurich: Manesse, 1950. [English translation: *Two Types of Faith,* 1952.]

————. *Two Types of Faith.* [German, 1950] Translated by N. Goldhawk. New York: Macmillan, 1952.

————. "Der Dialog zwischen Himmel und Erde." In *An der Wende.* Cologne: Hegner, 1952. [English translation: "The Dialogue Between Heaven and Earth." In *On Judaism.* 1972.]

————. "Die heimliche Frage." In *An der Wende.* Cologne: Hegner, 1952. [English translation: "The Silent Question." In *On Judaism.* 1972.]

————. *The Eclipse of God.* Translated by M. Friedman *et al.* New York: Harper and Row, 1952.

————. *Bilder von Gut und Böse.* Cologne: Hegner, 1952. [English translation: *Good and Evil.* 1953.]

————. *Good and Evil.* [German, 1952.] Translated by R. G. Smith. New York: Scribner's, 1953.

————. *Das echte Gespräch und die Möglichkeiten des Friedens.* Heidelberg: L. Schneider, 1953. [English translation: "Genuine Dialogue and the Possibilities of Peace." In *Pointing the Way.* 1974.]

————. "Zu einer Verdeutschung der Schrift." Beilage to *Die Fünf Bücher der Weisung.* Köln: Jakob Hegner, 1954.

———. "Elemente des Zwischenmenschlichen." *Schriften über des dialogische Prinzip.* 1954. [English translation: "Elements of the Interhuman." In *The Knowledge of Man.* 1965.]

———. "Nachwort." In *Die Schriften über das dialogische Prinzip.* Heidelberg: L. Schneider, 1954. [English translation: "Afterward: The History of the Dialogical Principle." In *Between Man and Man.* 1965.]

———. *"Der Mensch und sein Gebild."* Heidelberg: Lambert Schneider, 1955. [1962, *Werke* I.] [English translation: "Man and His Image-Work." In *The Knowledge of Man.* 1965.]

———. "Dem Gemeinschaftlichen folgen." *Die Neue Rundschau* LXVII/4 (Oct. 1956), 582–600. [1962, *Werke* I.] [English translation: "What Is Common to All." In *The Knowledge of Man.* 1965.]

———. "Der Chassidismus und der abendländische Mensch," *Merkur.* X/10 (1956), 933–43. [English translation: "Hasidism and Modern Man." In *Hasidism and Modern Man.* 1966.]

———. *The Tales of Rabbi Nachman.* [German, 1906 and 1918.] Translated by M. Friedman. New York: Horizon, 1956.

———. *I and Thou.* [German, 1923] Translated by R. G. Smith. New York: Scribner's Sons, 1958.

———. *Moses: The Revelation and the Covenant.* [Hebrew, 1945] New York: Harper and Row, 1958.

———. *Paths in Utopia.* [Hebrew, 1947.] Translated from the German [1950] by R. F. C. Hull. Boston: Beacon, 1958.

———. *Begegnung: Autobiographische Fragmente.* Stuttgart: W. Kohlhammer, 1960. [English translation: "Autobiographical Fragments." In Schilpp and Friedman, eds., *The Philosophy of Martin Buber.* 1967.]

———. *The Prophetic Faith.* [Hebrew 1942] Translated from the German [1950] by C. Witten-Davies. New York: Harper and Row, 1960.

———. "Das Wort, das gesprochen wird." *Wort und Wirklichkeit.* Edited by R. Oldenbourg. Munich: Bayerische Akademie der Schönen Künste. 1960. [1962, *Werke* I.] [English translation: "The Word That Is Spoken." In *The Knowledge of Man.* 1965.]

———. *Werke I Erster Band: Schriften zur Philosophie.* Heidelberg: Lambert Schneider, 1962.

———. *Israel and the World.* Translated by O. Marx. New York: Schocken, 1963.

———. "Interpreting Hasidism." *Commentary.* 36:3 (Sept. 1963), 218–25.

———. "Antwort." *Martin Buber: Philosophen des XX. Jahrhunderts.* Edited by P. Schilpp and M. Friedman. Stuttgart: W. Kohlhammer, 1963. [English translation: "Replies to My Critics." In Schilpp and Friedman, eds., *The Philosophy of Martin Buber.* 1967.]

———. *Darkho shel Mikra.* Jerusalem: Mosad Bialik, 1964.

———. "The Leading Word and the Paradigmatic Form of Divine Speech" [Hebrew]. In *Darkho shel Mikra.* 1964.

———. *Werke II Zweiter Band: Schriften zur Bibel.* Heidelberg: Lambert Schneider, 1964.

———. "Interrogation of Martin Buber by M. Friedman," In S. and B. Rome. eds., *Philosophical Interrogations.* New York: Holt, Rinehart, Winston, 1964.

———. *The Knowledge of Man.* Edited by M. Friedman. Translated by M. Friedman and R.G. Smith. New York: Harper and Row, 1965.

———. *Between Man and Man.* Edited by Maurice Friedman. Translated by R. G. Smith. New York: Macmillan Co., 1965.

———. *Nachlese.* Heidelberg: Lambert Schneider, 1965. [English translation: *A Believing Humanism.* 1967.]

———. "Das Unbewusste." In *Nachlese.* 1965. [English translation: "The Unconscious." In *A Believing Humanism.* 1967.]

————. "Von der Verseelung der Welt." In *Nachlese.* 1965. [English translation: "On the Psychologizing of the World." In *A Believing Humanism.* 1967.]

————. *Hasidism and Modern Man.* Translated by M. Friedman. New York: Harper. 1966.

————. *A Believing Humanism.* Translated by M. Friedman. New York: Simon and Schuster, 1967.

————. *Kingship of God.* [German, 1932.] Translated by R. Scheimann. New York: Harper and Row, 1967.

————. "Zu einer neuen Verdeutschung der Schrift." [1st edition, 1954] Beilage to *"Die Fünf Bücher der Weisung."* Köln: Jakob Hegner, 1968.

————. *The Legend of the Baal-Shem.* [German, 1908 and 1920.] Translated by M. Friedman. New York: Schocken, 1969.

————. *I and Thou.* [German, 1923] Translated by W. Kaufmann. New York: Scribner's Sons, 1970.

————. *On Judaism.* Edited by N. Glatzer. Translated by E. Jospe. New York: Schocken, 1972.

————. *Meetings.* Translated and edited by M. Friedman. La Salle, IL: Open Court, 1973.

————. *Briefwechsel aus sieben Jahrzehnten,* Vol. I. Edited by G. Schaeder. Heidelberg: Lambert Schneider, 1972.

————. *Briefwechsel aus sieben Jahrzehnten,* Vol. II. Edited by G. Schaeder. Heidelberg: Lambert Schneider, 1973.

————. *Pointing the Way.* Edited and translated by M. Friedman. New York: Schocken, 1974.

————. *Briefwechsel aus sieben Jahrzehnten,* Vol. III. Edited by G. Schaeder. Heidelberg: Lambert Schneider, 1975.

————. *On the Bible.* Edited by N. Glatzer. New York: Schocken, 1982.

————. *A Land of Two Peoples.* Edited by P. Mendes-Flohr. Oxford: Oxford University Press, 1983.

————. *Ecstatic Confessions.* [German, 1921.] Edited by P. Mendes-Flohr. Translated by E. Cameron. San Francisco: Harper and Row, 1985.

Buber, Martin, and Franz Rosenzweig. *Die Schrift und ihre Verdeutschung.* Berlin: Schocken, 1936.

B. Other Works Cited

Abramovitch, Henry. "The Psychobiography of a Dialogue: Martin Buber and the Biblical Abraham." *Judaism,* 34:4 (Sept. 1985), 401–16.

Aichele, George, Jr. *The Limits of Story.* Chico, CA: Scholars Press, 1985.

Altizer, Thomas, *et al. Deconstruction and Theology.* New York: Crossroad, 1982.

Amir, Yehoshua. "The Finite Thou and the Eternal Thou in the Work of Buber," In H. Gordon and J. Bloch, eds., *Martin Buber: A Centenary Volume.* New York: KTAV, 1984.

Anderson, Bernard, ed. *The Old Testament and Christian Faith.* New York: Harper and Row, 1963.

Auerbach, Erich. *Mimesis.* Translated by W. Trask. Princeton: Princeton University Press, 1953.

Augustine, Saint. *Confessions.* Translated by R. S. Pine-Coffin. New York: Penguin, 1961.

Bakhtin, Mikhail. *Rabelais and His World.* Cambridge: MIT Press, 1968.

————. *The Dialogic Imagination.* Edited by M. Holquist. Translated by C. Emerson and M. Holquist. Austin: University of Texas Press, 1981.

————. *Problems of Dostoevsky's Poetics.* Edited and translated by C. Emerson. Minneapolis: University of Minnesota Press, 1984.

————. *Art and Answerability.* Edited by M. Holquist. Translated by V. Liapunov. Austin: University of Texas Press, 1990.

Band, Arnold. *Nahman of Bratslav: The Tales.* New York: Paulist Press, 1978.

Barthes, Roland. "Introduction to the Structural Analysis of Narratives." In *Image, Music, Text.* Translated by Stephen Heath. New York: Hill and Wang, 1977.

———. "The Death of the Author." In *Image, Music, Text.* Translated by Stephen Heath. New York: Hill and Wang, 1977.

Bellah, Robert, *et al. Habits of the Heart.* Berkeley: University of California Press, 1985.

Ben-Amos, Dan, and Jerome Mintz. *In Praise of the Baal-Shem Tov.* Bloomington: Indiana University Press, 1970.

Benveniste, Emile. *Problems in General Linquistics.* Translated by E. Meck, Coral Gables, FL: University of Miami Press, 1971.

Berger, Peter. *The Sacred Canopy.* New York: Anchor, 1969.

Bernstein, Richard. *Beyond Objectivism and Relativism: Science, Hermeneutics and Praxis.* Philadelphia: University of Pennsylvania Press, 1983.

Berry, Donald. *Mutuality: The Vision of Martin Buber.* Albany: SUNY Press, 1985.

Bialik, Chaim. *Halakhah and Aggadah.* London: Zionist Federation, 1944.

Blettgen, Hans Hermann. "Der Rabbi und Sein Sohn: Martin Bubers Verarbeitung einer Geschichte des Rabbi Nachman von Bratzlaw." In M. Brocke, ed., *Beter und Rebellen Aus 1000 Jahren Judentum in Polen.* Berlin: Institut Kirche und Judentum, 1983.

Bloom, Harold. "Introduction." In Martin Buber, *On the Bible.* Edited by N. Glatzer. New York: Schocken, 1982.

Bloom, Harold, *et al.,* eds. *Deconstruction and Criticism.* New York: Seabury, 1979.

Booth, Wayne. *The Rhetorics of Fiction.* Chicago: University of Chicago Press, 1961.

———. *Critical Understanding: The Powers and Limits of Pluralism.* Chicago: University of Chicago Press, 1979.

Bouchard, Larry. *Tragic Method and Tragic Theology.* University Park: Pennsylvania State University Press, 1989.

Breslauer, Daniel. *The Chrysalis of Religion: A Guide to the Jewishness of Buber's I and Thou.* Nashville, Abingdon, 1980.

Brice, Charles. "Pathological Modes of Human Relating and Therapeutic Mutuality: A Dialogue Between Buber's Existential Theory and Object-Relations Theory." *Psychiatry,* 47:2 (1984), 109–23.

Brocke, Michael. "Martin Bubers *Misreading* des R. Nachman von Bratzlaw: *Die unbekannte 'Geschichte von der fahrenden Prinzessin.'* " *Spiel—Räume.* Edited by H. G. Heimbrock. Neukirchener Verlag, 1983.

Bultmann, Rudolf. "The Problem of Hermeneutics." In *New Testament and Mythology.* Translated and edited by S. Ogden. Philadelphia: Fortress Press, 1984.

Capps, Donald. "Parabolic Events in Augustine's Autobiography." *Theology Today,* XL/3 (October 1983), 260–72.

Chatman, Seymour. *Story and Discourse.* Ithaca: Cornell University Press, 1978.

Clark, Katerina, and Michael Holquist. *Mikhail Bakhtin.* Cambridge, MA: Harvard University Press, 1984.

Cohen, Arthur, and Paul Mendes-Flohr, eds. *Contemporary Jewish Religious Thought.* New York: Scribner's, 1987.

Cohler, Bertram. "Personal Narrative and Life Course." In P. Baltes and O. Brim, eds., *Life-Span Development and Behavior.* Vol. 4. New York: Academic Press, 1982.

Cohn, Margot, and Raphael Buber, eds. *Martin Buber: A Bibliography of His Writings.* Jerusalem: Magnes Press, 1980.

Comstock, Gary. "Two Types of Narrative Theology." *Journal of the American Academy of Religion,* 55:4 (Winter 1987), 687–717.

Crites, Stephen. "The Narrative Quality of Experience." *Journal of the American Academy of Religion,* 39:3 (Sept. 1971), 291–311.

Derrida, Jacques. *L'Écriture et la différénce.* Paris: Seuil, 1967.

———. *De la Grammatologie.* Éditions du Minuit, 1967.

———. "Structure, Sign and Play in the Discourse of the Human Sciences." In R. Macksey and E. Donato, eds., *The Languages of Criticism and the Sciences of Man.* Baltimore: Johns Hopkins University Press, 1970.

Dilthey, Wilhelm. *Die grosse Phantasiedichtung.* Edited by H. Nohl. Göttingen: Vandenhoeck und Ruprecht, 1954.

———. "Die Entstehung der Hermenutik." [1900] *Gesammelte Schriften,* Vol. 5. *Die geistige Welt* I. Edited by B. Groethuysen. Stuttgart: Teubner, 1957.

———. *Gesammelt Schriften,* Vol. 6. *Die geistige Welt* II. Edited by G. Misch. Stuttgart: Teubner, 1958.

———. *Gesammelte Schriften,* Vol. 7. *Der Augbau der geschichtlichen Welt in den Geisteswissenschaften.* Edited by B. Groethuysen. Stuttgart: Teubner, 1958.

———. *Gesammelte Schriften.* Vol. 1. *Einleitung in die Geisteswissenschaften.* Edited by B. Groethuysen; Stuttgart: Teubner, 1959.

———. *Gessammelte Schriften,* Vol. 8. *Weltanschauungslehre Abhandlungen zur Philosophie der Philosophie.* Edited by B. Groethuysen. Stuttgart: Teubner, 1960.

———. *W. Dilthey: Selected Writings.* Translated and edited by H. P. Rickman. London: Cambridge University Press, 1976.

———. "Fragments of a Poetics." In *Selected Works,* Vol. 5. *Poetry and Experience.* Edited by R. Makkreel and F. Rodi. Princeton: Princeton University Press, 1985.

Eliade, Mircea. *The Myth of the Eternal Return.* Translated by W. Trask. Princeton: Princeton University Press, 1971.

Erikson, Erik. *Childhood and Society.* New York: Norton, 1963.

Ermarth, Michael. *William Dilthey: The Critique of Historical Reason.* Chicago: University of Chicago Press, 1978.

Estess, Ted. "The Inenarrable Contraption." *Journal of the American Academy of Religion,* 42:3 (Sept. 1974), 415–34.

Fackenheim, Emil. *God's Presence in History.* New York: Harper, 1970.

———. *The Jewish Return into History.* New York: Schocken, 1978.

———. *To Mend the World.* New York: Schocken, 1982.

Fischer-Barnicol, Hans. " '. . . und Poet dazu.' *Die Einheit von Denken und Dichten bei Martin Buber."* *Bulletin des Leo Baeck Instituts,* IX/33. Tel Aviv: Bitaon, 1966.

Fishbane, Michael. "Martin Buber as an Interpreter of the Bible." *Judaism,* 27:2 (1978), 184–95.

———. *Biblical Interpretation in Ancient Israel.* Oxford: Clarendon Press, 1984.

———. "Introduction." In Martin Buber, *Moses.* Atlantic Highlands, NJ: Humanities Press, 1987.

———. *Garments of Torah.* Bloomington: Indiana University Press, 1987.

Fleishman, Avrom. *Figures of Autobiography.* Berkeley: University of California Press, 1983.

Flohr, Paul R. "From *Kulturmystik* to Dialogue. An Inquiry into the Formation of Martin Buber's Philosophy of I and Thou." Diss., Brandeis University, 1973.

Flohr, Paul, and Bernard Susser. "*Alter und neue Gemeinschaft:* An Unpublished Buber Manuscript." *AJS Review,* 1 (1976), 41–57.

Foucault, Michel. *Madness and Civilization.* Translated by R. Howard. New York: Random, 1965.

———. "What Is an Author?" In D. Bouchard, ed., *Language, Counter-Memory, Practice.* Ithaca: Cornell University Press, 1977.

———. *Power/Knowledge.* Edited by C. Gordon. Brighton, UK: Harvester Press, 1980.

Fox, Everett. "Technical Aspects of the Translation of Genesis of Martin Buber and Franz Rosenzweig." Diss., Brandeis University, 1975.

———. *In the Beginning: A New English Rendition of the Book of Genesis.* Translated with Commentary and Notes by Everett Fox. New York: Schocken, 1983.

———. *Now These Are the Names: A New English Rendition of the Book of Exodus.*

Translated with Commentary and Notes by Everett Fox. New York: Schocken, 1986.

Frank, Joseph. "The Voices of Mikhail Bakhtin." *New York Review of Books*, XXXIII/16 (Oct. 1986), 56–60.

Frankl, Victor. *Man's Search for Meaning*. New York: Simon and Schuster, 1962.

Frei, Hans. *Eclipse of Biblical Narrative*. New Haven: Yale University Press, 1974.

Freud, Sigmund. "Lecture to Society of B'nai Brith." [1926] *Standard Edition of the Complete Psychological Works*. Vol. 20. Translated by J. Strachey. London: Hogarth Press, 1959.

———. *Dora: An Analysis of a Case of Hysteria*. New York: Macmillan, 1963.

Friedman, Maurice. "Introduction." In Martin Buber, *The Knowledge of Man*. New York: Harper, 1965.

———. "Introduction." In Martin Buber, *Meetings*. La Salle, IL: Open Court, 1973.

———. *Martin Buber's Life and Work: The Early Years, 1878–1923*. New York: Dutton, 1981.

———. *Martin Buber's Life and Work: The Middle Years*. New York: Dutton, 1983.

———. *Martin Buber's Life and Work: The Later Years*. New York: Dutton, 1983.

———. *The Confirmation of Otherness*. New York: Pilgrim Press, 1983.

———. "Philosophical Anthropology and Dialogue." Unpublished lecture.

Gadamer, Hans-Georg. *Wahrheit und Methode*. [1960] Tübingen: J.C.B. Mohr, 1965. Second Edition.

———. "On the Scope and Function of Hermeneutical Reflection." *Continuum*, 8:1 (Spring 1970).

———. *Dialogue and Dialectic: Eight Hermeneutical Studies of Plato*. New Haven: Yale University Press, 1980.

———. *Truth and Method*. New York: Crossroad, 1982.

Genette, Gérard. *Nouveau Discours du Récit*. Paris: Seuil, 1983.

Gerhart, Mary, and Allan Russell. *Metaphoric Process: The Creation of Scientific and Religious Understanding*. Fort Worth: Texas Christian University Press, 1984.

Glatzer, Nahum. *Franz Rosenzweig: His Life and Thought*. New York: Schocken, 1961.

———. "Buber as an Interpreter of the Bible." In P. Schilpp and M. Friedman, eds., *The Philosophy of Martin Buber*. 1967.

Goldberg, Michael. *Theology and Narrative*. Nashville: Abingdon, 1981.

Gordon, Haim, and Jochanan Bloch, eds. *Martin Buber: A Centenary Volume*. New York: KTAV, 1984.

Graff, Gerald. "Determinancy/Indeterminancy." In F. Lentricchia and T. McLaughlin, eds., *Critical Terms for Literary Study*. Chicago: University of Chicago Press, 1990.

Grant, Robert, and David Tracy. *A Short History of the Interpretation of the Bible*. Philadelphia: Fortress Press, 1984.

Green, Arthur. *Tormented Master: A Life of Rabbi Nahman of Bratslav*. University, AL: University of Alabama Press, 1979.

Greenberg, Irving. "Cloud of Smoke, Pillar of Fire: Judaism, Christianity, and Modernity After the Holocaust." In E. Fleischner, ed., *Auschwitz: Beginning of a New Era?* New York: KTAV, 1977.

———. "Judaism and History: Historical Events and Religious Change." In S. Kazan and N. Stampfer, eds., *Perspectives in Jewish Learning*, Vol. 1. Chicago: Spertus College Press, 1977.

Greenstein, Edward. "Biblical Narratology." *Prooftexts*, 1:2 (May 1981), 201–09.

Greimas, Algirdas-Julien. *On Meaning: Selected Writings in Semiotic Theory*. Translated by P. Perron and F. Collins. Minneapolis: University of Minnesota Press, 1987.

Gunn, Giles. *The Culture of Criticism and the Criticism of Culture*. New York: Oxford University Press, 1987.

Gunn, Janet Varner. *Autobiography: Toward a Poetics of Experience*. Philadelphia: University of Pennsylvania Press, 1982.

————. "The Religious Hermeneutic of Autobiography." In R. Detweiler, ed., *Art/ Literature/Religion*, JAAR Thematic Studies, 49:2. Chico, CA: Scholars Press, 1983.

Gusdorf, Georges. "Conditions and Limits of Autobiography." In J. Olney, ed., *Autobiography: Essays Theoretical and Critical*. Princeton: Princeton University Press, 1980.

Gutman, H. "Rousseau's Confessions: A Technology of the Self." In L. Martin, H. Gutman, and P. Hutton, eds., *Technologies of the Self*. Amherst: University of Massachusetts Press, 1988.

Habermas, Jürgen. "Summation and Response." *Continuum*, 8:1 (Spring 1970).

————. "On Systematically Distorted Communication." *Inquiry*, 13:3 (Autumn 1970), 205–19.

————. "Introductory Remarks for a Theory of Communicative Competence." *Inquiry*, 13:4 (Winter 1970), 360–76.

————. *Knowledge and Human Interests*. Translated by J. Shapiro. Boston: Beacon, 1970.

————. *Hermeneutik und Ideologiekritic*. Frankfurt: Suhrkamp, 1971.

————. *Theory and Practice*. Translated by J. Viertel. Boston: Beacon, 1975.

————. "A Review of Gadamer's Truth and Method." In F. Dallmayr and T. McCarthy, eds., *Understanding and Social Inquiry*. Notre Dame: University of Notre Dame Press, 1977.

————. *Communication and the Evolution of Society*. Translated by T. McCarthy. Boston: Beacon, 1979.

————. *The Philosophical Discourse of Modernity*. Translated by F. Lawrence. Cambridge: MIT Press, 1987.

Hameln, Glueckel. *The Memoirs of Glueckel of Hameln*. Translated by M. Lowenthal. New York: Schocken, 1977.

Hammer, Louis. "The Relevance of Buber to Aesthetics." In P. Schilpp and M. Friedman, eds., *The Philosophy of Martin Buber*. 1967.

Handelman, Susan. *The Slayers of Moses*. New York: SUNY Press, 1982.

Heidegger, Martin. *Poetry, Language, Thought*. Translated by A. Hofstadter. San Francisco: Harper and Row, 1971.

Heinemann, Yitzchak. *Darkhei ha-Aggadah*. Jerusalem: Magnes, 1970.

Hempel, Carl. "The Function of General Laws in History." *The Journal of Philosophy*, 39 (1942), 35–48.

Herrmann, Ulrich. *Bibliographie Wilhelm Dilthey*. Weinheim: Beltz, 1969.

Heschel, Abraham J. *God in Search of Man*. New York: Harper and Row, 1955.

Hirsch, E. D. *Validity in Interpretation*. New Haven: Yale University Press, 1967.

Horwitz, Rivka. *Buber's Way to I and Thou*. Heidelberg: Lambert Schneider, 1978.

Howarth, William. "Some Principles of Autobiography." In J. Olney, ed., *Autobiography: Essays Theoretical and Critical*. 1980.

James, Henry. "Preface to Portrait of a Lady." *The Art of the Novel*. Edited by R. Blackmur. New York: Scribner's, 1934.

James, William. *The Varieties of Religious Experience*. New York: Penguin, 1982.

Jauss, Robert. *Toward an Aesthetic of Reception*. Minneapolis: University of Minnesota Press, 1982.

Jaynes, Julian. *The Origin of Consciousness in the Breakdown of the Bicameral Mind*. Boston: Houghton Mifflin, 1976.

Johnston, William. "Martin Buber's Literary Debut: 'On Viennese Literature.'" *The German Quarterly Review*, 47:4 (Nov. 1974), 556–66.

Jung, Carl G. *Modern Man in Search of a Soul*. Translated by W. F. Dell and C. F. Baynes. New York: Harcourt, Brace, 1933.

————. *Memories, Dreams, Reflections*. Translated by R. and C. Winston. New York: Vintage, 1963.

————. *Psychology and Religion.* New Haven: Yale University Press, 1972.

Kaplan, Lawrence. *Bibliography of American Autobiography.* Madison: University of Wisconsin Press, 1961.

Katz, Steven. *Post-Holocaust Dialogues.* New York: New York University Press, 1984.

Kelsey, David. *The Uses of Scripture in Recent Theology.* Philadelphia: Fortress Press, 1975.

Kepnes, Steven. "Telling and Retelling: The Use of Narrative in Psychoanalysis and Religion." In S. Kepnes and D. Tracy, eds., *The Challenge of Psychology to Faith.* New York: Seabury, 1982.

————. "Martin Buber's Stories and Contemporary Narrative Theory." Diss., University of Chicago, 1983.

————. "Bridging the Gap Between Understanding and Explanation Approaches to the Study of Religion." *Journal for the Scientific Study of Religion,* 25:4 (Dec. 1986), 504–12.

————. "A Hermeneutic Approach to the Buber-Scholem Controversy." *Journal of Jewish Studies,* 38:1 (Spring 1987), 81–98.

————. "Buber as Hermeneut: Relations to Dilthey and Gadamer." *The Harvard Theological Review,* 81:2 (May 1988), 193–213.

————. "A Narrative Jewish Theology." *Judaism,* 37:2 (Spring 1988), 210–17.

————. "In Pursuit of Dialogue." *Journal for the Scientific Study of Religion,* 27 (Dec. 1988), 645–50.

————. "Buber's Autobiographical Fragments: Becoming Self Through the Other." *Soundings,* 73:2–3 (Summer/Fall 1990), 407–22.

————. "Buber and Bakhtin: Towards a Dialogical Theory of Language and Interpretation." *The Journal of Jewish Thought and Philosophy,* 2:1 (1992).

————. "Buber's Ark: The Dialogic Self." In D. Capps and R. Fenn, eds., *The Endangered Self.* Philadelphia: Augsburg Fortress Press, 1992.

————. *Contemporary Critical Jewish Hermeneutics.* New York: New York University Press, 1992.

————. *The Social Self in Modern Jewish Philosophy* (forthcoming).

————. "Martin Buber and the Dialectic of Meeting and Mismeeting: A Psychological Portrait." In H. Abramovitch and S. Kepnes, eds., *The Healing Between.* Pittsburgh. Duquesne University Press (forthcoming).

Kermode, Frank. *The Sense of an Ending.* Oxford: Oxford University Press, 1966.

————. *The Genesis of Secrecy.* Cambridge, MA: Harvard University Press, 1979.

Kohn, Hans. *Martin Buber: Sein Werk und Sein Zeit.* Köln: Joseph Melzer, 1961.

Kramer, Kenneth. "Autobiographical World Theology." *Horizons.* 13:1 (Spring 1986), 104–15.

Lang, Berel. *Act and Idea in the Nazi Genocide.* Chicago: University of Chicago Press, 1990.

Lasch, Christopher. *The Culture of Narcissism.* New York: W. W. Norton, 1978.

Lentricchia, F., and T. McLaughlin, eds. *Critical Terms for Literary Study.* Chicago: University of Chicago Press, 1990.

Levinas, Emmanuel. "La trace de l'autre." In *En découvrant l'existence avec Husserl et Heidegger.* Paris: Vrin, 1967.

————. *Totality and Infinity.* Translated by A. Lingis. Pittsburgh: Duquesne University Press, 1979.

————. *Collected Philosophical Papers.* Translated by A. Lingis. Dordrecht: Martinus Nijhoff, 1987.

Levinas, E., and R. Kearney. "Dialogue with Emmanuel Levinas." In R. Cohen, ed., *Face to Face with Levinas.* New York: SUNY Press, 1986.

Lindbeck, George. *The Nature of Doctrine.* Philadelphia: Westminister, 1984.

Lyotard, Jean-François. *The Post-Modern Condition: A Report on Knowledge.* Translated by G. Bennington and B. Massumi. Minneapolis: University of Minnesota Press, 1984.

———. "Discussions, or Phrasing 'after Auschwitz.' " In A. Benjamin, ed., *The Lyotard Reader.* Oxford: Basil Blackwell, 1989. Pp.360–92.

McCarthy, Thomas. "Rationality and Relativism: Habermas's 'Overcoming' of Hermeneutics." In D. Held and J. Thompson, eds., *Habermas: Critical Debates.* Cambridge, MA: MIT Press, 1982.

McFague, Sallie TeSelle. *Speaking in Parables.* Philadelphia: Fortress Press, 1975.

Mack, Rudolf. "Intuition und Interpretation in Martin Bubers Umgang mit der Hebraeischen Bibel." *Vetus Testamentum Supplement,* 15:4 (1966), 22-31.

Mandel, Barrett. "Full of Life Now." In J. Olney, ed., *Autobiography: Essays Theoretical and Critical.* 1980.

Mead, George Herbert. *Selected Writings.* New York: Bobbs Merrill, 1964.

Mendes-Flohr, Paul. *Von der Mystik zum Dialog: Martin Bubers geistige Entwicklung bis hin zu "Ich und Du."* Köningstein/Ts.: Jüdischer Verlag bei Athenäum, 1978.

———. "Buber and Post-Traditional Judaism." *European Judaism,* 12:2 (Winter 1978), 4–6.

———. "Orientalism, the Ostjuden and Jewish Self-Affirmation." In J. Frankel, ed., *Studies in Contemporary Jewry,* Vol. I. Bloomington: Indiana University Press, 1984.

———. "Martin Buber's Conception of God." In A. Babolin, ed., *Teologia Filosofica E Filosofia Della Religione.* Perugia: Editrice Benucci, 1986.

———. "Martin Buber's Reception Among the Jews." *Modern Judaism,* 6:2 (May 1986), 111–27.

———. *From Mysticism to Dialogue.* Detroit: Wayne State University Press, 1989.

———. *"Nachwort."* In Martin Buber, *Die Geschichten des Rabbi Nachman.* Heidelberg: Lambert Schneider, 1989.

Mendes-Flohr, Paul, and Jehuda Reinharz, eds. *The Jew in the Modern World: A Documentary History.* Oxford: Oxford University Press, 1980.

Mesch, Barry. "Ta'amey Ha-Mitzvot and Ta'amey Hasippurim: The Biblical Narrative in Saadya, Halevi and Maimonides." Unpublished paper, 1989.

Mitchell, W. J. T. "Representation." In F. Lentricchia and T. McLaughlin, eds., *Critical Terms for Literary Study.* Chicago: University of Chicago Press, 1990.

Morse, B. J. *Martin Buber's Baalschem and Rilke's Ninth Duino Elegy.* Unpublished manuscript, Buber Archive, Ms. 258.

Mosse, George. *Germans and Jews.* New York: Fertig, 1970.

Mueller-Vollmer, Kurt, ed. and trans. *The Hermeneutics Reader.* New York: Continuum, 1985.

Muilenburg, James. "Buber as an Interpreter of the Bible." In P. Schilpp and M. Friedman, eds., *The Philosophy of Martin Buber.* 1967.

Myers, David. "The Scholem-Kurzweil Debate and Modern Jewish Historiography." *Modern Judaism,* 6:3 (October 1986), 261–87.

Nahman, Rabbi. *Sippurey Ma'asiyot.* Berlin: Hebräischer Verlag, 1922.

———. *Sippurey Ma'asiyot.* 14th ed. Jerusalem: Association of Bratslav Hasidism, 1969.

Nelson, Pamela. "The Scholar and the Philosopher: A Tale of Rabbi Nahman's Translators." Unpublished paper.

Nelson, Paul. *Narrative and Morality.* University Park: Pennsylvania State University Press, 1987.

Neusner, Jacob. *Between Time and Eternity.* Encino, CA: Dickenson, 1975.

———. *Scriptures of the Oral Torah.* New York: Harper, 1987.

Niebuhr, H. Richard. *The Meaning of Revelation.* New York: Macmillan, 1941.

Ochs, Peter. "A Rabbinic Pragmatism." In B. Marshall, ed., *Theology and Dialogue.* Notre Dame: Notre Dame University Press, 1990.

Olney, James. *Metaphors of Self: The Meaning of Autobiography.* Princeton: Princeton University Press, 1972.

———, ed. *Autobiography: Essays Theoretical and Critical.* Princeton: Princeton University Press, 1980.

———. "Autobiography and the Cultural Moment." In *Autobiography: Essays Theoretical and Critical.* 1980.

———. "The Style of Autobiography." In *Autobiography: Essays Theoretical and Critical.* 1980.

Ong, Walter. *The Presence of the Word.* New Haven: Yale University Press. 1967.

Pascal, Roy. *Design and Truth in Autobiography.* Cambridge, MA: Harvard University Press, 1960.

Perkins, Robert. "Buber and Kierkegaard: A Philosophic Encounter." In H. Gordon and J. Bloch, eds., *Martin Buber: A Centenary Volume.* 1980.

Perlina, Nina. "Mikhail Bakhtin and Martin Buber: Problems of Dialogic Imagination." *Studies in Twentieth Century Literature,* 9:1 (Fall 1984), 13–28.

Pfuetze, Paul. *Self, Society, Existence.* New York: Harper and Row, 1961.

Piekarz, Mendel. *Hasidut Braslav.* Jerusalem, 1972.

Reines, Chaim. "The Self and Other in Rabbinic Ethics." In M. Kellner, ed., *Contemporary Jewish Ethics.* New York: Sanhedrin, 1978.

Renza, Louis. "The Veto of the Imagination: A Theory of Autobiography." In J. Olney, ed., *Autobiography: Essays Theoretical and Critical.* 1980.

Ricoeur, Paul. *Symbolism of Evil.* Translated by E. Buchanan. Boston: Beacon, 1967.

———. "The Hermeneutical Function of Distanciation." *Philosophy Today,* 17:2/4 (Summer 1973), 129–42.

———. "Ethics and Culture." *Philosophy Today* 17:2/4 (Summer 1973), 153–66.

———. *Interpretation Theory.* Fort Worth: Texas Christian University Press, 1976.

———. "Explanation and Understanding." In *The Philosophy of Paul Ricoeur.* New York: Beacon, 1978.

———. "The Narrative Function." *Semeia,* 13 (1978), 177–202.

———. *Essays on Biblical Interpretation.* Philadelphia: Fortress Press, 1980.

———. "Narrative Time." *Critical Inquiry,* 7:1 (Autumn 1980), 169–90.

———. *Temps et Récit,* Vols. 1,2,3. Paris: Editions du Seuil, 1983, 1984, 1985.

———. *Time and Narrative,* Vol. 1. Translated by K. McLaughlin and D. Pellauer. Chicago: University of Chicago Press, 1984.

———. *Time and Narrative,* Vol. 2. Translated by K. McLaughlin and D. Pellauer. Chicago: University of Chicago Press, 1985.

———. *Time and Narrative,* Vol. 3. Translated by K. Blamey and D. Pellauer. Chicago: University of Chicago Press, 1988.

Rieff, Philip. *The Triumph of the Therapeutic.* New York: Harper and Row, 1966.

Robbe-Grillet, Alain. "New Novel New Man." In *For a New Novel.* Translated by R. Howard. New York: Grove, 1965

Rogers, Carl. *Client-Centered Therapy.* Boston: Houghton Mifflin, 1951.

Roitman, Betty. "Sacred Language and Open Text." In G. Hartman and S. Budick, eds., *Midrash and Literature.* New Haven: Yale University Press, 1986.

Rorty, Richard. *Philosophy and the Mirror of Nature.* Princeton: Princeton University Press, 1979.

———. *Contingency, Irony, and Solidarity.* Cambridge: Cambridge University Press, 1989.

Rosenzweig, Franz. *The Star of Redemption.* Translated by W. Hallo. Boston: Beacon, 1972.

Roskies, David. "Memory." In A. Cohen and F. Mendes-Flohr, eds., *Contemporary Jewish Religious Thought.* 1987.

Rowe, John Carlos. "Structure." In F. Lentricchia and T. McLaughlin, eds., *Critical Terms for Literary Study.* 1990.

Rubenstein, Richard. "The Dean and the Chosen People." In *After Auschwitz.* Indianapolis: Bobbs Merrill, 1968.

———. "The Promise and Pitfalls of Autobiographical Theology." In R. Detweiler, ed., *Art/Literature/Religion,* JAAR Thematic Studies, 49:2. Chico, CA: Scholars Press, 1983.

Said, Edward. *Beginnings*. New York: Basic, 1975.

Schaeder, Grete. *The Hebrew Humanism of Martin Buber*. Translated by N. Jacobs. Detroit: Wayne State University Press, 1973.

Schatz-Uffenheimer, Rivka. "Man's Relation to God and World in Buber's Rendering of the Hasidic Teaching." In P. Schilpp and M. Friedman, eds., *The Philosophy of Martin Buber*. 1967.

Schilpp, Paul, and Maurice Friedman, eds. *The Philosophy of Martin Buber*. La Salle, IL: Open Court, 1967.

Schleiermacher, Friedrich. *Werke* III. Berlin: Riemer, 1838.

———. *Hermeneutics: The Handwritten Manuscripts*. Edited by H. Kimmerle. Translated by J. Duke and J. Forstman. Missoula: Scholars Press, 1977.

Scholem, Gershom. *Major Trends in Jewish Mysticism*. New York: Schocken, 1946.

———. *On the Kabbalah and Its Symbolism*. New York: Schocken, 1969.

———. "Martin Buber's Interpretation of Hasidism." [1961] In *The Messianic Idea in Judaism*. 1971.

———. "The Neutralization of Messianism." [1970] In *The Messianic Idea in Judaism*. 1971.

———. *The Messianic Idea in Judaism*. Translated by M. Meyer. New York: Schocken, 1971.

———. "Martin Buber's Conception of Judaism." In *On Jews and Judaism in Crisis*. New York: Schocken, 1976.

Schopenhauer, Arthur. *The World as Will and Representation*. New York: Dover, 1966.

Schorske, Carl. *Fin-de-Siècle Vienna: Politics and Culture*. New York: Knopf, 1980.

Schrag, Calvin. *Communicative Praxis and the Space of Subjectivity*. Bloomington: Indiana University Press, 1986.

Schwarz-Bart, André. *The Last of the Just*. Translated by S. Baker. New York: Atheneum, 1960.

Scott, Nathan, Jr. "The New Trahison des Clercs: Reflections on the Present Crisis in Humanistic Studies." *The Virginia Quarterly Review*, 62:3 (Summer 1986), 402–22.

———. "The House of Intellect in an Age of Carnival: Some Hermeneutical Reflections." 1986 Presidential Address. *Journal of The American Academy of Religion*, 55:1 (Spring 1987), 3–21.

Silberstein, Laurence. *Martin Buber's Social and Religious Thought: Alienation and the Quest for Meaning*. New York: New York University Press, 1989.

Silko, Leslie Marmon. *Ceremony*. New York: Viking, 1977.

Smith, Ronald. *Martin Buber*. Richmond, VA: John Knox, 1967.

Smith, Roy Steinhoff. "The Becoming of the Person in Martin Buber's Philosophical Anthropology and Heinz Kohut's Psychology of Self." Diss., University of Chicago, 1985.

Spanos, William V., ed. *Martin Heidegger and the Question of Literature*. Bloomington: Indiana University Press, 1979.

Spero, Moshe. "Remembering and Historical Awareness, Part II." *Tradition*, 19:1 (Spring 1981), 59–75.

Stahmer, Harold. *"Speak that I May See Thee": The Religious Significance of Language*. New York: Macmillan, 1968.

Starobinski, Jean. "The Style of Autobiography." In J. Olney, ed., *Autobiography: Essays Theoretical and Critical*. 1980.

Steinsaltz, Adin. *Beggars and Prayers*. New York: Basic Books. 1985.

Stendhal, Henri Beyle, *The Life of Henri Brulard*. Translated by J. Stewart and B. C. J. G. Knight. New York: Minerva, 1968.

Stern, David. "Midrash and Indeterminacy." *Critical Inquiry*, 15:1 (Autumn 1988), 132–61.

Stern, Josef. "Language," In A. Cohen and P. Mendes-Flohr, eds., *Contemporary Jewish Religious Thought*. 1987.

Sternberg, Meir. *The Poetics of Biblical Narrative.* Bloomington: Indiana University Press, 1987.
Tanakh. New York: Jewish Publication Society, 1985.
Taylor, Charles. "Interpretation and the Sciences of Man." *Review of Metaphysics,* 25:1 (Sept. 1971), 3–51.
Theunissen, Michael. *Der Andere: Studien zur Sozialontologie der Gegenwart.* Berlin: W. de Gruyter, 1965.
———. *The Other: Studies in the Social Ontology of Husserl, Heidegger, Sartre, and Buber.* Translated by C. Macann. Cambridge: MIT Press, 1984.
Thiemann, Ronald. *Revelation and Theology.* Notre Dame: University of Notre Dame Press, 1985.
Thomas, Laurence. *Vessels of Evil.* Philadelphia: Temple University Press (forthcoming).
Tillich, Paul. *Systematic Theology.* Chicago: University of Chicago Press, 1967.
Todorov, Tzvetan. *Les Genres du Discours.* Paris: Seuil, 1978.
———. *Mikhail Bakhtin: The Dialogical Principle.* Translated by W. Godzich. Minneapolis: University of Minnesota Press, 1984.
Tönnies, Ferdinand. *Community and Society.* Translated by C. P. Loomis. New York: Harper, 1963.
Tracy, David. *Blessed Rage for Order.* New York: Seabury, 1975.
———. *The Analogical Imagination.* New York: Crossroad, 1981.
———. *Plurality and Ambiguity: Hermeneutics, Hope, Religion.* San Francisco: Harper and Row, 1987.
Udoff, Alan. "Introduction to New Edition." In Martin Buber, *The Knowledge of Man.* Edited by M. Friedman. Atlantic Highlands: Humanities Press, 1988. Pp. viii–xxii.
Uffenheimer, Benyamin. "Buber and Modern Biblical Scholarship." In H. Gordon and J. Bloch, eds., *Martin Buber: A Centenary Volume.* New York: KTAV, 1984.
Warnke, Georgia. *Gadamer: Hermeneutics, Tradition and Reason.* Cambridge, UK: Polity, 1987.
Watt, Ian. *The Rise of The Novel.* Berkeley: University of California Press, 1967.
Weintraub, Karl. "Autobiography and Historical Consciousness." *Critical Inquiry,* 1:4 (June 1975), 821–48.
———. *The Value of the Individual.* Chicago: University of Chicago Press, 1978.
White, Allon. "Bakhtin, Sociolinguistics, and Deconstruction." In F. Gloversmith, ed., *The Theory of Reading.* Totowa, NJ: Barnes and Noble, 1984.
White, Hayden. *The Tropics of Discourse.* Baltimore: Johns Hopkins University Press, 1978.
———. "The Value of Narrativity in the Representation of Reality." *Critical Inquiry,* 7:1 (Autumn 1980), 5–27.
Wiesel, Elie. *The Testament.* Translated by M. Wiesel. New York: Summit Books, 1981.
———. *The Summit.* Translated by M. Wiesel. New York: Summit Books, 1981.
Winch, Peter. *The Idea of a Social Science and Its Relation to Philosophy.* London: Routledge and Kegan Paul, 1964.
Wood, Robert. *Martin Buber's Ontology.* Evanston, IL: Northwestern University Press, 1969.
Wright, G. Ernest. *God Who Acts.* London: SCM Press, 1952.
Wyschogrod. Edith. *Spirit in Ashes: Hegel, Heidegger, and Man-Made Mass Death.* New Haven: Yale University Press, 1985.
Yerushalmi, Yosef. *Zakhor: Jewish History and Jewish Memory.* Seattle: University of Washington Press, 1982.
Young, James. *Writing and Rewriting the Holocaust.* Bloomington: Indiana University Press, 1988.
Zunz, Leopold. "Etwas über die rabbinische Literatur." *Gesammelte Schriften,* Vol. 1. Berlin: 1875. [English translation by A. Schwarz. In P. Mendes-Flohr and J. Reinharz, eds., *The Jew in the Modern World.* 1980.]

INDEX

Abraham, 129, 137
Abramovitch, Henry, 197n154
Actual occurrence (*Begebnis*), 64, 65
Adequacy of an interpretation, 77–78, 163n78
"Advice to Frequenters of Libraries" (1944), 71–72, 74, 148
Aesthetics, xiii, 23–26. *See also* Art
Aggadah, xv, 121, 198n21
Aichele, George Jr., 198n21
Aletheia, 28, 60
Alter, Robert, 151n4
Altizer, Thomas, 175n86
Amir, Yehoshua, 186n73
Ammi (my people), 129–30
Amos, 133–35, 136
Anderson, Gary, 166n1
Annales School, 179n39
Anti-novel, 100
Apocalypse, 98–99, 178n23, 181n84
Application, 76
Argument, 77
Aristotle: and *phronesis*, 39, 60; and plot, 104, 182n1, 182n2; on time, 91, 93
Aron, Raymond, 36
Art, 154n16, 181n90; and Buber, 5; as expression, 9, 161n28; folk, 4; interpretation of as art, 31; and I-Thou, 22–26, 177n1; Jewish, 4–5; as language, 30; mutuality in, 162n42; and spirit, 161n25; and the spoken word, 68; truth in, 26–27. *See also Geistige Wesenheiten*; Spirit
Ar Vif (mythological book), 71, 72
Ast, Friedrich, 164n93
Audience: original understanding of, 22, 29
Auerbach, Erich, 125, 179n46, 191n35
Augustine, Saint, 187n85; his *Confessions* as autobiography, 116–17; on time, 91, 92–93, 98
Author, 156n62, 173n54; in autobiography, 104–5, 112; and construction of a narrative, 94–95; death of, 186n58; and dialogue, 68, 75, 78; intention of, 7, 9, 29, 175n95; and the interpreter, 22, 157n72
Authority, charismatic, 193n81
"Autobiographical Fragments" (1960), xiv, 105–7, 110–11, 113, 115–19, 172n41, 182n95
Autobiography, 156n57, 183n25, 187n84, 187n85; the author in, 104–5, 112; defined, 106; Jewish, 188n89, 188n92; monumental, 108–9, 113, 117, 188n92; religious, 115–19; repetition in, 180n66; the self in, xiv, 104–5, 107–15; as unique in the West, 183n26

Baal-Shem, 17, 99, 157n66, 157n69
Babylonian Exile, 54, 136, 137
Bakhtin, Mikhail, 91; and the Bakhtin circle, 171n15; on the Bible, 70, 173n52; and Buber, 62, 170n1, 171n10, 171n13, 171n14, 172n23; and dialogue, xii–xiii, 61, 63–64, 66, 76; and heteroglossia, 65, 149; on interpretation, 69; on prose, 68; religious affiliations of, 171n16; his sociolinguistics, 172n27; on the spoken word, 65, 67; on the unity of language, 66–67; on utterance and situation, 67
Band, Arnold, 159n86
Barth, Karl, 192n46
Barthes, Roland, ix; and the death of the author, 186n58; and narrative, 177n20; and self, 112
Beckett, Samuel, 99
Beer-Hofmann, Richard, 5
Begebnis (actual occurrence), 64, 65
Beginnings, 181n74, 181n82
Being, 168n54; and dialogue, 20, 63; and Seeming, 73; and Time, 93; -toward-death, 98–99
Bellah, Robert, 184n33
Ben-Amos, Dan, 160n9
Ben-Gurion, David, 194n99
Benveniste, Emile, 91
Berlin, Adele, 151n4
Bernstein, Richard, 163n78
Berry, Donald, 162n42
Bialik, Chaim, 198n21
Bible: and contemporary Jews, 53–54, 122–25; and dialogical hermeneutics, xiii; as dialogue, 70, 173n52; its German translation, 40–41, 43–44, 46–47, 53, 54; and historical criticism, 40, 50–52; historicity of its figures, 123; and history, 125–27; interpreting methodologies for, 52–53 (*see also* Explanation, methods of); and I-Thou, 31, 122; and Jewish common memory, 122–23; multiple authorship of, 45, 48, 122–23; narrative in, 88, 125, 127, 192n46; other translations of, 44; spokenness of, 45, 55; stylistic unity of, 48, 123; technical devices used in its translation, 42–50; as Thou, 57–58; and time, 125; and tradition, 121
Biblical criticism, 53, 122–23
"Biblical Humanism" (1933), 55, 62
Blettgen, Hans Hermann, 158n83
Bloch, Ernst, 154n35
Bloch, Mark, 179n39
Bloom, Harold, 52, 126, 158n81, 175n86

Steven Kepnes is Assistant Professor of Philosophy and Religion at Colgate University. He is editor of *Contemporary Critical Jewish Hermeneutics* and coeditor, with David Tracy, of *The Challenge of Psychology to Faith.*